DANIEL BLUM'S

THEATRE WORLD

SEASON 1963-1964

CHILTON BOOKS

A Division of Chilton Company
Publishers
Philadelphia and New York

Library of Congress Catalog Card No. 46-13321

To

LUCILLE MARSH
HOLLENDER

with admiration
and affection

CHILTON BOOKS

EAST WASHINGTON SQUARE (525 LOCUST STREET) / PHILADELPHIA, PA., 19106

We would appreciate your sending
a copy of the publication in which
your review appears, or two copies
of your review, to CHILTON
BOOKS.

ATTN: PROMOTION DEPARTMENT

TITLE	THEATER WORLD, VOL 20
AUTHOR	DANIEL BLUM, ED.
PRICE	$7.50 PUBLICATION DATE SEPTEMBER 24, 1964

TABLE OF CONTENTS

Assistant Editor: John Willis

Associate: Carl Raymund

**Staff Photographers: Louis Mélançon, Friedman-Abeles,
Earle Forbes, Avery Willard**

THE NEW YORK SEASON

There was much cause to rejoice during the 1963-64 season. There were more plays produced on Broadway than in any one season in the past twelve years. There were more hits too. Every week during the entire season there were at least seven or eight attractions that were complete sell-outs. These included, among the musical comedies, "Hello, Dolly!" the biggest hit of the year, "Funny Girl," "High Spirits," and at the season's end "Fade Out—Fade In." Of the straight play sell-outs, there was Richard Burton's version of "Hamlet" which was on its way to breaking John Gielgud's long-run "Hamlet" record; there was the controversial drama "The Deputy," and also the two light comedy delights "Any Wednesday" and "Barefoot In The Park."

Other plays in the hit class were "Dylan," "Nobody Loves An Albatross," and "Baby Want A Kiss," and in the musical comedy field "What Makes Sammy Run?," "110 In The Shade," and "Here's Love."

"The Subject Was Roses" opened May 25, too late for gathering deserved awards. It was the best American play of the season and was showered with praise by all the critics who count; and it established Frank D. Gilroy as a fine playwright.

Moderate successes included "Luther," "A Case of Libel," and "The Private Ear and The Public Eye." Attractions that deserved a better fate were "The Rehearsal," a sparkling comedy by Anouilh, and beautifully played; and "Spoon River," Edgar Lee Masters' anthology which received critical acclaim but failed to draw in the customers.

The Actors Studio came into its own as producers with "Marathon '33," "Blues For Mister Charlie," and "Baby Want A Kiss." "Marathon '33" was a failure, "Baby Want A Kiss" a success, and at the season's end "Blues For Mister Charlie" was struggling for survival.

The Repertory Theatre of Lincoln Center was off to a bad start with "After The Fall," a revival of Eugene O'Neill's "Marco Millions," and "But For Whom Charlie," a new play by S.M. Behrman. "After The Fall" caused much argument, but the major opinions were that it was inferior Arthur Miller and in very bad taste. The controversy made for box office appeal. The other two productions were dismissed as unworthy. The acting company itself was, for the most part, hopelessly inadequate. The Repertory Theatre of Lincoln Center was, in all respects, a disappointment in its first year.

The National Repertory Theatre had moderate acclaim with a national tour, and played a short unprofitable spring engagement with two of its three offerings, "The Sea Gull" and "The Crucible." Eva LeGallienne was the guiding force of the company.

The New York State Theatre of Lincoln Center for The Performing Arts, a handsome edifice, opened its doors April 23, 1964, and added glamour to the metropolitan theatre scene. Opening with the New York City Ballet, and primarily a musical theatre, it also presented the Royal Shakespeare Company in "King Lear" and "The Comedy of Errors" for a short limited engagement.

An interesting footnote on the year was the abundance of theatres. At no time was there a theatre shortage, and during the entire season there were at least eight or ten choice theatres empty and available. Also, it was the season for the preview. Rather than face the expense of out of town tryouts, twenty productions had their "tryouts" in New York City by selling tickets to previews. It was also the year for fast closings. Six plays shut up shop after opening night. Mary Martin, beloved star, had her first notable flop on Broadway when "Jennie," an elaborate and expensive musical, ran only 82 performances.

Holdovers from past seasons that spanned this one included "Mary, Mary," with 1352 performances; "How To Succeed In Business Without Really Trying" with 1098 showings; "A Funny Thing Happened On The Way To The Forum" with 862; "Beyond The Fringe" with 673; "Never Too Late" with 631, and "Oliver" with 586 performances.

The City Center again came up with top-notch revivals of "My Fair Lady," "The King and I," "West Side Story," "Porgy and Bess," and Gilbert and Sullivan musicals. Also, the Theatre De France with Jean-Louis Barrault and Madeleine Renaud played repertory.

Off-Broadway continued its activities with many revivals and many new plays. Among the outstanding that deserve mention include "The Pinter Plays," "In White America," "The Blood Knot," "The Trojan Women," "Dutchman," and "Telemachus Clay," and musically, "Jerico-Jim Crow," "The Amorous Flea," "Trumpets of The Lord," "The Knack." Holdovers included "The Fantasticks," "The Blacks," "This Was Burlesque," "Six Characters In Search of An Author," and "The Boys From Syracuse."

The Phoenix Theatre had a good, though unappreciated, revival of William Gillette's "Too Much Johnson." It also housed the Association of Producing Artists repertory of excellent revivals of "The Lower Depths," "Right You Are If You Think You Are," "The Tavern," and "Scapin."

BROADWAY CALENDAR
June 1, 1963 to May 31, 1964

MOROSCO THEATRE

Opened Tuesday, August 27, 1963.°
Roger L. Stevens and T. Edward Hambleton by arrangement with Phoenix Theatre present:

OH DAD, POOR DAD, MAMMA'S HUNG YOU IN THE CLOSET AND I'M FEELIN' SO SAD

By Arthur Kopit; Directed by Jerome Robbins; Scenery by William and Jean Eckart;
Costumes, Patricia Zipprodt; Lighting, Thomas
Skelton; Music, Robert Prince; Sound Technician, Robert Buccalo.

CAST

Madame Rosepettle.................Hermione Gingold
Jonathan.............................Sam Waterston
Rosalie...................................Alix Elias
Commodore Roseabove.............Sandor Szabo
Head Bellboy...........................John Hallow
Bellboys........Jaime Sanchez, Thom Koutsoukos,
Gary Garth, Ernesto Aponte, Peter
Lenahan, Carl Guttenberger
UNDERSTUDIES: Madame, Carol Gustafson;
Commodore, John Hallow; Rosalie, Alexandra
Berlin; Jonathan, Carl Guttenberger; Head Bell-
boy, Donald Wesley.

A Comedy in three scenes without intermission. The action takes place in a hotel suite in
Port Royal, a city somewhere in the Caribbean.

General Manager: Victor Samrock
Company Manager: Thomas Bodkin
Press: Ben Kornzweig, Karl Bernstein
Stage Managers: Charles Forsythe, Don Wesley
°Closed October 5, 1963. (47 performances)
Opened Off-Broadway with Jo Van Fleet on
February 26, 1962, and closed March 31,
1963, after 454 performances. See THEATRE
WORLD, Vol. 18.

Henry Grossman Photos

Sam Waterston, Hemione Gingold, Alix Elias
Top: Sam Waterston, Alix Elias

Hermione Gingold

Cyril Ritchard, Roger C. Carmel,
Claudette Colbert

Robert Drivas, Margot Bennett
Top: Robert Drivas, Claudette Colbert,
Hilda Haynes, Cyril Ritchard

10

ETHEL BARRYMORE THEATRE

Opened Wednesday, September 18, 1963.°
Alfred de Liagre, Jr. presents:

THE IRREGULAR VERB TO LOVE

By Hugh and Margaret Williams; Directed by Cyril Ritchard; Setting and Lighting by Donald Oenslager; Costumes, Frank Thompson; Associate Producer, Orrin E. Christy, Jr.

CAST

Lucy Beckett	Kathryn Hays
Michael Vickers	William Kinsolving
Mrs. Couter	Hilda Haynes
Andrew Rankin	Robert Drivas
Fedra	Margot Bennett
Hedda Rankin	Claudette Colbert
Felix Rankin	Cyril Ritchard
Mr. Andrikos	Roger C. Carmel

A Comedy in two acts and four scenes. The action takes place in the Rankin's Maisonette, opposite the zoo in Regent's Park, London, at the present time.

General Manager: C. Edwin Knill
Press: Ben Washer, Phillip Bloom
Stage Manager: Ben Janney

°Closed December 28, 1963. (115 performances)

Friedman-Abeles Photos

Top: (L) William Kinsolving, Kathryn Hays, Cyril Ritchard (R) Robert Drivas, Cyril Ritchard, Claudette Colbert

Claudette Colbert, Cyril Ritchard

Jennifer Hilary, Alan Badel, Coral Browne, Keith Michell, Adrienne Corri
Top: Keith Michell, Coral Browne

ROYALE THEATRE

Opened Monday, September 23, 1963.°
David Merrick by arrangement with Tennent Productions, Ltd., presents:

THE REHEARSAL

By Jean Anouilh; Adapted by Pamela Hansford Johnson and Kitty Black; Sets Designed by Jane Graham; Costumes Designed by Tony Walton; Lighting and Supervision, Will Steven Armstrong; Directed by Peter Coe; Production Supervisor, Neil Hartley.

CAST

Footman	Guy Arbury
The Countess	Coral Browne
M. Damiens	Earl Montgomery
The Count	Keith Michell
Hortensia	Adrienne Corri
Hero	Alan Badel
Villebosse	Edward Bishop
Lucile	Jennifer Hilary

UNDERSTUDIES: Count, Hero, John Cullun; Countess, Hortensia, Gaye Jordan; Damiens, Guy Arbury; Villebosse, Robert Milli; Lucile, Suzanne Storrs.

General Manager: Jack Schlissel
Company Manager: Emanuel Azenburg
Press: Lee Solters, Harvey Sabinson, James D. Proctor, David Powers, Betty Lee Hunt
Stage Managers: Lucia Victor, Paul Phillips

°Closed December 28, 1963. (110 performances)

Top: (L) Coral Browne, Alan Badel,
Adrienne Corri
(R) Keith Michell, Jennifer Hilary

Jennifer Hilary, Alan Badel

Keith Michell, Adrienne Corri
in
"THE REHEARSAL"

14

CORT THEATRE
Opened Tuesday, September 24, 1963°
Roger L. Stevens and Herman Shumlin in
association with Nelson Morris and Randolph Hale present:

BICYCLE RIDE TO NEVADA

By Robert Thom; Based on Novel by Barnaby
Conrad; Directed by Herman Shumlin; Settings
and Lighting, Howard Bay; Costumes, Edith
Lutyens Bel Geddes; Production Assistant, Raymond A. League.

CAST

Austin	John Marriott
Lucha Morena	Lois Smith
Winston Sawyer	Franchot Tone
Phoebe Fletcher	Leona Powers
Victor	Paul McGrath
Elizabeth	Lulamae Hubbard
Basil	Leslie Redford
Sally Dawn	Barbara Mostel
Bentley	John Boruff
Chandler	Guy Repp
David Sawyer	Richard Jordan
Rip Calabria	Ron Leibman
Miriam Cooper Clyde	
(Mrs. Tiggy-Winkle)	Violet Dunn

UNDERSTUDIES: Winston, Michael O'Sulli-
van; Lucha, Sall Kirkland; David, Rip, Jere
Michael; Victor, John Boruff; Sally, Afnee
McClain; Bentley, Chandler, Basil, Austin,
Maxton Latham.

A Drama in three acts and five scenes. The
action takes place at the present time in a house
in Santa Barbara, California.

General Manager: Victor Samrock
Company Manager: Robert Alex Baron
Press: Samuel Lurie, Ruth Cage,
Judith Davidson, Stanley Kaminsky
Stage Managers: Michael Thoma,
Joseph Brownstone
°Closed September 24, 1963. (1 performance)

Friedman-Abeles Photos

Top: John Marriott, Franchot Tone,
Ron Leibman, Lois Smith
Right Center: Lois Smith, Richard Jordan

Franchot Tone, Lois Smith

15

Albert Finney, Glyn Owen

Frank Shelley, Lorna Lewis
Top: (Kneeling) Albert Finney

Opened Wednesday, September 25, 1963.°
David Merrick by arrangement with The
English Stage Company and Oscar Lewenstein presents:

LUTHER

By John Osborne; Directed by Tony Richardson; Sets and Costumes by Jocelyn Herbert; Supervised by Thea Neu; Music Composed and Arranged by John Addison; Choral Director, Max Walmer; Production Assistant, Jocelyn Tawse.

CAST

Knight	Glyn Owen
Prior	Ted Thurston
Martin	Albert Finney[†1]
Hans	Kenneth J. Warren[†2]
Lucas	Luis Van Rooten
Reader	Alfred Sandor
Weinand	John Heffernan[†3]
Tetzel	Peter Bull[†4]
Staupitz	Frank Shelley
Cajetan	John Moffatt[†5]
Miltitz	Robert Burr
Leo	Michael Egan
Eck	Martin Rudy
Katherine	Lorna Lewis
Children	Perry Golkin, Joseph Lamberta

MONKS, LORDS, PEASANTS: Thor Arngrim, Harry Carlson, Stan Dworkin, Roger Hamilton, Konrad Matthaei, Alfred Sandor.

SINGERS: Paul Flores, Dan Goggin, Robert L. Hultman, Marvin Solley (soloist).

UNDERSTUDIES: Miltitz, Thor Arngrim, Knight, Robert Burr; Lucas, Winand, Harry Carlson; Hans, Eck, Stan Dworkin; Prior, Pope, Roger Hamilton; Luther, John Heffernan; Katherine, Barbara Lester; Staupitz, Konrad Matthaei;Tetzel, Alfred Sandor.

A Drama in three acts and twelve scenes. The action takes place between 1506 and 1527.

General Manager: Jack Schlissel
Company Manager: Eugene Wolsk
Press: Lee Solters, Harvey Sabinson, David Powers
Stage Managers: Mitchell Erickson, B. Lester

°Closed March 28, 1964. (212 performances)
†Succeeded by : 1. John Heffernan, 2. George Mathews, 3. Harry Carlson, 4. Lionel Stander, 5. Hugh Franklin.

Henry Grossman and Friedman-Abeles Photos

Kenneth J. Warren (L), Albert Finney (R)
Top: Luis Van Rooten, Albert Finney,
John Heffernan, Kenneth J. Warren

Albert Finney, Frank Shelley

Albert Finney
in
"LUTHER"

Henry Grossman Photo

BOOTH THEATRE

Opened Sunday, September 29, 1963.°
(Moved November 19, 1963, to Belasco
Theatre)
Joseph Cates presents:

SPOON RIVER ANTHOLOGY

By Edgar Lee Masters; Conceived and Di-
rected by Charles Aidman; Lighting by Jules
Fisher; Original Songs: Music by Naomi Caryl
Hirshhorn, Lyrics by Charles Aidman; Hair
Styles, Michel Kazan; Production Supervised by
Robert Weiner; Production Assistant, Jan Gass-
man.

CAST

Betty Garrett   Robert Elston
Joyce Van Patten   Charles Aidman
Singers: Naomi Caryl Hirshhorn, Hal Lynch
Standbys: Barbara Gilbert, Robert Doyle
Readings from Edgar Lee Masters in two parts.

General Manager: Marshall Young
Press: Gertrude Kirschner, Violet Welles,
Saul Ostrove
Stage Managers: Robert Darnell, Robert Doyle
°Closed January 4, 1964. (111 performances)

Betty Garrett, Robert Elston, Joyce Van Patten, Charles Aidman
Top: Robert Elston, Betty Garrett

19

FIFTY-FOURTH STREET THEATRE

Opened Monday, September 30, 1963.°
Sandy Farber presents:

THE STUDENT GYPSY
or
THE PRINCE OF LIEDERKRANZ

Book, Music, Lyrics, and Direction by Rick Besoyan; Musical Numbers Staged by Ray Harrison; Sets and Costumes, Raoul Pene Du Bois; Lighting, Paul Morrison; Musical Direction, Shepard Coleman; Orchestrations and Arrangements, Arnold Goland; Production Associate, Edward Royce; Production Assistant, Doris Blum.

CAST

Papa Johann Sebastian Glockenspiel	Allen Swift
Ginger Glockenspiel	Mitzie Welch
Edelweiss Glockenspiel	Joleen Fodor
Merry May Glockenspiel	Eileen Brennan
Rudolph von Schlump	Don Stewart
Muffin T. Ragamuffin	Dom De Luise
Gryphon Allescu	Bill Fletcher
Zampa Allescu	Shannon Bolin
Col. Helmet Blunderbuss	Dick Hoh
Pfc. Wolfgang Humperdinck	Edward Miller
Osgood the Good	Donald Babcock
Elsie Umlaut	Linda Segal

THE GLOCKENSPIEL GIRLS: Rosemary McNamara, Mary Jay, Jean Palmerton, Maria Graziano, Jacque Dean, Ann Collins, Jean Middlebrooks, Katherine Sutter, Jamie Simmons.
PRIVATES IN THE ROYAL GRENADIERS: Ralph Vucci, Doug Robinson, Robert Edsel, Marc Destin, Richard Marshall, William Wheless, Nino Galanti, Tony Marlowe, Arnold Whyler.
UNDERSTUDIES: Merry May, Joleen Fodor; Papa, Colonel, Osgood, Walter Kattwinkel; Anne Nunnally and Edward Royce.
MUSICAL NUMBERS: Welcome Home Anthem, Singspielia, Romance, Somewhere, It's A Wonderful Day To Do Nothing, The Gypsy Life, The Grenadiers' Marching Song, Greetings, Kiss Me, Ting-A-Ling Dearie, Merry May, Seventh Heaven Waltz, Gypsy Dance, Walk-On, You're A Man, A Whistle Works, Gypsy of Love, Our Love Has Flown Away, A Woman Is A Woman Is A Woman, Very Much In Love, My Love Is Yours, There's Life In The Old Folks Yet, The Drinking Song, Finale.

A Musical Comedy in two acts and twenty-one scenes. The action takes place late in the nineteenth century in the Kingdom of Singspielia.

General and Company Manager: David Lawlor
Press: Robert Larkin
Stage Managers: Duane Camp, Tony Manzi, Richard Marshall

°Closed October 12, 1963. (16 performances)

Martha Swope Photos

Allen Swift, Shannon Bolin, Donald Babcock
Above: Eileen Brennan, Dom DeLuise
Top: (L) Shannon Bolin (R) Dom DeLuise,
Eileen Brennan, Shannon Bolin

20

Gary Bond, Derek Fowlds
in
"CHIPS WITH EVERYTHING"

21

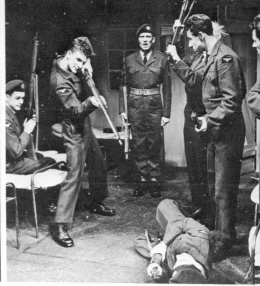

PLYMOUTH THEATRE

Opened Tuesday, October 1, 1963.°
Morton Gottlieb and Helen Bonfils present
The Royal Court Theatre and Bob Swash
production of:

CHIPS WITH EVERYTHING

By Arnold Wesker; Directed by John Dexter;
Designed by Jocelyn Herbert; Supervised by Ed
Wittstein; Assistant to the Director, Braham
Murray.

CAST

Corporal Hill	Alan Dobie
Cannibal (Archie)	George Innes
Wingate (Charles)	Derek Fowlds
Thompson (Pip)	Gary Bond
Seaford (Wilfie)	Terence Taplan
McClure (Andrew)	Frank Wylie
Richardson (Whitey)	John Noakes
Cohen (Dodger)	John Levitt
Smith (Dickey)	Michael Standing
Washington (Smiler)	Ronald Lacey
Wing Commander	Dallas Cavell
Squadron Leader	Robert Hewitt
Pilot Officer	Corin Redgrave
P.T. Instructor Flt. Sgt.	Tony Caunter
Recruit	Patrick Ellis
Night Guard	James Luck
1st Corporal	George Layton
2nd Corporal	Christopher Timothy
Airmen	Barry Evans, Edward Burrell, Gerald McNally, Norman Allen, John Lane

UNDERSTUDIES: Hill, Squadron Leader, Tony
Caunter; Pip, Archie, George Layton; Smiler,
Charles, Patrick Ellis; Pilot Officer, Sgt., Chris-
topher Timothy; Airmen, John Lane; Wilfie,
Andrew, Cpls., Gerald McNally; Whitey, Edward
Burrell; Dodger, Norman Allen; Dickey, James
Luck.

A Comedy in two acts. The action takes place
at the present time at a Royal Air Force Station
in England.

General Manager: Richard Seader
Press: Dorothy Ross, Tom Trenkle,
Richard O'Brien
Stage Managers: Julian Oldfield,
Edward Burrell, Norman Allen, Gerald McNally
°Closed February 8, 1964. (149 performances)

Top: (L) Patrick Ellis, John Levitt, Terence
Taplin, George Innes, (R) Barry Evans, Terence
Taplin, Alan Dobie, John Noakes, George
Innes, Frank Wylie

John Levitt, George Innes
Above: Corin Redgrave,
Gary Bond

John Noakes
Above: Alan Dobie

Valerie Lee, Laurence Naismith
in
"HERE'S LOVE"

23

Center: Craig Stevens, Valerie Lee,
Laurence Naismith
Above: Craig Stevens

SAM S. SHUBERT THEATRE
Opened Thursday, October 3, 1963.*
Stuart Ostrow presents:

HERE'S LOVE

Book, Music, and Lyrics by Meredith Willson; Book based on "Miracle On 34th Street"; Story by Valentine Davies, and Screenplay by George Seaton; Directed by Stuart Ostrow; Settings, William and Jean Eckart; Costumes, Alvin Colt; Lighting, Tharon Musser; Musical Direction and Vocal Arrangements, Elliot Lawrence; Orchestrations, Don Walker; Dance Music Arranged by Peter Howard; Dances and Musical Numbers Staged by Michael Kidd; Hairstyles, Ernest Adler.

CAST

Mr. Kris Kringle	Laurence Naismith
Fred Gaily	Craig Stevens†1
Susan Walker	Valerie Lee
Marvin Shellhammer	Fred Gwynne
Doris Walker	Janis Paige†2
Clerks	Michael Bennett, Gene Kelton, Bill Stanton, Patrick Cummings, Diane Ball, Sandra Roveta, Patti Pappathatos, Elaine Cancilla
R. H. Macy	Paul Reed
Harry Finfer	Sal Lombardo
Mrs. Finfer	Mara Landi
Hendrika	Kathy Cody
Hendrika's New Mother	Suzanne France
Miss Crookshank	Reby Howells
Mr. Psawyer	David Doyle†3
Governor	Darrell Sandeen
Mayor	Hal Norman
Mr. Gimbel	William Griffis
Policeman	Bob McClure
Clara	Mary Louise†4
Judge Martin Group	Cliff Hall
D.A. Thomas Mara	Larry Douglas
Tammany O'Halloran	Arthur Rubin†5
Nurse	Leesa Troy
Marines	John Sharpe, Bob McClure, Darrell Sandeen
Girl Scout Leader	Mara Landi
Bailiff	Del Horstman
Mailman	Hal Norman
Thomas Mara, Jr.	Ronnie Kroll†6
Murphy	William Griffis

CHILDREN: Debbie Breen, Kathy Cody, Sal Lombardo, Ronnie Kroll, Terrin Miles.

DANCERS: Diane Ball, Michael Bennett, Duane Bodin, Elaine Cancilla, Patrick Cummings, Suzanne France, Reby Howells, Gene Kelton, Baayork Lee, David Lober, Bill Louther, Patti Pappathatos, Sandra Roveta, John Sharpe, Bill Stanton, Carolsue Shaer.

SINGERS: Ceil Delli, Penny Gaston, Del Horstman, Mara Landi, Mary Louise, Bob McCure, Hal Norman, Darrell Sandeen, Leesa Troy.

UNDERSTUDIES: Fred, Larry Douglas; Doris, Leesa Troy; Kris, William Griffis; Macy, Hal Norman; Shellhamer, Bob McClure; Psawyer, Del Horstman; Susan, Debbie Breen; Judge, William Griffis; Tammany, Bob McClure; D.A., Darrell Sandeen; Gimbel, Del Horstman.

MUSICAL NUMBERS: "The Big Clown Balloons," "Arm In Arm," "You Don't Know," "The Plastic Alligator," "The Bugle," "Here's Love," "My Wish," "Pine Cones and Holly Berries," "Look, Little Girl," "Expect Things To Happen," "The Party," "She Hadda Go Back," "That Man Over There," "My State," "Nothin In Common."

A Musical in two acts and twenty-one scenes. The action takes place at the present time on Thanksgiving Day.

General Manager: Joseph Harris
Press: Harvey B. Sabinson, Harry Nigro, David Powers
Stage Managers: Terence Little, Arthur Rubin, Ralph Linn

*Still playing May 31, 1964. (271 performances)
†Succeeded by: 1. Richard Kiley, 2. Lisa Kirk, 3. Dom DeLuise, 4. Ceil Delli, 5. William Griffis, 6. Dewey Golkin.

Friedman-Abeles Photos

Top Left: (C) Laurence Naismith

Craig Stevens, Valerie Lee, Laurence Naismith
Above: Janis Paige, Valerie Lee

Paul Reed, Janis Paige, Cliff Hall,
Fred Gwynne, Arthur Rubin
Top: Laurence Naismith (C)

25

THE MUSIC BOX

Opened Monday, October 7, 1963.°
David Black and Nicholas A. Strater in association with Jerome Rosenfeld by arrangement with Oscar Lewenstein, L.O.P.
Ltd, and Donald Albery present The Coventry Belgrade Theatre Company in association with the Arts Council of Great
Britain in:

SEMI-DETACHED

By David Turner; Directed by Anthony Richardson; Designed by Kenneth Bridgeman; Lighting and Design Supervision by Will Steven
Armstrong.

CAST

Hilda Midway	Gillian Raine
Fred Midway	Leonard Rossiter
Tom Midway	Bryan Stanyon
Eileen Midway	Thelma Whiteley
Robert Freeman	Peter French
Avril Hadfield	Bridget Turner
Mrs. Garnet Hadfield	Antonia Pemberton
Nigel Hadfield	Donald Gee
Arnold Makepiece	Leon Sinden

A Comedy in three acts. The action takes
place on a Sunday morning in the home of Fred
Midway at 12 Woody Lane, Dowlihull, England
in the Spring of 1963.

General Manager: A. Gino Giglio
Press: Seymour Krawitz, Merle Debuskey,
Madi Ross
Stage Managers: Jose Vega, Doreen Richards
°Closed October 19, 1963. (16 performances)

Richard Sadler Photos

Donald Gee, Antonia Pemberton
Leonard Rossiter

Top: Thelma Whiteley, Gillian Raine
Leonard Rossiter

26

Geraldine McEwan, Barry Foster, Brian Bedford
in
"THE PRIVATE EAR"

MOROSCO THEATRE

Opened Wednesday, October 9, 1963.°
Roger L. Stevens by arrangement with H. M. Tennent, Ltd., presents:

THE PRIVATE EAR and THE PUBLIC EYE

By Peter Shaffer; Directed by Peter Wood; Decor by Richard Negri; Supervision by Klaus Holm; Associate Producers, Lyn Austin, Victor Samrock.

"The Private Ear"

CAST

Tchaik..Brian Bedford
Ted..Barry Foster
Doreen...Geraldine McEwan

The action takes place in Tchaik's bed-sitting room in Belsize Park, North London

"The Public Eye"

CAST

Cristoforou...Barry Foster
Charles...Moray Watson
Belinda...Geraldine McEwan

The action takes place in the office of Charles Sidley, chartered accountant, in Bloomsbury, London.

UNDERSTUDIES: Jane Henderson, Michael Sinclair.

Company Manager: Ben Rosenberg
Press: Samuel Lurie, Ruth Cage, Judith Davidson, Stanley Kaminsky
Stage Managers: John Drew Devereaux, Michael Sinclair

°Closed February 29, 1964. (163 performances) The same company opened at the Biltmore in Los Angeles on Monday, March 3, 1964, and closed at the Denver, Colo., Auditorium April 11, 1964.

Brian Bedford, Geraldine McEwan
Above: Geraldine McEwan, Moray Watson

Top: (L) Moray Watson, Geraldine McEwan
Barry Foster (also R)

Sidney Blackmer, Van Heflin, Larry Gates
in
"A CASE OF LIBEL"

Friedman-Abeles Photo

M'el Dowd, Joseph Julian, Joel Crothers, John Randolph, Van Heflin
Top: Sidney Blackmer, Philip Bourneuf

LONGACRE THEATRE
Opened Thursday, October 10, 1963.°
Roger L. Stevens and Joel Schenker present:

A CASE OF LIBEL

By Henry Denker; Based on Louis Nizer's Book "My Life In Court"; Directed by Sam Wanamaker; Settings and Lighting, Donald Oenslager; Costumes, Ann Roth; Production Assistant, Raymond League.

CAST

Claire Marshall	Camila Ashland
Abner Coles	Joseph Julian
David Strong	Joel Crothers
Robert Sloane	Van Heflin
Dennis Corcoran	John Randolph
Anita Corcoran	M'el Dowd†2
James Baldwin	Alexander Clark
Miss Brand	Lesley Woods
Paul Cleary	Sidney Blackmer†1
Boyd Bendix	Larry Gates
The Judge	Wynn Wright
Cleary's Assistant	Tom Hammond
Court Clerk	Douglas McLean
Court Stenographer	William Hindman
Colonel Douglas	Philip Bourneuf
Fred Alston	Richard McMurray
Foreman of Jury	Keith Parnell

UNDERSTUDIES: Bendix, Cleary, Wendell K. Phillips; Douglas, Alexander Clark; Anita, Claire, Lesley Woods; Dennis, Richard McMurray; Abner, Fred, Baldwin, William Hindman, Strong, Tom Hammond; Judge, Douglas McLean.

A Drama in three acts and eight scenes. The action takes place in the private office of Robert Sloane in New York City, and in a court room of the New York State Supreme Court.

General Manager: Victor Samrock
Company Manager: John Larson
Press: Nat Dorfman, Irvin Dorfman, Marcia Taradash
Stage Managers: Henri Caubisens, Jack Woods
°Closed May 9, 1964. (242 performances)
†Succeeded by: 1. Paul McGrath, 2. Audra Lindley.

Friedman-Abeles Photos

Top: Joseph Julian, Camila Ashland, Joel Crothers, Van Heflin

John Randolph, Richard McMurray, Joseph Julian, Joel Crothers, Van Heflin

31

ANTA THEATRE

Opened Monday, October 14, 1963.°
Michael Ellis and William Hammerstein present:

THE ADVOCATE

By Robert Noah; Directed by Howard Da Silva; Scenery and Lighting, J. Michael Travis; Costumes, Ralph Alswang.

CAST

Ed Hughes	Martin Brooks
Giovanni Bertelli	Paul Stevens
Warren Curtis	James Daly
Tom Stark	Allen Nourse
Bartolomeo Vanzetti	Dino Fazio
A Guard	Walter P. Brown
Miss Evans	Lynn Brinker
Judge Ballantine	Joseph Warren
Rosa Sacco	Tresa Hughes
Nicola Sacco	Dolph Sweet
A Guard	Ernest Stone
Flint	Luther James
Celestino Madeiros	Conrad J. Bromberg
Inspector Matthews	Leslie Litomy
Al Tuttle	Stuart A. Germain
Captain Riordan	John Crowley
Court Clerk	Stuart A. Germain
George Schreiber	Charles Baxter
Adam Schuyler	Wilson Brooks
Samuel Carter	Ernest Stone
Charles Sherman	Rufus Smith
Sergeant-at-Arms	Alan Ansara
Arthur Burns	John Cecil Holm
A Secretary	Alan Ansara
The Governor	Barnard Hughes
The Warden	Leslie Litomy
Assistant Warden	Alan Ansara

UNDERSTUDIES: Hughes, Conrad Bromberg; Bertelli, Wilson Brooks; Curtis, Charles Baxter; Stark, Rufus Smith; Vanzetti, Alan Ansara; Judge, Wilson Brooks; Rosa, Lynn Brinker; Sacco, Conrad Bromberg; Governor, Rufus Smith.

A Drama in three acts. The action occurs in various places in and around Boston, Massachusetts, from September 1923 to August 1927.

General Manager: Elias Goldin
Company Manager: Leonard Mulhern
Press: Abner D. Klipstein, Howard Roy
Stage Managers: Leonard Patrick, Bernard Pollock, Leslie Litomy

°Closed October 19, 1963. (8 performances)

Friedman-Abeles Photos

Top: (L) Tresa Hughes, Dolph Sweet
(R) Barnard Hughes, Tresa Hughes, James Da▌
Left Center: James Daly

Mary Martin
in
"JENNIE"

Friedman-Abeles Photo

33

George Wallace, Connie Scott, Mary Martin
Top: Ethel Shutta, Mary Martin

George Wallace, Mary Martin (also at top)

Opened Thursday, October 17, 1963.°
Cheryl Crawford and Richard Halliday
present:

JENNIE

Lyrics and Music by Howard Dietz and Arthur
Schwartz; Book by Arnold Schulman; Suggested
by "Laurette" by Marguerite Courtney by arrangement with Alan J. Pakula; Directed by
Vincent J. Donehue; Choreography, Matt Mattox; Settings, George Jenkins; Costumes, Irene
Sharaff; Lighting, Jean Rosenthal; Musical Director, John Lesko; Orchestrations, Philip J. Lang
and Robert Russell Bennett; Dance Music and
Vocal Arrangements by Trude Rittman.

CAST

"The Mountie Gets His Man"
or
"Chang Lu, King of The White Slavers"

The Evil Chang Lu	Kirby Smith
Randolph of The Royal Mounted	George Wallace
Lu Wong	Gerald Teijelo
Dong Foo	Robert Murray
Our Melissa	Mary Martin
The Bear	Jeremiah Morris
Wicked Owner of a House of Ill Repute	Elaine Swann
A Tragic Virgin Sold into White Slavery	Linda Donovan
A Sinful Woman of Ill Repute	Sharon Vaughn
A Croupier	Stephen Elmore
A Woodsman	Rico Froehlich
A Pioneer Woman	Julie Sargant
Jennie Malone	Mary Martin
James O'Connor	George Wallace
Bessie Mae Sue	Elaine Swann
Stella	Linda Donovan
Sydney Harris	Jeremiah Morris
Frank Granada	Rico Froehlich
Casey O'Harrison	Stephen Elmore
Gregory Hyman	Kirby Smith
Sheriff Pugsley	Jay Velie
Abe O'Shaughnessy	Jack De Lon
Kevin O'Connor	Brian Chapin
Lois Houser	Imelda De Martin
O'Connor's Wardrobe Mistress	Bernice Saunders
Deputies	Martin Ambrose, Oran Osburn
Linda O'Connor	Connie Scott
Nellie Malone	Ethel Shutta

Delivery Man	Stephen Elmore
Charlie The Juiceman	Stan Watt
Flower Girl	Debbie Scott
Rita Bradley	Diane Coupe
Christopher Lawrence Cromwell	Robin Bailey
Shine Boy	Robert Murray
Teddy	Sean Peters
Gentleman	Jay Velie
Stage Manager	Stan Watt
Piano Player	Woody Kessler
The Pony	Misty
Fire Chief	Jay Velie

"The Sultan's 50th Bride"

Sultan	Kirby Smith
Harem Girls	Diane Coupe, Sally Ackerman, Linda Donovan
Guardians	Gerald Teijelo, Robert Murray, Al Sambogna
Eunuchs	Blair Hammond, Martin Ambrose
Indian Fakir	Jeremiah Morris
Shalamar	Mary Martin
Omar	George Wallace

DANCING ENSEMBLE: Sally Ackerman, Diane
Coupe, Mollie Sterns, Blair Hammond, Robert
Murray, Al Sambogna, Gerald Teijelo.
SINGING ENSEMBLE: Lispet Nelson, Julie
Sargant, Bernice Saunders, Sharon Vaughn,
Martin Ambrose, Stephen Elmore, Rico Froeh-
lich, Oran Osburn.
UNDERSTUDIES: Miss Martin, Christine Lind;
Mr. Wallace and Mr. Bailey, Jon Cypher.
MUSICAL NUMBERS: "Waitin' For The Eve-
ning Train," "When You're Far Away From
New York Town," "I Still Look At You That
Way," "For Better Or Worse," "Born Again,"
"Over Here," "Before I Kiss The World Good-
bye," "Sauce Diable," "Where You Are," "The
Jig," "See Seattle," "High Is Better Than Low,"
"The Night May Be Dark," "I Believe In Takin'
A Chance," "Welcome," "Lonely Nights."

A Musical in two acts and fourteen scenes.
The action takes place in a small town in South
Dakota, in New York City, and Seattle in 1906.

General Manager: Herman Bernstein
Company Manager: Thomas Kilpatrick
Press: Ben Washer
Stage Managers: Randall Brooks, Steven
Meyer, Paul Bertelsen, Richard Via

°Closed December 28, 1963. (82 performances)

Friedman-Abeles Photos

George Wallace, Mary Martin

BROOKS ATKINSON THEATRE

Opened Sunday, October 20, 1963.°
S. Hurok presents by arrangement with the
Government of the French Repubic:

MARIE BELL AND HER COMPANY in PHEDRE

By Jean Racine; Directed by Raymond Gerome; Decor and Costumes by Jacques Dupont;
Musique Concrete by Raymond Scheaffer.

CAST

Phedre	Marie Bell
Oenone	Henriette Barreau
Aricie	Danielle Volle
Ismene	Florence Ennery
Thesee	Alain Cuny
Hippolyte	Claude Giraud
Theramene	Tristani
Panope	Alain Lionel

A Drama in five acts. The action takes place
in 1677 at Trezenes near Athens

Company Manager: Oliver W. Nicoll
Press: Martin Feinstein, Michael Sweeley
Stage Manager: Edy Nichola

°Closed Sunday, October 27, 1963, after a limited engagement of 11 performances.

BROOKS ATKINSON THEATRE

Opened Tuesday, October 29, 1963.°
S. Hurok presents by arrangement with the
Government of the French Republic:

BERENICE

By Jean Racine; Directed by Andre Barsacq;
Scenery and Costumes by Diane Esmond.

CAST

Berenice, Queen of Palestine	Marie Bell
Phenice	Florence Ennery
Titus, Emperor of Rome	Claude Giraud
Antiochus, King of Commagene	Jean-Francois Calve
Paulin	Serge Bossac
Arsace	Alain Lionel
Rutile	Tristani

A Drama in five acts presented with one
intermission.

Company Manager: Oliver W. Nicoll
Press: Martin Feinstein, Michael Sweeley
Stage Manager: Edy Nicolas

°Closed Sunday, November 3, 1963, after a
limited engagement of 8 performances.

Bernand Photos

**Left: Alain Cuny, Marie Bell, Alain Lionel
in "Phedre"**

Marie Bell

Marie Bell, Claude Giraud in "Phedre"
Top Left: Marie Bell, Florence Ennery
in "Berenice"

Claude Giraud

36

Claude Giraud, Marie Bell
in
"BERENICE"

37

BELASCO THEATRE

Opened Tuesday, October 22, 1963.°
Stevens Productions presents:

A RAINY DAY IN NEWARK

By Howard Teichmann; Staged by Albert Marre; Designed by Ed Wittstein.

CAST

Sidney Rice	Gene Hackman
Harry Untermeyer	Tom Ahearne
Edward L. Voorhees	John McMartin
John T. Kodiak	Eddie Mayehoff
Brewster	Mary McCarty
Elizabeth Lamb	Dody Goodman
Maurice Endicott	Ivor Francis
Milo Boulton	Milo Boulton
TV Technician	Don Lochner
Henry Cotton	Zachary Scott
Lionel Davis	Rex Everhart

UNDERSTUDIES: Kodiak, Rex Everhart; Elizabeth, Brewster, Kip McArdle; Voorhees, Cotton, John Garner; Endicott, Untermeyer, Davis, Don Lochner; Rice, Boulton, Daniel Walker.

A Comedy in two acts with a prologue and epilogue. The action takes place at the present time in Endicott, N. J.

General Manager: Victor Samrock
Company Manager: Mitchell Brower
Press: Samuel Lurie, Judith S. Davidson, Ruth Cage, Stanley Kaminsky
Stage Managers: James Gelb, Joseph Olney, Daniel Walker

°Closed October 26, 1963. (6 performances)

Friedman-Abeles Photos

Left: Eddie Mayehoff, Dody Goodman, Zachary Scott, Mary McCarty

Ivor Francis, Mary McCarty, Dody Goodman
Top: Dody Goodman, John McMartin, Eddie Mayehoff

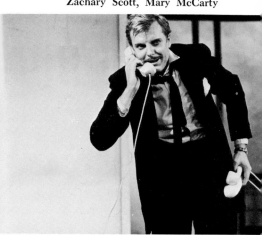

John McMartin
Top: Mary McCarty, Zachary Scott

Robert Redford, Elizabeth Ashley
in
"BAREFOOT IN THE PARK"

Elizabeth Ashley, Kurt Kasznar

Kurt Kasznar, Mildred Natwick
Top: Mildred Natwick, Elizabeth Ashley,
Kurt Kasznar, Robert Redford

BILTMORE THEATRE

Opened Wednesday, October 23, 1963.°
Saint Subber presents:

BAREFOOT IN THE PARK

By Neil Simon; Setting Designed by Oliver
Smith; Lighting, Jean Rosenthal; Costumes, Donald Brooks; Directed by Mike Nichols.

CAST

Corie Bratter	Elizabeth Ashley
Telephone Man	Herbert Edelman
Delivery Man	Joseph Keating
Paul Bratter	Robert Redford
Mrs. Banks	Mildred Natwick
Victor Velasco	Kurt Kasznar

UNDERSTUDIES: Paul, Gene Rupert; Corie,
E. J. Peaker; Victor, Herbert Edelman; Mrs.
Banks, Ruth Gregory.

A Comedy in three acts and four scenes. The
action takes place in the Bratter apartment on
East 48th Street in New York City at the present
time.

General Manager: C. Edwin Knill
Company Manager: William Craver
Press: Harry Nigro, Harvey Sabinson,
David Powers
Stage Managers: Harvey Medlinsky, Joseph
Keating

°Still playing May 31, 1964. (252 performances)

Friedman-Abeles Photos

**Top: Elizabeth Ashley, Robert Redford
Center: (L) Mildred Natwick
(R) Elizabeth Ashley**

urt Kasznar

Robert Redford

Inga Swenson, Stephen Douglass,
Robert Horton, Will Geer

BROADHURST THEATRE
Opened Thursday, October 24, 1963.°
David Merrick presents:

110 IN THE SHADE

By N. Richard Nash; Music, Harvey Schmidt;
Lyrics, Tom Jones; Based on the Play "The
Rainmaker" by N. Richard Nash; Directed by
Joseph Anthony; Musical Numbers Staged by
Agnes De Mille; Settings by Oliver Smith; Cos-
tumes, Motley; Lighting, John Harvey; Musical
Director, Donald Pippin; Orchestrations, Hershy
Kay; Dance Music, William Goldenberg; Vocal
Arranger, Robert De Cormier; Hair Styles,
Michel Kazan.

CAST

Toby	George Church
File	Stephen Douglass
H. C. Curry	Will Geer
Noah Curry	Steve Roland
Jimmie Curry	Scooter Teague
Lizzie Curry	Inga Swenson[1]
Snookie	Lesley Warren
Mrs. Jensen	Diane Deering
Phil Mackey	Seth Riggs
Tommy	Christopher Votos
Belinda	Renee Dudley
Geshy Toops	Don Crabtree
Gil Demby	Jerry Dodge[2]
Olive Barrow	Leslie Franzos
Wally Skacks, 3rd	Loren Hightower[3]
Maurine Toops	Evelyn Taylor
Bo Dollivon	Vernon Lusby
Mr. Curtis	Robert Shepard[4]
Bill Starbuck	Robert Horton
Wally Skacks	Carl Nicholas
Hannah	Dori Davis

TOWNSPEOPLE: Lynne Boradbent, Leslie
Franzos, Lucia Lambert, Paula Lloyd, Evelyn
Taylor, Esther Villavicencio, Florence Willson,
Don Atkinson, Frank Derbas, Jerry Dodge, Ben
Gillespie, Loren Hightower, Vernon Lusby,
Arthur Whitfield, Barbara Bossert, Gretchen
Cryer, Dori Davis, Diane Deering, Carolyn Kemp,
Urylee Leonardos, Donna Sanders, Clifford Fearl,
David London, Carl Nicholas, Stan Page.

UNDERSTUDIES: Lizzie, Joan Fagan; Starbuck,
Seth Riggs; File, Stan Page; H. C. Robert Shepard; Jimmie, Jerry Dodge; Noah, Don Crabtree;
Snookie, Florence Willson; Toby, Vernon Lusby
and Carl Nicholas.

MUSICAL NUMBERS: "Another Hot Day,"
"Lizzie's Coming Home," "Love, Don't Turn
Away," "Poker Polka," "Hungry Men," "The
Rain Song," "You're Not Foolin' Me," "Raunchy,"
"A Man and a Woman," "Old Maid," "Every-
thing Beautiful Happens At Night," "Melisande,"
"Simple Little Things," "Little Red Hat," "Is It
Really Me?," "Wonderful Music."

A Musical Play in two acts and eleven scenes.
The action takes place in a western state from
dawn to midnight of a summer day in a time
of drought.

General Manager: Jack Schlissel
Press: Lee Solters, Harvey Sabinson,
David Powers
Stage Managers: Bill Ross, Charles Blackwell,
May Muth, Seth Riggs

° Still playing May 31, 1964.
(251 performances)
† Succeeded by: 1. Joan Fagan, 2. Arthur Whitfield, 3. Bob Bishop, 4. Robert Spelvin.

Friedman-Abeles Photos

Top Left: Robert Horton, Inga Swenson
Stephen Douglass
Center: Robert Horton, Inga Swenson

Lesley Warren, George Church
Above & Top: Lesley Warren, Scooter Teague

Inga Swenson, Robert Horton (also top)
Above: Adriane Rogers, Stephen Douglass

43

Friedman-Abeles Photo

44

Robert Horton, Inga Swenson
in
"110 IN THE SHADE"

Colleen Dewhurst
in
"THE BALLAD OF THE SAD CAFE"

Friedman-Abeles Photo

45

MARTIN BECK THEATRE
Opened Wednesday, October 30, 1963.°
Lewis Allen and Ben Edwards present:

THE BALLAD OF THE SAD CAFE

Adapted by Edward Albee from the Novella of Carson McCullers; Directed by Alan Schneider; Scenery, Ben Edwards; Lighting, Jean Rosenthal; Music Composed by William Flanagan; Costumes, Jane Greenwood; Production Associate, Harry Rigby; Assistant Director, Melvin Bernhardt; Boxing Coordinator, Max Kleven.

CAST

The Narrator	Rosco Lee Browne
Rainey 1	Louis W. Waldon
Rainey 2	Deane Selmier
Stumpy MacPhail	John C. Becher
Henry Macy	William Prince
Miss Amelia Evans	Colleen Dewhurst
Cousin Lymon	Michael Dunn
Emma Hale	Enid Markey
Mrs. Peterson	Jenny Egan
Merlie Ryan	Roberts Blossom
Horace Wells	William Duell
Henry Ford Crimp	David Clarke
Rosser Cline	Griff Evans
Lucy Willins	Nell Harrison
Mrs. Hasty Malone	Bette Henritze
Marvin Macy	Lou Antonio
Henrietta Ford Crimp, Jr.	Susan Dunfee

TOWNSPEOPLE: Ernest Austin, Alice Drummond, Jack Kehoe.

MUSICIANS: Raymond Crisara, Stanley Drucker, Laura Newell, Julius Baker, Herb Harris, Seymour Barab.

UNDERSTUDIES: Amelia, Rosemary Murphy; Henry, David Clarke; Marvin, Louis W. Waldon; Lymon, Julian Miller; Emma, Bette Henritze; Stumpy, Griff Evans; Mrs. Peterson and Townswomen, Alice Drummond; Merlie, William Duell; Rainey 1, Ernest Austin; Rainey 2 and Townsmen, Jack Kehoe.

A Drama presented without intermission.

Company Manager: Tom Bodkin
Press: Howard Atlee, Michael Sean O'Shea,
Robert Larkin, Paul Solomon
Stage Managers: John Maxtone-Graham,
Don Gilliland, Ernest Austin
°Closed February 15, 1964. (123 performances)

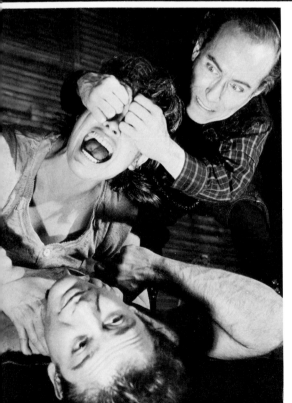

Lou Antonio, Colleen Dewhurst, Michael Dunn

46

Friedman-Abeles and Henry Grossman Photos

Michael Dunn, Colleen Dewhurst
Top: Colleen Dewhurst, Lou Antonio

Lou Antonio, William Prince
Above: William Prince, Michael Dunn

47

LITTLE THEATRE

Opened Saturday, November 2, 1963.*
Joel Schenker and Hexter Productions, Inc.,
in association with Sydney S. Baron
present:

TAMBOURINES TO GLORY

By Langston Hughes; Adapted from his Novel;
Music, Jobe Huntley; Directed by Nikos Pschar-
opoulos; Settings and Costumes, John Conklin;
Lighting, Peter Hunt; Choral Director, Clara
Ward; Dance Assistant, Judd Jones; Musical
Consultant, Abba Bogin.

CAST

C. J. Moore	Robert Guillaume
Marshalls	Rudy Challenger, Garwood Perkins
Essie Belle Johnson	Rosetta LeNoire
Youth	Clyde Williams
Mattie Morningside	Rosalie King
Laura Wright Reed	Hilda Simms
Policeman	Rudy Challenger
Big-Eyed Buddy Lomax	Louis Gossett
Birdie Lee	Clara Ward
Gloria Dawn	Anna English
The Gloriettas	Helen Ferguson, Tina Sattin
Bartender	Garwood Perkins
Brother Bud	Brother John Sellers
Brother Clyde	Clyde Williams
Marietta Johnson	Micki Grant
Deacons	Clark Morgan, Garwood Perkins,
	Brother John Sellers, Laurence Watson
Deaconess Lucy Mae Hobbs	Lynn Hamilton
Chicken-Crow-For-Day	Joseph Attles
Ministers of Music	Clyde Williams,
	Alton Williams
Prison Warden	Garwood Perkins

CHOIR, PASSERSBY: Rudy Challenger, Voyla
Crowley, Dorothy Drake, Helen Ferguson, Alma
Hubbard, Judd Jones, Rosalie King, Theresa
Merritt, Clark Morgan, Garwood Perkins, Tina
Sattin, Laurence Watson.

A Gospel Singing Play in two acts and twelve
scenes. The action takes place in Harlem, New
York City, some time in the past.

General Manager: Arthur Waxman
Company Manager: Dick Campbell
Press: Nat and Irvin Dorfman, Ted Goldsmith,
Marcia Taradash
Stage Managers: Richard Blofson, Otis Young,
Clark Morgan

*Closed November 23, 1963. (24 performances)

Martha Holmes Photos

Louis Gossett, Hilda Simms, Clara Ward
Top: Micki Grant, Louis Gossett,
Robert Guillaume

LUNT-FONTANNE THEATRE

Opened Monday, November 11, 1963.°
David Merrick presents:

ARTURO UI

By Bertolt Brecht; Adapted by George Tabori;
Directed by Tony Richardson; Designed by
Rouben Ter-Arutunian; Music by Jule Styne;
Orchestrations, Ray Ellis; Associate Producer,
Neil Hartley.

CAST

The Barker	Paul Michael
Dogsborough	Michael Constantine
Giuseppe Givola	Elisha Cook
Manuele Giri	Lionel Stander
Arturo Ui	Christopher Plummer
Mulberry	George Cotton
Butcher	Henry Lascoe
Flake	James Frawley
Sheet	William Shust
Clark	Hugh Franklin
Young Dogsborough	Oliver Clark
Ernesto Roma	Murvyn Vye
Dockdaisy	Dossie Hollingsworth
Arturo's Bodyguards	Tom Pedi, Harold Gary
Ragg	Louis Guss
Bowl	Sandy Baron
Goodwill	Paul Michael
Gaffles	Warren Wade
O'Casey	James Coco
The Actor	Roger DeKoven
Jim Crockett	John Marriott
The Woman	Beah Richards
Judge	Warren Wade
Fish	Leonardo Cimino
Doctor	Glenn Stensel
Defense Counsel	David O'Brien
Betty Dullfeet	Madeleine Sherwood
Inna	Chuck Haren
Shorty	John Karlen
Ignatius Dullfeet	Robert Weil
Priests	Sandy Baron

GROCERS, GUNMEN, GUARDS, REPORTERS,
SPECTATORS: Sandy Baron, Leonardo Cimino,
James Coco, James Frawley, Louis Guss, Chuck
Haren, Diane Higgins, Bobby Dean Hooks, John
Karlen, Frank Loren, Gubi Mann, John Marriott,
David O'Brien, Anthony Ponzini, William Shust,
Jim Stark, Glenn Stansel.

A Drama in two acts and sixteen scenes. The
action takes place in and around Chicago in
the early 1930's.

General Manager: Jack Schlissel
Company Manager: A. Gino Giglio
Press: Lee Solters, Harvey B. Sabinson,
Leo Stern, David Powers
Stage Managers: Bernard Gersten, Jim Stark,
Anthony Ponzini

°Closed November 16, 1963. (8 performances)

Murvyn Vye, Christopher Plummer, Harold
Gray, Lionel Stander, Elisha Cook
Above: Madeleine Sherwood, Hugh Franklin,
Christopher Plummer
Top: Christopher Plummer, Murvyn Vye

49

Jane Downs, Charles Boyer   Louise Sorel, Barry Justice (also at top)

BROOKS ATKINSON THEATRE
Opened Tuesday, November 12, 1963.°
    Alexander H. Cohen and H. M. Tennent
    Ltd. present:

MAN AND BOY

By Terence Rattigan; Suggested by Robert
Shaplen's "Kreuger Genius and Swindler"; Directed by Michael Benthall; Setting and Lighting, Ralph Alswang; Associate Producers, Gabriel Katzka, Andre Goulston; Production Assistants, Annette Segal, Robin Rudd.

CAST

Carol Penn	Louise Sorel
Basil Anthony	Barry Justice
Gregor Antonescu	Charles Boyer
Sven Johnson	Geoffrey Keen
Mark L. Herris	Austin Willis
David Beeston	William Smithers
Countess Antonescu	Jane Downs

UNDERSTUDIES: Herris, Johnson, Beeston,
Stuckmann; Basil, John Milligan; Carol, Countess, Beverlee McKinsey.

A Drama in three acts. The action takes
place in a basement apartment in Greenwich
Village, New York, during a July evening in
1934.

    General Manager: Roy A. Somlyo
Press: David Rothenberg, Michael Alpert
Stage Managers: Herman Shapiro, Eugene
                Stuckmann
°Closed December 28, 1963. (54 performances)

Angus McBean Photos

Top: Charles Boyer, Jane Downs

Charles Boyer, Barry Justice

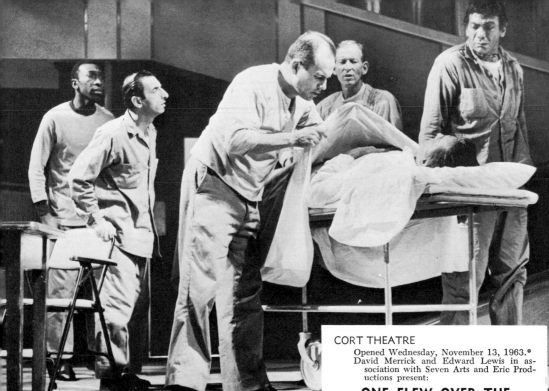

Astrid Wilsrud, Kirk Douglas, Joan Tetzel

CORT THEATRE

Opened Wednesday, November 13, 1963.°
David Merrick and Edward Lewis in association with Seven Arts and Eric Productions present:

ONE FLEW OVER THE CUCKOO'S NEST

By Dale Wasserman; Based on Novel by Ken
Kesey; Directed by Alex Segal; Scenery and
Lighting, Will Steven Armstrong; Costumes,
Noel Taylor; Incidental Music, Teiji Ito; Hair
Styles, Michel Kazan; Party Dance Staged by
Rhoda Levine.

CAST

Chief Bromden	Ed Ames
Aide Warren	Lincoln Kilpatrick
Aide Williams	Leonard Parker
Nurse Ratched	Joan Tetzel
Nurse Flinn	Astrid Wilsrud
Dale Harding	William Daniels
Ellis	Arnold Soboloff
Billy Bibbit	Gene Wilder
Scanlon	Malcolm Atterbury
Cheswick	Gerald S. O'Loughlin
Martini	Al Nesor
Ruckly	William Gleason
Fredericks	Wesley Gale
Sefelt	Charles Tyner
Colonel Matterson	Paul Huber
Randle P. McMurphy	Kirk Douglas
Dr. Spivey	Rex Robbins
Aide Turkle	Milton J. Williams
Candy Starr	Arlene Golonka
Nurse Nakamura	Michi Kobi
Technician	Clifford Cothren
Sandra	K. C. Townsend
Aide	Peter Gumeny

UNDERSTUDIES: Randle, Gerald S. O'Lough-
lin; Cheswick, William Gleason; Bromden, Clif-
ford Cothren; Harding, Bibbit, Spivey, Robert
Boxill; Fredericks and Aides, Dougles Turner;
Scanlon, Paul Huber; Martini, Arnold Soboloff;
Sefelt, Ruckly, Matterson, Ellis, Peter Gumeny.

A Drama in three acts. The action takes place
in a ward in a State mental hospital in the
Pacific Northwest at the present time.

General Manager: Jack Schlissel
Company Manager: Harold Kusell
Press: Lee Solters, Harvey Sabinson,
David Powers
Stage Managers: Del Hughes, Clifford
Cothren, Peter Gumeny
°Closed January 25, 1964. (82 performances)

Henry Grossman Photos

Foreground: Kirk Douglas, Arnold Soboloff
Top: Malcolm Atterbury, Gerald O'Loughlin,
Al Nesor, Gene Wilder, Kirk Douglas, Arnold
Soboloff, William Daniels, William Gleason

Kirk Douglas, Joan Tetzel, Gene Wilder
Above: Kirk Douglas, Ed Ames

53

LYCEUM THEATRE

Opened Monday, November 18, 1963.°
Arthur Cantor and E. E. Fogelson present:

THE GOLDEN AGE

Devised by Richard Johnson; Directed by
Douglas Campbell; Music Devised and Directed
by Sydney Beck; Production Associate, Kip
Cohen; Produced by Santa Fe Productions, Inc.;
Assistant to The Producers, Lois Bianchi; Pro-
duction Assistant, Benjamin Siegler; Technical
Consultant, Robert Buccolo; Men's Evening
Wear by After Six; Gowns by Domingo A.
Rodriguez.

CAST

Douglas Campbell	Nancy Wickwire
Douglas Rain	Lester Rawlins

UNDERSTUDIES: Gordon Myers, Betty Wilson.
SINGERS: Betty Wilson, James Stover, Gordon
Myers.
Consort of Instruments: Blanche Winogron,
James Tyler, Leonid Bolotine, Robert Kuehn.

An Entertainment in the words and music of
the Elizabethan Age presented in two acts:
Spring and Summer, Fall and Winter.

General Manager: Ken Myers
Company Manager: Tony Geiss
Press: Arthur Cantor, Artie Solomon
Stage Managers: Edward Payson Call,
Douglas Rain

°Closed November 23, 1963. (7 performances)

Werner J. Kuhn Photos

**Top: Douglas Campbell, Lester Rawlins,
Nancy Wickwire, Douglas Rain**

Douglas Campbell, Douglas Rain

BOOTH THEATRE

Opened Wednesday, November 20, 1963.°
Jon Burgin and Bruno di Cosmi present:

ONCE FOR THE ASKING

By Owen G. Arno; Directed by Reginald
Denham; Designed and Lighted by Feder; Costumes by Audre.

CAST

Michele Robbins	Donna Scott
Ashley Robbins	Scott McKay
Gretchen	Janet Fox
Madelaine Robbins	Jan Sterling
Alex Krumbull	Russell Nype
Mrs. Goolsby	Dorothy Sands
Sondi	Bonnie Jones
Bradford	Martin Ross
Martin Hollingshead	Ralph Dunn
Doreen Krumbull	Fayne Blackburn
Grace Hollingshead	Leona Powers
Eddie	Richard Poston
A Little Girl	Jeanne Tanzy
George Richardson	Humphrey Davis
A Taxi Driver	Maurice Brenner
A Stranger	Walter Flanagan

UNDERSTUDIES: Madelaine, Fayne Blackburn; Ashley, Alex, Richard Poston; Sondi,
Doreen, Bibi Besch; Fretchen, Goolsby, Grace,
Hazel Jones; Michele, Little Girl, Jennifer
Stone; Martin, Humphrey Davis; Eddie, George,
Cabbie, Stranger, Norman Shelly.

A Comedy in three acts and eight scenes.
The action takes place at the present time in
the Long Island home of Ashley Robbins, and
his Manhattan office.

General Manager: Elias Goldin
Company Manager: Leonard Mulhern
Press: Nat and Irvin Dorfman, Ted Goldsmith,
Marcia Taradash
Stage Managers: Mortimer Halpern,
Norman Shelly

°Closed Wednesday, November 20, 1963.
(1 performance)

Friedman-Abeles Photos

**Top: Donna Scott, Scott McKay, Jan Sterling,
Janet Fox**

Ralph Dunn, Fayne Blackburn, Russell Nype

55

THE MUSIC BOX
Opened Monday, December 2, 1963.°
Joseph Kipness and Richard W. Krakeur in association with David Kaufman present:

HAVE I GOT A GIRL FOR YOU!

By Irving Cooper; Based on a Story by Helen Cooper; Directed by Don Richardson; Design and Lights, Sam Leve; Costumes, Willa Kim; Wigs and Hairstyles, R. Keith; Production Assistant, Marge-Toni Hesse; Associate Producer, Bernard Howard.

CAST
Rose Garfield	Nancy R. Pollock
Joe Garfield	Simon Oakland
Sam Garfield	Michael Gorrin
Sally Jordan	Paula Laurence
Steve Kozlek	Tom Ligon
Ruby Pulaski	Dick Van Patten
Jonas Wells	Donald Mitchell
Helen Baker	Karen Thorsell
Ben Garfield	Bernard Kates
Emily Garfield	Patricia Benoit
Mitzi Jordan	Mary Linn Beller
Ted Barker	Hal Riddle
Thad MacKenzie	Joseph Boland
Western Union Messenger	Tedd King

UNDERSTUDIES: Joe, Ben, Ruby, Messenger, Allan Miller; Sam, Thad, Ted, Ben Basenko; Helen, Mitzi, Emily, Marge-Toni Hesse; Sally, Beatrice Pons; Jonas, Steve, Tedd King.

A Comedy in three acts and ten scenes. The action takes place at the present time in the Bronx apartment of the Garfields, and in the athletic director's office in Fremont High School on New York's East Side.

General Manager: Ben Boyar
Press: Karl Bernstein, Ben Kornzweig
Stage Managers: Richard B. Shull, Tedd King, Donald Mitchell

°Closed Monday, December 2, 1963.
(1 performance)

Friedman-Abeles Photos

Paula Laurence, Nancy R. Pollock
Above: Nancy R. Pollock, Michael Gorrin

Top: (L) Karen Thorsell, Simon Oakland
(R) Nancy R. Pollock, Michael Gorrin

56

Tessie O'Shea
in
"THE GIRL WHO CAME TO SUPPER"

Jose Ferrer, Chris Gampel, Florence
Henderson, Sean Scully

BROADWAY THEATRE
Opened Sunday, December 8, 1963.°
Herman Levin presents:

THE GIRL WHO CAME TO SUPPER

Music and Lyrics, Noel Coward; Book, Harry Kurnitz; Based on Play, "The Sleeping Prince," by Terence Rattigan; Staged by Joe Layton; Scenery, Oliver Smith; Costumes, Irene Sharaff; Lighting, Peggy Clark; Musical Direction and Vocal Arrangements, Jay Blackton; Orchestrations, Robert Russell Bennett; Dance Music Arranged by Genevieve Pitot; Hair Styles, Ronald DeMann; Production Assistant, Eleanore Saidenberg.

CAST

Jessie Maynard	Marian Haraldson
Mary Morgan	Florence Henderson
Tony Morelli	Jack Eddleman
Mr. Grimes	Peter Pagan
Violetta Vines	Maggie Worth
Peter Northbrook	Roderick Cook
Colonel Hofmann	Chris Gampel
Grand Duke Charles, Prince Regent of Carpathia	Jose Ferrer
First Girl	Donna Monroe
Second Girl	Ruth Shepard
Major-Domo	Carey Nairnes
King Nicholas III	Sean Scully
Simka	Murray Adler
Queen Mother	Irene Browne
Ada Cockle	Tessie O'Shea
Baroness Brunheim	Lucie Lancaster
Lady Sunningdale	Ilona Murai

DANCERS: Nancy Lynch, Julie Drake, Sheila Forbes, Jami Landi, Sandy Leeds, Carmen Morales, Ilona Murai, Mari Shelton, Gloria Smith, Mary Zahn, Ivan Allen, Robert Fitch, Jose Gutierrez, Peter Holmes, Scott Ray, Paul Reid Roman, Dan Siretta, Mike Toles.

SINGERS: Jeremy Brown, Kellie Brytt, Carol Glade, Marian Haraldson, Elaine Labour, Donna Monroe, Ruth Shepard, Maggie Worth, Jack Eddleman, John Felton, Dell Hanley, Barney Johnston, Art Matthews, Bruce Peyton, Jack Rains, Mitchell Taylor.

UNDERSTUDIES: Charles, David Brooks; Mary, Dran Seitz; Queen Mother, Lucie Lancaster; Peter, Peter Pagan; King, Mike Toles; Ada, Kellie Brytt; Colonel, Robert Fitch; Grimes, Barney Johnston; Baroness, Elaine Labour; Major-Domo, Jose Gutierrez; Prince Regent, Jack Eddleman.

MUSICAL NUMBERS: "Swing Song," "Yasni Kozkolai," "My Family Tree," "I've Been Invited to A Party," "When Foreign Princes Come To Visit Us," "Sir or Ma'am," "Soliloquies," "Lonely," "London Is A Little Bit Of All Right," "Waltz," "What Ho, Mrs. Brisket," "Don't Take Our Charlie For The Army," "Saturday Night At The Rose and Crown," "Here and Now," "Coronation Chorale," "How Do You Do, Middle Age?," "The Stingaree," "Curt, Clear, and Concise," "Tango," "The Coconut Girl," "Welcome To Pootzie Van Doyle," "Paddy MacNeil and His Automobile," "Swing Song," "Six Lillies Of The Valley," "The Walla Walla Boola," "This Time It's True Love," "I'll Remember Her."

A Musical Comedy in two acts and sixteen scenes. The action takes place in London, just prior to and during the Coronation of H.M. George V, June 21-22, 1911.

General Manager: Philip Adler
Company Manager: S. M. Handelsman
Press: Richard Maney, Martin Shwartz
Stage Managers: Samuel Liff, Jerry Adler, Marnel Sumner, Geoffrey Johnson

°Closed March 14, 1964. (112 performances)

Friedman-Abeles Photos

Top Left: Irene Browne (with crown), Jo[se]
Ferrer, Florence Henderson, Roderick Coo[k]
(with cape)
Left Center: Jose Ferrer, Florence Henderso[n]

Jose Ferrer, Irene Browne, Florence Henderson
Top: Tessie O'Shea (C)

Larry Parks, Dennis Cooney

THE MUSIC BOX

Opened Wednesday, December 18, 1963.*
Dore Schary presents:

LOVE AND KISSES

By Anita Rowe Block; Directed by Dore
Schary; Setting and Lighting, Marvin Reiss;
Costumes, Helene Pons; Associate Producer,
Walter Reilly.

CAST

Jeff Pringle_____Larry Parks
Rosemary Cotts_____Alberta Grant
Nanny_____Katharine Raht
Carol Pringle_____Mary Fickett
Elizabeth Pringle_____Susan Browning
Buzzy Pringle_____Dennis Cooney
Freddy Winters_____Bert Convy
T. J. Jones_____Michael Currie

UNDERSTUDIES: Jeff, Michael Currie; Rosemary, Janice Carson; Elizabeth, Pamela Raymond; Nanny, Elsa Walden.

A Comedy in three acts and seven scenes.
The entire action takes place in the living room
of the Pringle home in Elmsdale, a suburb of
Detroit, at the present time.

General Manager: Edward Choate
Press: Nat and Irvin Dorfman, Ted Goldsmith,
Marcia Taradash
Stage Managers: Jeb Schary, Louis Kosman,
Elsa Walden

*Closed December 28, 1963. (13 performances)

Friedman-Abeles Photos

Top: Alberta Grant, Bert Convy, Susan
Browning, Mary Fickett, Dennis Cooney

Robert Preston, Marie Wallace, Leslye Hunter
in
"NOBODY LOVES AN ALBATROSS"

Friedman-Abeles Photo

61

Leslye Hunter, Robert Preston, Constance Ford

Phil Leeds, Robert Preston, Leon Janney
Top: Robert Preston, Richard Mulligan,
Carol Rossen, Marian Winters

LYCEUM THEATRE

Opened Thursday, December 19, 1963.°
Elliot Martin and Philip Rose present:

NOBODY LOVES
AN ALBATROSS

By Ronald Alexander; Directed by Gene Saks;
Scenery and Lighting, Will Steven Armstrong;
Costumes, Florence Klotz; Production Assistant,
Ronnie Kramer.

CAST

Nat Bentley	Robert Preston†
Diane Bentley	Leslye Hunter
Sarah Washington	Gertrude Jeannette
Jean Hart	Carol Rossen
Phil Matthews	Richard Mulligan
Hildy Jones	Constance Ford
L. T. Whitman	Frank Campanella
Marge Weber	Marian Winters
Bert Howell	Barnard Hughes
Mike Harper	Leon Janney
Sean O'Loughlin	Jack Bittner
Linda	Marie Wallace
Victor Talsey	Phil Leeds

UNDERSTUDIES: Jean, Linda, Beverly Penberthy; Hildy, Marge, Evelyn Russell; Mike, Victor, Barnard Hughes; Whitman, Sean, Phil, Bert, Joseph Bernard; Diane, Joy Stark; Sarah, Jeannette DuBois.

A Comedy in two acts and four scenes. The action takes place at the present time in the Beverly Hills livingroom of Nathaniel Bentley.

General Manager: Walter Fried
Press: Merle Debuskey, Seymour Krawitz, Madi Ross
Stage Managers: Leonard Auerbach, Joseph Bernard

° Still playing May 31, 1964.
(188 performances)
† Succeeded by Barry Nelson

Friedman-Abeles Photos

Top: (L) Barnard Hughes, Robert Preston, Constance Ford
(R) Robert Preston, Carol Rossen

Leslye Hunter, Robert Preston, Carol Rossen, Gertrude Jeannette

63

ANTA THEATRE

Opened Monday, December 22, 1963.°
The Actors Studio, Inc., presents:

MARATHON '33

By June Havoc; Staged by Miss Havoc; Entire Production under the supervision of Lee Strasberg; Assistant Director, Tim Everett; Music by Conrad Janis and His Tail Gate 5; Setting, Peter Larkin; Lighting, Tharon Musser; Costumes, Noel Taylor; Production Coordinator, Fred Stewart.

CAST

Mike, Marathon Trainer	Philip Kenneally
Beezer, Marathon Trainer	Peter Masterson
Ruddy, Band Leader-M.C.	Conrad Janis
Eve Adamanski	Olive Deering
Lusty "One Punch" Hutchinson	Tom Avera
"Sugar Hips" Johnson	Margaret O'Neill
Banty Binks	Brooks Morton
Robin Greenaman, his Partner	Robin Howard
Rita Marimba	Maya Kenin
Scotty Schwartz	Don Fellows
Pearl Schwartz	Patricia Quinn
Schnozz Wilson	Logan Ramsey
Rae Wilson	Doris Roberts
Al Marciano	Gabriel Dell
Flo Marciano	Pat Randall
Abe O'Brien	Tim Everett
His Girl "The Mick"	Lane Bradbury
Bozo Bazoo	Iggie Wolfington
Helen Bazoo	Lucille Patton
Mr. Dankle	Lonny Chapman
Red	John Strasberg
His Partner Ida	Libby Dean
Beefy Bancroft, Acrobat	Dick Bradford
Petrushka Patrick	Robert Heller
Patsy, Marathon Top Banana	Lee Allen
June	Julie Harris
Mr. James	Joe Don Baker
Mr. Burke	Gordon Phillips
Mrs. Beckett-Jones	Adelaide Klein
Mr. Forbes	Will Hare
Pinky	Marcella Dodge
Angel	Janet Luoma
Hinky	Robert Heller
Joe	Dick Bradford
Minister	Ralph Waite
Melba Marvel	Libby Dean
Night Club Star	Janice Mars

SPECTATORS, ROUSTABOUTS, WHORES, PIMPS, ETC.: Sally Alex, Dick Bradford, Marcella Dodge, Philip Dorian, Will Hare, Janet Luoma, Brooks Morton, Janice Mars, Gordon Phillips, James Rado, Ralph Waite.

TAIL GATE 5: Ahmed Abdul-Malik, Eddie Barefield, Kenny Davern, David "Panama" Francis, Conrad Janis, John Letman, Dick Wellstood, Johnny Windhurst.

A Comedy with music in two acts. The action takes place in the early Spring of 1933 in the United States.

Press: Bill Doll & Co., Robert Ganshaw, Midori Tsuji, Shirley Herz
Stage Managers: Martin Fried, Bernard Pollack, Gordon Phillips, John Strasberg

°Closed February 1, 1964. (48 performances)

Martha Holmes Photos

Lee Allen, Julie Harris, Lucille Patton, Iggie Wolfington, Tim Everett
Above: Julie Harris, Lee Allen

Top: (L) Olive Deering, Julie Harris, Lonnie Chapman
(R) Tim Everett, Iggie Wolfington, Conrad Ja[nis]

Julie Harris

LITTLE THEATRE

Opened Thursday, December 26, 1963.°
Josephine Forrestal Productions, Inc. presents:

DOUBLE DUBLIN

Supervised by Gus Schirmer, Jr.; Musical Direction, Baldwin Bergersen; Setting and Lighting, Helen Pond, Herbert Senn; Musical Numbers Edited by David Nillo; Music Arranged and Played by Baldwin Bergersen.

CAST

John Molloy   Noel Sheridan
Deirdre O'Callaghan   Patricia Brogan

PROGRAM

ACT I: Audience Reflections, Window Dressing, 100,000 Welcomes, Darts, Rural Character, Gaelic Air, The Importance of Behan, Amateur Theatricals, Joyce's Dublin, Dublin Saunter, Irish Jig.

ACT II: Irish Station Break, Four Portraits, Bonnet Trimmed With The Blue, Folk Singer, Keeping Up With The Hones, The Fish Gutter, I Was Strolling, Portrait In Oils, The Green Bushes, Matchmaker, Finale.

General Manager: Robert Kamlot
Press: Betty Lee Hunt, Diane Judge,
Earl Butler
Stage Manager: Mike Foley

°Closed Saturday, December 28, 1963.
(4 performances)

Friedman-Abeles Photos

Top: (L) John Molloy, Noel Sheridan
(R) John Molloy

Noel Sheridan

BROOKS ATKINSON THEATRE

Opened Wednesday, January 1, 1964.°
David Merrick presents:

THE MILK TRAIN DOESN'T STOP HERE ANYMORE

By Tennessee Williams; Directed by Tony
Richardson; Designed by Rouben Ter-Arutunian;
Music, Ned Rorem; Associate Producer, Neil
Hartley; Lighting, Martin Aronstein; Hair Styles,
Michel Kazan.

CAST

Stage Assistants	Bobby Dean Hooks, Konrad Matthaei
Mrs. Goforth	Tallulah Bankhead
Blackie	Marian Seldes
Rudy	Ralph Roberts
Christopher Flanders	Tab Hunter
Witch of Capri	Ruth Ford

UNDERSTUDIES: Mrs. Goforth, Witch, Nancy
Cushman; Flanders, Konrad Matthaei; Blackie,
Laurinda Barrett; Stage Assistants, John Karlen.

A Drama in two acts. The action takes place
in Mrs. Goforth's villa on the Divina Costiera
of Italy.

General Manager: Jack Schlissel
Company Manager: Gene Wolsk
Press: Richard Maney, Martin Shwartz
Stage Managers: Kermit Kegley, John Karlen,
George Hyland

°Closed January 4, 1964. (5 performances)
Originally presented Jan. 16, 1963, at the
Morosco Theatre with Hermione Baddeley,
Paul Roebling, and Mildred Dunnock. Closed
March 16, 1963, after 69 performances.

Photos by Arnold Weissberger

p: Bobby Dean Hooks, Tallulah Bankhead,
Tab Hunter
ght Center: Tab Hunter, Tallulah Bankhead

Tab Hunter, Ruth Ford

67

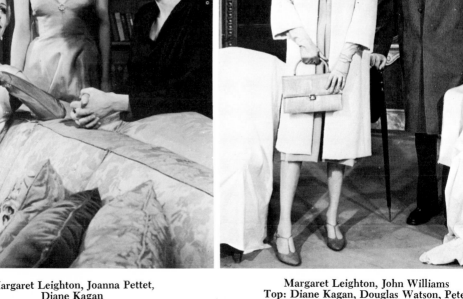

Margaret Leighton, Joanna Pettet,
Diane Kagan

Margaret Leighton, John Williams
Top: Diane Kagan, Douglas Watson, Peter
Donat, John Williams, Joanna Pettet, Margar
Leighton, James Olson, Alan Webb

ROYALE THEATRE

Opened Thursday, January 2, 1964.°
Roger L. Stevens presents:

THE CHINESE PRIME MINISTER

By Enid Bagnold; Directed by Joseph Anthony; Associate Producers, Lyn Austin, Victor Samrock; Setting, Oliver Smith; Costumes, Valentina; Lighting, Jean Rosenthal.

CAST

Bent	Alan Webb
Oliver	Peter Donat
She	Margaret Leighton
Roxane	Joanna Pettet
Alice	Diane Kagan
Tarver	Douglas Watson†
Red Gus Risko	James Olson
Sir Gregory	John Williams

UNDERSTUDIES: She, Brook Byron; Bent, Gregory, Guy Spaull; Oliver, Tarver, Roy R. Schneider; Alice, Roxane, Bibi Besch; Red, Joseph Maher.

A Comedy in three acts and four scenes. The action takes place in the drawing room of a once fashionable house in London.

Company Manager: James Awe
Press: Samuel Lurie, Ruth Cage, Judith Davidson, Stanley Kaminsky
Stage Managers: Bill Ross, Julian Barry

°Closed April 4, 1964. (108 performances)
†Succeeded by Roy Schneider

Top: Alan Webb, Margaret Leighton

Margaret Leighton

69

Charles Nelson Reilly, Eileen Brennan,
Jerry Dodge, Sondra Lee

ST. JAMES THEATRE

Opened Thursday, January 16, 1964.°
David Merrick presents:

HELLO, DOLLY!

Book, Michael Stewart; Music and Lyrics,
Jerry Herman; Suggested by Thornton Wilder's
Play "The Matchmaker"; Directed and Chore-
ographed by Gower Champion; Settings, Oliver
Smith; Costumes, Freddy Wittop; Lighting, Jean
Rosenthal; Musical Direction and Vocal Ar-
rangements, Shepard Coleman; Orchestrations,
Philip J. Lang; Dance and Incidental Music
Arranged by Peter Howard; Assistant to the
Director, Lucia Victor; Production Supervisor,
Neil Hartley; A David Merrick and Champion-
Five Inc., Production.

CAST

Mrs. Dolly Gallagher Levi	Carol Channing
Ernestina	Mary Jo Catlett
Ambrose Kemper	Igors Gavon
Horse	Jan LaPrade, Bonnie Mathis
Horace Vandergelder	David Burns
Ermengarde	Alice Playten
Cornelius Hackl	Charles Nelson Reilly
Barnaby Tucker	Jerry Dodge
Irene Molloy	Eileen Brennan
Minnie Fay	Sondra Lee
Mrs. Rose	Amelia Haas
Rudolph	David Hartman
Judge	Gordon Connell
Court Clerk	Ken Ayers

TOWNSPEOPLE, WAITERS, Etc.: Nicole Barth,
Monica Carter, Carvel Carter, Amelia Haas, Jan
LaPrade, Joan Buttons Leonard, Marilyne Mason,
Bonnie Mathis, Else Olufsen, Yolanda Poropat,
Bonnie Schon, Barbara Sharma, Mary Ann Snow,
Jamie Thomas, Pat Trott, Ken Ayers, Alvin
Beam, Joel Craig, Dick Crowley, Gene Gebauer,
Joe Helms, Richard Hermany, Neil Jones, Charles
Karel, Paul Kastl, Jim Maher, Joe McWherter,
John Mineo, Randy Phillips, Lowell Purvis,
Michael Quinn, Wil! Roy, Paul Solen, Ronnie
Young.

UNDERSTUDIES: Dolly, Jo Anne Worley;
Vandergelder, Gordon Connell; Cornelius, Charles
Karel, Mrs. Molloy, Mary Ann Snow; Minnie
Fay, Barbara Sharma; Barnaby, John Mineo;
Ambrose, Charles Karel; Judge, Michael Quinn;
Ernestina, Amelia Haas; Mrs. Rose, Jamie
Thomas.

MUSICAL NUMBERS: "I Put My Hand In,"
"It Takes A Woman," "Put On Your Sunday
Clothes," "Ribbons Down My Back," "Mother-
hood," "Dancing," "Before The Parade Passes
By," "Elegance," "The Waiters' Gallop," "Hello,
Dolly!," "Come and Be My Butterfly," "It Only
Takes A Moment," "So Long Dearie," Finale.

A Musical Comedy in two acts and fifteen
scenes. The action takes place in Yonkers and
in Manhattan.

General Manager: Jack Schlissel
Company Manager: Richard Highley
Press: Lee Solters, Harvey Sabinson,
Lila Glaser King, David Powers
Stage Managers: Frank Dudley, Pat Tolson,
David Hartman

° Still playing May 31, 1964.
(157 performances)

Eileen Darby—Graphic House Photos

**Left Center: Charles Nelson Reilly,
Carol Channing, Alice Playten, Igors Gavon**

Carol Channing (also top and center)

Sondra Lee, Carol Channing, Eileen Brennan
Above: Carol Channing, Charles Nelson Reilly
Top: Sondra Lee

David Burns, Carol Channing
in
"HELLO, DOLLY!"

Alec Guinness
in
"DYLAN"

Wallace Litwin Photo

PLYMOUTH THEATRE

Opened Saturday, January 18, 1964.°
George W. George and Frank Granat
present:

DYLAN

By Sidney Michaels; Directed by Peter Glenville; Scenery, Oliver Smith; Costumes, Ruth Morley; Music, Laurence Rosenthal; Lighting, Jack Brown; Production Assistant, Gloria Banta.

CAST

Dylan Thomas	Alec Guinness
Caitlin Thomas	Kate Reid
John Malcolm Brinnin	James Ray
Angus Marius	Martin Garner
Meg Stuart	Barbara Berjer
Annabelle Graham-Pike	Jenny O'Hara
Robert Mattack	Gordon B. Clarke
Bartender	Paul Larson†
Katherine Anne Porter	Carol Gustafson
Thelma Wonderland	Louisa Cabot
Elena Antone	Margaret Braidwood
Jay Henry Antone	Ernest Graves
Doctor	Grant Code
Nancy	Janet Sarno
Deck Officer	Jonathan Moore

REPORTERS, GUESTS, STUDENTS, Etc.: Susan Willis, Anthony Cannon, Louisa Cabot, Grant Code, Carol Gustafson, Paul Larson, Jonathan Moore, Janet Sarno.

UNDERSTUDIES: Dylan, Dana Elcar; Caitlin, Carol Gustafson; Brinnin, Jonathan Moore; Meg, Janet Sarno; Marius, Antone, Grant Code; Elena, Thelma, Susan Willis; Mattock, Paul Larson; Annabelle, Louisa Cabot.

A Drama in two acts. The entire action takes place in the early 1950's in America and Wales.

General Manager: Carl Fisher
Company Manager: Abe Cohen
Press: Lee Solters, Harvey Sabinson,
Mel Kopp, David Powers
Stage Managers: William Dodds, Roger
Johnson, Jr.

° Still playing May 31, 1964.
(152 performances)
† Succeeded by Alan North

Friedman-Abeles and Wallace Litwin Photos

Martin Garner, James Ray, Alec Guinness
Top: Alec Guinness, Kate Reid

Louisa Cabot, Alec Guinness, James Ray

Alec Guinness, Barbara Berjer
Top: Alec Guinness, Kate Reid

THE LITTLE THEATRE

Opened Monday, February 3, 1964.°
The Little Theatre, Inc., presents Habimah,
the National Theatre of Israel, in:

THE DYBBUK

By S. Ansky; Translated by H. N. Bialik;
Staged by I. Vachtangov; Settings, N. Altman;
Music, I. Engel; Choreography, Michedelov;
Production Supervised by Zvi Friedland; English
Translation Written by Raphael Rothstein with
the voices of Zvi Jagendorf and Sara Feinstein.

CAST

Talmudist I	Haim Amitai
Talmudist II	Shlomo Brook
Talmudist III	Avraham Ninio, Israel Rubinczyk
Meir	Nachum Buchman, Itzchak Bareket
Hanan	Jehuda Efroni, Nissim Azikri
Henoch	Nissim Azikri, Jehuda Efroni
Messenger	Ari Kutai
Gnessia	Judith Kronenfeld, Ada Tal
Reb Sender	Shmuel Rodensky
Sender's Relative	Itzchak Bareket
Leah	Eva Lion, Pnina Perah
Frieda	Bat-Ami
Gittel	Ada Tal
Batia	Tikva Mor
Asher	Shmuel Segal
Sondel	Haim Amitai
Shalom	Israel Rubinczyk
Berzik	Shlomo Brook
Raphael	Aharon Meskin
Dalfon	Raphael Klachkin
Dwossia	Niura Shein
Dresl	Judith Kronenfeld
Yachna	Ahuva Inbary
Elke	Yael Druyanof
Bobcha	Hanelle Hendler
Menashe	Shlomo Bar-Shavit
Nachman	David Baruch
Mendel	Shmuel Segal
Rabbi Azriel	Shimon Finkel
Michael	Raphael Klachkin
Shimshon	Shlomo Brook

A Drama in three acts. The action takes
place in Brainitz, a small Russian town, at the
turn of the century, in the synagogue, the
courtyard of Sender's home, and in Rabbi
Azriel's chambers.

Company Manager: Benjamin Rothman
Press: David Lipsky, Lawrence Witchel

°Closed Sunday, February 23, 1964, after a
limited engagement of 24 performances.

THE LITTLE THEATRE

Opened Wednesday, February 26, 1964.°
The Little Theatre, Inc., presents Habimah,
the National Theatre of Israel, in:

CHILDREN OF THE SHADOWS

By Ben-Zion Tomer; Directed by Israel
Becker; Scenery, David Sharir; Music, Zvi
Rosen; Lighting, Michael Lieberman; Artistic
Director, Julius Gellner; Administrative Director,
Asher Sharf; Simultaneous English translation
by Raphael Rothstein, based on English trans-
lation by Haim Glickstein.

CAST

Dr. Sigmund Rabinowitz	Aharon Meskin
Balloon Seller	Raphael Klachkin
Yoram	Amnon Meskin
Nurit	Yael Druyanof
Waiter	Shlomo Brook
Duby	Yehuda Efroni
Berele	Shmuel Segal
Helenka	Pnina Perah
Uncle Janek	Ari Kutai

A Drama in two acts and ten scenes. The
action takes place at the seashore of Tel-Aviv
in the spring of 1956.

Company Manager: Benjamin Rothman
Press: David Lipsky, Lawrence Witchel

°Closed Sunday, March 8, 1964, after a limited
engagement of 16 performances.

Aharon Meskin, Raphael Klachkin
in "Children of Shadows"

76

Top Left: The Zaddik and his Chassidim
Center: Eva Lion in "The Dybbuk"

THE LITTLE THEATRE

Opened Wednesday, March 11, 1964.°
The Little Theatre, Inc., presents Habimah,
The National Theatre of Israel, in:

EACH HAD SIX WINGS

By Hanoch Bartov; Directed by Avraham
Ninio; Decor by Yossel Bergner; Music by
Emanuel Amiran; Simultaneous English Version
by Raphael Rothstein and Hanoch Bartov;
Artistic Director, Julius Gellner; Administrative
Director, Asher Sharf.

CAST

Rakefet	Eva Lion
Gittel Klinger	Bat-Ami
Menashe Klinger	Nissim Azikri
Noah Klinger	Shmuel Rodensky
Aya	Ada Tal
Tzirkin	Shlomo Bar-Shavit
Vidal	David Baruch
Morris	Avraham Ninio
Hersheler	Itzchak Bareket
Dr. Stern	Nachum Buchman
Mitelman	Israel Rubinczyk
Mitelman's Mother	Hanelle Hendler
Glick	Haim Amitai
Mania	Judith Kronenfeld

A Drama in two acts. The action takes place
in the street and Rakefet's room during the
summer, autumn, and winter of 1949-50.

Company Manager: Benjamin Rothman
Press: David Lipsky, Lawrence Witchel

°Closed Sunday, March 22, 1964, after a
limited engagement of 16 performances.

**Top: Shlomo Bar-Shavit, Israel Rubinczyk,
Shmuel Rodensky, Bat-Ami, Itzchak Bareket**

Eva Lion, Nachum Buchman

BROOKS ATKINSON THEATRE

Opened Tuesday, February 4, 1964.°
Sherman S. Krellberg presents:

JOSEPHINE BAKER
and Her Company

Geoffrey Holder   Aviv Dancers
Larl Becham Trio

Musical Director, Gershon Kingsley; Lighting,
Michael Price; Production Consultant and Staged
by Felix S. Gerstman; Miss Baker's Costumes
by Dior, Balmain, House of Lanvin, and Balen-
ciaga; Scenery, Joseph Hansen.

PROGRAM

Part I: Introduction by The Orchestra; Miss
Baker singing "Avec," "Quand Tu M'embrasse,"
"Make Believe," "Quando, Quando"; Geoffrey
Holder; Miss Baker singing "Don't Touch My
Tomatoes"; Larl Becham Trio, Primitive and
Modern Dance Group; Miss Baker singing "La
Seine," "Hello Young Lovers," "Mon Bateau
Blanc," "Felicida"; The Aviv Dancers in "Is-
reali Festival," "Polynka"; Miss Baker singing
"Avril a Paris," "Addios, Addios," "Bill," "Je
Pars."

Part II: Miss Baker singing "Melodie Perdue,"
"Lucky Star," "EnEmerada," "Ja' Deux
Amours"; The Aviv Dancers; Miss Baker singing
"Hava Neguila"; Geoffrey Holder; Miss Baker
singing "Fan, Fan," "La Novia," "Et Pourtant,"
"Dans Mon Village," "J'Attendrai."

General Manager: Jesse Long
Press: Bill Doll, Midori Tsuji,
Robert Ganshaw, Shirley Herz, Dorothy Ross
Stage Manager, Pat Chandler

°Closed Sunday, February 16, 1964, after a
limited engagement of 16 performances. Reopened at Henry Miller's Theatre on Tuesday,
March 31, 1964, and closed Sunday, April 19,
1964 after 24 performances.

Fred Fehl Photos

Josephine Baker
(also top right)

MARK HELLINGER THEATRE

Opened Thursday, February 6, 1964.°
Alexander H. Cohen and Jack Hylton present:

RUGANTINO

Book, Lyrics, and Direction by Garinei and
Giovannini; Book in collaboration with Festa
Campanile and Franciosa; Music, Armando Tro-
vaioli; English Version by Alfred Drake; Lyric
Translation, Edward Eager; Scenery and Cos-
tumes, Giulio Coltellacci; Musical Numbers,
Dania Krupska; Musical Director, Anton Cop-
pola; Production Associate, Andre Goulston;
Scenic Supervision, Eldon Elder; Technical Di-
rection, Ralph Alswang; Production Managers,
Jean Barrere, Carlo Maresti; Lighting, Vannio
Vanni.

CAST

Rugantino	Nino Manfredi
Mariotto	Goffredo Spinedi
Rubastracci	Giuseppe Pennese
Strappalenzola	Fernando Martino
Brother Tappetto	Lino Benedetti
Bellachioma	Toni Ventura
The Brigadier	Willy Colombini
Chief Bandit	Armando Silverini
Rosetta	Ornella Vanoni
Gnecco	Renzo Palmer
Mastro Titta	Aldo Fabrizi
Bojetto	Carlo Delle Piane
Donna Marta Paritelli	Franca Tamantini
Don Nicolo Paritelli	Toni Ucci
Eusebia	Bice Valori
The Barber	Giorgio Zaffaroni
Thorwaldsen	Cesare Gelli
Don Fulgenzio	Giorgio Fabretti
The Troubador	Nunzio Gallo
The Lover	Marcello Serrallonga
Goat Keeper	Luciano Bonanni
Old Lady of The Cats	Simona Sorlisi
Cardinal Severini	Gino Mucci
Gentleman	Angelo Pericet
Gendarmes	Renato Ghigi, Angelo Michelotti

DANCERS AND SINGERS: Goffredo Spinedi,
Toni Ventura, Willy Colombini, Giorgio Zaffar-
oni, Marcello Serrallonga, Angelo Infanti, Luci-
ano Bernardi, Fernando Martino, Franco Di
Toro, Gabriele Villa, Giuseppe Pennese, Lino
Benedetti, Josephine Spinedi, Gianna Zorini,
Lettie Zaffaroni, Gina Sampieri, Lida Vianello,
Renata Zamengo, Brigitte Kirfel, Gabriella Pan-
enti, Carla Russo, Barbara Schaub, Yvonne De
Vintar, Maurizia Camilli.

CHORUS OF NORA ORLANDI: Armando
Silverini, Ercole Vulpiani, Margherita Brancucci,
Raffaella Caratelli.

UNDERSTURIES: Rugantino, Toni Ucci; Ros-
etta, Franca Tamantini; Titta, Renzo Palmer;
Eusebia, Angela Luce; Gnecco, Goffredo Spi-
nedi; Paritelli, Cesare Gelli; Thorwaldsen, Gino
Mucci; Marta, Simona Sorlisi; Mariotto, Angelo
Infanti; Troubadour, Giorgio Zaffaroni.

MUSICAL NUMBERS: "The Game of Morra,"
"Rugantino In The Stocks," "A House Is Not
The Same Without A Woman," "Nothing To
Do," "Just Look!," "The Saltarello," "Tirrallal-
lera," "The Headsman and I," "Ciumachella,"
"Lantern Night," "Roma," "I'm Happy," "Just
Stay Alive," "San Pasquale," "Passatella," "It's
Quick and Easy," "Dance of the Candle Killers,"
"Boy and Man," Finale.

A Roman Musical Spectacle in two acts and
twenty-four scenes. The action takes place in
Rome in the year 1830 during the reign of Pope
Pius VIII.

General Manager: Roy A. Somlyo
Company Managers: A. Gino Giglio, Carlo
Saviotti
Press: David Rothenberg, Michael Alpert,
Romano Camilli
Stage Managers: Harry Young, Jack Harrold,
Gian Pace, Carlo Maresti
°Closed February 29, 1964. (28 performances)

Friedman-Abeles Photos

Ornella Vanoni and chorus
Above: Nino Manfredi, Ornella Vanoni,
Aldo Fabrizi

79

CORT THEATRE

Opened Monday, February 10, 1964.°
Herbert Swope, Jr., in association with Bufman and Seiden presents:

FAIR GAME FOR LOVERS

By Richard Dougherty; Directed by Paul Shyre;
Sets, Lighting, and Costumes by Ralph Alswang;
Associate Producer, Teresa Calabrese; Women's
Clothes by The Clothes Parlour; Presented by ar-
rangement with Charles Rappaport.

CAST

Prudence Witten	Pegeen Lawrence
Benny	Alan Alda
Brigid	Sylvia Gassel
Chester Witten	Leo Genn
Maggie Becker	Maggie Hayes
Hollis Engrin	Forrest Tucker
Mrs. Bennington	Jane Hoffman
Dr. Bennington	Ralph Bell

UNDERSTUDIES: Chester, Hollis, Doctor,
Lawrence Weber; Maggie, Mrs. Bennington,
Sylvia Gassel; Prudence, Maggie Howard; Ben-
ny, Dan Scott; Brigid, Jacqueline Donnet.

A Comedy in three acts and eight scenes. The
action takes place in Chester Witten's house on
the east side of Manhattan Island at the present
time.

General Manager: Paul Vroom
Press: S. J. Friedman, Ralph Lycett,
Jane Friedman
Stage Managers: Steven Meyer, Jacqueline
Donnet
°Closed February 15, 1964. (8 performances)

Ray Fisher Photos

Leo Genn, Maggie Hayes, Pegeen Lawrence,
Forrest Tucker

Top: Maggie Hayes, Leo Genn, Forrest Tucker,
Pegeen Lawrence, Alan Alda, Jane Hoffman

ETHEL BARRYMORE THEATRE

Opened Tuesday, February 11, 1964.°
Arthur Cantor and E. E. Fogelson, and
Mark Lawrence present:

THE PASSION OF JOSEF D

Written and Directed by Paddy Chayefsky;
Sets and Lighting, Will Steven Armstrong; Costumes, Domingo A. Rodriguez; Original Music
by David Amram; Associate Director, John Allen;
Makeup Supervisor, Richard Corson; Production
Associate, Kip Cohen.

CAST

Soloist	Carol Wilder
Constable Kentinov	Alvin Epstein
Stalin	Peter Falk
Muranov	Gene Gross
Kamenev	Milt Kamen
Kapinsky	Michael McGuire
Klurman	Jon Silo
Bronsky	Bruce Kimes
Brustein	Rico Froehlich
Mirsky	Anthony Palmer
Rusikov	Mervyn Williams
Alliluyev	Ramon Bieri
Olga Evgeyvna	Betty Walker
Nadezhda	Elizabeth Hubbard
Chugurin	Don Wesley
Molotov	Simm Landres
Rykov	John A. Coe
Sukhanov	Nicholas Saunders
Skobelov	Mervyn Williams
Cheidze	Rico Froehlich
Lenin	Luther Adler
Krupskaya	Betty Walker
Grigori Nikitin	Milt Kamen
Alexander Lomov	Alvin Epstein
General Kornilov	Jon Silo
Sailors	John Carver, Frank Bouley
Orjonikidze	Nicholas Saunders
Zinoviev	Michael Enserro
Sverdlov	Gene Gross
Trotsky	Alvin Epstein

SOLDIERS, WORKERS, PEASANTS, ETC.:
Sean Allen, Robert Berdeen, Frank Bouley, John
Carver, John A. Coe, Carole Crook, Michael
Enserro, Janet Frank, Richard Frisch, Bruce
Kimes, Simm Landres, Penelope Laughton, Royce
Lenelle, Michael McGuire, Sylvia Saunders,
Peggy Steffans, Elaine Sulka, Carol Wilder,
Mervyn Williams, Stafford Wing.

UNDERSTUDIES: Stalin, Anthony Palmer;
Lenin, Klurman, Bruce Kimes; Kamenev, Nikitin, Gene Gross; Trotsky, Simm Landres; Kentinov, Lomov, Kornilov, John A. Coe; Nadezhda,
Penelope Laughton; Olga, Krupskaya, Gedda
Petry; Alliluyev, Richard Robbins.

A Drama in three acts and eleven scenes.
The action takes place in Russia between 1917
and 1924.

Company Manager: Harold Kusell
Press: Tony Geiss, Artie Solomon, Angela
Nardelli
Stage Managers: John Allen, William Krot,
Don Wesley

°Closed February 22, 1964. (15 performances)

Peter Falk, Alvin Epstein
Top: Peter Falk, Elizabeth Hubbard,
Luther Adler

Werner J. Kuhn and Henry Grossman Photos

Bert Lahr

Opened Sunday, February 16, 1964.°
David Merrick presents:

FOXY

Book by Ian McLellan Hunter and Ring Lardner, Jr.; Suggested by Ben Jonson's "Volpone"; Lyrics by Johnny Mercer; Music, Robert Emmett Dolan; Directed by Robert Lewis; Choreography and Musical Numbers Staged by Jack Cole; Scenery and Lighting, Robert Randolph; Costumes, Robert Fletcher; Musical Direction and Vocal Arrangements, Donald Pippin; Orchestrations, Edward Sauter and Hal Schaefer; Dance Music Arranged by Hal Schaefer; Production Supervisor, Neil Hartley.

CAST

Doc	Larry Blyden
Foxy	Bert Lahr
Bedrock	Robert H. Harris
Buzzard	Edward Greenhalgh
Shortcut	Gerald Hiken
Drunk	Tony Kraber
Mountie	John Hallow
Brandy	Cathryn Damon
Oliver	Will Parkins
Celia	Julienne Marie
First Prospector	Newt Sullivan
Second Prospector	Eddie James
Third Prospector	Herb Fields
Stirling	David Rounds
First Eskimo	John Waller
Second Eskimo	John Aristedes
Lord Rottingham	Anthony Kemble Cooper
Clergyman	John Taliaferro
Ben	John Davidson
Laurette	Mary Ann Corrigan
Marie	Constance Meng
Bellboy	John Taliaferro

PROSPECTORS: John Aristedes, Carlos Bas, Charles Cagle, George Del Monte, Lang Des Jardins, Herbert Fields, Tim Harum, Lee Howard, Eddie James, John Keatts, Robert LaCrosse, Will Parkins, Newt Sullivan, John Taliaferro, John Waller.

SALOON GIRLS: Helen Baisley, Mary Ann Corrigan, Virginia Craig, Judith Dunford, Alice Glenn, Marlena Lustik, Ethel Martin, Constance Meng, Nancy Myers, Shelly Rann, Sueanne Shirley, June Eve Story, Susan Terry.

UNDERSTUDIES: Foxy, Loney Lewis; Doc, David Rounds; Celia, Constance Meng; Ben, John Keats; Brandy, Virginia Craig; Bedrock, Buzzard, Shortcut, Tony Kraber; Stirling, John Hallow.

MUSICAL NUMBERS: Overture, Prologue, "Many Ways To Skin A Cat," "Rollin' In Gold," "My Weight In Gold," "Money Isn't Everything," "Larceny and Love," "Ebenezer McAfee III," "Talk To Me, Baby," "This Is My Night To Howl," "Bon Vivant," "It's Easy When You Know How," "Run, Run, Run Cinderella," "I'm Way Ahead Of The Game," "A Case of Rape," "In Loving Memory." Finale.

A Musical Comedy in two acts and fourteen scenes. The action takes place in Alaska.

General Manager: Jack Schlissel
Company Manager: Emanuel Azenberg
Press: Lee Solters, Harvey B. Sabinson, David Powers, Bob Ullman
Stage Managers: Perry Bruskin, Henry Velez, John Hallow

°Closed April 18, 1964. (72 performances)

Eileen Darby-Graphic House Photos

Larry Blyden, Bert Lahr

John Davidson, Julienne Marie
Above: Cathryn Damon, Larry Blyden
Top: Cathryn Damon (L), Bert Lahr

Ann Harding, Bill Travers

BELASCO THEATRE
Opened Monday, February 17, 1964.*
Walter Fried and Helen Jacobson present:

ABRAHAM COCHRANE

By John Sherry; Scenery and Lighting, Robert
O'Hearn; Costumes, Domingo A. Rodriguez;
Production Supervised by Harold Stone; Production Assistant, Wanda Davie.

CAST

Alice	Audrey Ward
Dr. Thomas Barrett	Richard Nicholls
Myra Holliday	Ann Harding
Samuel Holliday	John Griggs
Helen Balcon	Nancy Wickwire
Roger Balcon	Peter Adams
Abraham Cochrane	Bill Travers
Brock Holliday	Franklin Cover
Gregory Lawton	Jerome Collamore
Anne Dowling	Olympia Dukakis

UNDERSTUDIES: Myra, Audrey Ward; Samuel, Barrett, Lawton, Edwin Cooper; Helen, Olympia Dukakis; Roger, Brock, Ian Cameron; Ann, Alice, Lois Markle.

A Drama in three acts and four scenes. The action takes place in the library of the Holliday home located in the environ of a large American city along the eastern seaboard at the present time.

Company Manager: Robert Kamlot
Press: Seymour Krawitz, Merle Debuskey, Madi Ross
Stage Managers: Richard Evans, Ian Cameron
*Closed Monday, February 17, 1964. (1 performance)

Friedman-Abeles Photos

Top: Bill Travers, Ann Harding, Nancy Wickwire

Sandy Dennis
in
"ANY WEDNESDAY"

Wallace Litwin Photo

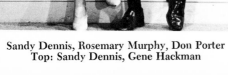

Sandy Dennis, Rosemary Murphy, Don Porter
Top: Sandy Dennis, Gene Hackman

Gene Hackman, Don Porter
Top: Rosemary Murphy, Don Porter

86

THE MUSIC BOX

Opened Tuesday, February 18, 1964.°
George W. George and Frank Granat and
Howard Erskine, Edward Specter
Productions,
Peter S. Katz present:

ANY WEDNESDAY

By Muriel Resnik; Directed by Henry Kaplan;
Scenery, Robert Randolph; Costumes, Theoni V.
Aldredge; Lighting, Tharon Musser; Hair Styles,
Kenneth; Production Assistant, Nelle Nugent.

CAST

John Cleves	Don Porter
Ellen Gordon	Sandy Dennis
Cass Henderson	Gene Hackman
Dorothy Cleves	Rosemary Murphy

UNDERSTUDIES: Ellen, Cynthia Harris; Dorothy, Lucy Prentis; John, John Dutra.

A Comedy in two acts and four scenes. The
action takes place at the present time in a garden
apartment in the East Sixties in Manhattan.

General Manager: Edward H. Davis
Press: Lee Solters, Harvey Sabinson,
Mel Kopp, David Powers
Stage Manager: Porter Van Zandt

° Still playing May 31, 1964.
(119 performances)

Wallace Litwin Photos

Top: Gene Hackman, Sandy Dennis,
Don Porter, Rosemary Murphy

Gene Hackman, Sandy Dennis, Don Porter

BROOKS ATKINSON THEATRE

Opened Wednesday, February 26, 1964.°
Herman Shumlin, Alfred Crown and Zvi
Kolitz present:

THE DEPUTY

By Rolf Hochhuth; Adapted by Jerome Rothenberg; Directed by Herman Shumlin; Designed
by Rouben Ter-Arutunian; Costumes, Edith Lutyens Bel Geddes; Lighting, John Harvey.

CAST

Papal Nuncio in Berlin	Reynolds Evans
Father Riccardo Fontana	Jeremy Brett†
Monk	David Thomas
S.S. Lt. Kurt Gerstein	Thomas A. Carlin
Jacobson	Stefan Gierasch
Doctor	James Mitchell
Vittorio	Idwal Bowen
Photographer	Guy Repp
Count Fontana	Carl Low
Cardinal	Fred Stewart
Officer of Pope's Guard	Gerald E. McGonagill
Brother Irenaeus	Richard Bengal
Father General	Ian Wolfe
Captain Salzer	Ron Leibman
Sergeant Witzel	Jock Livingston
Italian Militiamen	Victor Arnold, Ion Berger
A Girl	Maria Tucci
A Prisoner	Ben Hammer
Another Prisoner	Albert M. Ottenheimer
Pope Pius XII	Emlyn Williams
Officer of Papal Guard	Guy Repp
The Scribe	Gerald E. McGonagill
A Woman	Pepa Kantor
Guards	Roger Hamilton, Victor Arnold, Ion Berger, Paul Flores
Little Girl	Denise Joyce

UNDERSTUDIES: Pope, Nuncio, Father Gen-
eral, Prisoner, David Thomas; Fontana, Ion Ber-
ger; Gerstein, Doctor, Gerald E. McGonagill;
Count, Guy Repp; Cardinal, Jock Livingston;
Salzer, Witzel, Roger Hamilton; Monk, Vittorio,
Prisoner, Scribe, Richard Bengal; Jacobson,
Irenaeus, Guard, Victor Arnold; Militiamen,
Photographer, Officer of Papal Guard, Paul
Flores; Woman, Barbara Schneider; Little Girl,
Bianca Flores.

A Drama in two acts and seven scenes. The
action takes place in 1942 and 1943 in Germany
and Italy.

Company Manager: Alex Baron
Press: David Lipsky, Lawrence Witchel,
Ted Goldsmith, Bill Doll, Robert Ganshaw
Stage Managers: Howard Whitfield, Jerome
Michael, Paul Flores

° Still playing May 31, 1964.
  (117 performances)
† Succeeded by David Carradine

Friedman-Abeles Photos

Denise Joyce, Jeremy Brett, James Mitchell
Above: Emlyn Williams, Fred Stewart

88

Top: Ion Berger, Victor Arnold, Jack
Livingston, Ben Hammer, Albert M.
Ottenheimer, Pepa Kantor

Ian Wolfe, Ron Leibman, Jeremy Brett
Top: Emlyn Williams, Gerald McGonagill,
Jeremy Brett

Emlyn Williams, Fred Stewart

89

Emlyn Williams, Fred Stewart, Jeremy Brett
in
"THE DEPUTY"

Robert Alda, Sally Ann Howes, Steve Lawrence
in
"WHAT MAKES SAMMY RUN?"

FIFTY-FOURTH STREET THEATRE

Opened Thursday, February 27, 1964.°
Joseph Cates presents:

WHAT MAKES SAMMY RUN?

Book by Budd and Stuart Schulberg; Based on The Novel by Budd Schulberg; Music and Lyrics, Ervin Drake; Musical Staging, Matt Mattox; Director, Abe Burrows; Settings and Lighting, Herbert Senn and Helen Pond; Costumes, Noel Taylor; Vocal Arrangements, and Musical Direction, Lehman Engel; Orchestrations, Don Walker; Dance Arrangements, Arnold Goland; Production Manager, Michael Thoma; Production Supervised by Robert Weiner; A Gates Brothers Production in Association with Beresford Productions Ltd; Production Associate, Rick Mandell; Production Assistant, Jan Gassman; Hair Styles, Frank Reynolds.

CAST

Al Manheim	Robert Alda
Sammy Glick	Steve Lawrence
O'Brien	Edward McNally
Osborn	John Dorrin
Bartender	Ralph Vucci
Julian Blumberg	George Coe
Rita Rio	Graciela Daniele
Tracy Clark	Richard France
Lucky Dugan	Edward McNally
Shiek Orsini	Barry Newman
Technical Advisor	Bob Maxwell
Sidney Fineman	Arny Freeman
Kit Sargent	Sally Ann Howes
H. L. Harrington	Walter Klavun
Laurette Harrington	Bernice Massi
Seymour Glick	Mace Barrett
Swing Couple	Lynn Gremmler, Doug Spingler

SINGING ENSEMBLE: Lillian Bozinoff, Natalie Costa, Judith Hastings, Jamie Simmons, Darrell J. Askey, John Dorrin, Richard Terry, Ralph Vucci.

DANCING ENSEMBLE: Diaan Ainslee, Nancy Carnegie, Barbara Gine, Lavina Hamilton, Bella Shalom, Maralyn Thoma, Jean Blanchard, Marco Gomez, Buck Heller, Nat Horne, Jack Kresy.

UNDERSTUDIES: Sammy, Richard France; Kit, Judith Hastings; Al, Mace Barrett; Laurette, Natalie Costa; Tracy, Buck Heller; Rita, Diaan Ainslee; O'Brien, Lucky, Fineman, Harrington, John Dorrin.

MUSICAL NUMBERS: "A New Pair Of Shoes," "You Help Me," "The Work Song," "A Tender Spot," "Lites—Camera—Platitude," "My Hometown," "Monsoon," "I See Something," "Maybe Some Other Time," "You Can Trust Me," "A Room Without Windows," "Kiss Me No Kisses," "I Feel Humble," "Something To Live For," "Paint A Rainbow," "You're No Good," "The Friendliest Thing," "Wedding Of The Year," "Some Days Everything Goes Wrong."

A Musical Comedy in two acts. The action takes place a generation ago in New York and Hollywood.

General Manager: Marshall Young
Press: Gertrude Kirschner, Violet Welles
Stage Managers: George Thorn, Bob Maxwell
° Still playing May 31, 1964.
(109 performances)

Henry Grossman Photos

Top Left: Steve Lawrence, Sally Ann Howes, Robert Alda
Center: Steve Lawrence, Bernice Massi

Steve Lawrence, Robert Alda, Sally Ann Howes

92

Steve Lawrence, Robert Alda, Sally Ann Howes
Top: Richard France, Graciela Daniele

Robert Alda, Steve Lawrence, Barry Newman

Pierre Olaf, Lauri Peters, Jane Hoffman

MOROSCO THEATRE

Opened Wednesday, March 25, 1964.*
Jeff Britton presents:

A MURDERER AMONG US

By Yves Jamiaque; Adapted by George White;
Directed by Sam Wanamaker; Settings and
Lighting, David Hays; Costumes, Fred Voelpel;
Music, Paul Reif; Production Assistant, Thomas
H. Diringer.

CAST

Mlle. Suisson	Jane Hoffman
Louisette	Lauri Peters
Mayor	Loring Smith
Cabouche	Tom Bosley
Marolles	George S. Irving
Pertuiset	Dana Elcar
Madame Maille	Edith King
Jerome Lahutte	Pierre Olaf
Birgasse	Severn Darden
Policeman	Michael Flanagan

Understudies: Nancy Haywood, Michael Flanagan

A Comedy in three acts and five scenes. The
action takes place at the present time in the
small town of Bellefontaine in Provence, France.

General Manager: Irving Cooper
Company Manager: Warren O'Hara
Press: Harvey Sabinson, Lee Solters,
Jerry Gold, David Powers
Stage Managers: Joseph Brownstone, Michael
Flanagan

*Closed March 25, 1964. (1 performance)

Friedman-Abeles Photos

Top: Tom Bosley, Loring Smith, Dana Elca
Edith King, Jane Hoffman, George S. Irvin

Barbra Streisand
in
"FUNNY GIRL"

Henry Grossman Photo

Jean Stapleton, Kay Medford, Danny Meehan

Sydney Chaplin, Barbra Streisand
Top: Barbra Streisand, Kay Medford
Danny Meehan, Joyce O'Neil

WINTER GARDEN

Opened Thursday, March 26, 1964.*
Ray Stark presents:

FUNNY GIRL

Book and Story by Isobel Lennart; Music,
Jule Styne; Lyrics, Bob Merrill; Directed by
Garson Kanin; Musical Numbers Staged by Carol
Haney; Scenery and Lighting, Robert Randolph;
Costumes, Irene Sharaff; Musical Director, Milton
Rosenstock; Orchestrations, Ralph Burns; Vocal
Arrangements, Buster Davis; Dance Orchestra-
tions, Luther Henderson; Associate Producer, Al
Goldin; Associate Director, Lawrence Kasha;
Presented in association with Seven Arts Prod-
uctions; Hairstyles, Ronald DeMann.

CAST

Fanny Brice	Barbra Streisand
John	Robert Howard
Emma	Royce Wallace
Mrs. Brice	Kay Medford
Mrs. Strakosh	Jean Stapleton
Mrs. Meeker	Lydia S. Fredericks
Mrs. O'Malley	Joyce O'Neil
Tom Keeney	Joseph Macaulay
Eddie Ryan	Danny Meehan
Heckie	Victor R. Helou
Workmen	Robert Howard, Robert Henson
Snub Taylor	Buzz Miller
Trombone Smitty	Blair Hammond
Five Finger Finney	Alan E. Weeks
Trumpet Soloist	Dick Perry
Bubbles	Shellie Farrell
Polly	Joan Lowe
Maude	Ellen Halpin
Nick Arnstein	Sydney Chaplin
Showgirls	Sharon Vaughn, Diana Lee Nielsen
Stage Director	Marc Jordan
Florenz Ziegfeld, Jr.	Roger DeKoven
Mimsey	Sharon Vaughn
Ziegfeld Tenor	John Lankston
Ziegfeld Lead Dancer	George Reeder
Adolph	John Lankston
Mrs. Nadler	Rose Randolf
Paul	Larry Fuller
Cathy	Joan Cory
Vera	Lainie Kazan
Jenny	Diane Coupe
Ben	Buzz Miller
Mr. Renaldi	Marc Jordan
Mike Halsey	Robert Howard

REPORTERS: Blair Hammond, Albert Zimmerman, Alan Peterson, Victor R. Helou, Stephanie
Reynolds.

SHOWGIRLS: Prudence Adams, Joan Cory,
Diane Coupe, Lainie Kazan, Diana Lee Nielsen,
Sharon Vaughn, Rosemarie Yellen.

SINGERS: Lydia S. Fredericks, Mary Louise,
Jeanne McLaren, Joyce O'Neil, Rose Randolf,
Stephanie Reynolds, Victor R. Helou, Robert
Henson, Robert Howard, Marc Jordan, John
Lankston, Albert Zimmerman.

DANCERS: Edie Cowan, Christine Dalsey,
Shellie Farrell, Ellen Halpin, Rosemary Jelincic,
Karen Kristen, Joan Lowe, Jose Ahumada, Bud
Fleming, Larry Fuller, Blair Hammond, John
Nola, Alan Peterson, Alan E. Weeks.

UNDERSTUDIES: Fanny, Lainie Kazan; Arn-
stein, George Reeder.

MUSICAL NUMBERS: "If A Girl Isn't Pretty,"
"I'm The Greatest Star," "Eddie's Fifth En-
core," "Cornet Man," "Who Taught Her Every-
thing," "His Love Makes Me Beautiful," "I
Want To Be Seen With You Tonight," "Henry
Street," "People," "You Are Woman," "Don't
Rain On My Parade," "Sadie, Sadie," "Find
Yourself A Man," "Rat-Tat-Tat-Tat," "Who Are
You Now?," "The Music That Makes Me Dance."

A Musical in two acts and twenty-four
scenes.

General Manager: Al Goldin
Company Manager: John Larson
Press: Frank Goodman
Stage Managers: Richard Evans, Tom Stone,
Joseph Dooley, Robert Howard

* Still playing May 31, 1964.
(76 performers)

Henry Grossman Photos

Danny Meehan, Barbra Streisand

EUGENE O'NEILL THEATRE

Opened Saturday, March 28, 1964.°
Paul Vroom, Buff Cobb, Albert Marre
present:

NEVER LIVE OVER A PRETZEL FACTORY

By Jerry Devine; Staged by Albert Marre;
Setting and Lighting, Howard Bay; Costumes,
Frank Thompson; Music, Mitch Leigh; Men's
Fashions by Petrocelli.

CAST

Rick	Gino Conforti
Benny	Marc Marno
Sam	Lawrence Pressman
Winona	Nancy Franklin
Mike	Martin Sheen
Musicians	The Panama Francis Quartet
Bartender	Robert Jepson
Robert Miller	Dennis O'Keefe
Cheryl	Lanna Saunders
Edwards	Robert Getz
Mr. Balzac	Sidney Armus
The Inspector	Alan North
Mr. Callahan	Paul Huber
Bel Air Bonnie	Lorna Thayer
Myrna	Gloria Bleezarde
Rhonda	Sally Ackerman
Carlotta	Charlene Ryan
Attendants	Robert Jepson, Richard Higgs
Aunt Martha	Kitty Barling

UNDERSTUDIES: Balzac, Callahan, Alan
North; Winona, Gloria Bleezarde; Cheryl, Bon-
nie, DeAnn Mears; Sam, Mike, Rick, Robert
Getz.

A Comedy in three acts and four scenes. The
action takes place at the present time in the
basement of a building in downtown Manhattan.

General Manager: Paul Vroom
Press: David Lipsky, Ted Goldsmith,
Lawrence Witchel
Stage Managers: Burry Fredrik, Robert Getz,
Richard Higgs

°Closed April 4, 1964. (9 performances)

Friedman-Abeles Photos

Lawrence Pressman, Dennis O'Keefe,
Martin Sheen
Above: Dennis O'Keefe, Paul Huber, Lorna
Thayer, Charlene Ryan, Sally Ackerman,
Gloria Bleezarde

98

Top: Dennis O'Keefe, Nancy Franklin, Martin
Sheen, Lawrence Pressman, Gino Conforti

CORT THEATRE

Opened Thursday, April 2, 1964.*
Mary K. Frank presents:

SPONONO

By Alan Paton and Krishna Shah; Directed by Krishna Shah; Settings, Pamela Lewis; Costumes Supervised by John Boyt; Supervision and Lighting, Paul Morrison; Costumes Designed by Ruth St. Mortiz; Traditional Chants Arranged by Gideon Nxumalo. Additional Chants Composed by Fela Sowande, John Knox Bokwe, J. P. Mohapeloa, Gideon Nxumalo.

CAST

Sponono	Cocky Tlhotlhalemaje
Principal	Michael Goodliffe
Elizabeth	Ruth Nkonyeni
Walter	Joe Ngoetjana
Spike Moletsane	Ferdinand Mafata
Ha' penny	Philemon Hou
Mr. Mabaso	Lionel Ngakane
Mr. Makatini	Obed Dira
Mrs. Makatini	Phyllis Mqomo
Johannes Mofoking	Sidney Motha
Sangoma Diviner	Vinah Bendile
Imbongi	Douglas Xaba
Chief Counsellor	Paul Makgoba
Chief Attendant	Victor Shange

COURT ATTENDANTS: Barney Qhobosheane, Gideon Manana, Caiphus Semenya, John Sithebe.

REFORMATORY BOYS: Osborne Ferdinand, Paul Makgoba, Herbert Manana, Gideon Manana, Ernest Mohlomi, Sidney Motha, Barney Qhobosheane, Caiphus Sememya, John Sithebe, Victor Shange, Douglas Xaba.

CHOIR: Osborne Ferdinand (leader), Maria Khule, Virginia Mablane, Margaret Mcingane, Betty Mthombeni, Ernest Mohlomi, Gideon Manana, Herbert Manana, Paul Makgoba, Caiphus Semenya.

A Drama in three acts and fourteen scenes. The action takes place at the present time in the Reformatory, and in Victoriatown, a Johannesburg Township.

Manager: Victor Samrock
Press: Ben Washer
Stage Managers: Ben Janney, Meshack Mosia
*Closed April 18, 1964. (20 performances)

Eileen Darby—Graphic House Photos

Ruth Nkonyeni, Joe Ngoetjana
Above: Ruth Nkonyeni, Cocky Thotlhalemaje
Top: Michael Goodliffe, Ferdinand Mafata

MAJESTIC THEATRE

Opened Saturday, April 4, 1964.*
Kermit Bloomgarden and Diana Krasny
present:

ANYONE CAN WHISTLE

Book by Arthur Laurents; Music and Lyrics
by Stephen Sondheim; Scenery, William and
Jean Eckart; Costumes, Theoni V. Aldredge;
Lighting, Jules Fisher; Dances and Musical
Numbers Staged by Herbert Ross; Entire Prod-
uction Directed by Arthur Laurents; Orchestra-
tions, Don Walker; Vocal Arrangements and
Musical Direction, Herbert Greene; Dance Ar-
rangements, Betty Walberg; Associate Producer,
Arlene Sellers; Production Assistant, Jon De
Hart; Hairstyles, Ronald DeMann.

CAST

Sandwich Man	Jeff Killion
Baby Joan	Jeanne Tanzy
Mrs. Schroeder	Peg Murray
Treasurer Cooley	Arnold Soboloff
Chief Magruder	James Frawley
Comptroller Schub	Gabriel Dell
Cora Hoover Hoople	Angela Lansbury
The Boys	Sterling Clark, Harvey Evans, Larry Roquemore, Tucker Smith
Fay Apple	Lee Remick
J. Bowden Hapgood	Harry Guardino
Dr. Detmoid	Don Doherty
George	Larry Roquemore
June	Janet Hayes
John	Harvey Evans
Martin	Lester Wilson
Old Lady	Eleonore Treiber
Telegraph Boy	Alan Johnson
Osgood	Georgia Creighton

COOKIES, TOWNSPEOPLE, TOURISTS: Susan
Borree, Georgia Creighton, Janet Hayes, Bettye
Jenkins, Patricia Kelly, Barbara Lang, Paula
Lloyd, Barbara Monte, Odette Phillips, Hanne-
Marie Reiner, Eleonore Treiber, Sterling Clark,
Eugene Edwards, Harvey Evans, Dick Ensslen,
Loren Hightower, Alan Johnson, Jeff Killion,
Jack Murray, William Reilly, Larry Roquemore,
Tucker Smith, Don Stewart, Lester Wilson.

UNDERSTUDIES: Fay, Barbara Lang; Cora,
Peg Murray; Cooley, Tucker Smith; Detmoid,
Harvey Evans; Magruder, Dick Ensslen; Baby
Joan, Bettye Jenkins; Mrs. Schroeder, Georgia
Creighton; Hapgood, Don Stewart.

MUSICAL NUMBERS: "I'm Like The Bluebird,"
"Me and My Town," "Miracle Song," "Simple,
A-1 March," "Come Play Wiz Me," "Anyone
Can Whistle," "A Parade In Town," "Every-
body Says Don't," "I've Got You To Lean On,"
"See What It Gets You," "The Cookie Chase,"
"With So Little To Be Sure Of," Finale.

A Musical Comedy in three acts and twelve
scenes. The action takes place in a not too
distant town at the present time.

General Manager: Joseph Harris
Press: James D. Proctor, Louise Weiner
Stage Managers: James S. Gelb, Don Doherty,
Louis Kosman

*Closed April 11, 1964. (9 performances)

Fred Fehl and Friedman-Abeles Photos

Angela Lansbury, Harry Guardino (and above)
Top: Harry Guardino, Lee Remick

Harry Guardino, Lee Remick

Eva LeGallienne
in
"THE SEA GULL"

101

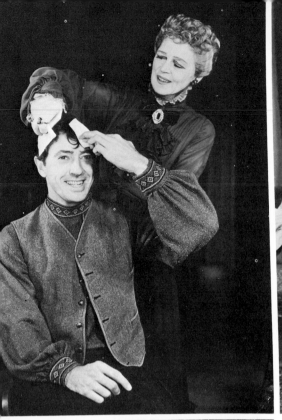

BELASCO THEATRE

Opened Sunday, April 5, 1964.°
The American National Theatre and Academy presents the National Repertory Theatre in:

THE SEAGULL

By Anton Chekhov; Translated by Eva Le Gallienne; Directed by Miss Le Gallienne; Sets by Peter Larkin; Costumes by Alvin Colt; Lighting, Tharon Musser; Producers, Michael Dewell and Frances Ann Dougherty.

CAST

Masha _____ Barbara Stanton
Semyon Semyonovitch Medvedenko Ben Yaffee
Pyotr Nikolayevitch Sorin _____ Thayer David
Konstantin Gavrilovitch Treplev __ Farley Granger
Yakov _____ Fred Ainsworth
Nina Mihailovna Zaretchnaya ____ Anne Meacham
Polina Andreyevna _____ Betty Sinclair
Yevegeny Sergeyevitch Dorn _____ G. Wood
Irina Nikolayevna Arkadina
  (Madame Treplev) _____ Eva Le Gallienne
Boris Alexeyevitch Trigorin ___ Denholm Elliott
Ilya Afanasyevitch Shamraev ___ Jerome Raphel
A Cook _____ Richard Bowler
A Housemaid _____ Susan Carr

A Drama presented in two parts and four scenes. The action takes place on Sorin's country estate in Russia, during the 1890's.

Van Williams Photos

Top: Eva LeGallienne with Farley Granger (L Denholm Elliott (R)

Anne Meacham, Farley Granger
Above: Betty Sinclair, G. Wood

Opened Monday, April 6, 1964.

THE CRUCIBLE

By Arthur Miller; Directed by Jack Sydow; Sets by Peter Larkin; Costumes, Alvin Colt; Lighting, Tharon Musser.

CAST

Betty Parris	Pamela Gruen
Reverend Parris	Ben Yaffee
Tituba	Osceola Archer
Abigail Williams	Kelly Jean Peters
Mrs. Ann Putnam	Mary Hara
Thomas Putnam	G. Wood
Mercy Lewis	Susan Carr
Mary Warren	Barbara Stanton
John Proctor	Farley Granger
Rebecca Nurse	Betty Sinclair
Giles Corey	George Turner
Reverend John Hale	Denholm Elliott
Elizabeth Proctor	Anne Meacham
Ezekiel Cheever	Richard Bowler
Marshal Willard	Clinton Anderson
Judge Hathorne	Jerome Raphel
Deputy Governor Danforth	Thayer David
Sara Good	Mary Hara
Hopkins	Fred Ainsworth

A Drama in two acts and five scenes. The action takes place in Salem, Massachusetts, in 1692.

Company Manager: Boris Bernardi
Press: Solters, O'Rourke and Sabinson, Mary Ward
Stage Managers: William Armitage, Helen Page Camp

*Closed May 2, 1964, after a limited engagement of 32 performances, In addition to these two productions, the company presented "Ring Round The Moon" in repertory on tour beginning October 10, 1963.

For the original New York production of "The Crucible," see THEATRE WORLD, Vol. 9. In the cast were Walter Hampden, Arthur Kennedy, E. G. Marshall, Maureen Stapleton, and Beatrice Straight. It ran for 197 performances.

Richard Bowler, Thayer David, Jerome Raphel, Denholm Elliott, Farley Granger, Barbara Stanton
Above: Kelly Jean Peters, Pamela Gruen, Ben Yaffee, Denholm Elliott, George Turner
Top: Farley Granger, Anne Meacham
(R) Barbara Stanton, Thayer David, Pamela Gruen, Susan Carr, Kelly Jean Peters

ALVIN THEATRE

Opened Tuesday, April 17, 1964.*
Lester Osterman, Robert Fletcher and
Richard Horner present:

HIGH SPIRITS

Music, Lyrics, and Book by Hugh Martin
and Timothy Gray; Based on Play "Blithe
Spirit" by Noel Coward; Directed by Noel Co-
ward; Settings and Costumes, Robert Fletcher;
Miss Grimes' Costume, Valentina; Lighting, Jules
Fisher; Musical Direction, Fred Werner; Vocal
Direction and Arrangements, Hugh Martin and
Timothy Gray; Orchestrations, Harry Zimmer-
man; Dance Music, William Goldenberg; Dances
and Musical Numbers Staged by Danny Daniels;
Hair Stylist, Phil Leto.

CAST

Charles Condomine	Edward Woodward
Edith	Carol Arthur
Ruth Condomine	Louise Troy
Mrs. Bradman	Margaret Hall
Dr. Bradman	Lawrence Keith
Madame Arcati	Beatrice Lillie
Elvira	Tammy Grimes
Bob	Robert Lenn
Beth	Beth Howland
Rupert	Gene Castle

SINGING-DANCING ENSEMBLE: Adrienne
Angel, Syndee Balaber, Gene Castle, Jerry Craig,
Jackie Cronin, Altovise Gore, Judith Haskell,
Beth Howland, Jack Kauflin, Bill Kennedy, Al
Lanti, Miriam Lawrence Renee Lee, Robert
Lenn, Alex MacKay, Jaqueline Maria, Stan
Mazin, Joe McGrath, Don Percassi, Kathy Pres-
ton, Sybil Scotford, Tom Thornton, Ronnie
Walken, Anne Wallace.

UNDERSTUDIES: Mme. Arcati, Beulah Garrick;
Elvira, Iva Withers; Ruth, Lynne Stuart; Charles,
Lawrence Keith; Mrs. Bradman, Adrienne Angel;
Dr. Bradman, Robert Lenn; Edith, Jacqueline
Maria.

MUSICAL NUMBERS: "Was She Prettier Than
I?," "The Bicycle Song," "You'd Better Love
Me," "Where Is The Man I Married?," "The
Sandwich Man," "Go into Your Trance," "For-
ever And A Day," "Something Tells Me," "I
Know Your Heart," "Faster Than Sound," "If
I Gave You," "Talking To You," "Home Sweet
Heaven," "Something Is Coming To Tea," "The
Exorcism," "What In The World Did You
Want?"

An Improbable Musical Comedy in two acts
and twelve scenes. The action takes place at
the present time in the Condomine home, The
Inner Circle, the Roof Garden of the Grove-
chester Hotel, and in Madame Arcati's bedroom.

Production Manager: Jose Vega
Press: Harvey Sabinson, Lee Solters,
Leo Stern, David Powers
Stage Managers: Frank Gero, Bruce Laffey

* Still playing May 31, 1964.
(71 performances)

Friedman-Abeles Photos

Louise Troy, Lawrence Keith, Edward
Woodward, Beatrice Lillie, Margaret Hall
Above: Tammy Grimes, Beatrice Lillie,
Edward Woodward

Top: (L) Edward Woodward, Tammy Grimes
and (R) with Beatrice Lillie

Beatrice Lillie

LUNT-FONTANNE THEATRE

Opened Thursday, April 9, 1964.°
Alexander H. Cohen presents:

HAMLET

By William Shakespeare; Directed by John
Gielgud; Designed by Ben Edwards; Clothes by
Jane Greenwood; Lighting, Jean Rosenthal; Pro-
duction Associates, Gabriel Katzka, Andre Goul-
ston; Produced in Association with Frenman
Productions; Fencing Master, Charles Bellin.

CAST

Bernardo	Robert Burr
Francisco	Michael Ebert
Marcellus	Bernard Hughes
Horatio	Robert Milli
Claudius	Alfred Drake
Voltimand	Philip Coolidge
Cornelius	Hugh Alexander
Laertes	John Cullum
Polonius	Hume Cronyn
Hamlet	Richard Burton
Gertrude	Eileen Herlie
Ophelia	Linda Marsh
Ghost	The Voice of John Gielgud
Reynaldo	Dillon Evans
Rosencrantz	Clement Fowler
Guildenstern	William Redfield
Player King	George Voskovec
Player Prologue	John Hetherington
Player Queen	Christopher Culkin
Lucianus	Geoff Garland
Fortinbras	Michael Ebert
A Gentleman	Richard Sterne
First Gravedigger	George Rose
Second Gravedigger	Hugh Alexander
Priest	Barnard Hughes
Osric	Dillon Evans
English Ambassador	Hugh Alexander

LORDS, LADIES, OFFICERS, ATTENDANTS:
Robert Burr, Alex Giannini, Frederick Young,
Claude Harz, John Hetherington, Gerome Ragni,
Linda Seff, Carol Teitel.

UNDERSTUDIES: Hamlet, Robert Burr; Ger-
trude, Carol Teitel; Polonius, Philip Coolidge;
Claudius, Barnard Hughes; Guildenstern, Claude
Harz; Gravedigger, Geoff Garland; Player King,
Frederick Young; Rosencrantz, John Hethering-
ton; Reynaldo, Geoff Garland; Marcellus, Alex
Giannini; Fortinbras, Frederick Young; Horatio,
Gerome Ragni; Ophelia, Linda Seff; Laertes,
Richard Sterne; Lucianus, Alex Giannini.

This is a "Hamlet" presented in two parts,
and acted in rehearsal clothes, stripped of all
extraneous trappings, unencumbered by a recon-
struction of any particular historical period. This
performance is conceived as a final "run-through,"
as actors call it.

General Manager: Roy A. Somlyo
Production Manager: Jean Barrere
Company Manager: Seymour Herscher
Press: David P. Rothenberg, Michael Alpert
Stage Managers: Harry Young, Nathaniel White,
Jake Hamilton

° Still playing May 31, 1964.
(61 performances)

Friedman-Abeles Photos

**William Redfield, Alfred Drake, Eileen Herlie,
Clement Fowler**

Top: (L) William Redfield, Clement Fowler,
Richard Burton (R) Hume Cronyn
Richard Burton

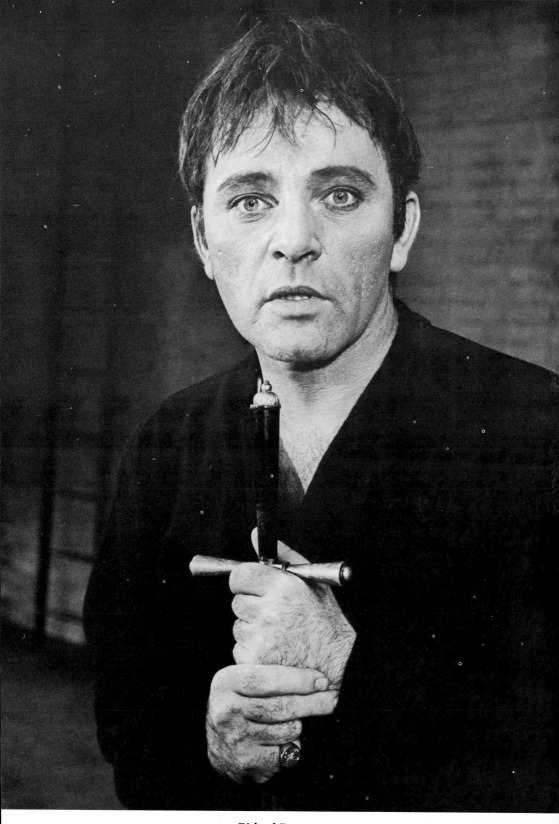

Richard Burton

MARTIN BECK THEATRE
Opened Friday, April 17, 1964.*
Philip Rose and Swanlee present:

CAFE CROWN

Book by Hy Kraft, based on his Play; Music, Albert Hague; Lyrics, Marty Brill; Scenery and Lighting, Sam Leve; Directed by Jerome Eskow; Choreography, Ronald Field; Costumes, Ruth Morley; Dance Music, Albert Hague; Orchestrations, Hershy Kay; Vocal Arrangements and Musical Direction, Gershon Kingsley; Production Associate, Jeanne Otto; Hair Styles, Dorman Allison; Additional Orchestrations, Bill Stegmeier, Jack Andrews, Jay Brower.

CAST

Mr. Morris	Ted Thurston
1st Woman	Shirley Leinwand
2nd Woman	Fay Reed
3rd Woman	Stephanie Winters
Passerby	Ken Richards
Bloom The Fiddler	Joe Ross
Dr. Irving Gilbert	Alan Alda
Rubin	Robert Penn
Beck	Roy Stuart
Nathan The Waiter	Norman Shelly
Kaplan	Val Avery
Mendel Polan	Wood Romoff
Mrs. Perlman	Francine Beers
Mr. Toplitz	Martin Wolfson
Hymie The Busboy	Sam Levene
Lipsky	Michael Vale
Ida Polan	Renee Orin
Norma Roberts	Monte Amundsen
David Cole	Tommy Rall
Mme. Cole	Brenda Lewis
Ship's Captain	John Anania
Petty Officer	Val Avery
Sarah	Betty Aberlin
Samuel Cole	Theodore Bikel
Burton	Edwin Bruce

SINGERS: Marilyn Murphy, Bonnie Brody, Betty Aberlin, Fay Reed, Ann Marisse, Shirley Leinwand, Stephanie Winters, John Wheeler, Ken Richards.

DANCERS: Geri Spinner, Betty Rosebrock, Bonnie Walker, Cheryl Kilgren, Patsi King, Luigi Gasparanetti, Ean Benjamin, Robert Avian, Keith Stewart, Terry Violino.

MUSICAL NUMBERS: Overture, "What's The Matter With Buffalo?," "All Those Years," "Make The Most Of Spring," "Au Revoir Poland—Hello New York!," "So Long As It Isn't Shakespeare," "A Lifetime Love," "I'm Gonna Move," "A Mother's Heart," "On This Wedding Day," "What's Gonna Be Tomorrow," "A Man Must Have Something To Live For," "That's The Life For Me," "Someone's Waiting," "King Lear Ballet," "On A Day Such As This," "Magical Things In Life," Finale.

A Musical Comedy in two acts and thirteen scenes. The action takes place in and around the Cafe Crown at the corner of Second Avenue and Twelfth Street in New York City in the early 1930's.

General Manager: Walter Fried
Company Manager: Sam Handelsman
Press: Merle Debuskey, Seymour Krawitz, Madi Ross
Stage Managers: Leonard Auerbach, Mortimer Halpern, Norman Shelly, Edwin Bruce

*Closed April 18, 1964. (3 performances). The original play without music was directed by Elia Kazan and opened at the Cort Theatre on January 23, 1942, with Sam Jaffe and Morris Carnovsky. It ran for 141 performances.

Friedman-Abeles Photos

Top Left: (C) Theodore Bikel, Sam Levene, Brenda Lewis
Center: Monte Amundsen, Alan Alda Tommy Rall

Tommy Rall, Sam Levene, Theodore Bikel

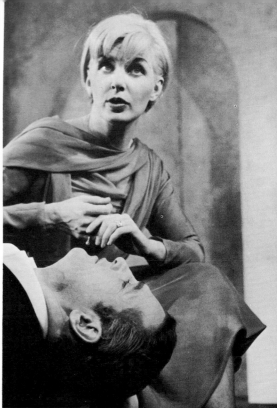

LITTLE THEATRE

Opened Sunday, April 19, 1964.*
The Actors Studio Inc., presents:

BABY WANT A KISS

By James Costigan; Directed by Frank Corsaro; Scenery and Costumes, Peter Harvey; Lighting, David Hays; Fencing Choreography, Guy Burton.

CAST

Barney (A Dog) .... Patrick
Edward .... James Costigan
Mavis .... Joanne Woodward
Emil .... Paul Newman

UNDERSTUDIES: Edward, Will Hare; Mavis, Alexandra Holland; Emil, J. R. Crawford.

A Comedy in two acts. The action takes place at the present time in the sitting room of Edward's house in the country.

General Manager: Arthur Waxman
Press: Samuel Lurie, Judith S. Davidson, Stanley F. Kaminsky
Stage Managers: Richard Blofson, J. R. Crawford

* Still playing May 31, 1964.
(49 performances)

Top: Paul Newman, Joanne Woodward

Joanne Woodward, Paul Newman, James Costigan

ANTA THEATRE

Opened Thursday, April 23, 1964.°
The Actors Studio, Inc., presents The
Actors Studio Theatre production of:

BLUES FOR MISTER CHARLIE

By James Baldwin; Directed by Burgess Mere-
dith; Design and Lighting by Feder; Musical
Coordinator, Robert Cordier; Assistants to the
Director, Ira Cirker, Talley Beatty; Special Con-
sultant, Jerome Smith; Executive Assistant,
Richard R. Chandler.

CAST

Disc Jockey	Frankie (Downbeat) Brown
Lyle Britten	Rip Torn
Richard Henry	Al Freeman, Jr.
Rev. Meridian Henry	Percy Rodriguez
Tom	Wayne Grice
Arthur	Clyde Williams
Ken	Otis Young
Mother Henry	Rosetta LeNoire
Juanita	Diana Sands
Pete	Lincoln Kilpatrick
Lorenzo	David Baldwin
Parnell	Pat Hingle
Jo Britten	Ann Wedgeworth
Papa D	John McCurry
Hazel	Pat Randall
Susan	Patricia Quinn
Ralph	Ralph Waite
Ellis	Joe Don Baker
Lillian	Ann Hennessey
Rev. Phelps	Bill Moor
Judge	Ralph Waite
Court Stenographer	Pat Corley
The State	Dick Bradford
Counsel for the Bereaved	Otis Young
Trombonist	Grachan Moncur III
Drummer	Frankie (Downbeat) Brown
Townspeople	Billie Allen, Pat Corley,

Grachan Moncur III, Bill Moor, Pearl Reynolds

UNDERSTUDIES: Lyle, Ralph Waite; Jo, Pat-
ricia Quinn; Parnell, Dick Bradford; Ralph, Pat
Corley, Bill Moor; Phelps, Joe Don Baker; Ellis,
Pat Corley; Richard, Otis Young; Juanita, Billie
Allen; Meridian, John McCurry; Lorenzo, Pete,
Wayne Grice; Mother Henry, Hilda Haynes;
Arthur, Ken, Ted, Grachan Moncur III; Papa D,
Richard Ward; The State, Bill Moor; Counsel,
Wayne Grice; Stenographer, Judge, Bill Moor.

A Drama in three acts. The action takes place
both in the present and past in a small Southern
town.

General Manager: Arthur Waxman
Company Manager: Eugene Wolsk
Press: Samuel Lurie, Judith S. Davidson,
Stanley F. Kaminsky
Stage Managers: John Strasberg, Martin Gold,
Otis Young, Wayne Grice

° Still playing May 31, 1964.
(46 performances)

Ann Wedgeworth, Rip Torn, Pat Hingle
Above: Diana Sands, Al Freeman, Jr.

Top: (L) Al Freeman, Jr., Rosetta LeNoire
(R) Pat Hingle, Rip Torn

David Brooks, Paula Trueman

MOROSCO THEATRE

Opened Wednesday, May 13, 1964.°
Cornelius Productions, Inc., presents:

THE SUNDAY MAN

By Louis S. Bardoly; Adapted from the Hungarian "A Nadrag" by Ferenc Dunai; Directed by Alexander Dore; Designed by Donald F. Jensen; Production Assistant, Judy Insel.

CAST

Jim	David Brooks
Penny	Vivienne Martin
Miss Mulligan	Paula Trueman
Peter	Stephen Strimpell
Georgia	Jen Nelson
Harry	Dean Dittmann

UNDERSTUDIES: Penny, Georgia, Lynne Charnay; Jim, Harry, John Garner; Peter, Don Pomes.

A Comedy in three acts. The entire action of the play takes place between 10:30 A.M. and 3 P.M. on Sunday in an apartment in a brownstone house off Sutton Place in early summer.

General Manager: Paul Vroom
Company Manager: Richard Osorio
Press: David Lipsky, Lawrence Witchel, Ted Goldsmith
Stage Managers: Joseph Olney, John Garner
°Closed Wednesday, May 13, 1964. (1 performance)

Friedman-Abeles Photos

Top: Vivienne Martin, David Brooks, Stephen Strimpell

HENRY MILLER'S THEATRE

Opened Tuesday, May 19, 1964.°
Gilbert Miller, Helen Bonfils, and
Morton Gottlieb present:

"The WHITE HOUSE"

By A. E. Hotchner; Directed by Henry Kaplan; Sets and Costumes, Ed Wittstein; Lighting, Jules Fisher; Music Composed and Selected by Lee Hoiby; Original Lyrics, A. E. Hotchner.

THE PLAYERS AND THEIR PARTS

Helen Hayes—Abigail Adams, Dolley Madison, Rachel Jackson, Mrs. Franklin Pierce, Leonora Clayton, Mary Todd Lincoln, Julia Grant, Mrs. James G. Blaine, Mrs. Grover Cleveland, Mrs. Benjamin Harrison, Mrs. Theodore Roosevelt, Edith Wilson.

Fritz Weaver—Thomas Jefferson, Andrew Jackson, Millard Fillmore, Franklin Pierce, Abraham Lincoln, Mark Twain, Captain Sigsbee, Woodrow Wilson.

James Daly—George Washington, James Monroe, Martin Van Buren, William Henry Harrison, James Buchanan, Andrew Johnson, Grover Cleveland, Theodore Roosevelt.

Sorrell Booke—Daniel Webster, Reverend Fuller, Stephen A. Douglas, Ulysses S. Grant, Dr. W. W. Keen, John Hay, a Senator.

Eric Berry—John Adams, James K. Polk, Nathaniel Hawthorne, Alexander Graham Bell, Chester A. Arthur, William McKinley, George Bernard Shaw.

Gene Wilder—John Quincy Adams, John Van Buren, John Tyler, Vernon, Robert Lincoln, Rutherford B. Hayes.

Michael O'Sullivan—Washington Irving, The Drover, Henry Clay, Prosecuting Attorney, Charles Guiteau, a Senator.

Bette Henritze—First Fitter, Priscilla Tyler, Mary Ames, Lucy Webb Hayes, Mrs. McBurke.

Eugene Roche—White House Butler, French John, Zachary Taylor, Dr. Grayson.

Nancy Franklin—White House Maid, Martha Jefferson, Second Fitter, Miss Thorndyke.

The setting is in, out and around the White House, before, during, and after the occupancy of the men and women who lived at 1600 Pennsylvania Avenue. The events depicted, relevant and irrelevant, reverent and irreverent, are based upon letters, diaries, and documents written by the Presidents and their ladies, or about them by their contemporaries. Presented in two acts.

General Manager: George Banyai
Company Manager: Richard Seader
Press: Dorothy Ross, Richard O'Brien
Stage Managers: Warren Crane, Robert Crawley

° Still playing May 31, 1964.
(14 performances)

Werner J. Kuhn Photos

Helen Hayes   **James Daly**

BOOTH THEATRE

Opened Thursday, May 21, 1964.*
Fryer, Carr & Harris, Inc., and
John Herman present:

ROAR LIKE A DOVE

By Lesley Storm; Directed by Cyril Ritchard;
Setting and Lighting, Herbert Senn and Helen
Pond; Costumes, Michael Travis; Hair Styles,
Ronald DeMann; Production Associate, Robert
Linden; Assistant to the Producers, John Bowab.

CAST

Jane	Christopher Norris
MacIntosh	Neil Fitzgerald
Lady Dungavel	Betsy Palmer
Cousin Edward	Roderick Cook
Lord Dungavel	Derek Godfrey
Muriel Chadwick	Jessie Royce Landis
Tom Chadwick	Charlie Ruggles
Bernard Taggart-Stuart	William Kinsolving

UNDERSTUDIES: Lady Dungavel, Martha
Randall; Muriel, Constance Carpenter; Tom,
MacIntosh, Jon Richards; Robert, Edward, Bern-
ard, Jonathan Frid; Jane, Bridget Knapp.

A Comedy in three acts. The action takes
place at the present time in the library of Dungavel Castle in the Western Highlands of Scotland.

General Manager: Richard Grayson
Press: Betty Lee Hunt
Stage Managers: Robert Linden, Jonathan Frid
* Still playing May 31, 1964.
(12 performances)

Friedman-Abeles Photos

Right: Charlie Ruggles, Jessie Royce Landis,
Derek Godfrey, Betsy Palmer

Derek Godfrey, Betsy Palmer

Neil Fitzgerald, Christopher Norris,
Derek Godfrey

113

Martin Sheen

Irene Dailey Top with Martin Sheen,
Jack Albertson

ROYALE THEATRE
Opened Monday, May 25, 1964.°
Edgar Lansbury presents:

THE SUBJECT WAS ROSES

By Frank D. Gilroy; Directed by Ulu Gros-
bard; Scenery, Edgar Lansbury; Lighting, Jules
Fisher; Costumes, Donald Foote; Production
Assistants, Linda Gaydos, Al Isaac.

CAST

John Cleary_____Jack Albertson
Nettie Cleary_____Irene Dailey
Timmy Cleary_____Martin Sheen
UNDERSTUDIES: John, Joseph Sullivan; Nettie,
Peg Murray; Timmy, Matt Clark.

A Play in two acts and seven scenes. The
action takes place in May 1946 in a middle
class apartment.

General Manager: Joseph Beruh
Press: Max Eisen, Jeannie Gibson Merrick,
Dan Rosen, Paul Solomon
Stage Managers: Paul Leaf, Matt Clark

° Still playing May 31, 1964.
(8 performances)

Bert Andrews Photos

**Top: Irene Dailey, Jack Albertson,
Martin Sheen**

Irene Dailey, Martin Sheen

115

MARK HELLINGER THEATRE
Opened Tuesday, May 26, 1964.°
Lester Osterman and Jule Styne present:

FADE OUT—FADE IN

Book and Lyrics by Betty Comden and Adolph Green; Music by Jule Styne; Directed by George Abbott; Dances and Musical Numbers Staged by Ernest Flatt; Settings and Lighting, William and Jean Eckart; Costumes, Donald Brooks; Hair Styles, Ernest Adler; Musical Direction, Orchestrations, Ralph Burns and Ray Ellis; Vocal Arrangements, Buster Davis; Dance Music Arranged by Richard De Benedictis; Production Co-ordinator, Dorothy Dicker; Production Assistant, Joe Regan.

CAST

Byron Prong	Jack Cassidy
Teenagers	Jodi Perselle, Judy Newman
Woman	Diana Ede
Man	Darrell J. Askey
Autograph Kids	Roger Allan Raby, Charlene Mehl
Helga Sixtrees	Judy Cassmore
Pops	Frank Tweddell
Rosco	Bob Neukum
Billy Vespers	Glenn Kezer
Lyman	John Dorrin
Hope Springfield	Carol Burnett
Rex	Darrell J. Askey
Chauffeur	William Louther
1st Girl	Wendy Taylor
1st Cowboy Extra	Stephen Elmore
2nd Cowboy Extra	Fred Cline
Gangster Extra	Gene Varrone
Ralph Governor	Mitchell Jason
Rudolf Governor	Dick Patterson
George Governor	Howard Kahl
Frank Governor	John Dorrin
Harold Governor	Gene Varrone
Arnold Governor	Stephen Elmore
Waiters	Fred Cline, Richard Frisch, Roger Allan Raby
Publicity Men	Sean Allan, Darrell J. Askey
Convicts	Gene Kelton, William Louther, Ed Pfeiffer, James Von Weiss
Myra May Melrose	Virginia Payne
Seamstress	Diane Arnold
Miss Mallory	Jo Tract
Custer Corkley	Dan Resin
Approval	Smaxie
Photographer	Sean Allan
Max Welch	Richard Frisch
Lou Williams	Tiger Haynes
Dora Dailey	Aileen Poe
Lionel Z. Governor	Lou Jacobi
Dr. Anton Traurig	Reuben Singer
Gloria Currie	Tina Louise
Madame Barrymore	Penny Egelston
Lead Dancer	Don Crichton

SINGING ENSEMBLE: Sean Allan, Jackie Alloway, Darrell J. Askey, Fred Cline, John Dorrin, Trish Dwelley, Stephen Elmore, Richard Frisch, Howard Kahl, Carolyn Kemp, Betty Kent, Glenn Kezer, Mari Nettum, Bob Neukum, Roger Allan Raby, Jo Tract, Gene Varrone.

DANCING ENSEMBLE: Virginia Allen, Diane Arnold, Judy Cassmore, Diana Ede, Ernie Horvath, Gene Kelton, William Louther, Charlene Mehl, Judy Newman, Jodi Perselle, Ed Pfeiffer, Carolsue Shaer, Patricia Sigris, Roy Smith, Bill Stanton, Wendy Taylor, James Von Weiss.

UNDERSTUDIES: Hope, Carolyn Kemp; Byron, Gene Varrone; Rudolf, Don Crichton; Gloria, Judy Cassmore; Traurig, Richard Frisch; Lou, William Louther; Smaxie, Maxie.

MUSICAL NUMBERS: "The Thirties," "It's Good To Be Back Home," "Fear," "Call Me Savage," "The Usher From The Mezzanine," "I'm With You," "My Fortune Is My Face," "Lila Tremaine," "Go Home Train," "Close Harmony," "You Mustn't Be Discouraged," "The Dangerous Age," "L. Z. In Quest of His Youth," "The Fiddler and The Fighter," "Fade Out—Fade In."

A Musical Comedy in two acts and nineteen scenes. The action takes place in New York and Hollywood in the mid-1930's.

General Manager: Richard Horner
Press: Harvey B. Sabinson, Lee Solters, David Powers
Stage Managers: John Allen, William Krot, Nicholas A. B. Gray
°Still playing May 31, 1964. (7 performances)

Friedman-Abeles Photos

Carol Burnett, Jack Cassidy, Don Crichton
Above: Carol Burnett, Dick Patterson

Top: Carol Burnett and Smaxie

LILA TREMAINE

Tina Louise (C)
Above: Bob Neukum, Carol Burnett
Top: (C) Carol Burnett

Jack Cassidy, Tina Louise
Above: Tina Louise, Lou Jacobi, Don Crichton
Top: Tiger Haynes, Carol Burnett 117

HELEN HAYES THEATRE

Opened Wednesday, March 8, 1961.°
Roger L. Stevens presents:

MARY, MARY

By Jean Kerr; Directed by Joseph Anthony;
Designed by Oliver Smith; Costumes, Theoni V.
Aldredge; Lighting, Peggy Clark; Hair Styles,
Kenneth of Lilly Daché; Associate Producer, Lyn
Austin; Produced in association with Collin
Productions.

CAST

Bob McKellaway	Tom Poston†1
Tiffany Richards	Ellen Weston†2
Oscar Nelson	Hiram Sherman†3
Dirk Winsten	Edward Mulhare†4
Mary McKellaway	Diana Lynn†5

A Comedy in three acts. The action takes
place at the present time in Bob McKellaway's
livingroom in a New York apartment building.

Company Manager: Ben Rosenberg
Press: Samuel Lurie, Judith S. Davidson,
Stanley F. Kaminsky
Stage Managers: Wayne Carson, Joe Hanrahan
°Still playing May 31, 1964. (1352 performances)
For original production, see THEATRE
WORLD, Vol. 17.
†Succeeded by: 1. Murray Hamilton, 2. Eliza-
beth St. Clair, 3. Alan Bruce, Clinton Sund-
berg, 4. Tom Helmore, 5. Mindy Carson.

Friedman-Abeles Photos

Tom Poston, Diana Lynn
Top: Biff McGuire, Hiram Sherman,
Ellen Weston

FORTY-SIXTH STREET THEATRE

Opened Saturday, October 14, 1961.°
Feuer and Martin in association with Frank Productions Inc. present:

HOW TO SUCCEED IN BUSINESS WITHOUT REALLY TRYING

Book by Abe Burrows, Jack Weinstock, Willie Gilbert; Based on the Book by Shepherd Mead; Music and Lyrics, Frank Loesser; Directed by Abe Burrows; Musical Staging, Bob Fosse; Choreography, Hugh Lambert; Scenery and Lighting, Robert Randolph; Costumes, Robert Fletcher; Musical Direction, Abba Bogin; Orchestrations, Robert Ginzler.

CAST

Finch	Robert Morse[1]
Gatch	Ray Mason
Jenkins	Hal Englund[2]
Tackaberry	David Collyer
Peterson	Casper Roos
J. B. Biggley	Rudy Vallee
Kittridge	Lanier Davis
Rosemary	Michele Lee
Bratt	Walter Klavun[3]
Smitty	Claudette Sutherland
Frump	Charles Nelson Reilly[4]
Miss Jones	Leta Bonynge
Mr. Twimble	Sammy Smith
Hedy	Joy Claussen
Scrubwomen	Virginia Perlowin[5], Silver Saundors[6]
Miss Krumholtz	Mara Landi[5]
Toynbee	Ray Mason
Ovington	Lanier Davis
Policeman	Bob Murdock[7]
Womper	Sammy Smith

SINGERS: Richard Barclay, David Collyer, Lanier Davis, Harris Hawkins, Casper Roos, Fairfax Mason, Alice Evans, Carole Lindsey, Renee Gorsey, Nanette Workman.

DANCERS: Nick Andrews, Don Emmons, Richard Korthaze, Darrell Notara, Gene Cooper, Ron Stratton, Merritt Thompson, Carol Jane Abney, Elaine Cangilla, Iva March, Alice Shanahan, Mickey Gunnersen, Enid Hart, Kaarlyn Kitch.

UNDERSTUDIES: Finch, Richard Barclay; Rosemary, Nanette Workman; Hedy, Fairfax Mason; Frump, Darrell Notara; Smitty, Carole Lindsey; Bratt, David Collyer; Twimble, Lanier Davis; Jones, Alice Evans; Womper, Casper Roos.

MUSICAL NUMBERS: "How To," "Happy To Keep His Dinner Warm," "Coffee Break," "The Company Way," "A Secretary Is Not A Toy," "Been A Long Day," "Grand Old Ivy," "Paris Original," "Rosemary," "Finaletto," "Cinderella, Darling," "Love From A Heart of Gold," "I Believe In You," "Brotherhood of Man," Finale.

A Musical Comedy in two acts. The entire action takes place in the new Park Avenue office building of World Wide Wickets Company, Inc.

Manager: Ira Bernstein
Press: Merle Debuskey, Seymour Krawitz, Madi Ross
Stage Managers: Phil Friedman, Herman Magidson, Lanier Davis, Darrell Notara

°Still playing May 31, 1964. (1098 performances) For original production, see THEATRE WORLD, Vol 18.

†Succeeded by: 1. Darryl Hickman, 2. Ronnie Welsh, Richard Barclay, 3. Bruce Mackay, 4. Ralph Purdum, 5. Carole Lindsey, 6. Alice Evans, 7. Harris Hawkins.

Friedman-Abeles Photos

Top Right: (C) Rudy Vallee, Darryl Hickman
Leta Bonynge
Center: Rudy Vallee, Darryl Hickman

Darryl Hickman, Michele Lee, Rudy Vallee

ALVIN THEATRE

Opened Tuesday, May 8, 1962.°
(Moved Monday, March 9, 1964, to the Mark Hellinger Theatre, and to the Majestic Theatre on Tuesday, May 12, 1964.)
Harold Prince presents:

A FUNNY THING HAPPENED ON THE WAY TO THE FORUM

Book, Burt Shevelove, Larry Gelbart; Based on Plays of Plautus; Music and Lyrics, Stephen Sondheim; Directed by George Abbott; Settings and Costumes, Tony Walton; Lighting, Jean Rosenthal; Musical Direction, Harold Hastings; Orchestrations, Irwin Kostal, Sid Ramin; Dance Music Arrangements, Hal Schaefer; Additional Dance Music, Betty Waldberg.

CAST

Prologue	Zero Mostel†1
The Proteans	Eddie Phillips, George Reeder,†2 David Evans
Senex	David Burns†3
Domina	Ruth Kobart
Hero	Brian Davies†4
Hysterium	Jack Gilford
Lycus	John Carradine†5
Pseudolus	Zero Mostel†1
Tintinabula	Roberta Keith†6
Panacea	Lucienne Bridou†7
The Geminae	Lisa James, Judy Alexander†8
Philia	Preshy Marker
Vibrata	Myrna White†9
Gymnasia	Gloria Kristy
Erronius	Raymond Walburn†10
Miles Gloriosus	Ronald Holgate

UNDERSTUDIES: Pseudolus, Danny Dayton; Hysterium, Eddie Phillips; Senex, Horace Cooper, Danny Dayton; Domina, Julia Ross; Philia, Linda Donovan; Miles, Ron Ross; Gymnasia, Julia Ross; Courtesans, Gretl Bauer; Hero, David Evans; Proteans, George Martin.

MUSICAL NUMBERS: "Comedy Tonight," "Love, I Hear," "Free," "The House of Marcus Lycus," "Lovely," "Pretty Little Picture," "Everybody Ought To Have A Maid," "I'm Calm," "Impossible," "Bring Me My Bride," "That Dirty Old Man," "That'll Show Him," "Funeral Sequence and Dance."

A Musical Comedy in two acts. The action takes place 200 years before the Christian era on a day in spring, in a street in Rome in front of the houses of Erronius, Senex, and Lycus.

General Manager: Carl Fisher
Company Manager: Clarence Jacobson
Press: Sol Jacobson, Lewis Harmon, Earl Butler
Stage Managers: Ruth Mitchell, James Bronson, George Martin

° Still playing May 31, 1964. (862 performances). For original production, see THEATRE WORLD, Vol. 18.

† Succeeded by: 1. Jerry Lester, Dick Shawn, 2. Ron Ross, 3. Frank McHugh, 4. Harry David Snow, 5. Erik Rhodes, Danny Dayton, 6. Ethel Martin, 7. Barbara London, 8. Lisa Ackerman, 9. Sally Neal, 10. Horace Cooper.

Van Williams Photos

Dick Shawn, Horace Cooper, Jack Gilford

Dick Shawn with Courtesans, and above with Barbara London

120

Fred Burrell, Orson Bean, Paul Ford
Left: Maureen O'Sullivan, Leona Maricle
Top Left: Paul Ford, Maureen O'Sullivan,
John Alexander, Leona Maricle

THE PLAYHOUSE

Opened Tuesday, November 27, 1962.*
Eliot Martin and Daniel Hollywood
present:

NEVER TOO LATE

By Sumner Arthur Long; Directed by George
Abbott; Setting and Lighting, William and Jean
Eckart; Costumes, Florence Klotz; "Never Too
Late Cha-Cha" by Jerry Bock and Sheldon
Harnick; Incidental Music, John Kander.

CAST

Grace Kimbrough	Leona Maricle
Harry Lambert	Paul Ford†1
Edith Lambert	Maureen O'Sullivan†2
Dr. James Kimbrough	House Jameson
Charlie	Orson Bean†3
Kate	Fran Sharon
Mr. Foley	Wallace Engelhardt
Mayor Crane	John Alexander
Policeman	Ed Griffith†4

UNDERSTUDIES: Edith, Lorraine MacMartin;
Charlie, Fred Burrell; Mayor, House Jameson;
Grace, Lorraine MacMartin; Doctor, Wallace
Engelhart.

A Comedy in three acts and five scenes. The
action takes place in the living room of the
Lambert home in Calverton, Massachusetts, at
the present time.

General Manager: C. Edwin Knill
Company Manager: Helen Richards
Press: Mary Bryant
Stage Managers: Wally Peterson, Wallace
Engelhardt

*Still playing May 31, 1964. (631 performances)
For original production, see THEATRE
WORLD, Vol. 19.

† Succeeded by: 1. Dennis O'Keefe, 2. Martha
Scott, 3. Will Hutchins, 4. Fred Burrell.

Van Williams and Friedman-Abeles Photos

Dennis O'Keefe, Martha Scott, Will Hutchins

IMPERIAL THEATRE

Opened Sunday, January 6, 1963.°
David Merrick and Donald Albery present:

OLIVER!

Book, Music, and Lyrics by Lionel Bart; Freely adapted from Charles Dickens' "Oliver Twist"; Directed by Peter Coe; Designed by Sean Kenny; Orchestrations, Eric Rogers; Musical Director, Donald Pippin; Technical Supervisor, Ian Albery; Lighting, John Wyckham; Costumes, M. Berman, Ltd.; Production Supervisor, Neil Hartley.

CAST

Oliver Twist	Bruce Prochnik†1

At The Workhouse:

Mr. Bumble	Willoughby Goddard
Mrs. Corney	Hope Jackman†2
Old Sally	Ruth Maynard

At the Undertaker's:

Mr. Sowerberry	Robin Ramsay
Mrs. Sowerberry	Helena Carroll†3
Charlotte	Cherry Davis
Noah Claypole	Terry Lomax

At the Thieves' Kitchen:

Fagin	Clive Revill†4
The Artful Dodger	David Jones
Nancy	Georgia Brown†5
Bet	Alice Playten†6
Bill Sikes	Danny Sewell

At the Brownlow's:

Mr. Brownlow	Geoffrey Lumb
Dr. Grimwig	John Call
Mrs. Bedwin	Dortha Duckworth

WORKHOUSE BOYS AND FAGIN'S GANG: Bobbie Bradley, Eugene Endon, Bryant Fraser, Stuart Getz, Bart Larsen, Christopher Month, Blaise Morton, Patrick O'Shaughnessy, Jackie Perkuhn, George Priolo, Robbie Reed, Malcolm Taylor, Christopher Votos.

LONDONERS: Linda Barrie, Johnny Borden, Jack Davison, James Glenn, Lucille Cole, Lesley Hunt, John M. Kimbro, Allan Lokos, Richard Miller, Moose Peting, Ruth Ramsey, Michael Roberts, Terry Robinson, Ann Tell, Ray Tudor, Maura K. Wedge.

UNDERSTUDIES: Fagin, Robin Ramsay, Richard Miller; Nancy, Maura K. Wedge; Bumble, John Call; Mrs. Corney, Ann Tell; Brownlow, Alan Lokos; Grimwig, John M. Kimbro; Bill, Michael Roberts; Mrs. Sowerberry, Ann Tell; Oliver, Eugene Endon, Blaise Morton; Artful Dodger, George Priolo, Malcolm Taylor; Charlotte, Lesley Hunt; Noah, Michael Lamont; Sally, Ruth Ramsey; Bet, Lesley Hunt; Mrs. Bedwin, Ruth Ramsey.

MUSICAL NUMBERS: "Food, Glorious Food," "Oliver," "I Shall Scream," "Boy For Sale," "That's Your Funeral," "Where Is Love?," "Consider Yourself," "You've Got To Pick A Pocket Or Two," "It's A Fine Life," "I'd Do Anything," "Be Back Soon," "Oom-Pah-Pah," "My Name," "As Long As He Needs Me," "Who Will Buy?," "Reviewing The Situation," Finale.

A Musical in two acts.

General Manager: Jack Schlissel
Press: Lee Solters, Harvey Sabinson, Lila Glaser King, David Power
Stage Managers: Ross Bowman, Edward Hastings, Moose Peting

° Still playing May 31, 1964. (586 performances) For original production, see THEATRE WORLD, Vol. 19.

† Succeeded by: 1. Paul O'Keefe, then Ronnie Kroll, 2. Helena Carroll, 3. Ruth Maynard, 4. Robin Ramsay during 2 weeks vacation, 5. Maura K. Wedge during 2 weeks vacation, 6. Joan Lombardo.

Left Center: Clive Revill, Georgia Brown

David Jones

Georgia Brown

PLAYS FROM OTHER SEASONS THAT CLOSED DURING THIS SEASON

Play	Opened	Closed	Performances
The Sound of Music	Nov. 16, 1959	June 15, 1963	1443
Beyond The Fringe	Oct. 27, 1962	May 30, 1964	673
Who's Afraid of Virginia Woolf?	Oct. 13, 1962	May 16, 1964	664
A Man For All Seasons	Nov. 22, 1961	June 1, 1963	640
No Strings	Mar. 15, 1962	Aug. 3, 1963	580
Stop The World–I Want To Get Off	Oct. 3, 1962	Feb. 1, 1964	556
Enter Laughing	Mar. 13, 1963	Mar. 14, 1964	419
She Loves Me	Apr. 23, 1963	Jan. 11, 1964	302
Mr. President	Oct. 20, 1962	June 8, 1963	265
Tovarich	Mar. 18, 1963	Nov. 9, 1963	264
Little Me	Nov. 17, 1962	June 29, 1963	257
Photo Finish	Feb. 12, 1963	June 29, 1963	159
Dear Me, The Sky Is Falling	Mar. 2, 1963	July 10, 1963	151
Strange Interlude	Mar. 11, 1963	June 29, 1963	97
Too True To Be Good	Mar. 12, 1963	June 1, 1963	94
Rattle of A Simple Man	Apr. 17, 1963	July 6, 1963	94
Pajama Tops	May 31, 1963	July 13, 1963	72
Pal Joey (City Center)	May 29, 1963	June 9, 1963	15

SPECIAL ATTRACTIONS

Sergei Obratsov

BROADWAY THEATRE
Opened Wednesday, October 2, 1963.°
S. Hurok presents:

OBRATSOV RUSSIAN PUPPET THEATRE

Conceived and Produced by Sergei Obratsov;
Text of conferencier by Alexander Bondi; Text
for acts by Zinovy Gerdt; Choreography by Semyon Samodur; Settings by Valentin Andreivich
and Vera Terekhova; Music by Grigory Teplitsky;
Orchestra Conducted by Arthur Lief.

PROGRAM
PART I: Overture, The Conferencier, The Can-
tata, Peredielkin, The Coloratura Soprano, The
Tango, The Baritone, The Wunderkind, The
Gypsies.
PART II: The Performing Animals, The Operetta
Scene, The Illusionist, The Tap Dancers, Jazz
Singer and Combo, The Wild-Beast Tamer,
Finale.

Company Manager: Edward A. Perper
Press: Martin Feinstein, Michael Sweeley
Stage Managers: Pavel Nashelsky, Galina
Badich, Nicolai Gzhelsky
°Closed November 30, 1963. (76 performances)

Opened Wednesday, June 12, 1963.*

THE KING AND I

Music by Richard Rodgers; Book and Lyrics by Oscar Hammerstein 2nd; Based on Novel "Anna and The King of Siam" by Margaret Landon; Directed by John Fearnley; Musical Director and Conductor, Pembroke Davenport; Choreography, Jerome Robbins; Scenery, Jo Mielziner; Choreography reproduced by Yuriko; Costumes, Irene Sharaff; Supervised by Stanley Simmons; Lighting, Peggy Clark; Orchestrations, Robert Russell Bennett; Hairstyles, Ernie Adler.

CAST

Captain Orton	Sam Kirkham
Louis Leonowens	Tommy Leap
Anna Leonowens	Eileen Brennan
The Interpreter	Paul Flores
The Kralahome	Ken LeRoy
The King	Manolo Fabregas
Phra Alack	John Garces
Lun Tha	L. D. Clements
Tuptim	Joy Clements
Lady Thiang	Anita Darian
Prince Chululongkorn	Ramon Caballero
Princess Ying Yoawalak	Lisa Jo Abe
Sir Edward Ramsay	John D. Seymour

PRINCES AND PRINCESSES: David Aguilar, Paula Chin, Delfino DeArco, Capri Hermany, Roma Hermany, Vivian Hernandez, Lawrence Kikuchi, Susan I. Kikuchio, Peter Martinez, Ado Sato, Ramon Torres.

ROYAL DANCERS: Susan Aschieri, Hadassah Badoch, Mavis Ray Booth, Noemi Chiesa, Miriam Cole, Barbara Creed, Victor Duntiere, Carol Fried, Phyllis A. Gutelius, Edith Jerell, Marion Jim, Loi Leabo, Jim E. McMillan, Paul E. Olson, Clive Thompson.

SINGERS, WIVES, PRIESTS, ETC: Faith Daltry Compo, Harris W. Davis, James Fels, Helen Guile, Janet Hayes, Bill Kennedy, Joy Lynne Sica, Sharon Vaughn, Lynn Wendell.

UNDERSTUDIES: King, Paul Flores; Thiang, Helen Guile; Tuptim, Joy Sica; Lun Tha, Bill Kennedy; Kralahome, Jim McMillan; Topsy, Little Eva, Carol Fried; Eliza, Marion Jim; Simon, Edith Jerell; Angel, Bettina Dearborn; Uncle Thomas, Barbara Creed; Prince, Peter Martinez, Orton, Interpreter, Paul Olson, Ramsey, Harris Davis.

MUSICAL NUMBERS: "I Whistle A Happy Tune," "My Lord and Master," "Hello, Young Lovers," "March of The Siamese Children," "A Puzzlement," "Getting To Know You," "We Kiss In A Shadow," "Shall I Tell You What I Think Of You?," "Something Wonderful," "Western People Funny," "I Have Dreamed," "The Small House of Uncle Thomas Ballet," "Shall We Dance?," Finale.

General Manager: Buford Armitage
Company Manager: Zelda Dorfman
Press: Diane Judge
Stage Managers: Herman Shapiro, Bill Fields, Tom Ellis

*Closed Sunday, June 23, 1963.
(15 performances)

Original production opened on Broadway March 29, 1951, and closed March 20, 1954, after 1246 performances. Yul Brynner and Gertrude Lawrence originated the leading roles. Last revival was at the City Center in 1960.

Alix Jeffry Photos

Top and Center: Eileen Brennan, Manolo Fabregas

Anita Darian, Manolo Fabregas, Eileen Brennan

NEW YORK CITY CENTER

Opened Tuesday, February 11, 1964.°
S. Hurok presents:

MAZOWSZE

Polish Song and Dance Company

PROGRAM

PART I: Chodzony, Oberek, Dance from Kurpie Region, Spindle Polka, Dances and Songs from Wielkopolska, Tatra Dances and Songs, Polonaise, Songs from Lancut Region, Here Come The Guests, Wooers, Poleczka from Warsaw Suburbs, Jokes and Dances from Podegrodzie, Cracow Dances and Songs, Krakowiak.

PART II: Polonaise, Mazurka, Cieszyn Songs, Kujawiak, Carnival in Wilamowice, Dances from Biskupizna Wielkopolska, Songs and Dances from Lowicz, Get Married Mary, Matthew Is A Lucky Man, The Lowicz Maiden, Mazurka, Oberek, Finale.

Company Manager: Oscar Berlin
Press: Martin Feinstein, Michael Sweeley, Edward Parkinson
Stage Managers: Waclaw Zukowski, John Scott

° Closed Sunday, February 23, 1964, after a limited engagement of 16 performances.

Madeleine Renaud, Jean-Louis Barrault
in
"LE MARIAGE DE FIGARO"

127

NEW YORK CITY CENTER
Opened Tuesday, February 25, 1964.°
S. Hurok presents, by arrangement with the
Government of The French Republic,
The Theatre De France in:

LE MARIAGE DE FIGARO

By Beaumarchais; Decor, Pierre Delbée; Costumes, Yves Saint-Laurent; Incidental Music from the Eighteenth Century; Directed by Jean-Louis Barrault; Choreography, Jose Torres.

CAST

Count Almaviva	Jean-Louis Barrault
The Countess	Madeleine Renaud
Figaro	Jean Desailly
Suzanne	Simone Valere
Marceline	Denise Benoit
Antonio	Robert Lombard
Fanchette	Dominique Arden
Cherubin	Bernard Laik
Bartholo	Regis Outin
Bazile	Henri Gilabert
Don Guzman Brid'Oison	Pierre Bertin
Double-Main	Michael Bertay
A Court Crier	Georges Coste
Gripe-Soleil	Andre Batisse
Young Shepherdess	Sabine Lods
Pedrille	Luis Masson

Chorus........Dominique Santarelli, Jean Winckler, Jean-Guy Henneveux, Stanislas Staskewitsch, Sarah Sanders, Jane Martel, Claudie Bourlon, Judith Alexandre

ANDROMAQUE

By Racine; Directed by Jean-Louis Barrault; Scenery and Costumes by Bernard Dayde. Opened Friday, February 28, 1964.

CAST

Andromaque	Maria Mauban
Pyrrhus, King of Epirus	Jean Desailly
Orestes	Jean-Louis Barrault
Hermione	Genevieve Page
Pylade	Henri Gilabert
Cleone	Christiane Carpentier
Cephise	Sarah Sanders
Phoenix	Jean-Roger Tandou

Followers of Orestes and Pyrrhus

LA VIE PARISIENNE

By Meilhac and Halevy; Music by Jacques Offenbach; Decor and Costumes, Jean-Denis Malcles; Directed by Jean-Louis Barrault; Dances Arranged by Roger Stefani; Orchestra Conducted by Andre Girard. Opened Tuesday, March 10, 1964.

CAST

Bobinet	Jean-Pierre Granval
Gardefeu	Jean Desailly
The Baron	Pierre Bertin
The Brazilian	Jean-Louis Barrault
Frick, Prosper, Alfred	Jean Paredes
Gontran, Urbain	Dominique Santarelli
Joseph	Robert Lombard
Alphonse	Regis Outin
The Man Who Waits	Michel Bertay
Metella	Suzy Delair
The Baroness	Sarah Sanders
Gabrielle	Simone Valere
Pauline	Denise Benoit
The Sweeper	Marie-Helene Daste

CHORUS AND FRENCH-CANCAN: Judith Alexandre, Dominique Arden, Paulette Attie, Christine Bottai, Claudie Bourlon, Josette Grisy, Sabine Lods, Jane Martel, Nicole Nevat, Celine Salles, Andre Batisse, Georges Coste, Henri Gilabert, Jean-Guy Henneveux, Bernard Laik, Gilbert Lefevre, Luis Masson, Gerard Quenez, Stanislas Staskewitsch, Jean Winckler.

Company Manager: Edward A. Perper
Press: Martin Feinstein, Michael Sweeley
Stage Manager: Charles Maryan
° Closed Sunday, March 15, 1964.
(24 performances)

Simone Valere, Jean Paredes, Pierre Bertin, Denise Benoit, Jean Pierre Granval in "La Vie Parisienne"

128 Above: Simone Valere, Jean Desailly in "Le Mariage De Figaro"

Top: Simone Valere, Bernard Laik, Madelei Renaud in "Le Mariage De Figaro"

LE PIETON DE L'AIR
(The Pedestrian of the Air)

By Eugene Ionesco; Directed by Jean-Louis
Barrault; Decor and Costumes, Jacques Noel;
Music, Georges Delerue; Special Effects, Guy
Bert. Opened Tuesday, March 3, 1964.

CAST

M. Berenger	Jean-Louis Barrault
Mme. Berenger	Madeleine Renaud
Mlle. Berenger	Dominique Arden
English Journalist	Luis Masson
First Englishman	Jean Paredes
His Wife	Sabine Lods
Second Englishman	Robert Lombard
His Wife	Jane Martel
John Bull	Dominique Santarelli
First Old English Lady	Christiane Carpentier
Second Old English Lady	Marie-Helene Daste
Uncle Doctor	Regis Outin
Undertaker's Employee	Michel Bertay
Apparition from Anti-World	Georges Coste
Judge	Georges Coste
Man in White	Henri Gilabert
Second Man in White	Andre Batisse

Presented with:

SALUT A MOLIERE

A Presentation by Jean-Louis Barrault with
the Theatre De France Company.

CAST

Narrators	Madeleine Renaud, Jean-Louis Barrault, Jean Desailly
An Actor	Jean-Guy Henneveux
The Valet	Luis Masson
Monsieur Jourdain	Dominique Santarelli
Madame Jourdain	Marie-Helene Daste
Don Luis	Henri Gilabert
Le Marquis	Jean-Pierre Granval
Lucrece	Georges Coste
Sganarelle	Jean Paredes
Martine	Denise Benoit
Monsieur Robert	Michel Bertay
Lycarsis	Andre Batisse
Sganarelle	Pierre Bertin
Geronimo	Regis Outin
Georgette	Sabine Lods
Alain	Robert Lombard
Artiste	Jean Desailly
Angelique	Jane Martel
Agnes	Domininque Arden
Arnolphe	Jean-Louis Barrault
Celimene	Madeleine Renaud
Alceste	Jean-Louis Barrault
Monsieur de Fonandres	Georges Coste
Monsieur Tomes	Michel Bertay
Monsieur Filerin	Henri Gilabert
Bary	Jean-Pierre Granval
Elomire	Jean Paredes
Mlle. Moliere	Jane Martel
The Valet	Luis Masson
Tartuffe	Pierre Bertin
Dorine	Denise Benoit
Elmire	Simone Valere
On Hypocrisy	Bernard Laik
Sganarelle	Jean-Pierre Granval
Don Juan	Jean Desailly
The Pauper	Regis Outin
Argan	Robert Lombard
Beralde	Michel Bertay
Geronte	Pierre Bertin
Scapin	Luis Masson
Madeleine Bejart	Madeleine Renaud
Moliere	Jean-Louis Barrault
L'Amour	Georges Coste
Psyche	Simone Valere

Photos by Photo Pic

Madeleine Renaud, as Madeleine Bejart,
Jean-Louis Barrault as Moliere
in "Salut A Moliere"

Top: "Le Pieton De L'Air"
Left Center: Jean Desailly, Genevieve Page
in "Andromaque"

Opened Wednesday, March 25, 1964.

PATIENCE

Book by W. S. Gilbert; Music, Arthur Sullivan; Staged by Dorothy Raedler; Scenery and Costumes, Motley; Solo Dance Choreography, Thomas Andrew; Conductor, Julius Rudel.

CAST

Colonel Calverley	William Chapman
Major Murgatroyd	James Wilson
Lt. Duke of Dunstable	Richard Krause
Reginald Bunthorne	Emile Renan
Archibald Grosvenor	David Smith
Mr. Bunthorne's Solicitor	Thomas Andrew
Lady Angela	Marlena Kleinman
Lady Saphir	Helen Guile
Lady Ella	Virginia Bitar
Lady Jane	Claramae Turner
Patience	Lee Venora

Chorus of Rapturous Maidens and Officers.

Opened Saturday afternoon, March 28, 1964.

THE PIRATES OF PENZANCE

Book, W. S. Gilbert; Music, Arthur Sullivan; Staged by Dorothy Raedler; Scenery, H. A. Condell; Conductor, Herbert Grossman.

CAST

Major-General Stanley	Emile Renan
Pirate King	William Chapman
Samuel	William Ledbetter
Frederic	Charles Hindsley
Sergeant of Police	Herbert Beattie
Mabel	Anne Elgar
Edith	Virginia Bitar
Kate	Mary Burgess
Isabel	Helen Guile
Ruth	Muriel Greenspon

Chorus of Pirates, Police, Wards.

Opened Friday afternoon, April 3, 1964.

IOLANTHE

Book by W. S. Gilbert; Music, Arthur Sullivan; Staged by Dorothy Raedler; Scenery and Costumes, Micunis; Bee Dance Choreography, Thomas Andrew; Conductor, William Jonson.

CAST

The Lord Chancellor	Norman Kelley
Lord Mountararat	David Smith
Lord Tolloller	Richard Krause
Private Willis	George Gaynes
Strephon	William Ledbetter
Queen of the Fairies	Claramae Turner
Iolanthe	Marlena Kleinman
Celia	Virginia Bitar
Lelia	Mary Burgess
Fleta	Beverly Evans
The Bee	Rochelle Zide
The Dragonfly	Hanna Owen
The Butterfly	Helen Guile
Phyllis	Carol Bergey

Chorus of Dukes, Noblemen, Fairies.

COMPANY ROSTER: Raymond Allen, Sean Barker, Carol Bayard, Herbert Beattie, Carol Bergey, Virginia Bitar, Mary Burgess, Lee Cass, William Chapman, William Diard, Anne Elgar, George Gaynes, Muriel Greenspon, Charles Hindsley, Mary Jennings, Norman Kelley, Marlena Kleinman, Richard Krause, William Ledbetter, Kellis Miller, Theodore Morill, Herbert Pordum, Frank Porretta, Donna Precht, Emile Renan, Robert Rounseville, Evelyn Sachs, David Smith, Claramae Turner, Paul Ukena, Lee Venora, James Wilson.

CHORUS: Barbara Beaman, Paul Corder, Harris Davis, Marceline Decker; Anthea de Forest, Glen Dowlen, Robert Edwards, Beverly Evans, Fredric Griesinger, Helen Guile, Don Henderson, Lila Herbert, David Hicks, Lynda Jordan, Robert Lee Kelly, Kellis Miller, Hanna Owen, Richard G. Park, Charlotte Povia, Lourette Raymon, Anthony Safina, Alexander Savchuck, John Smith, Dale Westerman, Lou Ann Wyckoff, Marie Young.

Company Manager: George Zorn
Press: Dorfman Associates
Stage Managers: Hans Sondheimer, Bill Field, J. Edgar Joseph, Frank Wicks

° Closed Sunday, April 5, 1964, after a limited engagement of 27 performances.

Beatrice Krebs, William Diard
in "Pirates of Penzance"
Above: "Pinafore"
Top: "The Mikado"

mile Kenan, Claramae Turner in "Patience"
Above: George Gaynes, Evelyn Sachs in "Yeomen"
Top: Norman Kelley, Richard Fredricks, Claramae Turner in "Iolanthe"

Opened Wednesday, March 18, 1964.°
The City Center Gilbert and Sullivan
Company present:

THE YEOMEN OF THE GUARD

Book by W. S. Gilbert; Music by Arthur
Sullivan; Staged by Allen Fletcher; Scenery by
Stephen O. Saxe; Costumes, Alvin Colt; Conducted by Julius Rudel.

CAST

Sir Richard Cholmondely	Paul Ukena
Colonel Fairfax	Robert Rounseville
Sergeant Meryll	George Gaynes
Leonard Meryll	Richard Krause
Jack Point	Norman Kelley
Wilfred Shadbolt	Herbert Beattie
The Headsman	Thomas Andrew
First Yeoman	Herbert Pordum
Second Yeoman	Sean Barker
First Citizen	Harris Davis
Second Citizen	Glen Dowlen
Elsie Maynard	Mary Jennings
Phoebe Meryll	Mary Burgess
Dame Carruthers	Evelyn Sachs
Kate	Virginia Bitar

Chorus of Yeomen of the Guard

Opened Friday, March 20, 1964.

H.M.S. PINAFORE

Book by W. S. Gilbert; Music by Arthur
Sullivan; Staged by Allen Fletcher; Scenery and
Costumes, Patton Campbell; Conductors, Felix
Popper and Charles Wilson.

CAST

The Rt. Hon. Sir Joseph Porter	Raymond Allen
Captain Corcoran	William Chapman
Ralph Racktsraw	Robert Rounseville
Dick Deadeye	Paul Ukena
Bill Bobstay	Sean Barker
Bob Becket	Lee Cass
Josephine	Anne Elgar
Cousin Hebe	Marlena Kleinman
Little Buttercup	Muriel Greenspon

First Lord's Sisters, Cousins, Aunts, and Sailors

Opened Sunday afternoon, March 22, 1964.

THE MIKADO

Book, W. S. Gilbert; Music, Arthur Sullivan;
Staged by Dorothy Raedler; Scenery, Donald
Oenslager; Costumes, Patton Campbell; Conductor, Dean Ryan.

CAST

The Mikado of Japan	George Gaynes
Nanki-Poo	William Diard
Ko-Ko	Norman Kelley
Pooh-Bah	Herbert Beattie
Pish-Tush	David Smith
Yum-Yum	Carol Bergey
Pitti-Sing	Mary Burgess
Peep-Bo	Marlena Kleinman
Katisha	Evelyn Sachs

Chorus of Schoolgirls, Nobles, Guards

Opened Friday afternoon, March 27, 1964.

THE GONDOLIERS

Book by W. S. Gilbert; Music, Arthur Sullivan; Staged by Dorothy Raedler; Scenery and
Costumes, Ed Wittstein; Cachucha Dance Choreography, Thomas Andrew; Conductor, Felix
Popper.

CAST

The Duke of Plaza-Toro	Norman Kelley
Luiz	Theodore Morill
Don Alhambra Del Bolero	George Gaynes
Marco Palmieri	Charles Hindsley
Guiseppe Palmieri	Sean Barker
Antonio	David Smith
Francesco	Herbert Pordum
Giorgio	John Smith
The Duchess of Plaza-Toro	Claramae Turner
Casilda	Donna Precht
Gianetta	Mary Jennings
Tessa	Marlena Kleinman
Fiametta	Virginia Bitar
Vittoria	Mary Burgess
Giulia	Beverly Evans
Inez	Charlotte Povia
Solo Cachucha Dancers	Rochelle Zide, Thomas Andrew

Chorus of Gondoliers, Contadine, Heralds, Pages.

NEW YORK CITY CENTER

Opened Wednesday, April 8, 1964.*
The New York City Center Light Opera
Company (Jean Dalrymple, Director)
presents:

WEST SIDE STORY

Book by Arthur Laurents; Based on a conception by Jerome Robbins; Music, Leonard Bernstein; Lyrics, Stephen Sondheim; Entire Production Directed and Choreographed by Jerome Robbins; This Production Staged by Gerald Freedman; Choreography Re-Mounted by Tom Abbott; Original Co-Choreographer, Peter Gennaro; Musical Director, Charles Jaffe; Original Scenery by Oliver Smith; This Production, Peter Wolf; Costumes, Irene Sharaff; Supervised by Stanley Simmons; Lighting, Jean Rosenthal.

CAST

The Jets:
Riff, The Leader	James Moore
Tony	Don McKay
Action	Joe Bennett
A-Rab	Mark Jude Sheil
Baby John	Steve Curry
Snowboy	Barry Burns
Big Deal	Larry Moss
Diesel	Hamp Dickens
Gee-Tar	Danny Lockin
Mouth Piece	Joe Corby
Tiger	John McCook

Their Girls:
Graziella	Wilma Curley
Velma	Tobie Lynn
Minnie	Barbara Rogers
Clarice	Gloria Kaye
Pauline	Eileen Casey
Anybody's	Erin Martin

The Sharks:
Bernardo, The Leader	Jay Norman
Maria	Julia Migenes
Chino	B. J. DeSimone
Pepe	Noel Schwartz
Indio	Tim Ramirez
Luis	Jo Jo Smith
Anxious	Kent Thomas
Nibbles	Carlos Gorbea
Juano	Richard Balin
Toro	Carmine Terra
Moose	Eliot Feld

Their Girls:
Anita	Luba Lisa
Rosalia	Marilyn Cooper
Consuelo	Carmen Morales
Teresita	Ella Thompson
Francisca	Diana Corto
Estella	Lolli Hinton
Marguerita	Tina Faye

The Adults:
Doc	Harry Davis
Schrank	Ted Gunther
Krupke	Frank Downing
Gladhand	Brooks Morton

UNDERSTUDIES: Tony, Joe Corby; Maria, Diana Corto; Anita, Carmen Morales; Riff, Joe Bennett; Action, Al DeSio; Doc, Brooks Morton; Bernardo, Carmine Terra; Anybody's, Gloria Kaye; Schrank, Frank Downing; Chino, Noel Schwartz; Krupke, Brooks Morton; Baby John, Al DeSio; Rosalia, Carmen Morales; A-Rab, Al DeSio; Gladhand, John McCook; Graziella, Tobie Lynn.

MUSICAL NUMBERS: "Prologue," "Jet Song," "Something's Coming," "The Dance At The Gym," "Maria," "Tonight," "America," "Cool," "One Hand, One Heart," "The Rumble," "I Feel Pretty," "Somewhere," "Gee, Officer Krupke," "A Boy Like That," "I Have A Love," "Taunting," Finale.

A Musical in two acts with prologue and fifteen scenes. The action takes place on the West Side of New York City during the last days of summer.

General Manager: Buford Armitage
Company Manager: Zelda Dorfman
Press: Tom Trenkle
Stage Managers: Herman Shapiro, Lo Hardin, Alfred DeSio

* Closed Sunday, May 3, 1964, after a limited engagement of 31 performances.
For the original New York production, see THEATRE WORLD, Vol. 14.

Jay Norman, Luba Lisa, James Moore (R)
Above: Julia Migenes, Don McKay

Alix Jeffry Photos

NEW YORK CITY CENTER

Opened Wednesday, May 6, 1964.°
The New York City Center Light Opera
Company presents:

PORGY AND BESS

Music, George Gershwin; Libretto, DuBose Hey-
ward; Lyrics, DuBose Heyward and Ira Gersh-
win; Based on Play "Porgy" by Dorothy and
DuBose Heyward; Directed by John Fearnley;
Musical Director, Julius Rudel; Choral Director
and Associate Conductor, William Johnson;
Settings, Stephen O. Saxe; Costumes, Stanley
Simmons; Lighting, Nan Porcher; Production
Assistant, Keith Holzman.

CAST

Clara	Marie Young
Mingo	Tony Middleton
Sportin' Life	Robert Guillaume
Jake	Irving Barnes
Serena	Gwendolyn Walters
Robbins	Eugene Edwards
Jim	Garwood Perkins
Peter	Garrett Morris
Lily	Frances Haywood
Maria	Carol Brice
Porgy	William Warfield, Irving Barnes
Crown	William Dillard
Bess	Veronica Tyler, Barbara Smith Conrad
Policemen	David Hicks, John Smith
Detective	Walter Riemer
Undertaker	Wanza King
Annie	Alyce Webb
Frazer	Al Fann
Strawberry Woman	Kay Barnes
Crabman	Clyde Turner
Scipio	William Harris
Pearl	Lillian Hayman

CHILDREN: Deborah Hall, Benjamin Hines,
Norman Hines, Antonell Jones.

RESIDENTS OF CATFISH ROW: Ruby Green
Aspinall, Kaye Barnes, Phyllis Bash, Elijah
Bennett, Joseph Bryant, Paul Corder, Marceline
Decker, Beverly Evans, Don Forrest, Beno
Foster, Claretta Freemon, Carol Joy George,
Carrie Glover, Helen Guile, William G. Harris,
Afrika Hayes, Lillian Hayman, Frances W.
Haywood, Annette B. Jackson, Martin Jewell,
Marva Josie, Wanza King, Thomas Laidman,
Dorothy Lane, Garrett Morris, Caryl Paige,
Garwood Perkins, Lucinda Ransom, John Rich-
ardson, Edna Ricks, Anthony Safina, Clyde
Turner, Eliose C. Uggams, James Wamen,
Laurence Watson, Alyce Webb, Pauline Weekes,
James Wilson, William Wright, Lou Ann Wyc-
koff.

UNDERSTUDIES: Serena, Phyllis Bash; Jake,
Eugene Edwards; Robbins, Anthony Safina;
Bess, Dorothy Lane; Sportin' Life, John Rich-
ardson; Mingo, Lillian Hayman; Serena, Afrika
Hayes; Maria, Lillian Hayman; Clara, Lou Ann
Wyckoff; Crown, James Wamen; Jake, Don
Forrest; Robbins, James Wilson; Policemen, John
Smith; Peter, Beno Foster; Lily, Edna Ricks;
Undertaker and Frazer, Garwood Perkins.

MUSICAL NUMBERS: "Summertime," "A
Woman Is A Sometime Thing," "They Pass By
Singing," "Crap Game Fugue," "Gone, Gone,
Gone," "My Man's Gone Now," "Overflow,"
"Rowing Song," "I Got Plenty Of Nuttin',"
"Buzzard," "Bess, You Is My Woman Now,"
"Oh I Can't Sit Down," "Ha da da," "Leavin'
Fo' de Promis' Lan'," "It Ain't Necessarily So,"
"What You Want With Bess," "Time and Time
Again," "Street Cries," "I Love You, Porgy,"
"Oh de Lawd Shake de Heaven," "A Red
Headed Woman," "Oh Doctor Jesus," "Clara
Don't You Be Downhearted," "There's A Boat
That's Leavin' Soon For New York," "Occupa-
tional Humoresque," "Where's My Bess?," "I'm
On My Way."

A Musical in two acts. The action takes
place on Catfish Row.

General Manager: Buford Armitage
Company Manager: George Zorn
Press: Tom Trenkle
Stage Managers: Bill Field, Walter Riemer,
Alyce Webb

°Closed Sunday, May 17, 1964.
(15 performances)

Alix Jeffry Photos

Robert Guillaume
Center: William Warfield, Veronica Tyler

133

Opened Wednesday, May 20, 1964.*
The New York City Center Light Opera
Company presents:

MY FAIR LADY

Adapted from Bernard Shaw's Play "Pygmalion" and Gabriel Pascal's motion picture "Pygmalion"; Book and Lyrics, Alan Jay Lerner; Music, Frederick Loewe; Directed by Samuel Liff; Choreography and Musical Numbers, Hanya Holm; Musical Director, Anton Coppola; Designed by Oliver Smith; Costumes, Cecil Beaton; Supervised by Stanley Simmons; Lighting, Feder; Musical Arrangements, Robert Russell Bennett and Phil Lang; Dance Music Arranged by Trude Rittman.

CAST

Buskers	Jerry Trent, Myron Curtis, Kiki Minor
Mrs. Eynsford-Hill	Claire Waring
Eliza Doolittle	Marni Nixon
Freddy Eynsford-Hill	Russell Nype
Colonel Pickering	Byron Webster
Bystander	Raymond Allen
Henry Higgins	Myles Eason
Selsey Man	Charles Penman
Hoxton Man	Henry Lawrence
Another Bystander	Robert Fitch
First Cockney	William Krach
Second Cockney	Stokely Gray
Third Cockney	Richard H. Goodlake
Fourth Cockney	Barney Johnston
Bartender	Jack Eddleman
Harry	Charles Penman
Jamie	Raymond Allen
Alfred P. Doolittle	Reginald Gardiner
Mrs. Pearce	Dorothy Sands
Mrs. Hopkins	Olive Reeves-Smith
Butler	Stokely Gray
Servants	Jeremy Broun, Margaret Broderson, Joyce Dahl, Ruth Shepard, Art Martinson, Stokely Gray
Mrs. Higgins	Margery Maude
Chauffeur	Harry Woolever
Footmen	William Krach, Richard Park
Lord Boxington	Charles Penman
Lady Boxington	Olive Reeves-Smith
Constable	Harry Woolever
Flower Girl	Kiki Minor
Zoltan Karpathy	Sandor Szabo
Flunkey	Richard Park
Queen of Transylvania	Terry Marone
Ambassador	Raymond Allen
Bartender	Barney Johnston
Mrs. Higgins' Maid	Margaret Cuddy

SINGING ENSEMBLE: Jeremy Broun, Margaret Broderson, Diane Chase, Joyce Dahl, Elaine Labour, Terry Marone, Donna Monroe, Ruth Shepard, Jack Eddleman, Richard H. Goodlake, Stokely Gray, Barney Johnston, William Krach, Henry Lawrence, Art Martinson, Richard Park.

DANCING ENSEMBLE: Judi Allison, Emily Byrne, Margaret Cuddy, Katia Geleznova, Audrey Hays, Adriana Keathley, Kiki Minor, Molly Molloy, Mari Shelton, Esther Villavicencio, Dick Colacino, Myron Curtis, Bob Fitch, Ronn Forella, Dennis Lynch, Joe Nelson, Jerry Trent, R. Michael Steele, Mark West, Harry Woolever.

UNDERSTUDIES: Eliza, Helen Ahola; Higgins, Raymond Allen; Doolittle, Pickering, Charles Penman; Freddy, Richard Goodlake; Karpathy, Jack Eddleman; Mrs. Pearce, Olive Reeves-Smith; Mrs. Higgins, Claire Waring.

MUSICAL NUMBERS: "Street Entertainers," "Why Can't The English?" "Wouldn't It Be Loverly," "With A Little Bit Of Luck," "I'm An Ordinary Man," "Just You Wait," "The Rain In Spain," "I Could Have Danced All Night," "Ascot Gavotte," "On The Street Where You Live," "The Embassy Waltz," "You Did It," "Show Me," "Get Me To The Church On Time," "A Hymn To Him," "Without You," "I've Grown Accustomed To Her Face."

A Musical Comedy in two acts and eighteen scenes. The action takes place in London in 1912.

General Manager: Buford Armitage
Company Manager: George Zorn
Press: Tom Trenkle
Stage Managers: Herman Shapiro, Daniel S. Broun, Marnel Sumner

*Still playing May 31, 1964. (16 performances)
For original New York production, see THEATRE WORLD, Vol. 12.

134

Russell Nype, Marni Nixon, Margery Maude
Above: Reginald Gardner, Marni Nixon
Top: Marni Nixon, Margery Maude,
Myles Eason

Alix Jeffry Photos

ANTA WASHINGTON SQUARE
THEATRE

Opened Thursday, January 23, 1964.°
Repertory Theatre of Lincoln Center
presents:

AFTER THE FALL

By Arthur Miller; Directed by Elia Kazan;
Production and Lighting Designed by Jo Miel-
ziner; Costumes, Anna Hill Johnstone; Music,
David Amram; Make-up, hair styles, and wigs,
The House of Revlon.

CAST

Quentin	Jason Robards, Jr.
Felice	Zohra Lampert
Holga	Salome Jens
Mother	Virginia Kaye
Dan	Michael Strong
Father	Paul Mann
Nurses	Faye Dunaway, Diane Shalet
Doctor	Scott Cunningham
Maggie	Barbara Loden
Elsie	Patricia Roe
Louise	Mariclare Costello
Lou	David J. Stewart
Mickey	Ralph Meeker
Man in the park	Stanley Beck
Carrie	Ruth Attaway
Chairman	David Wayne or Lou Frizzell
Rev. Harley Barnes	Hal Holbrook or Harold Scott
Porter	Jack Waltzer
Secretary	Crystal Field
Lucas	Harold Scott
Clergyman	James Greene

OTHERS: Stanley Beck, Scott Cunningham,
Faye Dunaway, Crystal Field, Lou Frizzell,
James Greene, Clinton Kimbrough, John Phillip
Law, Barry Primus, Harold Scott, Diane Shalet,
Jack Waltzer.

UNDERSTUDIES: Stanley Beck, Scott Cunning-
ham, Faye Dunaway, Crystal Field, Lou Frizzell,
James Greene, Patricia Roe, Harold Scott, Diane
Shalet, Morgan Sterne, Jack Waltzer.

A Drama in two acts. The action takes place
in the mind, thought, and memory of Quentin,
a contemporary man.

General Manager: Oscar Olesen
Press: Barry Hyams, Robert Pasolli
Stage Managers: Howard Fischer, Bruce W.
Stark, Robert Downing
°Still playing May 31, 1964. (59 performances)

Inge Morath Photos

**Left: Jason Robards, Salome Jens, Mariclare
Costello, David Stewart, Michael Strong,
Ralph Meeker, Paul Mann
Top: Robards, Barbara Loden**

Jason Robards, Jr., Michael Strong,
Virginia Kaye, Paul Mann

Zohra Lampert, Jason Robards, Jr.,
Barbara Loden

ANTA WASHINGTON SQUARE
THEATRE

Opened Thursday, February 20, 1964.°
Repertory Theatre of Lincoln Center presents:

MARCO MILLIONS

By Eugene O'Neill; Directed by José Quintero; Production and Lighting Designed by David Hays; Costumes, Beni Montresor; Music Composed by Doris Schwerin; Musical Arrangements by La Noue Davenport and Doris Schwerin; Make-up, Hair Styles, and Wigs by The House of Revlon; Movement and Gesture by Sophia Delza.

CAST

A Christian Merchant	James Greene
A Magian Merchant	Jack Waltzer
A Buddhist Merchant	Graham Jarvis
A Corporal	John McCurry
Princess Kukachin	Zohra Lampert
Marco Polo	Hal Holbrook
Donata	Crystal Field
Nicolo Polo	Lou Frizzell
Maffeo Polo	Michael Strong
Tedaldo	David J. Stewart
A Dominican Monk	Barry Primus
A Papal Courier	Scott Cunningham
First Ali Brother	James Greene
Second Ali Brother	Graham Jarvis
(also two Buddhist and two Tartar Merchants)	
A Prostitute	Virginia Kaye
A Dervish	Jim Ray-James
Emissary from Kublai Khan	Barry Primus
Kublai, the Great Khan	David Wayne
Chu-Yin	Joseph Wiseman
A Boatswain	Barry Primus
Ghazan, Khan of Persia	Harold Scott
General Bayan	Stanley Beck
A Chamberlain	Scott Cunningham
Courier from Persia	Barry Primus
Paulo Loredano	Graham Jarvis
Priest of Tao	Scott Cunningham
Priest of Confucius	James Greene
Priest of Buddha	John McCurry
Priest of Islam	Jack Waltzer
Tartar Chronicler	Barry Primus

LADIES, GENTLEMEN, SOLDIERS, SLAVES, Etc.: Mariclare Costello, Lee Delmer, Frank DeSal, Rene Enriquez, Patricia Fay, Phillip H. Frey, John Garces, Linda Hodes, Richard Khan, Leonora Landau, Noemi Lapzeson, Don McGovern, Sasha Pressman, Jim Ray-James, Patricia Roe, Diane Shalet.

UNDERSTUDIES: Lee Delmer, Patricia Fay, Phillip H. Frey, Lou Frizzell, John Garces, James Greene, Graham Jarvis, Richard Khan, Barbara Loden, Don McGovern, Barry Primus, Jim Ray-James, Diane Shalet.

MUSICIANS: Jacob Maxin, Richard Serbagi, Robert Montesi, Harry Smyles, Fred Braverman, Fred King.

A Drama in three acts and eleven scenes with prologue.

General Manager: Oscar Olesen
Press: Barry Hyams, Robert Pasolli
Stage Managers: Frederic De Wilde, Frank Hamilton, Jonathan Anderson, Donald McGovern
°Still playing May 31, 1964. (38 performances)

Martha Swope Photos

Joseph Wiseman, Zohra Lampert, David Wayne, Hal Holbrook
Above: David Wayne, Hal Holbrook
Top: Hal Holbrook, Zohra Lampert

David Stewart, Hal Holbrook, Lou Frizzell, Michael Strong

ANTA WASHINGTON SQUARE THEATRE

Opened Thursday, March 12, 1964.°
Repertory Theatre of Lincoln Center presents:

BUT FOR WHOM CHARLIE

By S. N. Behrman; Directed by Elia Kazan; Production and Lighting Designed by Jo Mielziner; Music Arranged by David Amram; Costumes, Anna Hill Johnstone; Make-up, Hair Styles, and Wigs by The House of Revlon.

CAST

Naomi Saunders	Patricia Roe
Seymour Rosenthal	Jason Robards, Jr.
Anna	Diane Shalet
Charles Taney	Ralph Meeker
Faith Prosper	Faye Dunaway
Willard Prosper	Clinton Kimbrough
Gilian Prosper	Salome Jens
Brock Dunnaway	David Wayne
Harry Lorch	Michael Strong
Sheila Maloney	Barbara Loden

A Comedy in three acts. The action takes place in the headquarters of the Seymour Rosenthal Foundation in the East Sixties in New York City, at the present time.

General Manager: Oscar Olesen
Press: Barry Hyams, Robert Pasolli, Susan Bloch
Stage Managers: Robert Downing, Howard Fischer, Bruce Stark
°Still playing May 31, 1964. (34 performances)

Martha Swope Photos

Top: (L) Faye Dunaway, Clinton Kimbrough (R) Salome Jens, Ralph Meeker

Jason Robards, Jr., Faye Dunaway, Ralph Meeker
Above: Michael Strong, Jason Robards, Jr., David Wayne

NEW YORK STATE THEATRE LINCOLN CENTER

Opened Wednesday, May 20, 1964.

THE COMEDY OF ERRORS

By William Shakespeare; Directed by Clifford Williams; Setting and Lighting by John Wyckham and Clifford Williams; Costumes, Anthony Powell; Music, Peter Wishart; Assistant to the Director, Sandy Black; Music recorded by English Chamber Orchestra conducted by Guy Woolfenden.

CAST

Solinus, Duke of Ephesus	Michael Murray
Aegeon, Merchant of Syracuse	Tony Church
Antipholus of Ephesus	Ian Richardson
Antipholus of Syracuse	Alec McCowen
Dromio of Ephesus	Clifford Rose
Dromio of Syracuse	Barry MacGregor
Balthazar	Michael Burrell
Angelo	Ken Wynne
First Merchant	Ian Lindsay
Second Merchant	John Harwood
Pinch	Michael Williams
An Officer	John Church
A Messenger	Peter Blythe
A Gaoler	Brian Osborne
Aemilia, Abbess at Ephesus	Pauline Jameson
Adriana	Diana Rigg
Luciana	Julie Christie
Luce	Caroline Maud
A Courtesan	Elizabeth Spriggs

WITH: Trevor Bowen, John Cobner, Ian Lindsay, Peter Tory, John Church, Michael Jenkinson, Lyn Pinkney, Philippa Urquhart, Jennifer Clulow, Wyn Jones, Leslie Southwick.

A Comedy presented in two parts. The action takes place in Ephesus.

General Manager: Oscar Olesen
Company Managers: Peter Davis, Hal Rogers
Press: Richard Maney, Martin Shwartz
Stage Managers: Fred Hebert, David Brierley, Ruth Atkinson, Ann Fosbrooke, Roger Howells, Diane Seaney

✦Closed June 6, 1964, after a limited engagement of 24 performances.

Alec McCowen, Barry MacGregor
Above: Julie Christie, Clifford Rose, Diana Rigg
Top: Diana Rigg, Alec McCowen

NEW YORK STATE THEATRE
LINCOLN CENTER

Opened Monday, May 18, 1964.°
Bonard Productions and Donald Seawell by
arrangement with the governors of the
Royal Shakespeare Theatre Stratford-Upon-
Avon present The Royal Shakespeare Com-
pany in:

KING LEAR

By William Shakespeare; Directed and De-
signed by Peter Brook; Costumes in collaboration
with Kegan Smith; Music, Guy Woolfenden;
Assistant Designer, Adele Hankey; Assistant
Director, Charles Marowitz; Fight arranged by
John Barton.

CAST

The Earl of Kent	Tom Fleming
The Earl of Gloucester	John Laurie
Edmund	Ian Richardson
Lear King of Britain	Paul Scofield
Goneril	Irene Worth
The Duke of Albany	Clifford Rose
Regan	Pauline Jameson
The Duke of Cornwall	Tony Church
Cordelia	Diana Rigg
The Duke of Burgundy	Michael Murray
The King of France	Barry MacGregor
Edgar	Brian Murray
Oswald	Michael Williams
Knight attending Lear	Michael Murray
Fool	Alec McCowen
Curan	John Harwood
Servant to Cornwall	John Cobner
Old Man tenant to Gloucester	Ken Wynne
Doctor	Michael Burrell
Messenger to Cordelia	Ian Lindsay
Captain to Edmund	John Church
Herald	Peter Blythe

British Captains ....Leslie Southwick, Peter Tory
KNIGHTS, SOLDIERS, SERVANTS: Peter
Blythe, Trevor Bowen, John Church, John Cob-
ner, Michael Jenkinson, Wyn Jones, Ian Lindsay,
Brian Osborne, Leslie Southwick, Peter Tory.
MUSICIANS: Joseph Currie, Geoffrey Mason,
Derek Oldfield, Martyn Shields, Norman Wallis.
A Drama presented in two parts. The action
takes place in Britain.

(R) Paul Scofield holding Diana Rigg
Above: Paul Scofield, Irene Worth
Top: Paul Scofield, Tom Fleming,
Alec McCowen

Angus McBean Photos

THE DANCE ON BROADWAY

MADISON SQUARE GARDEN
Opened Thursday, October 10, 1963.°
S. Hurok presents:

STARS OF THE
BOLSHOI BALLET

Under the Direction of Asaf Messerer, with
Symphony Orchestra Conducted by Georgi
Zhemchuzhin; Associate Conductor, Igor Bout-
nikoff; Pianist, Vladimir Kudryavtsev.

PROGRAM
Swan Lake, The Nutcracker, Russian Dance,
Don Quixote, Three Moods, Gopak, Waltz, Ballet
School, Chopiniana, Walpurgis Night.
Press: Martin Feinstein, Michael Sweeley
°Closed October 12, 1963, after a limited en-
gagement of 4 performances.

Shamil Yagudin
Above: Vladimir Nikonov

Vladimir Tikhonov, Yelena Riabinkina
Top: "Ballet School"
Center: Raissa Struchkova

LUNT-FONTANNE THEATRE

Opened Sunday, October 13, 1963.°
The B. de Rothschild Foundation presents:

MARTHA GRAHAM
And Her Dance Company

Bertram Ross	Helen McGehee
Robert Cohan	Ethel Winter
Yuriko	Linda Hodes
Mary Hinkson	David Wood
Robert Powell	Gene McDonald
Clive Thompson	Richard Gain
Takako Asakawa	Peter Randazzo
Phyllis Gutelius	Juliet Fisher
Noemi Lapzeson	Dudley Williams
Carol Fried	

Rosalia Maresca, Soprano
Mario Laurenti, Baritone
Robert Irving, Conductor

Lighting, Jean Rosenthal; Assistant Conductor and Musical Adviser, Eugene Lister; Produced by Gertrude Macy; Production Assistant, Marion Kinsella.

PROGRAM

Circe, Secular Games, Phaedra, Diversion of Angels, Legend of Judith, Night Journey, Seraphic Dialogue, Clytemnestra, Acrobats of God, Embattled Garden.

Company Manager: Gertrude Macy
Press: Isadora Bennett

Stage Managers: Anne Sullivan, William H. Batchelder

° Closed Sunday, October 27, 1963, after a limited engagement of 17 performances.

Jack Mitchell Photos

Top: (L) "Secular Games"
(R) Martha Graham

Martha Graham (R) in "Phaedra"
Above: Mary Hinkson as "Circe"

141

PROMISING PERSONALITIES
THEATRE WORLD AWARD WINNERS

1944-45

Richard Davis	John Lund	Margaret Phillips	Donald Murphy
Judy Holliday	Betty Comden	Richard Hart	Nancy Noland
Bambi Linn	John Raitt	Charles Lang	

1945-46

Burt Lancaster	Barbara Bel Geddes	Marlon Brando	Beatrice Pearson
Patricia Marshall	Wendell Corey	Mary James	Paul Douglas
Bill Callahan			

1946-47

Patricia Neal	David Wayne	Keith Andes	Ann Crowley
James Mitchell	Marion Bell	John Jordan	George Keane
Ellen Hanley	Peter Cookson	Dorothea MacFarland	

1947-48

Douglas Watson	Valerie Bettis	Ralph Meeker	June Lockhart
Meg Mundy	Whitfield Connor	Peggy Maley	Mark Dawson
James Whitmore	Patrice Wymore	Edward Bryce	Estelle Loring

1948-49

Carol Channing	Gene Nelson	Julie Harris	Cameron Mitchell
Tod Andrews	Allyn Ann McLerie	Richard Derr	Jean Carson
Mary McCarty	Byron Palmer	Doe Avedon	Bob Scheerer

1949-50

Charlton Heston	Grace Kelly	Charles Nolte	Nancy Andrews
Priscilla Gillette	Don Hanmer	Lydia Clarke	Phil Arthur
Rick Jason	Marcia Henderson	Roger Price	Barbara Brady

1950-51

Richard Burton	Maureen Stapleton	Jack Palance	Pat Crowley
Barbara Ashley	Eli Wallach	Marcia Van Dyke	James Daly
Russell Nype	Isabel Bigley	Martin Brooks	Cloris Leachman
	William Smithers		

1951-52

Audrey Hepburn	Ronny Graham	Kim Stanley	Eric Sinclair
Tony Bavaar	Virginia de Luce	Conrad Janis	Helen Wood
Patricia Benoit	Charles Proctor	Diana Herbert	Peter Conlow
	Marian Winters	Dick Kallman	

1952-53

Paul Newman	Geraldine Page	John Kerr	Sheree North
Eileen Heckart	Ray Stricklyn	Gwen Verdon	Richard Kiley
John Stewart	Edie Adams	Peter Kelley	Gloria Marlowe
	Rosemary Harris	Penelope Munday	

1953-54

Eva Marie Saint	James Dean	Harry Belafonte	Ben Gazzara
Leo Penn	Kay Medford	Carol Haney	Joan Diener
Elizabeth Montgomery	Orson Bean	Jonathan Lucas	Scott Merrill

1954-55

Anthony Perkins	Julie Andrews	Christopher Plummer	Barbara Cook
Jacqueline Brookes	Dennis Patrick	Loretta Leversee	Jack Lord
Page Johnson	Shirl Conway	David Daniels	Mary Fickett

1955-56

Jayne Mansfield	Laurence Harvey	Sarah Marshall	Frtiz Weaver
Anthony Franciosa	Susan Johnson	Andy Griffith	Gaby Rodgers
Susan Strasberg	John Michael King	Diane Cilento	Earle Hyman
	Al Hedison	Dick Davalos	

1956-57

George Grizzard	Peggy Cass	Cliff Robertson	Bradford Dillman
Carol Lynley	Peter Palmer	Pippa Scott	Sylvia Daneel
Sydney Chaplin	Inga Swenson	Jason Robards, Jr.	Peter Donat

1957-58

Anne Bancroft	Robert Morse	Carol Lawrence	Timmy Everett
George C. Scott	Joan Hovis	Warren Berlinger	Wynne Miller
Colleen Dewhurst	Eddie Hodges	Jacqueline McKeever	Richard Easton

1958-59

Rip Torn	Paul Roebling	Tammy Grimes	Larry Hagman
Dolores Hart	France Nuyen	William Shatner	Susan Oliver
Lou Antonio	Ben Piazza	Ina Balin	Roger Mollien
	Pat Suzuki	Richard Cross	

1959-60

Carol Burnett	Jane Fonda	Warren Beatty	George Maharis
Donald Madden	John McMartin	Anita Gillette	Patty Duke
Eileen Brennan	Elisa Loti	Dick Van Dyke	Lauri Peters

1960-61

Robert Goulet	James MacArthur	Dennis Cooney	Bruce Yarnell
Joyce Bulifant	June Harding	Joan Hackett	Nancy Dussault
	Ron Husmann		

1961-62

Barbara Harris	Peter Fonda	Janet Margolin	Robert Redford
John Stride	Karen Morrow	Sean Garrison	James Earl Jones
Brenda Vaccaro	Don Galloway	Elizabeth Ashley	Keith Baxter

1962-63

Dorothy Loudon	Alan Arkin	Liza Minnelli	Swen Swenson
Stuart Damon	Estelle Parsons	Bob Gentry	Melinda Dillon
Julienne Marie	Robert Drivas	Diana Sands	Brandon Maggart

PROMISING PERSONALITIES

GILBERT PRICE
of
"Jerico-Jim Crow"

BARBARA LODEN
of
"After The Fall"

ALAN ALDA
of
"Fair Game For Lovers"

JENNIFER WEST
of
"Dutchman"

JOHN TRACY
of
"Telemachus Clay"

147

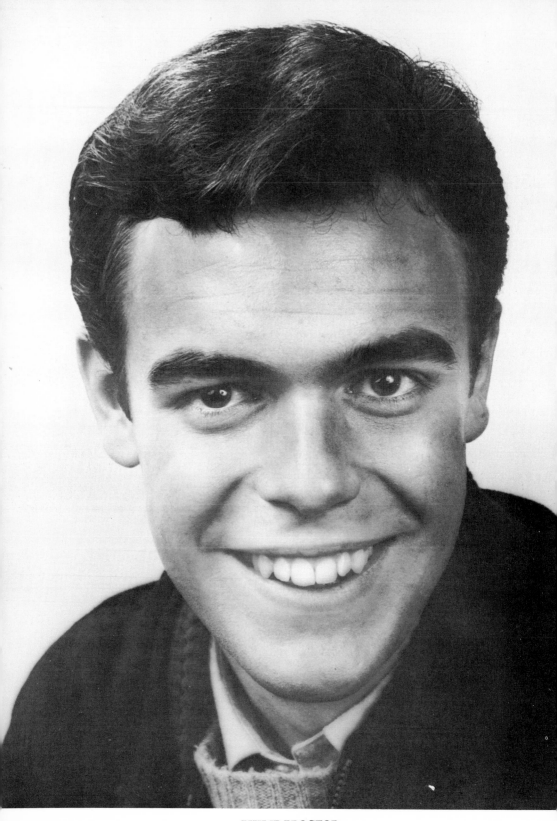

PHILIP PROCTOR
of
"The Amorous Flea"

IMELDA DE MARTIN
of
"The Amorous Flea"

LAWRENCE PRESSMAN
of
"Never Live Over A Pretzel Factory"

KETTY LESTER
of
"Cabin In The Sky"

151

CLAUDE GIRAUD
of
"Phedre"

GLORIA BLEEZARDE
of
"Never Live Over A Pretzel Factory"

Victor Helou Photo

153

MY FAIR LADY

Book and Lyrics by Alan Jay Lerner; Adapted from George Bernard Shaw's "Pygmalion"; Music, Frederick Loewe; Staged by Moss Hart; Choreography and Musical Numbers by Hanya Holm; Designed by Oliver Smith; Costumes by Cecil Beaton; Musical Arrangements, Robert Russell Bennett and Phil Lang; Lighting, Feder; Dance Music Arranged by Trude Rittman; Musical Director, Aaron Benar; Presented by Herman Levin. Opened March 18, 1957, at the Rochester, N. Y., Auditorium, and closed December 14, 1963, at the O'Keefe Theatre in Toronto, Canada.

CAST

Buskers	Ed Kerrigan[1], Earl Clayton, Jean Bledsoe[2]
Mrs. Eynsford-Hill	Eleanor Phelps[3]
Eliza Doolittle	Gaylea Byrne
Freddy Eynsford-Hill	Richard Young
Colonel Pickering	Hugh Dempster[4]
Bystander	John Duarte[5]
Henry Higgins	Ronald Drake
Selsey Man	Charles Penman
Hoxton Man	Luis de Ybarrondo
Another Bystander	Eric Brotherson[6]
First Cockney	David Waner[7]
Second Cockney	Robert Hocknell[8]
Third Cockney	John Duarte[9]
Fourth Cockney	Ted Bloecher[10]
Bartender	Reese Burns[11]
Harry	Charles Penman
Jamie	Eric Brotherson[6]
Alfred P. Doolittle	Charles Victor
Mrs. Pearce	Katherine Hynes
Mrs. Hopkins	Margaretta Warwick[12]
Butler	William Gibson[9]
Servants	Susan Cashman, Marilyn Newberg, Pamela Eden, Patricia Hall, Richard Norse, Ken Fields
Mrs. Higgins	Margaret Bannerman
Chauffeur	Richard Maxon[13]
Footmen	David Hartman[10], John Duarte[5]
Lord Boxington	Charles Penman
Lady Boxington	Margaretta Warwick[12]
Constable	Richard Maxon[13]
Flower Girl	Debra Lyman
Zoltan Karpathy	Leland Howard
Flunkeys	David Hartman[10], John Duarte[5]
Queen of Transylvania	Phyllis Battleson[14]
Ambassador	Reese Burns[8]
Bartender	John Duarte[5]
Mrs. Higgins' Maid	Jean Bledsoe[15]

SINGING ENSEMBLE: Ed Belson, Reese Burns, Susan Cashman, Mary Jane Caveny, Pamela Eden, Ken Fields, Pat Hall, Rosemary Harvey, Roland Ireland, Marilyn Newberg, Richard Norse, Wilson Robey.

DANCING ENSEMBLE: Hugh Brown, Earl Clayton, Jack Craig, Kathleen Doherty, Dolores Hamperian, Van Kelley, Dee Kirkpatrick, Debra Lyman, Grehan Pearce, Hal Pittard, Betty Ann Rapine, Mel Spinney, Luis de Ybarrondo, Elyse Zorgo.

UNDERSTUDIES: Higgins, Leland Howard; Eliza, Susan Cashman; Doolittle, Charles Penman; Pickering, Stanley Tackney; Mrs. Higgins, Christine Thomas; Mrs. Pearce, Mrs. Eynsford-Hill, Blanche Collins; Freddy, Wilson Robey; Mrs. Hopkins, Lady Boxington, Rosemary Harvey; Karpathy, Stanley Tackney; Jamie, Roland Ireland; Harry, Selsey Man, Lord Boxington, Reese Burns.

MUSICAL NUMBERS: "Street Entertainers," "Why Can't The English?," "Wouldn't It Be Lovely?," "With A Little Bit Of Luck," "I'm An Ordinary Man," "Just You Wait," "The Rain In Spain," "I Could Have Danced All Night," "Ascot Gavotte," "On The Street Where You Live," "The Embassy Waltz," "You Did It," "Show Me," "Get Me To The Church On Time," "A Hymn To Him," "Without You," "I've Grown Accustomed To Her Face."

A Musical Comedy in two acts and seventeen scenes. The action takes place in London in 1912.

General Manager: Philip Adler
Company Manager: Joseph M. Grossman
Press: Richard Maney, Martin Shwartz, Joseph Shea, Nate Schenker
Stage Managers: Pat Chandler, Stanley Tackney, Luis de Ybarrondo

†Succeeded by: 1. Jack Craig, 2. Debra Lyman, 3. Christine Thomas, 4. Eric Brotherson, 5. Reese Burns, 6. Robert Hocknell, 7. Wilson Robey, 8. Roland Ireland, 9. Richard Norse, 10. Ed Belson, 11. Luis de Ybarrondo, 12. Blanche Collins, 13. Hal Pittard, 14. Mary Jane Caveny, 15. Kathleen Doherty.

For original New York production, see THEATRE WORLD, Vol. 12.

Top: Caroline Dixon, Ronald Drake
Center: Charles Victor, Gaylea Byrne

CAMELOT

Book and Lyrics, Alan Jay Lerner; Music, Frederick Loewe; Staged by Moss Hart; Choreography and Musical Numbers by Hanya Holm; Scenic Production, Oliver Smith; Costumes, Adrian and Tony Duquette; Lighting, Feder; Musical Director, Dobbs Franks; Orchestrations, Robert Russell Bennett and Philip J. Lang; Dance and Choral Arrangements, Trude Rittman; Hair Styles, Ernest Adler; Assistant to Producers, Stone Widney; Based on "The Once and Future King" by T. H. White; Presented by The Messrs. Lerner, Loewe, and Hart. Opened Monday, January 8, 1963, at the Fisher Theatre in Detroit, and still touring May 31, 1964.

CAST

Sir Dinadan	Bob Rue[1]
Sir Lionel	Frederic Griesinger[2]
Merlyn	Byron Webster
Arthur	Louis Hayward[3]
Guenevere	Kathryn Grayson[4]
Nimue	Marie Grasso[5]
Lady Anne	Maureen Bailey
Lancelot	Robert Peterson
Mordred	Christopher Cary
A Page	Jimmy Stiles[6]
Dap	Thomas Barry
Pellinore	Arthur Treacher
Clarius	Don Strong
Lady Sybil	Jane Coleman
Sir Sagramore	Charles Vick[7]
A Page	Ricky Cameron
Herald	Don Strong
Lady Catherine	Ginny Gagnon
Morgan Le Fey	Jan Moody
Tom	Arthur Sussis[8]
Horses	Don Strong, George Tregre

SINGERS: Maureen Bailey, Jane Coleman, Paula Coonen, Marie Grasso, Anne Doughty, Ginny Gagnon, Kathryn Humphreys, Julie Stomne, Abbie Todd, Thomas Barry, Ed Becker, Peter Costanza, Frederic Griesinger, Bill James, Dugan Miller, Laried Montgomery, Byrne Piven, Rob Rue, Charles Vick.

DANCERS: Pat Drylie, Audrey Hayes, Marion Hunter, Joan Kall, Elaine King, Marcia Paterson, Carol Perea, Zoya Terzetta, Eileen Woliner, Joan Volkman, Myron Curtis, Paul Gleason, Jerry Kent, Ed Kerrigan, Gerard Leavitt, George Mozer, Haydon Smith, Don Strong, George Tregre, Jerry Trent.

UNDERSTUDIES: Guenevere, Jan Moody; Arthur, Byrne Piven; Lancelot, Bob Rue; Pellinore, Byron Webster; Morgan, Pat Drylie; Merlyn, Herald, Frederic Griesinger; Dinadan, Peter Costanza; Lionel, Charles Vivk; Tom, Ricky Cameron; Nimue, Paula Coonen; Dap, Charles Vick; Mordred, Byrne Piven.

MUSICAL NUMBERS: "I Wonder What The King Is Doing Tonight?," "The Simple Joys Of Maidenhood," "Camelot," "Follow Me," "C'est Moi," "The Lusty Month Of May," "How To Handle A Woman," "The Jousts," "Before I Gaze At You Again," "If Ever I Would Leave You," "The Seven Deadly Virtues," "What Do Simple Folk Do?," "The Persuasion," "I Loved You Once In Silence." "Guenevere," Finale.

A Musical in two acts and nineteen scenes. The action takes place in Camelot, a long time ago.

General Manager: C. Edwin Knill
Company Manager: James S. Miller
Press: Robert Reud
Stage Managers: Edmund Baylies, Tom Larson, Edward Becker

† Succeeded by: 1. Peter Costanza, 2. Charles Vick, 3. George Wallace, 4. Anne Jeffreys, 5. Kathryn Humphreys, 6. Marc Castle, 7. William James, 8. Royston Thomas.

For original New York production, see THEATRE WORLD, Vol. 17.

Friedman-Abeles Photos

Top: Robert Peterson, Arthur Treacher, Louis Hayward, Kathryn Grayson
Right Center: Kathryn Grayson, Arthur Treacher

Kathryn Grayson, Robert Peterson

MILK AND HONEY

Book by Don Appell; Music and Lyrics by Jerry Herman; Presented by Gerard Oestreicher; Staged by Albert Marre; Choreographed by Donald Saddler; Settings and Lighting, Howard Bay; Costumes, Miles White; Orchestrations, Hershy Kay and Eddie Sauter; Choral Arrangements, Robert de Cormier; Musical Director, Theodore Saidenberg; Dance Arrangements, Genevieve Pitot; Production Assistant, Rose Kovner; Opened Tuesday, January 29, 1963, at the Shubert Theatre, Philadelphia, and closed at the Biltmore Theatre, Los Angles, September 7, 1963.

CAST

Porter	George Smiley
Shepherd Boy	Martin Ross
Policeman	Charles Karel
Ruth	Terry Saunders
Phil	Robert Weede
Clara Weiss	Molly Picon
The Guide	Nada Rowand
Mrs. Weinstein	Justine Johnston
Mrs. Strauss	Joyce Lynn
Mrs. Breslin	Dorothy Richardson
Mrs. Segal	Diane Goldberg
Mrs. Kessler	Terry Marone
Mrs. Perlman	Helene Winston
Barbara	Monte Amundsen
David	Tommy Rall
Adi	Marc Hertsens
Zipporah	Frances Spanier
Cantor	Lou Polacek
Maid of Honor	Nancy Stevens
Wedding Couples	Carlos Macri, Jane Meserve, Don Rehg, Ciya Challis
Arab	Renato Cibelli
Man of the Moshav	Charles Karel
Mr. Horowitz	Rueben Singer

SOLDIERS, TOURISTS, ARABS, ETC: Terry Marone, Patti Winston, Jane Meserve, Joyce Lynn, Jeanne McLarin, Joan Musselman, Margot Harley, Ciya Challis, Edwina Fontaine, Nancy Stevens, Nada Rowand, Renato Cibelli, John Grigas, Carlos Macri, Allan Byrns, George Smiley, John Mandia, Louis Gasparinetti, Ted Forlow, Charles Karel, Martin Ross, Alphonse Pater, Don Rehg, William Wendt, Nancy Haywood.

UNDERSTUDIES: Phil, Bruce MacKay; Ruth, Patti Winston; Mrs. Weiss, Diane Goldberg; David, Ted Forlow; Adi, Martin Ross; Barbara, Zipporah, Margot Harley; Horowitz, George Spelvin; Mrs. Perlman, Patti Winston; Mrs. Breslin, Jeanne McLaren; Mrs. Strauss, Nada Rowand.

MUSICAL NUMBERS: "Shepherd's Song," "Shalom," "Independence Day Hora," "Milk and Honey," "There's No Reason In The World," "Chin Up, Ladies," "That Was Yesterday," "Let's Not Waste A Minute," "The Wedding," "Like A Young Man," "I Will Follow You," "Hymn To Hymie," "As Simple As That."

A Musical Comedy in two acts and twelve scenes.

General Manager: Philip Adler
Company Manager: S. M. Handelsman
Press: Fred Weterick
Stage Managers: David Kanter, Bob Burland, Renato Cibelli

For original New York production, see THEATRE WORLD, Vol. 18.

Friedman-Abeles Photos

Top Right: Terry Saunders, Robert Weede

Molly Picon

156

HOW TO SUCCEED IN BUSINESS WITHOUT REALLY TRYING

Book by Abe Burrows, Jack Weinstock, Willie Gilbert; Based on Novel by Shepherd Mead; Music and Lyrics, Frank Loesser; Directed by Abe Burrows; Choreography, Hugh Lambert; Scenery and Lighting, Robert Randolph; Costumes, Robert Fletcher; Musical Direction, Fred Werner; Orchestrations, Robert Ginzler; Musical Staging, Bob Fosse; Presented by Feuer and Martin in association with Frank Productions, Inc. Opened Monday, February 4, 1963, at the Hanna Theatre in Cleveland, Ohio, and still touring May 31, 1964.

CAST

Finch	Dick Kallman
Gatch	Stanley Simmonds
Jenkins	I. W. Klein
Tackaberry	Larry Pool
Peterson	William Sisson
Kittridge	Larry Devon
J. B. Biggley	Willard Waterman
Rosemary	Dyan Cannon†
Bratt	Tom Batten
Smitty	Pat McEnnis
Frump	William Major
Miss Jones	Lilian Fields
Mr. Twimble	Joe Cowan
Hedy	Maureen Arthur
Scrubwomen	Carole Lindsey, Fayn LeVeille
Miss Krumholtz	Carole Lindsey
Toynbee	Lee Barry
Ovington	Larry Devon
Policeman	Bill Joyce
Womper	Joe Cowan

SINGERS: Lee Barry, Larry Devon, Joe Evans, I. W. Klein, Larry Pool, Stanley Simmonds, William Sisson, Jill Alexander, Eleanor Edie, Judith Leamon, Fayn LeVeille, Carole Lindsey, Anne Nathan.

DANCERS: Ted August, Gene Foote, Curtis Hood, Bill Joyce, Ronald Stratton, Buddy Vest, Lou Zeldis, Felice Camargo, Natasha Grishin, Enid Hart, Diane Hull, Karen Miller, Renata Powers, Elyn Tia.

MUSICAL NUMBERS: "How To," "Happy To Keep His Dinner Warm," "Coffee Break," "The Company Way," "A Secretary Is Not A Toy," "Been A Long Day," "Grand Old Ivy," "Paris Original," "Rosemary," Finaletto, "Cinderella, Darling," "Love From A Heart of Gold," "I Believe In You," "The Yo Ho Ho," "Brotherhood of Man," Finale.

A Musical Comedy in two acts. The entire action takes place in the new Park Avenue office building of World Wide Wickets Company, Inc.

General Manager: Donald Loze
Company Manager: Milton Pollack
Press: Merle Debuskey, Seymour Krawitz, Madi Ross
Stage Managers: Charles Durand, Hal Halvorsen, Larry Pool, Ted August

† Succeeded by Suzanne Menke

For original New York production, see THEATRE WORLD, Vol. 18.

Friedman-Abeles Photos

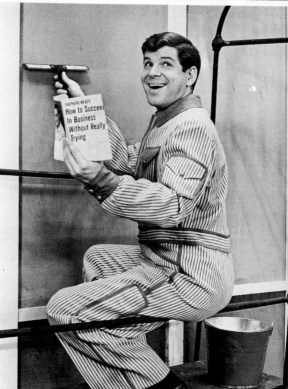

Top Right: Pat McEnnis, Dyan Cannon, Dick Kallman, Tom Batten
Center: Dick Kallman

Dick Kallman, Willard Waterman

STOP THE WORLD—I WANT TO GET OFF

Book, Music, and Lyrics by Leslie Bricusse and Anthony Newley; Setting and Lighting, Sean Kenny; Musical Supervision, Ian Fraser; Musical Director, Oscar Kosarin; Orchestrations, Ian Fraser with David Lindup, Burt Rhodes, Gordon Langford; John Broome's Choreography Restaged by Virginia Mason; Directed by Anthony Newley; Presented by David Merrick in association with Bernard Delfont. Opened Monday, March 25, 1963, at the Pabst Theatre, Milwaukee, Wisc., and closed at the Forrest Theatre in Philadelphia on April 18, 1964.

CAST

Joel Grey†1	Julie Newmar†2
Janet Allman	Shelley Payton
Jennifer Allman	Audrey Saxon
Karen Hopper	Beverlee Weir
Karen Johnson	Virginia Mason
Sherry Lambert	Mark Month
Geri O'Gorman	Michael Month

STANDBYS: Barry Dennen, Leigh Stewart, Virginia Mason.

MUSICAL NUMBERS: Overture, "The A. B. C. Song," "I Want To Be Rich," "Typically English," "A Special Announcement," "Lumbered," "Welcome To Sludgepool," "Gonna Build A Mountain," "Glorious Russian," "Meilinki Meilchick," "Family Fugue," "Typische Deutsche," "Nag! Nag! Nag!" "All American," "Once In A Lifetime," "Mumbo Jumbo," "Welcome To Sunvale," "Someone Nice Like You," "What Kind Of Fool Am I?"

A Musical in two acts.

General Manager: Jack Schlissel
Company Manager: Manuel Davis
Press: Lee Solters, Harvey Sabinson, Allan Dalzell
Stage Managers: David Clive, Leigh Stewart, Barry Dennen
Wardrobe Mistress: Ethel Sayles

†Succeeded by: 1. Kenneth Nelson, 2. Joan Eastman.

For original New York production, see THEATRE WORLD, Vol. 19.

Friedman-Abeles Photos

Left: Julie Newmar, Joel Grey

THE BLACKS

By Jean Genet; Directed by Gene Frankel; Sets and Lighting, Gene Rudolph; Costumes and Masks, Patricia Zipprodt; Music arranged by Charles Gross; Movement by Talley Beatty; Presented by The Edgewater Beach Playhouse by arrangement with Sidney Bernstein. Opened Tuesday, July 16, 1963, at the Studebaker Theatre in Chicago, and closed there on Sunday, August 18, 1963.

CAST

Archibald Wellington	Louis Gossett
Deodatus Village	Lincoln Kilpatrick
Adelaide Bobo	Helen Martin
Edgar Alas Newport News	Nick Smith
Augusta Snow	Ethel Ayler
Felicity Trollop Pardon	Brunetta Barnett
Stephanie Virtue Diop	Nichelle Nichols†1
Diouf	Clebert Ford
Missionary	Lex Monson
Judge	Raymond St. Jacques
Governor	Fred Pinkard
Queen	Roxie Roker†2
Valet	Harold Scott
Drummer	Charles Campbell

A Drama in two acts. The action takes place somewhere in Africa.

General Manager: Joseph H. Salyers
Press: Herbert M. Kraus
Stage Manager: Maxwell Glanville

†Succeeded by: 1. Yvette Hawkins, 2. Melva Williams

For original New York production, see THEATRE WORLD, Vol. 17.

Bert Andrews Photo

Nichelle Nichols, Lincoln Kilpatrick, Helen Martin, Louis Gossett, Ethel Ayler, Clebert Ford in "The Blacks"

A MAN FOR ALL SEASONS

By Robert Bolt; Directed by Noel Willman; Settings and Costumes by Motley; Lighting by Paul Morrison; A Robert Whitehead-Roger L. Stevens Production by Arrangement with H. M. Tennent Ltd. presented by American National Theatre and Academy. Opened at the Greek Theatre, Los Angeles, on Tuesday, July 23, 1963, and closed May 30, 1964, at the Blackstone Theatre in Chicago.

CAST

The Common Man	George Rose†
Sir Thomas More	William Roderick
Richard Rich	William Bogert
The Duke of Norfolk	Albert Dekker
Alice More	Sarah Burton
Margaret More	Moira Wylie
Cardinal Wolsey	Edgar Daniels
Thomas Cromwell	Bruce Gordon
Signor Chapuys	Frederic Warriner
His Attendant	John Swearingen
William Roper	Laurence Luckinbill
King Henry VIII	Michael Lewis
The Woman	Mae Marmy
Cranmer, Archbishop of Canterbury	
	William Callan

UNDERSTUDIES: More, Cranmer, Alex Reed; Man, Wolsey, Alfred Hinckley; Norfolk, Henry, Attendant, William Mooney; Cromwell, Chapuys, William Callan; Rich, Roper, John Swearingen; Alice, Mae Marmy; Margaret, Woman Dorothy James.

A Drama in two acts. The action takes place in England in the Sixteenth Century.

General Managers: Stanley Gilkey,
Oscar Olesen
Press: Lillian Libman
Stage Managers: Paul A. Foley,
Alfred Hinckley, William Mooney

†Succeeded by Richard A. Dysart.
This company interrupted its tour to play the New York City Center for two weeks, opening Monday, January 27, 1964, and closing Sunday, February 9, 1964, after a limited engagement of 17 performances.

For the original New York production, see THEATRE WORLD, Vol. 18.

Moira Wylie, William Roderick
Top: with Sarah Burton, Michael Lewis,
Albert Dekker

Friedman-Abeles Photos

NEVER TOO LATE

By Sumner Arthur Long; Directed by George Abbott; Setting and Lighting, William and Jean Eckart; Costumes, Florence Klotz; Cha-cha by Jerry Bock and Sheldon Harnick; Incidental Music, John Kander; Presented by Elliot Martin and Daniel Hollywood. Opened Saturday, August 3, 1963, in the Central City Opera House, Central City, Colo., and closed at the Fisher in Detroit, Mich., on March 21, 1964.

CAST

Grace Kimbrough	Kate Wilkinson
Harry Lambert	William Bendix
Edith Lambert	Nancy Carroll
Dr. James Kimbrough	Royal Beal
Charlie	Will Hutchins
Kate	Janis Young
Mr. Foley	Robert Fitzsimmons
Mayor Crane	Larry Fletcher
Policeman	Robert Carraway

UNDERSTUDIES: Harry, Larry Fletcher; Edith, Kate Wilkinson; Charlie, Robert Carraway; Grace, Helen Bonstelle; Crane, Royal Beal; Kate, Kathryn Shawn; Doctor and Policeman, Robert Fitzsimmons.

A Comedy in three acts and five scenes. The action takes place in the livingroom of the Lambert home in Calverton, Massachusetts, at the present time.

General Manager: C. Edwin Knill
Company Manager: Morry Efron
Press: Mary Bryant
Stage Managers: Joe Calvan, Robert Carraway

For original New York production, see THEATRE WORLD, Vol. 19.

Left: William Bendix, Nancy Carroll, and above with Will Hutchins, Janis Young

BEYOND THE FRINGE

A Nine O'Clock Theatre Production presented by Alexander H. Cohen by arrangement with William Donaldson and Donald Albery; Staged by Alexander H. Cohen; Material by Alan Bennett, Peter Cook, Jonathan Miller, Dudley Moore; Setting, John Wyckham; Lighting, Ralph Alswang; Production Associates, Andre Goulston, Gabriel Katzka. Opened Monday, August 5, 1963, at the Huntington Hartford Theatre, Hollywood, Calif., and closed March 14, 1964, at the Capital Theatre, Montreal, Canada. Resumed, Monday, May 11, 1964 at the O'Keefe in Toronto, Canada, and still touring May 31, 1964.

CAST

Patrick Carter	Patrick Horgan
William Christopher	Paxton Whitehead

UNDERSTUDIES: William Bassett, John Aman

PROGRAM

PART I: Steppes In The Right Direction, Royal Box, Man Bites God, Fruits of Experience, Bollard, A Piece of My Mind, Deutscher Chansons, The Sadder and Wiser Beaver, Groves of Academe, The Prime Minister Speaks, And The Same To You, Aftermyth of War.

PART II: Civil War, Real Class, Little Miss Britten, The Suspense Is Killing Me, Porn Shopping, Studio 5, Sitting On The Bench, Men Only, Take A Pew, So That's The Way You Like It, The End of The World.

General Manager: Roy A. Somlyo
Company Manager: G. Warren McClane
Press: David Rothenberg, Harry Forwood
Stage Managers: Alan Hall, John Aman, William Bassett

For original New York production, see THEATRE WORLD, Vol. 19.

Friedman-Abeles Photo

Patrick Horgan, Paxton Whitehead, William Christopher, Patrick Carter

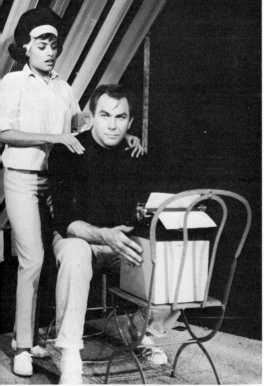

NO STRINGS

Music and Lyrics, Richard Rodgers; Book, Samuel Taylor; Directed and Choreographed by Joe Layton; Settings and Lighting, David Hays; Costumes, Fred Voelpel and Donald Brooks; Musical Direction, Jack Lee; Dance Arrangements, Peter Matz; Orchestration, Ralph Burns; Associate Choreographer, Buddy Schwab; Presented by Richard Rodgers in association with Samuel Taylor; Production Supervisor, Jerome Whyte; Hair Styles, Ronald DeMann. Opened Monday, August 5, 1963, at the Shubert in Boston, and closed January 4, 1964, at the Curan Theatre in San Francisco.

CAST

Barbara Woodruff	Barbara McNair
David Jordan	Howard Keel
Jeanette Valmy	Beti Seay
Luc Delbert	Juki Arkin
Mollie Plummer	Jane Van Duser
Mike Robinson	Robert Goss
Louis DePourtal	Ferdinand Hilt
Comfort O'Connell	Kit Smythe
Gabrielle Bertin	Anne Hodges
Marcello Agnolotti	Marc Scott

DANCERS: Rita Agnese, Annette Bachich, Donna Baccala, Eileen Casey, Martha Cutrufello, Grace Davidson, Jean Duguid, Mary Grace Ezell, Linda Rae Hager, Anne Hodges, Darla Fessler, April Nevins, Helene Parker, Louise Auick, Karen Yaffe, Jere Admire, Hamp Dickens, Jim Hovis, Marc Scott, Keith Stewart, Ron Tassone, Vernon Wendorf.

INSTRUMENTAL CHARACTERS: Flute and Clarinet, Spencer Sinatra; Drums, Bill Price; Trumpet, Bobby Nichols; Bassoon and Saxophone, Ronald Janelli; Trombone, Paul Selden.

UNDERSTUDIES: David, Robert Goss; Barbara, Beverly Todd; Jeanette, Donna Baccala; Mollie and Comfort, Anne Hodges; Louis, Joseph Hill; Luc, Marc Scott; Gabrielle, April Nevins; Marcello, Vernon Wendorf; Mike, Jim Hovis.

MUSICAL NUMBERS: "The Sweetest Sounds," "How Sad," "Loads of Love," "The Man Who Has Everything," "Be My Host," "La La La," "You Don't Tell Me," "Love Makes The World Go," "Nobody Told Me," "Look No Further," "Maine," "An Orthodox Fool," "Eager Beaver," "No Strings," "Maine."

A Musical Play in two acts. The action takes place at the present time in Paris, Monte Carlo, Honfleur, Deauville, and St. Tropez.

General Manager: Morris Jacobs
Company Manager: Maurice Winters
Press: Al Butler
Stage Managers: Fred Smith, Harry Clark, Joseph Hill

For original New York production, see THEATRE WORLD, Vol. 19.

Friedman-Abeles Photos

Howard Keel, Kit Smythe, Robert Goss
Above: Barbara McNair, Howard Keel

WHO'S AFRAID OF VIRGINIA WOOLF?

By Edward Albee; Presented by Theatre 1964; Directed by Alan Schneider; Designed by William Ritman; Costumes Supervised by Theoni V. Aldredge. Opened Monday, September 2, 1963, in the Colonial Theatre, Boston, and still touring May 31, 1964.

CAST
Evening Company
Martha	Nancy Kelly
George	Shepperd Strudwick
Honey	Barbara Dana
Nick	Ken Kercheval

Matinee Company
Martha	Michaele Myers
George	Kendall Clark
Honey	Barbara Dana
Nick	Ken Kercheval

Understudies: Eddie Jones, Judith Kercheval

A Drama in three acts. The action takes place at the present time in the home of Martha and George in a university town.

Company Manager: Paul Groll
Press: John L. Toohey
Stage Managers: Gerald O'Brien,
Joseph Kapfer, Eddie Jones

For original New York production, see THEATRE WORLD, Vol. 19.

Left: Nancy Kelly, Barbara Dana, Shepperd Strudwick, Ken Kercheval (also at top)

MARY, MARY

By Jean Kerr; Directed by Joseph Anthony; Presented by Roger L. Stevens; Designed by Oliver Smith; Costumes, Theoni V. Aldredge; Lighting, Peggy Clark; Associate Producers, Lyn Austin, Victor Samrock; Associate Director, William Ross. Opened at the Huntington Hartford Theatre, Los Angeles, Monday, September 9, 1963, and closed Friday, December 6, 1963, in Wheeling, West Virginia.

CAST
Bob McKellaway	Pirie MacDonald
Tiffany Richards	Elizabeth St. Clair
Oscar Nelson	Clinton Sundberg
Dirk Winsten	Jeffrey Lynn
Mary McKellaway	Mindy Carson

UNDERSTUDIES: Elizabeth MacDonald, Andy Rasbury.

A Comedy in three acts. The action takes place at the present time in Bob McKellaway's living room in a New York apartment.

General Manager: Victor Samrock
Company Manager: James Awe
Press: Arthur Brilant
Stage Managers: Jack Moorehead, Andy Rasbury
Wardrobe Mistress: Fanny Flaumonhaft

For original New York production, see THEATRE WORLD, Vol. 17.

Friedman-Abeles Photos

Jeffrey Lynn, Mindy Carson, Pirie MacDonald

A THOUSAND CLOWNS

By Herb Gardner; Directed by Fred Coe;
Scenery Designed and Lighted by George Jen-
kins; Costumes, Ruth Morley; Production Sup-
ervisor, Porter Van Zandt; Presented by Fred
Coe and Arthur Cantor. Opened Wednesday,
September 11, 1963, at the Playhouse, Wilming-
ton, Del., and closed April 18, 1964 at the
American, St. Louis.

CAST

Murray Burns..................................Dane Clark
Nick Burns...................................Barry Gordon
Albert Amundson.........................Conard Fowkes
Sandra Markowitz..................Margaret O'Brien
Arnold Burns................................Marc London
Leo Herman..............................Paul E. Richards
STANDBYS: Sandra, Ardyth Kaiser; Nick,
Barry Pearl; Albert, Arnold, Leo, Harry Basch.

A Comedy in three acts and five scenes. The
action takes place in Murray Burns' Manhattan
apartment at the present time.

General Managers: Joseph Harris, Ira Bernstein
Company Manager: Emmett Callahan
Press: George Deber
Stage Managers: Tom Porter, Harry Basch

For original New York production, see THEA-
TRE WORLD, Vol. 18.

Right: Dane Clark, Margaret O'Brien
Top: Gregg Weir, John Ireland, Nancy Douglas,
Sidney Rayder

A THOUSAND CLOWNS

By Herb Gardner; Directed by Porter Van
Zandt; Designed by Philip Rosenberg; Presented
by Lawrence Witchel and Kenneth J. Stein by
arrangement with Fred Coe and Arthur Cantor;
Associate Producer, James Travis; Production
Assistant, Betsy Katzin; Costume Consultant,
Marian Lathrop. Opened in Providence, R.I.,
on Monday, September 30, 1963, and closed
February 8, 1964, at the Rochester, N.Y.,
Auditorium.

CAST

Murray Burns...............................John Ireland
Nick Burns.....................................Gregg Weir
Albert Amundson.......................Sidney Rayder
Arnold Burns...............................Robert Alvin
Leo Herman................................Donald Barry
Sandra Markowitz.....................Nancy Douglas
UNDERSTUDIES: Sandra, Barbara Patin; Nick,
Robert Faller.

A Comedy in three acts and five scenes. The
action takes place in Murray Burns' apartment
and Arnold Burns' office in Manhattan at the
present time.

Company Manager: Carl Abraham
Press: Fred Weterick
Stage Managers: Philip Mandelker, John
Ireland, Jr.

For original New York production, see THEATRE
WORLD, Vol. 18.

Donald Barry, John Ireland

CAMELOT

Book and Lyrics, Alan Jay Lerner; Music, Frederick Loewe; Directed by Lawrence Kasha; Presented by Henry Guettel and Arthur Cantor by arrangement with Jenny Productions; Choreography and Musical Numbers by Hanya Holm; Scenic Production, Oliver Smith; Costumes, Stanley Simmons; Lighting, Feder; Orchestrations, Robert Russell Bennett and Philip J. Lang; Musical Directors, John Anderson, Edward Simons; Based on "The Once and Future King" by T. H. White; Opened Thursday, October 3, 1963, at the Masonic Temple, Scranton, Pa., and closed May 16, 1964 at The Playhouse in Wilmington, Del.

CAST

Sir Dinadan	George Hearn
Sir Lionel	Ewel Cornett
Merlyn	Gwyllum Evans
Arthur	Biff McGuire
Guenevere	Jeannie Carson
Nimue	Jane Bergerman
A Page	Daryl Alford
Lancelot	Sean Garrison
Dap	Charles May
Pellinore	Melville Cooper
Clarius	Dennis Wayne
Lady Anne	Yvonne Lynn
Sir Sagramore	Edgar Mastin
Mordred	Brendan Burke
Tom	Daryl Alford

LADIES OF THE COURT: Sue Babel, Jane Bergerman, Sandra Brewer, Laura Graham, Barbara Gregory, Gracia Littauer, Peff Modelski, Eva Marie Sage, Susanne Whitcomb, Marjorie Wood.

KNIGHTS OF THE COURT: Daryl Alford, Paul Glover, Jay Gregory, Don Lawrence, Arnott Mader, Andre St. Jean.

MUSICAL NUMBERS: "I Wonder What The King Is Doing Tonight," "The Simple Joys of Maidenhood," "Camelot," "Follow Me," "C'Est Moi," "The Lusty Month of May," "How To Handle A Woman," "The Jousts," "Before I Gaze At You Again," "If Ever I Would Leave You," "The Seven Deadly Virtues," "What Do The Simple Folks Do," "Fie On Goodness," "I Loved You Once In Silence," "Guenevere."

A Musical in two acts and eighteen scenes. The action takes place in Camelot a long time ago.

Company Manager: Charles Mooney
Stage Manager: Eddie Dimond

For original New York production, see THEATRE WORLD, Vol. 17.

Werner J. Kuhn Photos

Left: Sean Garrison, Jeannie Carson
Top: Jeannie Carson, Biff McGuire, Sean Garrison

Biff McGuire, Jeannie Carson

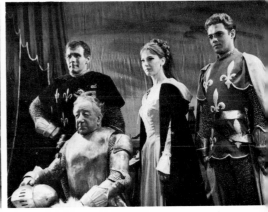

Biff McGuire, Melville Cooper, Jeannie Carson, Sean Garrison

SEIDMAN AND SON

By Elick Moll; Based on his Novel; Directed by Sam Levene; Associate Director, Loy Nilson; Scenery and Costumes, William Pitkin; Presented by Theatre Guild Productions, Joel Schenker, and Michael Kanin; Associate Producer, Elliott Martin; Production Assistant, Sylvia Kalegi. Opened at the Locust Theatre in Philadelphia, Monday, October 7, 1963, and closed at the Geary in San Francisco on February 22, 1964.

CAST

Morris Seidman	Sam Levene
Mamie	Ruth Warshawsky
Sophie Seidman	Janet Ward
Jenny Seidman	Elizabeth Bader
Harold Seidman	Richard Ideman
Miss Weintraub's Voice	Ruth Warshawsky
Mr. Karp	Morris Strassberg
Rosenzweig	Abe Vigoda
Laura Menken	Elizabeth Fleming
Tina	Lynne Roberts
Shelley	Barbara Sorensen
Larry Kogen	Chet London
Doreen	Susan Tabor
Wilenski	Alfred Leberfeld
Leo	E. M. Margolese
Mr. Magnuson	Lou Polan
Miss Kelley	Ruth Tate
Helen Sowolska	Sandy Walsh

UNDERSTUDIES: Morris, E. M. Margolese; Sophie, Ruth Warshawsky; Harold, B. J. De-Simone; Laura, Susan Tabor; Wilenski, Karp, E. M. Margolese; Larry, Leo, Rosenzweig, Barry Hoffman; Jenny, Doreen, Helen, Lynne Roberts; Mamie, Voice, Barbara Sorensen.

A Comedy in three acts and eight scenes. The action takes place at the present time in Morris Seidman's home and place of business.

General Manager: Robert Alex Baron
Company Manager: Maurice Costello
Press: Max Gendel
Stage Managers: Loy Nilson, Alfred Leberfeld, Barry Hoffman, E. M. Margolese

For original New York production, see THEATRE WORLD, Vol. 19.

Friedman-Abeles Photos

Right: Sam Levene, Chet London, Elizabeth Fleming
Top: Janet Ward, Sam Levene

Janet Ward, Richard Ideman, Elizabeth Bader, Ruth Warshawsky, Sam Levene

Sam Levene, Richard Ideman

Eva LeGallienne, Farley Granger

RING ROUND THE MOON

By Jean Anouilh; Translated by Christopher Fry; Directed by Jack Sydow; Music by Dean Fuller; Dance Assistant, Phillis Lear; Presented by The National Repertory Theatre. Opened Thursday, October 10, 1963, at Aycock Auditorium, Greensboro, N.C.

CAST

Joshua	George Turner
Hugo Frederic	Farley Granger
Diana Messerschmann	Barbara Stanton
Patrice Bombelles	Denholm Elliott
Lady India	Anne Meacham
Madame Desmermortes	Eva Le Gallienne
Capulat	Osceola Archer
Messerschmann	Thayer David
Romainville	G. Wood
Isabelle	Kelly Jean Peters
Her Mother	Betty Sinclair
A General	Jerome Raphel
Party Guests	Susan Carr, Pamela Gruen, Mary Hara, Clinton Anderson, Ben Yaffee

A Comedy in three acts and five scenes. The action takes place in the winter garden of Madame Desmermortes' chateau in Auvergne, France, in the spring of 1912.

Company Manager: Boris Bernardi
Press: Mary Ward
Stage Managers: William Armitage, Helen Page Camp

Presented in repertory with "The Seagull" and "The Crucible" which played a limited engagement on Broadway. See Broadway Calendar. For original Broadway production, see THEATRE WORLD, Vol. 7.

Van Williams Photos

Top: (L) G. Wood, Farley Granger, Kelly Jean Peters
(R) Anne Meacham, Denholm Elliott

HOW TO SUCCEED IN BUSINESS WITHOUT REALLY TRYING

Book by Abe Burrows, Jack Weinstock and Willie Gilbert; Based on Novel by Shepherd Mead; Music and Lyrics by Frank Loesser; Directed by Abe Burrows; Musical Staging by Bob Fosse; Presented by Feuer and Martin in association with Frank Productions. Opened at the Center Theatre, Norfolk, Va., October 14, 1963, and still touring May 31, 1964.

CAST

Finch	Hal England
Gatch	Fred Bennett
Jenkins	Earl Stam
Tackaberry	Thomas Boyd
Peterson	James Connor
Kittridge	Christian Grey
J. B. Biggley	Jeff De Benning
Rosemary	Kipp Hamilton
Bratt	Arthur Barnett
Smitty	Lynne Osborne
Frump	Bill Mullikin
Miss Jones	Maggie Task
Mr. Twimble	Jerry Mann
Hedy	Sandra O'Neill
Scrubwomen	Wanda Saxon, Roseann Bixler
Miss Krumholtz	Wanda Saxon
Ovington	Christian Grey
Policeman	Bill Richards
Womper	Jerry Mann

SINGERS: Fred Bennett, Thomas Boyd, James Connor, Christian Grey, Gerry O'Hara, Earl Stam, Michael Valenti, Roseann Bixler, Ann Davies, Del Green, Dorothy Henning, Leslie Mirin, Wanda Saxon.

DANCERS: Ray Becker, Gerard Brentte, Ray Chabeau, Jim Challendor, Charles Kalan, Gregg Owen, Bill Richards, Marilyn Charles, Brooke Roma, Susan Sigrist, Chris Stewart, Dean Taliaferro, Marlene Tyree, Laureen White.

UNDERSTUDIES: Finch, Michael Valenti; Rosemary, Roseann Bixler; Hedy, Dean Taliaferro; Frump, Gerry O'Hara; Smitty, Del Green; Bratt, Christian Grey; Twimble, Womper, Thomas Boyd; Miss Jones, Wanda Saxon.

MUSICAL NUMBERS: "How To," "Happy To Keep His Dinner Warm," "Coffee Break," "The Company Way," "A Secretary Is Not A Toy," "Been A Long Day," "Grand Old Ivy," "Paris Original," "Rosemary," "Cinderella, Darling," "Love From A Heart Of Gold," "I Believe In You," "Brotherhood of Man," Finale.

A Musical Comedy in two acts. The action takes place in the new Park Avenue office building of World Wide Wickets Company, Inc.

Business Manager: Donald Loze
Company Manager: Albert H. Rosen
Press: Merle Debuskey, Seymour Krawitz, Joseph Shea, Nate Schenker
Stage Managers: William Weaver, Jeffery Longe, Bill Richards, Gerry O'Hara

For original New York production, see THEATRE WORLD, Vol. 18.

Hal England, Sandra O'Neill, Jeff DeBenning
Top: Lynne Osborne, Hal England, Kipp Hamilton

BLACK NATIVITY

By Langston Hughes; Directed by Vinnette Carroll; Choreography by Talley Beatty; Costumes, Bill Hargate; Settings, Joe Eula; Lighting, Martin Aronstein; Pianist, Alberta Carter; Organist, Joe Washington; Presented by Martin Tahse by arrangement with Michael R. Santangelo-Barbara Griner Productions in association with Eric Franck. Opened Monday, October 14, 1963, at the Shubert Theatre in Boston, and closed Sunday, January 12, 1964, in Chicago.

CAST

Narrator	Ed Hall
Joseph	Matt Cameron
Mary	Hope Clark
A Woman	Henrietta Waddy
Shepherd	Philip Stamps
An Angel	Princess Stewart
The Stars of Faith	Kitty Parham, Frances Steadman, Henrietta Waddy, Mattie Williams, Marion Williams
The Bradford Singers	Alex Bradford, Judy Wilcox, Bernie Durant, Robert Pinkston, Kenneth Washington

A Gospel jamboree in two parts.

General Manager: Elizabeth Ireland McCann
Company Manager: Fred J. Cuneo
Press: Morton Langbord, Meredith Evans
Stage Manager: Nathan Caldwell, Jr.

Left: Marion Williams and top
with Alex Bradford

June Wilkinson, William Browder

PAJAMA TOPS

By Mawby Green and Ed Feilbert; Based on French farce "Moumou" by Jean De Le Traz; Staged by Richard Vath; Costumes by Vilma Auld; Presented by Abba Productions, Inc. Opened Monday, November 4, 1963, at the Geary Theatre in San Francisco, and still touring May 31, 1964.

CAST

Claudine Amour	Fabian Craig
Inspector Legrand	Don McArt
Yvonne Chauvinet	Lyn Statten
Georges Chauvinet	Richard Vath
Leonard Jolijoli	William Browder
Babette Latouche	June Wilkinson
Jacques Latouche	Carl Bensen

UNDERSTUDIES: Tom Anders, Joyce Langford.

A Farce in two acts and three scenes. The action takes place in the living room of the Chauvinet Villa + Deauville, France, at the present time.

General Manager: Lee Hewitt
Company Manager: Ann Hewitt
Press: Paul Montague
Stage Manager: Charles Belian, Jr.

For New York production, see **THEATRE WORLD**, Vol. 19.

A FUNNY THING HAPPENED ON THE WAY TO THE FORUM

Book by Burt Shevelove and Larry Gelbart; Based on plays of Plautus; Music and Lyrics, Stephen Sondheim; Directed by George Abbott; Choreography and Musical Staging, Jack Cole; Settings and Costumes, Tony Walton; Lighting, Jean Rosenthal; Musical Director, Joseph D. Lewis; Orchestrations, Irwin Kostal and Sid Ramin; Dance Music Arranged by Hal Schaefer; Presented by Martin Tashe by arrangement with Harold Prince. Opened at the Forrest Theatre, Philadelphia on December 25, 1963, and still touring May 31, 1964.

CAST

Prologus	Jerry Lester
Proteans	David Neuman, Scott Hunter, Eric Kelly
Senex	Paul Hartman
Domina	Justine Johnston
Hero	Bert Stratford
Hysterium	Arnold Stang
Lycus	Erik Rhodes
Pseudolus	Jerry Lester
Tintinabula	Tisa Chang
Panacea	Gloria Mills
The Geminae	Helen Levit, Pamela Hayford
Vibrata	Helen Sylvia
Gymnasia	Ricki Covette
Philia	Donna McKechnie
Erronius	Edward Everett Horton
Miles Gloriosus	Adair McGowen

UNDERSTUDIES: Erronius, Ross Hertz; Pseudous, David Huddleston; Senex, Ross Hertz; Hysterium, David Neuman; Lycus, Alan Louw; Proteans, Erik Howell; Domina, Emily Ruhberg; Hero, Erik Howell; Gymnasia, Emily Ruhberg; Philia, Nancy Mae Burns; Miles, Alan Louw; Tintinabula, Panacea, Vibrata, JaAnn Tenney.

MUSICAL NUMBERS: "Comedy Tonight," "Love, I Hear," "Free," "The House of Marcus Lycus," "Lovely," "Pretty Little Picture," "Everybody Ought To Have A Maid," "I'm Calm," "Impossible," "Bring Me A Bride," "That Dirty Old Man," "That'll Show Him," "Loverly," "Funeral Sequence and Dance," Finale.

A Musical Comedy in two acts. The action takes place on a street in Rome in front of the houses of Erronius, Senex and Lycus, on a day in spring, two hundred years before the Christian era.

General Manager: Elizabeth Ireland McCann
Company Manager: Fred J. Cuneo
Press: Morton Langbord, Meredith Evans
Stage Managers: Thelma Chandler, Henry Garrard, Ross Hertz

For original New York production, see THEATRE WORLD, Vol. 18.

Below top picture: **Paul Hartman, Arnold Stang, Jerry Lester, Erik Rhodes, Edward Everett Horton**

THE HOLLOW CROWN

Devised by John Barton; Music Arranged and Adapted by James Walker and Brian Priestman; Presented by Bonard Productions. Opened Monday, December 30, 1963, at McCarter Theatre, Princeton, N. J., and closed at the University of Maryland College Park on April 25, 1964.

CAST

Ann Firbank	Michael Gough
John Nettleton	John Warner
Richard Golding	John Lawrenson
Stephen Manton	Brian Priestman

A Royal Revue by and about the kings and queens of England.

Press: Abner D. Klipstein

For original New York production, see THEATRE WORLD, Vol. 19.

Ann Firbank, Michael Gough, John Warner

THE SOUND OF MUSIC

Music and Lyrics, Richard Rodgers and Oscar Hammerstein 2nd; Book, Lindsay and Crouse; Directed by John Fearnley; Musical Numbers Staged by Joe Layton; Scenic Production, Oliver Smith; Lighting, Jean Rosenthal; Costumes, Lucinda Ballard; Orchestrations, Robert Russell Bennett; Musical Director, Peter Laurini; Choral Arrangements, Trude Rittman; Presented by Henry Guettel. Opened at the Queen Elizabeth Theatre, Vancouver, Canada, on Monday, December 30, 1963, and closed at the Orpheum in Minneapolis, Minn., March 22, 1964.

CAST

Maria Reiner	Barbara Meister
Sister Berthe	Jessica Quinn
Sister Margaretta	Sally Cooke
The Mother Abbess	Katherine Hilgenberg
Sister Sophia	Jeanne Shea
Capt. George Von Trapp	John Van Dreelen
Franz	Roger Franklin
Frau Schmidt	Helen Noyes
Liesl	Ethelyne Dunfee
Friedrich	Vincent Alexander
Brigitta	Holly Sherwood
Kurt	John Messenger
Louisa	Alison Sherwood
Marta	Dawn Sherwood
Gretl	Mindy Sherwood
Rolf Gruber	Peter Van Hattum
Elsa Schraeder	Jen Nelson
Ursula	Hermine Warren
Max Detweiler	Wally Griffin
Herr Zeller	Larry Swanson
Baron Elberfeld	B. Walter Sherwood
A Postulant	Kyle Sherwood
Admiral Von Schreiber	Jack LeGrand

NEIGHBORS, NUNS, ETC.: Mary Alexander, Suzann Dyslin, Betty Janus, Dawn Joy Miller, Lynne Murray, Marcia O'Brien, Kyle Sherwood, Trudy Wallace, Hermine Warren, Joyce Withrow.

UNDERSTUDIES: Maria, Jeanne Shea; Captain, Roger Franklin; Mother Abbess, Frau Schmidt, Jessica Quinn; Elsa, Sally Cooke; Max, Zeller, Jack LeGrand; Rolf, Brooks Fountain; Franz, Larry Swanson; Liesl, Brigitta, Kyle Sherwood; Louisa, Holly Sherwood; Marta, Alison Sherwood; Gretl, Dawn Sherwood; Freidrich, Kurt, Frank Hubert; Berthe, Trudy Wallace; Margaretta, Joyce Withrow; Sophia, Betty Janus; Von Schreiber, B. Walter Sherwood.

MUSICAL NUMBERS: "Preludium," "The Sound of Music," "Maria," "My Favorite Things," "Do Re Me," "You Are Sixteen," "The Lonely Goatherd," "How Can Love Survive?," "So Long, Farewell," "Climb Every Mountain," "No Way To Stop It," "Ordinary Couple," "Processional," "Edelweiss."

A Musical in two acts and twenty scenes. The action takes place in Austria early in 1938.

Company Manager: Richard Grayson
Press: Mae S. Hong, Al Butler
Stage Managers: Bill O'Brien, Roger Franklin, Brooks Fountain, Jack LeGrand

For original New York production, see THEATRE WORLD, Vol. 16.

Helen Noyes, Shev Rodgers
Above: Katherine Hilgenberg, Barbara Meister
Top: Barbara Meister, John Van Dreelen;
Peter Van Hattum, Ethelyne Dunfee

Friedman-Abeles Photos

THE BOYS FROM SYRACUSE

Music, Richard Rodgers; Lyrics, Lorenz Hart; Book, George Abbott; Based on Shakespeare's "The Comedy of Errors"; Staged by Christopher Hewett; Choreography and Musical Numbers Staged by Bob Herget; Musical and Choral Direction, Joseph Klein; Settings, Herbert Senn and Helen Pond; Lighting, James Hamilton; Orchestrations, Ralph Burns, Larry Wilcox; Ballet Music, Peter Matz; Associate Producer, Hugh Fordin; Presented by National Performing Arts, Inc., in association with Len Bedsow and Hal Grossman. Opened at the Lyric Theatre, Allentown, Pa., Wednesday, January 8, 1964, and closed May 16, 1964 in Providence, R.I.

CAST

Sergeant	Rudy Vejar
Duke	Edward Greene
Aegeon	Wayne Adams
Antipholus of Ephesus	John Smolko
Dromio of Ephesus	Martin Ross
Tailor	Victor Duntiere
Antipholus of Syracuse	Chet Sommers
Dromio of Syracuse	Eddie Roll
Merchant of Syracuse	Ralph McWilliams
Apprentice	Virginia Klein
Angelo	Lonnie Davis
Corporal	Michael Mann, Jr.
Luce	Marcie Stringer
Adriana	Laurie Franks
Luciana	Carole Woodruff
Maids	June Helmers, Phyllis Ford, Virginia Klein
Sorcerer	Wayne Adams
The Courtesan	Norma Doggett
Fatima	Myrna Charles
Mirror Courtesan	Grace Mitchell
Jewel Courtesan	Joan Jaffee
Merchant of Ephesus	Victor Duntiere
Galatea	Grace Mitchell
Pygmalion	Ralph McWilliams
Amazons	Grace Mitchell, Joan Jaffee, Joann Lehmann, Phyllis Ford
Seeress	June Helmers

MUSICAL NUMBERS: "I Had Twins," "Dear Old Syracuse," "What Can You Do With A Man?," "Falling In Love With Love," "The Shortest Day of The Year," "This Can't Be Love," "Ladies' Choice Ballet," "Ladies of The Evening," "He and She," "You Have Cast Your Shadow On The Sea," "Come With Me," "Big Brother," "Sing For Your Supper," "Oh, Diogenes!," Finale.

A Musical Comedy in two acts and eleven scenes.

General Manager: Hal Grossman
Press: A. J. Clarke
Stage Managers: Elizabeth Caldwell, James Nygren

Wayne Adams, Norma Doggett, Joan Jaffe, Myrna Charles, Grace Mitchell

Left Center: (Kneeling) Eddie Roll, Martin Ross, Marcie Stringer (Standing) Carole Woodruff, Laurie Franks, Chet Sommers, Norma Doggett, John Smolko

LITTLE ME

Book by Neil Simon; Music, Cy Coleman; Lyrics, Carolyn Leigh; Based on Novel by Patrick Dennis; Scenery and Lighting, Robert Randolph; Costumes, Robert Fletcher; Musical Numbers and Dances Staged by Bob Fosse; Directed by Cy Feuer and Bob Fosse; Orchestrations, Ralph Burns; Dance Music Arranged by Fred Werner; Vocal Arrangements, Clay Warnick; Musical Direction, Charles Sanford; Presented by Feuer and Martin. Opened Thursday, January 30, 1964, at the Rochester, N. Y., Auditorium, and still touring May 31, 1964.

CAST

Butler	Burt Bier
Patrick Dennis	Grant Walden
Miss Poitrine, Today	Nancy Andrews
Belle	Virginia Martin
Momma	Alice Nunn
George Musgrove, as a boy	J. David Kirby
Brucey	Ross-Miles
Ramona	Barbara Doherty
Noble Eggleston	Sid Caesar
Mrs. Eggleston	Edith Gresham
Miss Kepplewhite	Marcia Gilford
Pinchley, Jr.	James Spann
Nurse	Leelyn Palmer
Mr. Pinchley	Sid Caesar
Newsboy	Terry Nicholson
Bernie Buchsbaum	Maurice Brenner
Bennie Buchsbaum	Lou Cuttell
Defense Lawyer	H. F. Green
Val Du Val	Sid Caesar
George Musgrove	Swen Swenson
Fred Poitrine	Sid Caesar
Preacher	Ripple Lewis
German Officer	H. F. Green
General	Dan Merriman
Courier	Bick Goss
Red Cross Nurse	Virginia Perlowin
Captain	H. F. Green
Steward	Mel Auston
Sailor	Wayne Boyd
Otto Schnitzler	Sid Caesar
Secretary	Susan Mora
Production Assistant	H. F. Green
Victor	Alexander Orfaly
Prince Cherney	Sid Caesar
Yulnick	H. F. Green
Baby	Virginia Martin
Noble, Junior	Sid Caesar

SINGERS: Marcia Gilford, Marlene Kay, Susan Mora, Virginia Perlowin, Mara Worth, Burt Bier, Ripple Lewis, Dick Moll, Alexander Orfaly, James Spann.

DANCERS: Ciya Challis, Kathryn Doby, Barbara Doherty, Carol Estey, Leelyn Palmer, Martha Pollak, Judy Shake, Mel Auston, Wayne Boyd, Gene Gavin, Bick Goss, J. David Kirby, Terry Nicholson, Ross-Miles, Dan Taylor.

UNDERSTUDIES: Mr. Caesar, H. F. Green; Miss Andrews, Alice Nunn; Miss Martin, Virginia Perlowin; Mr. Swenson, Gene Gavin; Messrs. Cutell and Brenner, Alexander Orfaly; Mr. Green, Burt Bier; Mr. Walden, Dan Merriman; Miss Nunn, Marcia Gilford.

MUSICAL NUMBERS: "The Truth," "The Other Side Of The Tracks," "Birthday Party," "I Love You," "Deep Down Inside," "Be A Performer!," "Dimples," "Boom—Boom," "I've Got Your Number," "Real Live Girl," "Poor Little Hollywood Star," "Little Me," "The Prince's Farewell," "Here's To US," Finale.

A Musical Comedy in two acts. The action takes place at the present at Belle's estate in Southampton, L.I., and in her past.

Company Manager: Milton M. Pollack
Press: F. Beverly Kelley
Stage Managers: Edmund Baylies, Bob Burland, Richard Hughes

For the original New York production, see THEATRE WORLD, Vol. 19.

Friedman-Abeles Photos

Sid Caesar, Virginia Martin
Above: Swen Swenson

172

Top Left: Alice Nunn, Virginia Martin,
Nancy Andrews, Sid Caesar

"IN ONE BED . . .
(And Out The Other)"

By Mawby Green and Ed Feilbert; Based on "Une Nuit Chez Vouz . . . Madame!" by Jean De Letraz; Directed by Jack Ragotzy; Designed by Leo B. Meyer; Lighting, Peter Sargent; Costumes, Bill Hargate; Presented by Zev Bufman and Stan Seiden. Opened Monday, February 17, 1964, at the Nixon Theatre, Pittsburgh, and closed May 16, 1964 at the Shubert in Cincinnati, Ohio.

CAST

Maurice	Rex Robbins
Huguette DuBois	Greta Thyssen
Gaston DuBois	Jules Munshin
Didier	Dale Helward
Clara	Merle Louise
Rosine	Grace Gaynor
Aunt Alice	Sibyl Bowan

A Comedy in three acts. The action takes place at the present time in the drawing room of Monsieur and Madame DuBois' apartment in the fashionable section of Paris.

General Manager: Lee Hewitt
Company Manager: Carl Abraham
Press: Richard Falk
Stage Managers: George Quick, Ralph Strait

Top Left: Sibyl Bowan, Greta Thyssen, Jules Munshin

ENTER LAUGHING

By Joseph Stein; Based on Novel by Carl Reiner; Directed by Gene Saks; Designed by Ed Wittstein; Presented by Morton Gottlieb. Opened at the Wilbur Theatre in Boston on Monday, March 16, 1964, and closed at the Geary in San Francisco, May 9, 1964.

CAST

Mr. Foreman	Irving Jacobson
David Kolowitz	Alan Arkin
Marvin	Marc Yohanna
Miss B	Judy Jordan
Pike	Charles Randall
Don Darwin	Bob Spencer
Don Baxter	Joe Young
Marlowe	Alan Mowbray
Angela	Yvonne DeCarlo
Mrs. Kolowitz	Mae Schoenfeld
Mr. Kolowitz	Marty Greene
Wanda	Freda Holloway
Waiter	Joe Young
Roger	Monroe Arnold
Lawyer	Tom Gorman

UNDERSTUDIES: Angela, Miss B, Mrs. Kolowitz, Fayne Blackburn; Morlowe, Pike, Tom Gorman; Mr. Foreman, Mr. Kolowitz, Joe Young; David, Marc Yohanna; Roger, Charles Randall; Wanda, Judy Jordan; Marvin, Bob Spencer.

A Comedy in two acts. The action takes place in the mid-1930's in New York during late spring.

General Manager: Richard Seader
Company Managers: David Wyler, Ronald Lee
Press: Dorothy Ross, Peggy Phillips, Richard O'Brien
Stage Managers: Iris O'Connor, Tom Gorman
For original New York production, see THEATRE WORLD, Vol. 19.

Werner J. Kuhn Photos

Center Left: Alan Arkin, Irving Jacobson, Marc Yohanna

Tom Gorman, Joe Young, Marc Yohanna, Alan Arkin, Yvonne DeCarlo, Alan Mowbray, Charles Randall

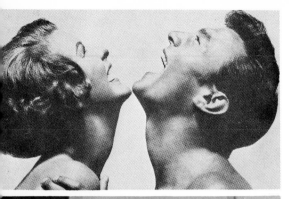

THE TIME OF THE BARRACUDAS

By Peter Barnes; Staged by Anthony Page, Fred Hebert; Scenery, Oliver Smith; Costumes, Theoni V. Aldredge; Lighting, Peggy Clark; Music, Miles Davis and Gil Evans; Presented by Frederick Brisson, Roger L. Stevens, and Donald Albery; Associate Producers, Lyn Austin, Victor Samrock. Opened Monday, October 21, 1963, at the Curran Theatre in San Francisco, and closed at the Huntington Hartford Theatre in Los Angeles, November 23, 1963.

CAST

Philip Wiere	Laurence Harvey
Jean	Christina Gillespie
Dr. Clayton	Rex O'Malley
Funeral Manager	Eugene Roche
Funeral Director	Robert van Hooton
Rev. Gosling	William Haddock
Insurance Agent	Eugene Roche
Insurance Manager	Robert van Hooton
Stella	Elaine Stritch
Police Sergeant	Eugene Roche
Police Inspector	Robert van Hooton

UNDERSTUDIES: Philip, Eugene Roche; Stella, Valerie French; Other Men, Geoff Garland.

A Comedy in two acts and five scenes. The action takes place at the present time in a Scottish highland honeymoon lodge.

General Manager: Victor Samrock
Company Manager: George Oshrin
Press: Peggy Phillips, Samuel Lurie Associates
Stage Managers: Charles Forsythe, Geoff Garland

Top Left: Elaine Stritch, Laurence Harvey

CONVERSATIONS IN THE DARK

By William Hanley; Directed by Daniel Petrie; Settings and Lighting, Ming Cho Lee; Costumes, Michael Travis; Presented by Theatre Guild Productions; Associate Producer, Don Herbert. Opened at the Walnut Street Theatre, Philadelphia, Monday, December 23, 1963, and closed there January 4, 1964.

CAST

Eddie Harmon	Jack Warden
Maude	Sandra Church
Ray Phillips	Jon Cypher
Claire	Barbara Barrie

STANDBYS: Suzanne Storrs, Gerald Metcalfe.

A Drama in three acts. The action takes place in summer, autumn, and winter in three apartments in New York City.

General Manager: Al Goldin
Company Manager: Leonard Mulhern
Press: Nat and Irvin Dorfman, Marcia Taradash
Stage Manager: Karl Nielsen, Gerald Metcalfe

Friedman-Abeles Photos

John Cypher, Barbara Barrie
Above: Jack Warden, Sandra Church

ZENDA

Book by Everett Freeman; Music, Vernon Duke; Lyrics, Lenny Adelson, Sid Kuller, Martin Charnin; Based on Anthony Hope's "The Prisoner of Zenda"; Producer, Edwin Lester; Dances and Musical Numbers Staged by Jack Cole; Scenery, Harry Horner; Costumes, Miles White; Lighting, Klaus Holm; Technical Director, Richard Rodda; Musical Direction, Pembroke Davenport; Arrangements and Orchestrations, Irwin Kostal; Dance Arrangements, Harper MacKay; Assistant Conductor, Irwin Webber; Production Manager, Tom Turner; Directed by George Schaefer. Opened Monday, August 5, 1963, at the Curran Theatre, San Francisco, and closed November 16, 1963, in the Pasadena Civic Auditorium.

CAST

Penelope	Susan Luckey
Judy	Virginia Justus
Sally	Gloria Mills
Celeste	Wanda Shannon
Diana	Jean Deeks
Gwynne	Barbara Andrews
Richard Rassendyl	Alfred Drake
Custom Officials	Rudy Vejar, Robert Avian
Newsboy	David Bean
Hawker	Eddie Gasper
Woman Tourist	Luce Ennis
Capt. Tarlenheim	Karl Redcoff
Rupert of Hentzau	Earl Hammond
King Rudolph V	Alfred Drake
Colonel Zapt	Frederic Worlock
Dr. Wesling	Truman Gaige
Josef	Eddie Gasper
Princess Flavia	Anne Rogers
Queen Mother Louise	Carmen Mathews
Gen. Michael Talchef	Jock Livington
Michael's Aides	Rudy Vejar, John Carver
Athena Constantine	Chita Rivera
Brazilian Attache	Marc Wilder
British Ambassador	Horace Guittard
Ambassador's Wife	Lynn Archer
Gobelik	Truman Gaige
Maria Madero	Joanne Horne
Italian Tenor	John Roberson
Madame Scarlatti	Gloria Enander
Premiere Danseur	Marc Wilder
German	Horace Guittard

DANCERS: Malanie Alexander, Millie Hamm, Odette Phillips, Brooke Robson, Wanda White, Heike Witting, Lorene Yarnell, Robert Avian, Robert Bakanic, David Bean, Terry De Mari, Eddie Gasper, James Senn, Michel Stuart.

SINGERS: Lynn Archer, Gloria Enander, Dorothy Emmerson, Luce Ennis, Stephanie Hill, Joanne Horne, John Carver, Phil Crummett, Larry Dean, William Gibson, Horace Guittard, Heber Jentzsch, Jack Martin, Evans Ray, John Roberson, Rudy Vejar.

UNDERSTUDIES: King Rudolph, Lawrence Brooks; Flavia, Luce Ennis; Athena, Jean Deeks; Louise, Lynn Archer; Zapt, Truman Gaige; Rupert, Karl Redcoff.

MUSICAL NUMBERS: "Bounce," "No More Love," "My Royal Majesty," "The Night Is Filled With Wonderful Sounds," "Alone At Night," "Now The World Begins Again," "Zenda," "A Whole Lot Of Happy," "Here and There" "A Royal Confession," "I Wonder What He Meant By That," "When Athena Dances," "Yesterday's Forgotten," "Let Her Not Be Beautiful," "Artists," "Born At Last," "No Ifs! No Ands! No Buts!," "Why Not?," "Command Performance," "Enchanting Girls," "Words, Words, Words!," Finale.

A Musical in two acts and twenty-one scenes. The action takes place in England, and in Zenda at the present time.

General Manager: Eleanor Pinkham
Press: Peggy Phillips, Thomas E. Earnfred
Stage Managers: Robert Merriman, Kenn Randall

Rothschild Photos

Top Right: Earl Hammond, Chita Rivera

Alfred Drake, and above with Anne Rogers

THREE CHEERS FOR THE TIRED BUSINESSMAN

Material by Jeff Harris, David Axelrod, Bruce Hart, Portia Nelson, Steven Vinaver, G. Wood, Herb Hartig, Lois Balk, Sam Pottle, Jay Thompson, Bill Penn, David Panich, Phil Springer; Directed by Bill Penn; Choreographer, Joyce Trisler; Designed by Boyd Dumrose; Costumes, Audre; Musical Supervision and Arrangements, Jay Thompson; Musical Director, Joe Clonick; Associate Producer, Barry Gordon; Production Associate, Kip Cohen; Production Assistants, Dennis Gibbs, James Dryden; Presented by Arthur Cantor and George Marienthal. Opened Thursday, December 26, 1963 at the Happy Medium Theater, Chicago, and still playing there May 31, 1964.

CAST

Joanne Beretta	Bob Shaver
Linda Harris	Bill Starr
Mary Jay	Matthew Tobin
Jack Metté	Ellen Travolta

Program

ACT I: Three Cheers For The Businessman, Personnel Interview, Mother's Day, Coffee Break, Sing Along, It Wouldn't Work, Lunch, Ballad to International Business Machine, Oldest Profession, First Day, Way of A Woman, Automation, The Patio Pretties Pageant.

ACT II: Top of The List, Death of The Traveling Salesman, Anniversary Dinner, What Became of Love, Monkey Business, Four Cheers For The Hell of It.

A Revue in two acts and twenty-one scenes.

Press: Arthur Cantor, Danny Newman
Stage Manager: Ken Solomon

Photos by David

Jack Metté, Linda Harris
Above: (Back) Jack Metté Mary Jay,
Joanne Beretta, Linda Harris, Bob Shaver
(Front) Bill Starr, Matthew Tobin,
Tom Williams, Ellen Travolta

Top: Jack Metté, Linda Harris, Matthew Tobin,
Joanne Beretta, Bill Starr, Mary Jay
Center: Ellen Travolta, Joanne Beretta

NEW YORK SHAKESPEARE FESTIVAL
Delacorte Theatre, Central Park, New York
June 13 through August 31, 1963
Produced by Joseph Papp

ANTONY AND CLEOPATRA

By William Shakespeare; Directed by Joseph Papp; Scenery and Lighting by Ming Cho Lee; Costumes by Theoni V. Aldredge; Music by David Amram; Dances arranged by Donald McKayle; Stage designed by Eldon Elder; Associate Producer, Bernard Gersten; Production Coordinator, Lathrop Robbins; Assistant to Mr. Papp, Esther Jackson; Hairstyling by Ronald DeMann.

CAST

Canidius	William H. Bassett
Taurus	Stan Dworkin
Cleopatra	Colleen Dewhurst
Mark Antony	Michael Higgins
Charmian	Bette Henritze
Alexas	Frank Shaw Stevens
Soothsayer	Robert Jackson
Enobarbus	Ramon Bieri
Iras	Ellen Holly
Scarus	George Hearn
Octavius Caesar	Michael Moriarty
Lepidus	Thomas Barbour
1st Messenger to Caesar	Herb Bernau
2nd Messenger to Caesar	Joe Allen Dorsey
Mardian	Clebert Ford
Maecenas	Albert Quinton
Agrippa	Mitchell Ryan
Pompey	Gerald E. McGonagill
Menas	Anthony Palmer
Octavia	Peggy Feury
Eros	Bill Gunn
Diomedes	Ray Stubbs
Old Soldier	Bert Conway
Egyptian	Maxwel Banks
Soldier	Leslie Sapiro
1st Watchman	Ken Hill
2nd Watchman	Allen Royce
Clown	Charles Durning

SOLDIERS AND ATTENDANTS: Les Carlson, John Robert Crawford, William Devane, Phillip H. Frey, Allan Frosch, David Hersey, Harry Kaiserlian, Colin Lee, Walter McGinn, Joseph Sullivan, William Wingate, Vera Cochran, Marguerite Davis, Margaret Heery, Connie Keyse.

FESTIVAL LINE SINGERS: Carole Demas, Alex Demas, Jonathan David Rosen, Paula Lani Rosen.

General Manager: Hilmar Sallee
Press: Merle Debuskey, Seymour Krawitz, Madi Ross
Stage Managers: Russell McGrath, Ron Bruncati, William Devane
Wardrobe Mistress: Florence Gabriel

Opened Thursday, June 13, 1963, and closed July 6, 1963. (21 performances)

Friedman-Abeles Photos

Colleen Dewhurst, and above with Michael Higgins

177

AS YOU LIKE IT

By William Shakespeare; Directed by Gerald
Freedman; Scenery and Lighting by Ming Cho
Lee; Costumes, Theoni V. Aldredge; Songs and
Music by John Morris; Choreography, Donald
McKayle; Associate Producer, Bernard Gersten;
Production Coordinator, Lathrop Robbins.

CAST

Orlando	Richard Jordan
Adam	Bert Conway
Oliver	Richard Benjamin
Dennis	Blaire Stauffer
Charles	Don Moore
Celia	Penny Fuller
Rosalind	Paula Prentiss
Touchstone	John Heffernan
Le Beau	Barry Bartle
Duke Frederick	Stan Dworkin
Duke Senior	Mitchell Ryan
Amiens	George Hearn
Forest Troubadour	Gerald Goodman
Foresters	Joe Dorsey, John Robert Crawford, David Hersey, William Wingate, Les Carlson
Lords, Guards	Colin Lee, Allan Frosch, Walter McGinn, Phillip H. Frey, Joseph Sullivan
Corin	Charles Durning
Silvius	Sam Waterston
Jacques	Frank Schofield
Audrey	K. C. Townsend
Sir Oliver Martext	John Robert Crawford
Phebe	Alix Elias
William	Jerry Zafer
Jack	Michael Moriarty
Dancers	Patricia Beatty, Harriet Clifford, Louanna Gardner, Carla Maxwell, Michael Podwal, Blaire Stauffer

General Manager: Hilmar Sallee
Press: Merle Debuskey, Seymour Krawitz,
Madi Ross
Stage Managers: John Fenn, Ron Bruncati
Wardrobe Mistress: Florence Gabriel
Opened Thursday, July 11, 1963, and closed
Saturday, August 3, 1963. (21 performances)

Friedman-Abeles Photos

Paula Prentiss, John Heffernan, Penny Fuller

178

**Top: Richard Jordan, Paula Prentiss,
Sam Waterston, Alix Elias**

THE WINTER'S TALE

By William Shakespeare; Directed by Gladys Vaughan; Scenery by Ming Cho Lee; Lighting, Martin Aronstein; Costumes by Theoni V. Aldredge; Music and Songs, David Amram; Dances by Mary Anthony; Associate Producer, Bernard Gersten; Production Coordinator, Lathrop Robbins.

CAST

Archidamus	Bill Gunn
Camillo	James Earl Jones
Polixines	Ramon Bieri
Leontes	Mitchell Ryan
Hermione	Salome Jens
Mamillius	DeWitt Nelson
Lady-in-Waiting	Connie Keyse
Emilia	Joan DeWeese
Lord and Court Officer	Bert Conway
Antigonus	John Ragin
Paulina	Bette Henritze
Gaoler	William Devane
Attendant to Mamillius	Bruce Edwards
Cleomenes	Anthony Palmer
Dion	Robert Jackson
Mariner	John Robert Crawford
Old Shepherd	John Heffernan
Clown	Charles Durning
Time	John Heffernan
Autolycus	Roscoe Lee Browne
Florizel	Michael Moriarty
Perdita	Dixie Carter
Dorcas	Mary Doyle
Mopsa	K. C. Townsend
Servant to Old Shepherd	William Devane
Attendant to Paulina	Herbert Foster

ATTENDANTS, LORDS, AND SHEPHERDS: Les Carlson, Harriet Clifford, Joe Allen Dorsey, Phillip H. Frey, Allan Frosch, David Hersey, Walter McGinn, Larry Sacharow, Fred Siretta, Joseph Sullivan.

General Manager: Hilmar Sallee
Press: Merle Debuskey, Seymour Krawitz, Madi Ross
Stage Managers: Russell McGrath, John Fenn, Ron Bruncati

Opened Thursday, August 8, 1963, and closed Saturday, August 31, 1963. (21 performances)

Friedman-Abeles Photos

Bette Henritze, John Heffernan, Mitchell Ryan, DeWitt Nelson, James Earl Jones, Ramon Bieri
Above: Mitchell Ryan, Salome Jens

Top: Mitchell Ryan, Bette Henritze, Michael Moriarty, Dixie Carter **179**

AMERICAN SHAKESPEARE FESTIVAL
Stratford, Connecticut
May 31 through September 15, 1963

KING LEAR

By William Shakespeare; Directed by Allen Fletcher; Scenery and Costumes by Will Steven Armstrong; Lighting by Tharon Musser; Music and Songs by Conrad Susa; Fights Staged by John Milligan; Helmets and Crowns by William Wallace Bellin.

CAST

Earl of Kent	Philip Bosco
Earl of Gloucester	Patrick Hines
Edmund	Douglas Watson
Ler, King of Britain	Morris Carnovsky
Goneril	Rosemary Murphy
Regan	Carrie Nye
Cordelia	Anne Draper
Duke of Albany	John Devlin
Duke of Cornwall	Tom Sawyer
Duke of Burgundy	Terence Scammell
King of France	Paxton Whitehead
Attendant to Gloucester	John Milligan
Edgar	James Ray
Oswald	Nicholas Martin
Attendant to Lear	Donald Gantry
Other Attendants to Lear	Miller Lide, Geddeth Smith, Richard Mathews, Harold Cherry
Fool	Lester Rawlins
Servant to Cornwall	Robert Benedict
Servants to Gloucester	Frank Converse, David Byrd
Messenger to Albany	Richard Mathews
Officer to Cordelia	Geddeth Smith
A Doctor	Harold Cherry
Officer to Goneril	Josef Sommer
A Herald	Miller Lide

KNIGHTS AND SERVANTS: Rob Bauer, Donald Briscoe, Richard Carroll, Todd Drexel, Jack Erthal, David Grimm, William Jacobson, Charles Lowry, James McDonald, Stuart Michaels, Gene Nye, Keith Perry, Leonard Raymond, Alex Rossman, Elaine Sulka, Norman Taffel, James Tripp.

Friedman-Abeles Photos

180

Morris Carnovsky, Patrick Hines
Top: Philip Bosco, Patrick Hines, Morris Carnovsky, Lester Rawlins

CAESAR AND CLEOPATRA

By George Bernard Shaw; Directed by Ellis Rabb; Scenery and Costumes by Lloyd Burlingame; Lighting, Gilbert V. Hamsley, Jr.; Music, Herman Chessid.

CAST

Julius Caesar	George Voskovec
Cleopatra	Carrie Nye
Ftatateeta	Rosemary Murphy
Charmian	Anne Draper
Iras	Patricia Peardon
Rufio	Philp Bosco
Pothinus	Patrick Hines
Ptolemy Dionysus	Nicholas Martin
Theodotus	David Byrd
Achillas	Frank Converse
Britannus	Richard Woods
Bel Affris	Miller Lide
Belzanor	Geddeth Smith
Major Domo	Terence Scammell
Music Master	Josef Sommer
Egyptian Courtier	Harold Cherry
Lucius Septimius	John Devlin
Wounded Soldier	Robert Benedict
Centurian	Donald Gantry
Sentinel	Rex Everhart
Apollodorus	James Ray
Apollodorus' Slave Girl	Betty Bendyk
1st Auxilliary Soldier	Richard Mathews
2nd Auxilliary Soldier	John Milligan

PRIESTESSES, PALACE WOMEN: Sally Amaru, Anne Gee, Claire Richard, Elaine Sulka, Anne Waldman.

EGYPTIAN SLAVES: Morris Alston, Donald Briscoe, Jack David, William Jackson, Stuart Michaels, Leonard Raymond, Norman Taffel, Dewey Amos.

APOLLODORUS' PORTERS: David Grimm, Don Hudson, Charles Lowry.

ROMAN SOLDIERS: Richard Carroll, Todd Drexel, John Erthal, William Jacobson, James McDonald, Keith Perry, Gene Nye, Alex Rossman, James Tripp.

Friedman-Abeles Photos

Carrie Nye, George Voskovec
Top: (L) James Ray, George Voskovec
Philip Bosco

181

COMEDY OF ERRORS

By William Shakespeare; Directed by Douglas Seale; Scenery and Costumes by Will Steven Armstrong; Lighting, Tharon Musser; Music by Herman Chessid; Choreography by Zenaide Trigg; Hats by Eve Shelley.

CAST

Solinus, Duke of Ephesus	Patrick Hines
Aegeon	Philip Bosco
Antipholus of Ephesus	Douglas Watson
Antipholus of Syracuse	Douglas Watson
Dromio of Ephesus	Rex Everhart
Dromio of Syracuse	Rex Everhart
1st Merchant	Richard Mathews
2nd Merchant	David Byrd
Balthazar	Josef Sommer
Angelo	Lester Rawlins
Doctor Pinch	Tom Sawyer
Sergeant	Miller Lide
Amelia	Betty Bendyk
Adriana	Carrie Nye
Luciana	Patricia Peardon
Luce	Anne Draper
A Courtesan	Rosemary Murphy
Servant to the Courtesan	Claire Richard
Militiamen	Donald Gantry, Terence Scammell
Harlequin	Richard Mathews
Columbine	Zenaide Trigg

Other Commedia Characters: Bob Bauer, Harold Cherry, Frank Converse, Nicholas Martin, Robert Benedict, Geddeth Smith, Paxton Whitehead

Gentleman in Blue	John Devlin
Servant in Green	John Milligan

TOWNSPEOPLE, NUNS, MILITIA, ETC: Sally Amaru, Donald Briscoe, Richard Carroll, Todd Drexel, Jack Erthal, Anne Gee, David Grimm, William Jacobson, Charles Lowry, James McDonald, Stuart Michaels, Gene Nye, Keith Perry, Leonard Raymond, Ann Rivers, Alex Rossman, Elaine Sulka, Norman Taffel, James Tripp.

Production Manager: Berenice Weiler
Press: Sol Jacobson, Lewis Harmon, Bob Larkin, Peggy Reddy, Carl Samrock
Stage Managers: David Bishop, John Seig, Wisner Washam

Rex Everhart, Douglas Watson, Carrie Nye
Top: Rex Everhart; Patrick Hines, Carrie Nye, Patricia Peardon; Rosemary Murphy

182

Friedman-Abeles Photos

HENRY V

By William Shakespeare; Directed by Douglas Seale; Scenery and Costumes by William Pitkin; Lighting by Tharon Musser; Music and Songs by Herman Chessid; Helmets and Crowns by Lohr Wilson.

CAST

Chorus	Tom Sawyer
King Henry V	James Ray
Duke of Gloucester	Robert Benedict
Duke of Bedford	Nicholas Martin
Duke of Exeter	John Devlin
Earl of Westmoreland	Frank Converse
Archbishop of Canterbury	Rex Everhart
Bishop of Ely	David Byrd
Earl of Cambridge	Josef Sommer
Lord Scroop	Terence Scammell
Sir Thomas Grey	Donald Gantry
Sir Thomas Erpingham	John Milligan
Captain Gower	Paxton Whitehead
Captain Fluellen	Lester Rawlins
Michael Williams	Rex Everhart
John Bates	Richard Mathews
Pistol	Philip Bosco
Nym	Harold Cherry
Bardolph	John Milligan
Boy	Rob Bauer
Charles VI of France	Patrick Hines
Lewis the Dauphin	Douglas Watson
Duke of Burgundy	Miller Lide
Duke of Orleans	Donald Gantry
Constable of France	David Byrd
Governor of Harfleur	Donald Gantry
Montjoy	Josef Sommer
French Ambassador	Geddeth Smith
A French Prisoner	Terence Scammell
Isabel, Queen of France	Betty Bendyk
Katharine	Patricia Peardon
Alice	Anne Draper
Mistress Quickly	Betty Bendyk

LADIES IN WAITING: Sally Amaru, Anne Gee, Claire Richard, Ann Rivers, Elaine Sulka.

LORDS, SOLDIERS, ETC: Donald Briscoe, Richard Carroll, Todd Drexel, Jack Erthal, David Grimm, William Jacobson, Charles Lowry, James McDonald, Stuart Michaels, Gene Nye, Keith Perry, Leonard Raymond, Alex Rossman, Norman Taffel, James Tripp.

Rosemary Murphy, Douglas Watson,
Nicholas Martin
p: Patricia Peardon, James Ray, Betty Bendyk

TROILUS AND CRESSIDA

By William Shakespeare; Directed by Michael Langham; Designed by Desmond Heeley; Music by Louis Applebaum; Fights arranged by Patrick Crean.

CAST

Prologue	Len Birman
Priam	Hugh Webster
Hecuba	Christine Bennett
Hector	John Colicos
Troilus	Peter Donat
Paris	James Douglas
Helenus	Joseph Shaw
Deiphobus	Edwin Stephenson
Cassandra	Kate Reid
Andromache	Amelia Hall
Aeneas	Donnelly Rhodes
Antenor	Nelson Phillips
Cressida	Martha Henry
Calchas	Joseph Shaw
Pandarus	William Hutt
Margarelon	Len Cariou
Alexander	Lewis Gordon
Servant to Troilus	Bob Nisbet
Servant to Paris	Ted Hodgeman
Agamemnon	Max Helpmann
Menelaus	Joseph Rutten
Ulysses	Douglas Rain
Nestor	William Needles
Diomedes	Len Birman
Achilles	Leo Ciceri
Ajax	Tony Van Bridge
Patroclus	Garrick Hagon
Thersites	Eric Christmas
Helen	Diana Maddox
Officer	Claude Bede

SOLDIERS, SERVANTS, MUSICIANS: David Britton, Al Kozlik, Joel Michaels, Louis Negin, Ken Pauli, Adrian Pecknold, Rick Quigley, Nicholas Simons, John Watts.

LADIES-IN-WAITING, SERVANTS, MUSICIANS: Bridget Blackwell, Norma Cartwright, Angela Fusco, Susan Learned, Claire Marshall, Kelly Ross.

Garrick Hagon, Eric Christmas, Leo Ciceri
Above: John Colicos, Leo Ciceri
Top: (L) Peter Donat, Martha Henry
(R) Douglas Rain, Peter Donat, Len Birman
Martha Henry

CYRANO DE BERGERAC

By Edmond Rostand; Translated by Brian Hooker; Adapted and Directed by Michael Langham; Designed by Tanya Moiseiwitsch and Desmond Heeley; Music by Louis Applebaum; Assistant to Mr. Langham, Fred Euringer; Fights arranged by Patrick Crean; Cadets' Song Staged by Alan Lund.

CAST

Porter	Mervyn Blake
Flower Girl	Claire Marshall
Citizen	Al Kozlik
Citizen's Son	Bob Nisbet
Pickpocket	Lewis Gordon
1st Musketeer	Len Birman
D'Artagnan	James Douglas
Cuigy	Max Helpmann
Brissaille	Claude Bede
Bellerose	Ken Pauli
First Fop	Jake Dengel
Second Fop	Garrick Hagon
Ligniere	Joseph Shaw
Christian De Neuvillette	Peter Donat
Ragueneau	Eric Christmas
Carbon De Castel-Jaloux	William Hutt
Roxane	Diana Maddox
Duenna to Roxane	Amelia Hall
Comte De Guiche	Leo Ciceri
Vicomte De Valvert	Donnelly Rhodes
Montfleury	William Needles
Jodelet	Hugh Webster
Cyrano de Bergerac	John Colicos
Lisa	Kate Reid
Journalist	Mervyn Blake
Capuchin Monk	Hugh Webster
Bertrandou	William Needles
Spanish Officer	Max Helpmann
Mother Marguerite	Christine Bennett
Sister Marthe	Kate Reid
Sister Claire	Amelia Hall

CADETS: Fred Euringer, Ted Hodgeman, Edwin Stephenson, Rick Quigley, Joseph Rutten, John Watts.

COOKS, ACTORS, NUNS, ETC: Moira Blackstock, Bridget Blackwell, David Britton, Len Cariou, Norma Cartwright, Clare Coulter, Angela Fusco, Rita Howell, Susan Learned, Joel Michaels, Louis Negin, Adrian Pecknold, Nelson Phillips, Kelly Ross, Nicholas Simons.

CHILDREN: Gleave Harris, Murray Scott, Donald Shipley.

STAGE MUSICIANS: Robert Comber, Donald Hyder, Eli Kassner, William Kuinka, Ronald Laurie.

Peter Smith Photos

William Hutt, John Colicos
Above: John Colicos, Donnelly Rhodes
op: Diana Maddox, John Colicos, Peter Donat

THE MIKADO

By W. S. Gilbert and Arthur Sullivan; Directed by Norman Campbell; Designed by Brian Jackson; Musical Director, Louis Applebaum; Musical Numbers Staged by Alan Lund.

CAST

Nanki-Poo	Andrew Downie
Pish-Tush	Arthur Sclater
Pooh-Bah	Howell Glynne
Koko	Eric House
Yum-Yum	Heather Thomson
Pitti-Sing	Kathryn Newman
Peep-Bo	Anne Linden
Katisha	Irene Byatt
The Mikado	Maurice Brown

SCHOOLGIRLS, NOBLES, GUARDS: Arthur Apy, Amie Apy, Vicki Berniolles, Jean Bonhomme, Garnet Brooks, Peter Brown, Robert Carley, Mary Carr, John Harcourt, Benita James, Leslie Mackey, Elizabeth Mawson, Howard Mawson, Sharon Meckling, Helen Murray, Joanna Myahl, Murray Olson, Donald Saunders, Barbara Strathdee.

Stage Managers: Mark Furness, Thom Trethewey

THE COMEDY OF ERRORS

By William Shakespeare; Directed by Jean Gascon; Designed by Robert Prevost and Mark Negin; Music by Gabriel Charpentier.

CAST

Solinus	William Needles
Aegeon	Tony van Bridge
Antipholus of Ephesus	James Douglas
Antipholus of Syracuse	Peter Donat
Dromio of Ephesus	Eric Christmas
Dromio of Syracuse	Douglas Rain
Balthazar	Nelson Phillips
Angelo	Mervyn Blake
First Merchant	Joseph Shaw
Second Merchant	Leo Ciceri
Pinch	Hugh Webster
Officer	Nicholas Simons
Adriana	Kate Reid
Luciana	Martha Henry
Nell	Amelia Hall
A Courtezan	Rita Howell
Aemilia	Christine Bennett
Novices	Claire Marshall, Norma Cartwright

PUNCHINELLOS: Jake Dengel, Lewis Gordon, Ted Hodgeman, Adrian Pecknold, Donnelly Rhodes.

MEMBERS OF COURT AND ATTENDANTS: Len Cariou, Al Kozlik, Joel Michaels, Louis Negin, Ken Pauli, John Watts.

SOLDIERS: David Britton, Rick Quigley, Edwin Stephenson.

MUSICIANS: Robert Comber, William Kuinka, Eli Kassner, Ronald Laurie.

Peter Smith Photos

Tony Van Bridge, Christine Bennett, Peter Donat, Douglas Rain

186

Douglas Rain, Rita Howell, Peter Donat
Above: Irene Byatt, Eric House
in "The Mikado"

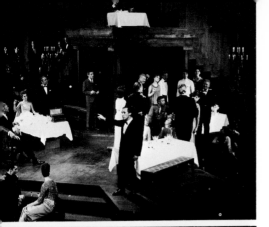

TIMON OF ATHENS

By William Shakespeare; Directed by Michael Langham; Designed by Brian Jackson; Music by Duke Ellington; Assistant to Mr. Langham, Fred Euringer; Dance Staged by Alan Lund.

CAST

A Poet	Joseph Shaw
A Painter	Len Birman
A Jeweller	Al Kozlik
A Merchant	Joseph Rutten
Flavius	Hugh Webster
Sempronius	Tony van Bridge
An Athenian	Adrian Pecknold
Ventidius	Ted Hodgeman
Flaminius	Lewis Gordon
Servilius	Len Cariou
Timon	John Colicos
Lucullus	Leo Ciceri
Lucius	Mervyn Blake
Caphis	Garrick Hagon
Apemantus	Douglas Rain
Alcibiades	William Hutt
Alcibiades' Officer	Donnelly Rhodes
Senators	Max Helpmann, Claude Bede, Nicholas Simons
Cupid	Fred Euringer
Timandra	Rita Howell
Phrynia	Martha Henry
Philotus	Ken Pauli
Titus	William Webster
Hortensius	David Britton
Servant to Isidore	Jake Dengel
Servant to Varro	Louis Negin
Baths Attendants	John Watts, Edwin Stephenson

GUARDS, SERVANTS, ATTENDANTS: Moira Blackstock, Bridget Blackwell, David Britton, Norma Cartwright, Helen Conway-Marmo, Clare Coulter, Jake Dengel, Angela Fusco, Gleave Harris, Susan Learned, Claire Marshall, Chela Matthison, Joel Michaels, Louis Negin, Bob Nisbet, Rick Quigley, Kelley Ross, Murray Scott, Sylvia Shaffer, Donald Shipley.

MUSICIANS: Clarence Brodhagen, Robert Comber, Paul Cross, Eli Kassner, William Kuinka, Horst Mueller.

Press: Jack Karr
Stage Managers: Jack Hutt, Thomas Bohdanetzky, Bill Kearns, Ronald Pollock, William Webster

Peter Smith Photos

Left: John Colicos, William Hutt

Douglas Rain, John Colicos

John Colicos, Mervyn Blake, Leo Ciceri, Tony Van Bridge

187

THE MINNESOTA THEATRE COMPANY
Minneapolis, Minn.
May 7 through September 22, 1963

TYRONE GUTHRIE THEATRE

Opened Tuesday, May 7, 1963.
The Minnesota Theatre Co. presents repertory:

HAMLET

By William Shakespeare; Directed by Tyr Guthrie; Designed by Tanya Moiseiwitsch; Msic, Herbert Pilhofer; Sound effects, Frank Andriello.

CAST

Francisco	William Po
Barnardo	Gordon Br
Horatio	Graham Bro
Marcellus	Paul Ballant
Ghost	Ken P
Claudius	Lee Richard
Gertrude	Jessica Ta
Cornelius	Charles C
Voltimand	John Le
Laertes	Nicolas Co
Polonius	Robert Past
Hamlet	George Grizza
Ophelia	Zoe Cald
Reynaldo	Clayton Corz
Rosencrantz	Alfred R
Guildenstern	Michael L
Player King	John Crom
Player Queen	Ruth Ne
Lucianus	John G
Prologue	James Linebe
Musicians	Katherine Emery, Carol Ems
Osric	Clayton Corz
Fortinbras	Claude Wool
Captain	William Po
Sailor	Charles C
1st Grave Digger	Ed Pr
2nd Grave Digger	Ken I
Priest	John Le

COURT LADIES: Helen Backlin, Judith D Janet MacLachlan, Joan van Ark, Selma F kins, Marion Miska.
OFFICERS: Donald Forsberg, Thomas Nyr Franklin Peters, Ronald Rogosheske, Ken Schuman, Charles Stanley, Hans Von Me
SAILORS: Hans Von Mende, Ronald Rogoshe
FOOTMEN: Edmond Poshek, Howard Mc

Presented in three parts, the action t place at Elsinore in Denmark.

Opened Wednesday, May 8, 1963.

THE MISER

By Moliere; Translated by George Grav Directed by Douglas Campbell; Designed Tanya Moiseiwitsch; Music, Paul Fetler.

CAST

Harpagon	Hume Cr
La Fleche	Paul Ballar
Jacques	Ed P
Prop Men	Alfred Rossi, William Po Graham B
Prop Girls	Judith Doty, Janet MacLac Carol Em
Valere	Claude Wool
Elise	Rita
Cleante	Clayton Cor
Mariane	Joan van
Frosine	Zoe Cald
Simon	Ken
Dame Claude	Judith
Brindavoine	Alfred
La Merluche	William P
Commissioner	Robert Pas
Clerk	George Griz
Lawyers	Charles Cioffi, Michael L John Going, James Linebe
Anselme	John Crom
Others	Gordon Bryars, John L

Presented in two parts. The action place in the house, garden, and mind Monsieur Harpagon.

Zoe Caldwell, Hume Cronyn in "The Miser"
Top: George Grizzard, Jessica Tandy in "Hamlet"

Opened Tuesday, June 18, 1963.

THE THREE SISTERS

By Anton Chekhov; Translated by Tyrone
Guthrie, and Leonid Kipnis; Directed by Tyrone Guthrie; Designed by Tanya Moiseiwitsch;
Musical Direction, Herbert Pilhofer; Sound effects, KUOM.

CAST

Olga	Jessica Tandy
Masha	Rita Gam
Irina	Judith Doty
Andrey	Charles Cioffi
Anfisa	Ruth Nelson
Ferapont	Ed Preble
Kulygin	Clayton Corzatte
Natasha	Zoe Caldwell
Col. Vershinin	Robert Pastene
Dr. Tchebutykin	Hume Cronyn
Capt. Solyony	George Grizzard
Lt. Tusenbach	Claude Woolman
Lt. Fedotik	Lee Richardson
Lt. Roday	Nicolas Coster
Maid	Carol Emshoff
Musicians	Katherine Emery, Hazel Lewin
Orderlies	Michael Levin, Graham Brown, James Lineberger, Alfred Rossi

Presented in four parts. The action takes
place at the Prozoroff house in a provincial
town in Russia.

Opened Tuesday, July 16, 1963.

DEATH OF A SALESMAN

By Arthur Miller; Directed by Douglas Campbell; Setting Designed by Randy Echols; Costumes, Carolyn Parker.

CAST

Willy	Hume Cronyn
Linda	Jessica Tandy
Happy	Nicolas Coster
Biff	Lee Richardson
Bernard	Ken Ruta
The Woman	Helen Backlin
Charley	Paul Ballantyne
Ben	John Cromwell
Howard	Alfred Rossi
Jenny	Janet MacLachlin
Stanley	Michael Levin
Miss Forsythe	Judith Doty
Letta	Joan van Ark
Switchboard Operator	Carol Emshoff
Waiter	John Lewin

Presented in two parts. The action takes
place in the house and mind of Willy Loman
during the past and present.

Press: Mary Jolliffe, Cynthia Maughan,
Kay Fliehr
Stage Managers: Rex Partington, Edward Call,
Gordon Smith

Nicolas Coster, Hume Cronyn
in "Death Of A Salesman"
Top: Charles Cioffi, Hume Cronyn, Ellen Geer,
Nicolas Coster, Lee Richardson
in "The Three Sisters"

189

SULLIVAN STREET PLAYHOUSE
Opened Tuesday, May 3, 1960.°
Lore Noto presents:

THE FANTASTICKS

Book and Lyrics by Tom Jones; Music, Harvey Schmidt; Suggested by the Play "Les Romantiques" by Edmond Rostand; Directed by Word Baker; Musical Direction and Arrangements, Julian Stein; Designed by Ed Wittstein; Associate Producers, Sheldon Baron, Dorothy Olim, Robert Alan Gold; Assistant to the Producer, Sherman Wayne.

CAST

The Narrator	John Cunningham
The Girl	Alice Cannon†1
The Boy	Ty McConnell†2
The Boy's Father	Charles Blackburn†3
The Girl's Father	John High†4
The Actor	Jay Hampton†5
The Man Who Dies	Don Pomes†6
The Mute	James Cook
The Handyman	Richard Drake
At The Piano	Glen Clugston†7
At The Harp	Henry Clay Fanelli

UNDERSTUDIES: The Boy, Richard Rothbard; The Girl, Sybil Lamb; The Narrator, George Ogee.

MUSICAL NUMBERS: Overture, "Try To Remember," "Much More," "Metaphor," "Never Say No," "It Depends On What You Pay," "Soon It's Gonna Rain," "Rape Ballet," "Happy Ending," "This Plum Is Too Ripe," "I Can See It," "Plant A Radish," "Round and Round," "They Were You," Finale.

A Musical in two acts.

Press: Harvey Sabinson, David Powers
Stage Managers: Geoffry Brown, Edward Garrabrandt, Ronald Link

° Still playing May 31, 1964.
(1703 performances)
For original production, see THEATRE WORLD, Vol. 16.

† Succeeded by: 1. Eileen Fulton, Royce Lenelle, 2. Jack Blackton, 3. George Riddle, 4. David Vaughan, Maurice Edwards, 5. Lowry Miller, 6. Robert A. Worms, 7. Nancy Ford.

Sam Siegel Photo

Top: James Cook, Keith Charles, Maurice Edwards, Jack Blackton, George Riddle, Robert A. Worms, Alice Cannon, Jay Hampton in "The Fantasticks"

ST. MARKS PLAYHOUSE
Opened Thursday, May 4, 1961.°
Sidney Bernstein, George Edgar, and Andre Gregory by arrangement with Geraldine Lust present:

THE BLACKS

By Jean Genet; Directed by Gene Frankel; Translated by Bernard Frechtman; Sets, Kim E. Swados; Lighting, Lee Watson; Costumes and Masks, Patricia Zipprodt; Movement, Talley Beatty; Music Supervised by Charles Gross; Production Associate, Alfred Manacher; Technical Assistant, Ivan Young.

CAST

Archibald Wellington	Louis Gossett†1
Deodatus Village	Lincoln Kilpatrick†2
Adelaide Bobo	Vinie Burrows†3
Edgar Alas Newport News	Morris Erby†4
Augusta Snow	Louise Stubbs
Felicity Trollop Pardon	Esther Rolle†5
Stephanie Virtue Diop	Thelma Oliver†6
Diouf	Clebert Ford†7
Missionary	Carl Byrd†8
Judge	Peter DeAnda†9
Governor	Moses Gunn†10
Queen	Lynn Hamilton†11
Valet	Harold Scott†12
Drummer	Marc Frasier†13

UNDERSTUDIES: Virtue, Snow, Bobo, Lea Scott; Governor, Judge, Missionary, Anthony Howard; Valet, Newport, Ivan Young; Queen, Loretta Pauker.

A Drama in two acts.

Press: Max Eisen
Stage Manager: Irving Vincent

°Still playing May 31, 1964. (1280 performances) For original production, see THEATRE WORLD, Vol. 18.

†Succeeded by: 1. Morris Erby, 2. Bobby Dean Hooks, Nick Smith, 3. Helen Martin, 4. Nathan George, 5. Dietrah Thomas, 6. Marlene Warfield, 7. Philip Lindsay, 8. Nick Smith, Bobby Dean Hooks, 9. Adolph Caesar, 10. Jay J. Riley, 11. Loretta Pauker, 12. Charles Gordone, 13. Charles Campbell.

Top: Marlene Warfield, Billy Dee Williams, Louise Stubbs in "The Blacks"

CASINO-EAST THEATRE

Opened Tuesday, March 6, 1962.*
Michael P. Iannucci presents:

THIS WAS BURLESQUE

A Musical Satire based on Ann Corio's Re-
collections as told to Joe DiMona and Suggested
by Eddie Jaffe; Entire Production Supervised
and Directed by Ann Corio; Choreography,
Paul Morokoff; Assistant to the Producer, E. C.
Oberg; Musical Conductor, Nick Francis.

CAST

Ann Corio

Steve Mills	Dexter Maitland
Harry Conley	Buddy Bryant
Mac Dennison	Pepper Powell
Reni Cooper	Penny Powers

THE CASINO CUTIES: Deanna Dunsmore,
Jan LaSalle, Junelee Graham, Reni Cooper,
Cathy Schopp, Bonnie Walker, Maria Bradley,
Gerri Marek, Nicole Jaffe, Trinka Morgan.

Program

ACT I: Overture, Prologue, Ann Corio, Hello
New York, The Carpenter, Ecdysiast, The
Detective Scene, Hotel De France, Danee De
L'Orient, The Cleopatra Scene, Penny Powers,
Les Poules, Jan LaSalle, The Courtroom Scene,
Feature Attraction, Finale, Candy Butcher.

ACT II: Powder My Back, Dodger Scene,
Penny Powers, Sutton Place, Twist and Shimmy,
Hall of Fame, Crazy House, Finale.

Company Manager: Clifford Hayman
Press: Lenny Traube, Eddie Jaffe
Stage Manager: Phil King

*Still playing May 31, 1964. (1160 performances)

Daniel Grossi Photo

MARTINIQUE THEATRE

Opened Thursday, March 7, 1963.*
Theodore Mann and Claude Giroux present:

SIX CHARACTERS IN SEARCH OF AN AUTHOR

By Luigi Pirandello; Translation by Paul
Avila Mayer; Directed by William Ball; Sets
and Costumes, Robert Darling; Lighting, Jules
Fisher; Technical Director, William H. Batchelder; Production Coordinator, Sylvia Price.

ACTING COMPANY

Director	Michael O'Sullivan[1]
Anne	Anne Lynn[2]
Al	Alfred Spindelman
Patsy	Patricia Hamilton
David	David Margulies
Paul	Paul Shenar
Herse	David Hersey
Higgins	John Higgins
Jan	Jan Moerel
Marg	Margery Shaw
Walt	Walter Brown

Six Characters

Step-daughter	Jacqueline Brookes[3]
Father	Richard A. Dysart[4]
Mother	Joan Croydon
Son	James Valentine[5]
Young Boy	Gregg Weir[6]
Young Girl	Diana Visco
Madame Pace	Angela Wood[7]

A Drama in two acts.

Press: Chester Fox
Stage Manager: Mark D. Healy

*Still playing May 31, 1964. (515 performances)
For original cast, see THEATRE WORLD,
Vol. 19.

[†]Succeeded by: 1. Jack Dodson, 2. Acting
Company: James Barnhill, Jean David, Diana
Muldaur, Paul Weidner, George McGrath,
Arthur Harris Miller, Viktor Allen, Carla
Shearer, Walter Allen, Ed McCloskey, 3.
Barbara Colby, 4. Daniel Keyes, 5. Paul
Shenar, 6. Philip Visco, 7. Judy Frank.

Bert Andrews Photo

Steve Mills, Ann Corio
in "This Was Burlesque"

"Six Characters In Search Of An Author"

191

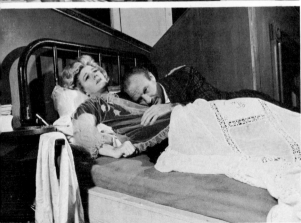

Opened Monday, April 15, 1963.°
Richard York presents:

THE BOYS FROM SYRACUSE

Book by George Abbott; Based on "The Comedy of Errors" by William Shakespeare; Music, Richard Rodgers; Lyrics, Lorenz Hart; Staged by Christopher Hewett; Choreography and Musical Numbers Staged by Bob Herget; Costumes, Guy Kent; Settings, Herbert Senn, Helen Pond; Orchestrations, Larry Wilcox; Ballet Music, Peter Matz; Musical and Choral Direction, Rene Wiegert.

CAST

Sergeant	Gary Oakes†1
Duke	Fred Kimbrough
Aegeon	Matthew Tobin†2
Antipholus of Ephesus	Clifford David†3
Dromio of Ephesus	Rudy Tronto†4
Tailor	James Pompeii†5
Antipholus of Syracuse	Stuart Damon†6
Dromio of Syracuse	Danny Carroll†7
Merchant	Richard Colacino†8
Apprentice	Jeane Deeks†9
Angelo	Richard Nieves
Corporal	Dom Salinaro
Luce	Karen Morrow†10
Adriana	Ellen Hanley†11
Luciana	Julienne Marie†12
Maids	Jeane Deeks†9, Betsy Hepburn, Svetlana McLee†13
Sorcerer	Matthew Tobin†2
Courtesan	Cathryn Damon†14
Fatima	Zebra Nevins
Courtesans	Violetta Landek, Charlene Carter
Merchant of Ephesus	James Pompeii
Galatea	Violetta Landek
Pygmalian	Richard Nieves
Amazons	Charlene Carter, Svetlana McLee†13, Jeane Deeks†9
Emilia	Betsy Hepburn

MUSICAL NUMBERS: "I Had Twins," "Dear Old Syracuse," "What Can You Do With A Man?," "Falling In Love With Love," "The Shortest Day of The Year," "This Can't Be Love," "Ladies Choice," "Ladies of The Evening," "He and She," "You Have Cast Your Shadow On The Sea," "Come With Me," "Big Brother," "Sing For Your Supper," "Oh, Diogenes," Finale.

A Musical Comedy in two acts and eleven scenes. The action takes place in Ephesus.

General Manager: Richard Horner Associates
Press: Bob Ullman
Stage Managers: Murray Gitlin, Richard Lyle
°Still playing May 31, 1964. (469 performances) For original cast, see THEATRE WORLD, Vol. 19.
†Succeeded by: 1. Eric Barnes, J. A. Boni, 2. Emory Bass, 3. Jay Stuart, 4. Angelo Mango, 5. Marc Scott, 6. Gary Oakes, Gene Bua, 7. Rudy Tronto, 8. Bob Scherkenback, 9. Isabelle Farrell, Mary Ann Niles, 10. Jane A. Johnston, 11. Karen Shepard, Luce Ennis, 12. Marie Santell, 13. Myrna Aaron, 14. Dorothy Frank, Ann Hodges.

Henry Grossman Photo
Top: Friedman-Abeles Photo

Opened Thursday, June 13, 1963.°
Judith Rutherford Marechal presents:

CAGES

By Lewis John Carlino; Directed by Howard Da Silva; Designed by Robin Wagner; Costume Supervision by Patricia Quinn Stuart; Music Composed by Al Cohn; Performed by Marty Lorin; Assistant to the Producer, Aldo Santoni.

CAST

Shelley Winters †1   Jack Warden†2

PROGRAM

Two one-act plays, "Snowangel" and "Epiphany," with two characters in each.
Press: Harvey Sabinson, David Powers
Stage Manager: Charles Maryan

°Closed Sunday, November 17, 1963. (176 performances)
†Succeeded by: 1. Mercedes McCambridge, 2. Michael Lombard, Morgan Sterne

Jim Marshall Photo

Shelley Winters, Jack Warden in "Cages"
Top: Karen Shepard, Jay Stuart
Center: Angelo Mango, Jane A. Johnston in "The Boys From Syracuse"

JAN HUS PLAYHOUSE

Opened Tuesday, June 4, 1963.*
Jeff Britton presents:

THE AMERICAN SAVOYARDS

In Gilbert and Sullivan Repertory; Staged and Directed by Dorothy Raedler; Music Directed by Ronald Bush; Settings by Pat Belew; Lighting, George Wojtasik; Costume Coordinator, Shelia Barry; At the Organ, Ronald Bush; At the Piano, Judith Somogi.

"The Gondoliers"

CAST

The Duke of Plaza-Toro	James Wilson
Luiz	James Spann
Don Alhambra Del Bolero	John Bridson
Marco Palmieri	Theodore Morrill
Giuseppe Palmieri	Sean Barker
Antonio	James Dowaliby
Francesco	Anthony Safina
Giorgio	Andrew Dirga
Annibale	Raymond Papay
Duchess of Plaza-Toro	Beverley Evans
Casilda	Ann Collins
Gianetta	Mary Ann Staffa
Tessa	Elizabeth McCarthy
Fiametta	Mary Manchester
Vittoria	Judith Massee
Giulia	Pat Hall
Inez	Shirley Perkins
Cachucha Dancers	Helen Andreu, Al Cohen

GONDOLIERS, CONTADINE, COURTIERS: Helene Andreu, Al Cohen, Andrew Dirga, James Dowaliby, Bob Fry, Pat Hall, Raymond Leiter, Mary Manchester, Judith Massee, Shirley Perkins, Raymond Papay, Naomi Robin, Anthony Safina.

"Patience"

CAST

Colonel Calverley	John Bridson
Major Murgatroyd	James Spann
Lt. The Duke of Dunstable	Theodore Morrill
Reginald Bunthorne	James Wilson
Archibald Grosvenor	Sean Barker
Mr. Bunthorne's Solicitor	Arthur Weiss
Lady Angela	Elizabeth McCarthy
Lady Saphir	Mary Manchester
Lady Ella	Ann Collins
Lady Jane	Beverley Evans
Patience	Mary Ann Staffa

MAIDENS AND OFFICERS: Helene Andreu, Al Cohen, Andrew Dirga, James Dowaliby, Bob Fry, Pat Hall, Raymond Leiter, Judith Massee, Shirley Perkins, Raymond Papay, Naomi Robin, Anthony Safina.

Alix Jeffry Photos

"The Mikado"

CAST

The Mikado	John Bridson
Nanki-Poo	Theodore Morrill
Ko-Ko	James Wilson
Pooh-Bah	Sean Barker
Pish-Tush	Andrew Dirga
Yum-Yum	Mary Ann Staffa
Pitti-Sing	Elizabeth McCarthy
Peep-Bo	Helene Andreu
Katisha	Beverly Evans

SCHOOL GIRLS AND NOBLES: Al Cohen, Ann Collins, James Dowaliby, Bob Fry, Pat Hall, Raymond Leiter, Mary Manchester, Elizabeth McCarthy, Judith Massee, Shirley Perkins, Raymond Papay, Naomi Robin, Anthony Safina, James Spann.

"The Pirates Of Penzance"

CAST

Major-General Stanley	James Wilson
The Pirate King	John Bridson
Samuel	James Spann
Frederick	Theodore Morrill
Sergeant of Police	Sean Barker
Mabel	Mary Ann Staffa
Edith	Ann Collins
Kate	Elizabeth McCarthy
Isabel	Mary Manchester
Ruth	Beverly Evans

PIRATES, POLICE, AND DAUGHTERS: Helene Andreu, Al Cohen, Ann Collins, Andrew Dirga, James Dowaliby, Bob Fry, Pat Hall, Raymond Leiter, Mary Manchester, Elizabeth McCarthy, Judith Massee, Shirley Perkins, Raymond Papay, Naomi Robin, Anthony Safina.

General Manager: Jeff Britton
Press: David Lipsky, Fred Weterick
Stage Manager: George Wojtasik

*Closed Sunday, September 1, 1963.
(112 performances)

Ginny Payne Photo

Theodore Morrill, Mary Ann Staffa,
James Wilson in "Ruddigore"

Top: Helene Andreu, Mary Ann Staffa,
Elizabeth McCarthy in "The Mikado"
Center: Mary Ann Staffa, Theodore Morrill,
John Bridson, Sean Barker, Elizabeth McCarthy
in "The Gondoliers"

GATE THEATRE

Opened Wednesday, June 5, 1963.°
The M F Company presents:

CHIAROSCURO

By Robert Gentile; Directed by Burt Lane; Scenery, Lighting, and Costumes by Fred Sammut; Technician, James N. Clark.

"Kitty, I Hardly Knew You"

He	Robert Gentile
She	Colleen Farrington

"The Judges"

The Boss	Jerry Parente
The Professionalist	George Reinholt
The Jury	Colleen Farrington
The Little Guy	Robert Gentile
The Judge	Lou Ciulla

"Maggie French Understands"

Maggie	Peggy Moore
Jenny	Colleen Farrington
Joe	Robert Gentile

The action of all three plays takes place here and now.

Press: Bernard and Avivah Simon
Stage Manager: Lou Ciulla

°Closed Saturday, June 8, 1963.
(5 performances)

Avery Willard Photo

ONE SHERIDAN SQUARE

Opened Thursday, June 6, 1963.°
Tanya Chasman and E. A. Gilbert present:

THE WORLD OF KURT WEILL IN SONG

Written and Directed by Will Holt; Featuring the Music of Kurt Weill; Lighting, John Morris; At the Piano, Abraham Stokman; Translations by Marc Blitzstein and Will Holt.

CAST

Martha Schlamme	Will Holt†

Press: Dorothy Ross
Stage Manager: Jeff Snider

° Closed Sunday, October 20, 1963.
(228 performances) Reopened with original cast Tuesday, May 12, 1964, at Jan Hus House with original cast, and still playing May 31, 1964.
† Succeeded by Scott Merrill.

WRITERS STAGE THEATRE

Opened Tuesday, June 18, 1963.°
Richard Everett Upton Productions, Inc., in association with Susan Eden and Tom Eyen present:

TOUR DE FOUR

Conceived and Directed by Tom Eyen; Musical Direction by Natalie Charlson; Costumes, Edward Charles; Lighting, Gene Tunezi; Associate Musical Director, Jim Hix, Jr.

CAST

Lyle O'Hara	Carol Fox
Paul Blake	Carl Crow

PROGRAM

ACT I: Tour De Four, Letters, Trio Con Brio, Cold Turkey, Bus Stop, Multi-colored Bush, This Time Next Year, D. and D. Rag, What I Want To Be, The Test, Cooperation, Fallout Shelter, Cleaning Man, Ode To A Scrapbook, Call of The Wild, That's Why.

ACT II: Whatever Happened, That Certain Look, Small Town Girl, You Came From Outer Space, Point Number, Baby John, Rapid Reading Rachel, Six O'Clock, 1600 Pennsylvania Avenue, Cuckoo Song, Good Ole Days, Theatres, Hollywood Folk Song, Beach Scene, You Have, Lyle's Wedding, Tour De Four.

Company Manager: Robert Thatcher
Press: Howard Atlee, Michael Sean O'Shea, Reuben Rabinovitch
Stage Manager: Robert Trenour

°Closed Sunday, June 30, 1963.
(16 performances)

Will Holt, Martha Schlamme
in "The World Of Kurt Weill In Song"

Colleen Farrington, Robert Gentile
in "Chiaroscuro"

Carl Crow, Carol Fox, Paul Blake
in "Tour De Four"

SHERIDAN SQUARE PLAYHOUSE

Opened Tuesday, July 9, 1963.*
The Greater New York Chapter of ANTA presents the Cheryl Crawford Production of:

BRECHT ON BRECHT

Arranged and Translated by George Tabori; Directed by Gene Frankel; Piano Accompaniment by Jane White; Assistant to the Producer, Richard Chandler.

CAST

Roscoe Lee Browne   Kathleen Murray
Anthony Costello   Dolores Sutton
Micki Grant   Joseph Warren

PROGRAM

Part I: Life: On Lighting, The Eternal Student, Written On The Wall, Conversations In Exile. Part II: The Theatre: On Casting, Advice To Actors, The Lion, On Critics, The Barbara Song, The Playwright's Song, The Old Hat, The Jewish Wife, Envoi.

General Manager: Joseph Beruh
Company Manager: Mike Weinberg
Press: Howard Atlee, Michael Sean O'Shea
Stage Manager: Quinton Raines.
*Closed August 18, 1963. (55 performances)
The original version was presented at the Theatre DeLys on November 14, 1961, and closed January 6, 1963, after 424 performances. See THEATRE WORLD, Vol. 17.

Alix Jeffry Photo

Joseph Warren, Anthony Costello, Dolores Sutton, Kathleen Murray in "Brecht On Brecht"

SHOWBOAT THEATRE

Opened Wednesday, August 28, 1963.*
Showboat Affiliates present:

THE PICTURE OF DORIAN GRAY

Adapted and Directed by Andy Milligan; Settings, Lighting, and Costumes by Gerald Jackson; Portrait by Frank Thompson.

CAST

Lord Henry Wotton................Jay Robinson
Basil Hallward................Madison Arnold
Parker................David Cole
Dorian Gray................T. J. Escott
Lord Fermor................Ira Rubin
Lady Wotton................Ricki Olshan
Sibyl Vane................Trisha Mortimer
Mrs. Vane................Fredi Dundee
James Vane................Ben Greer
Waiter................Roy Wilson
Victor................Carl Hoyer
Alan Campbell................Gerald Rome
Lady Narborough................Veronica Radburn
Adrian Singleton................Mike J. McGovern
Cockney Prostitute................Jeana Franks
Gladys, Duchess of Monmouth................Barbara Caruso

A Drama in two acts and fourteen scenes. The action takes place in London.
Press: Chester Fox, Max Karper
Stage Manager: Peter Rogan
*Closed Thursday, September 12, 1963. (23 performances)

Conrad Ward Photo

T. J. Escott, Ricki Olshan, Jay Robinson in "The Picture Of Dorian Gray"

JUDSON HALL

Opened Tuesday, September 10, 1963.*
Norman Seaman in association with Richard Roffman presents:

FIVE QUEENS

Conceived and Directed by Sala Staw; Translation of Racine, and adaptations of Schiller and Euripides by Sala Staw, with excerpts from Shakespeare; Costumes by Harry Phillips; Lighting, Liz Stearns; Production Assistants, Joy Seaman, Jean Flores.

CAST

Sala Staw
Assisted by Daniel Elliot
as the Troubadour

PART I: Lady Macbeth; PART II: Elizabeth of England, Mary of Scotland; PART III: Andromache, Phaedra.

Company Manager: Esther Prince
Press: Richard Falk
Stage Manager: Ira Zuckerman
*Closed Sunday, September 15, 1963. (8 performances)

Alix Jeffry Photo

Sala Staw in "Five Queens"

SHERIDAN SQUARE PLAYHOUSE

Opened Wednesday, September 11, 1963.
The New Playwrights Company presents:

A TIME OF THE KEY

By Milton Erskine; Directed by Gigi Cascio;
Sets and Lighting by James A. Taylor; Technical
Director, David Whitemore; Pottery by Ellen
King.

CAST

Rachel Clews............................Joyce Davis
Walter Barrett.....................Stephen Pearlman
F. S. Key................................Joe Davies
Angelo Nessa.......................Martin Priest
Dave Sweeney......................Brendan Fay
T. J. Hudson.........................Allan Louw
Dr. Brauer...........................Henry Oliver

A Drama in two acts and seven scenes. The
action takes place in New York City some years
from now.

Company Manager: Al Isaac
Press: Max Eisen
°Closed Sunday, September 15, 1963.
(7 performances)

Alix Jeffry Photo

Henry Oliver, Brendan Fay, Stephen Pearlman
Allan Louw in "A Time Of The Key"

SECOND CITY AT SQUARE EAST

Opened Thursday, September 12, 1963.°
Bernard Sahlins and Paul Sills present:

WHEN THE OWL SCREAMS

Scenes and Dialogue Created by the Company; Music Composed and Played by Tom
O'Horgan; Theatre and Stage Designed by
Ralph Alswang; Directed by Paul Sills; Lighting
by Dan Butt.

CAST

Bob Dishy   Barbara Harris
MacIntyre Dixon   Andrew Duncan
Paul Dooley   Anthony Holland

General Manager: Allen Levine
Press: Seymour Krawitz, Merle Debuskey,
Madi Ross
°Closed Sunday, January 19, 1964.
(204 performances)

Friedman-Abeles Photo

Andrew Duncan, Paul Dooley, MacIntyre
Dixon, Bob Dishy, Anthony Holland, Barbar
Harris in "When The Owl Screams"

FORTY-FIRST STREET THEATRE

Opened Thursday, September 26, 1963.°
Arch Lustberg presents:

A POLITICAL PARTY

Directed by Arch Lustberg; Written by
C. D. B. Bryan, Gwen Gibson Schwartz, Sidney
Schwartz, Shirley Grossman, Bob Vigoda, Hir-
schel Horowitz, Pierce Rollins, Antony Matar-
rese, Jean Anne, Richard Lingeman; Musical
Director, Daniel Ruslander; Costumes, Jean
Anne; Special Choreography, Gloria Contreras,
Penelope Hunter.

CAST

Jean Anne   Bill Holter
Arch Lustberg   Daniel Ruslander

PROGRAM

ACT I: Washington Is Your Home, A Tour of
Washington, PEnnsylvania 1600, An Office In
The White House, Where The Mona Lisa Was
Hung, An Important Announcement, This Is
The Premier, A Rilly Great Shew, Under Sec-
retary, Rent-a-crowd, Mississippi U, Where Is
The News?, Project Moon Shot, News Flash,
The Culture Twist, Thy Neighbor and Thy
Shelter, Youth Speaks Out, The Medicare Rock,
The Rocky Road To The White House, Little
Black Tshombe, Hootenanny with Peter, Paul
and Irving.
ACT II: Filibuster, Cocktail Party Types, The
Ins and The Outs, Friendship For Dulles, The
Red Visitors, Lady Bird Fly Away Home, Very
Influential Politicos, News Flash, Father Dear
Father Stop Testing, Cuba Si Yanqui No,
Minorities Is No Damm Good, The Ballad of
Federal City, Avant Garbage, A Tour of The
World, The Church of Birch, Exeunt Omnes.

A Revue in two acts.

Company Manager: Henry Sutton
Press: Mike Merrick, Sandy Hochberg
Stage Manager: Gustav Sabin
°Closed Sunday, October 13, 1963.
(14 performances)

Ed Rooney Photo

Jean Anne, Arch Lustberg
in "A Political Party"

Andrew Dunbar, Eleanor Phelps
in "Color Of Darkness"

Alix Jeffry Photo

Fran Malis, William V. Metzo
in "The Bald Soprano"

GATE THEATRE

Opened Tuesday, September 17, 1963.°
The Second Company presents:

THE BALD SOPRANO

By Eugene Ionesco; Translated by Donald M.
Allen; Staged by James Nisbet Clark.

CAST

Mr. Smith	Gerald E. McGonagill
Mrs. Smith	Fran Malis
Mary	Jane Cronin
Mrs. Martin	Thea Ruth
Mr. Martin	George Reinholt
The Fire Chief	William V. Metzo

with

THE LESSON

The Young Pupil	Thea Ruth
The Maid	Fran Malis
The Professor	Ronald Weyand

General Manager: Lily Turner
Stage Manager: Jeffery Douglas
°Closed Sunday, October 27, 1963.
(53 performances)

WASHINGTON SQUARE THEATRE

Opened Tuesday, September 24, 1963.°
Harold Bloom and Ned Hendrickson present:

THE SPOTS OF THE LEOPARD

By James K. Baxter; Directed and Designed
by Robert Dahdah; Lighting, Daniel T. Frankel;
Masks, Charles Loubier; Assistant to the Producers, Lenny Sandow.

CAST

Peter Yeoman	Ronald Colby
Students	Barry Bonner, Gary Haynes, Elaine Lawrence, Jeffrey Gorney, Kip Kirby, Valerie Haynes
Katinka	Sandra Gardner
Furies	Barry Bonner, Gary Haynes, Kip Kirby, Elaine Lawrence, Jeffrey Gorney, Valerie Haynes, Pat Roberts
Dr. Vaughan	Lee Shaw
Miss Clagg	Maureen Drew
Concrete Grady	Ron Faber
Barney Flynn	Stevenson Phillips
Tom	Allister Whitman
Bertha Yeoman	Jan Owens
Shona Yeoman	Pat Roberts
A Fury	Barry Bonner
Prof. Carmody	Willard Trask
Miss Appleby	Elaine Lawrence
Mr. Copplestone	Jeffrey Gorney
Miss McLaren	Kip Kirby
Mr. Obolonsky	Barry Bonner
Miss Albion	Valerie Haynes
Mr. Gosling	Gary Haynes
Mr. Finkel	Ron Faber
Sonia	Tilla Frueh
Tony	Gordon Gray
Susan	Kip Kirby
Harold	Jeffrey Gorney
Author	Allister Whitman
Albert	Barry Bonner
Albert's Girl	Valerie Haynes
Algie	Gary Haynes
Alice	Elaine Lawrence
Clerk	Maureen Drew
A Fury	Elaine Lawrence
A Clubwoman	Maureen Drew

A Comedy in two acts and nine scenes. The
action takes place at the present time in
Wellington, New Zealand.

Press: Ivan Black
Stage Managers: Virginia English, Barry Bonner
°Closed Sunday, September 29, 1963.
(8 performances)

WRITERS' STAGE THEATRE

Opened Monday, September 30, 1963.°
Harvest Productions presents:

COLOR OF DARKNESS

An Evening In The World of James Purdy

and

CRACKS

By James Purdy; Arranged and Adapted by
Ellen Violett; Directed by William Francisco;
Sets and Costumes, Lloyd Evans; Lighting, Peter
Hunt; Music, Ned Rorem; Production Assistant,
Betty Bradley; Masks by Burton Wolfe; Pro-
ducer, Margaret Barker.

CAST

Doris Roberts	Eleanor Phelps
Mary Michael	Tom Brennan
Ann Hegira	Vincent Milana
Kevin Mitchell	Walter Rhodes

ACT I: Sermon, Don't Call Me By My Right
Name, Everything Under The Sun, You Reach
For Your Hat.
ACT II: Encore, Cracks.

General Manager: Robert Mathews
Press: Barry Hyams
Stage Manager: Frank Geraci
°Closed Sunday, October 27, 1963.
(32 performances)

EAST END THEATRE

Opened Wednesday, October 2, 1963.°
Erni Brown presents:

OPENING NIGHT
and
A MATTER OF LIKE LIFE AND DEATH

By John Cromwell; Directed by Paul E. Davis; Designed by Don Manfredi; Production Associate, Charles McDaniel.

"Opening Night"
CAST

Fanny Ellis..Peggy Wood
Hecky..Ruth Gates

The action takes place a half hour before the opening curtain of a revival of "The Seagull" in the star's dressing room.

"A Matter Of Like Life And Death"
CAST

Dean Maveeda.....................................James Karen
Lois..Frances Sternhagen
A Third Person...............................Marlene Warfield

The action takes place underground on a spring evening.

Press: Howard Atlee, Paul Solomon
Stage Manager: Gian Pace

°Closed Sunday, November 10, 1963.
(47 performances)

Harvey Lloyd Photo

Ruth Gates, Peggy Wood in "Opening Night"

PHOENIX THEATRE

Opened Sunday, October 6, 1963.°
T. Edward Hambleton and Martin Tahse present:

MORNING SUN

Book and Lyrics by Fred Ebb; Based on Story by Mary Deasy; Music by Paul Klein; Directed by Daniel Petrie; Dances and Musical Numbers Staged by Donald Saddler; Musical Director, John Strauss; Settings, Eldon Elder; Lighting, Eldon Elder and Martin Aronstein; Costumes, Patricia Zipprodt; Orchestrations and Vocal Arrangements by Fred Karlin; Ballet and Incidental Music Arranged by Sol Berkowitz.

CAST

Rome...Bert Convy
Mother..Patricia Neway
Halleck...David Aguilar
Thad...Danny Lockin
Mary..Ave Maria Megna
Robert...Sammy Bayes
Mrs. Peabody...............................Nancy Cheevers
Virginia......................................Elizabeth Wullen
Mr. Haskins.....................................David Thomas
Sarah...Nancy Haywood
Emily...Kitty Sullivan
Margaret..Jan Tanzy
Elvira...Joan August
John Atzel..................................Will Mackenzie
Melissa...Carole Demas
Alex..Stuart Hodes
Mr. Simpson..........................Richard Hermany
Will..Michael Maurer
Jailor...Sammy Bayes

UNDERSTUDIES: Mother, Joan August; Rome, Will Mackenzie; John, Michael Maurer; Thad, Sammy Bayes; Melissa, Sarah, Kitty Sullivan; Haskins, Richard Hermany; Mary, Jan Tanzy.

MUSICAL NUMBERS: "Morning Sun," "This Heat!," "Tell Me Goodbye," "New Boy In Town," "Good As Anybody," "Mr. Chigger," "Pebble Waltz," "Follow Him," "Missouri Mule," "Square Dance," "Seventeen Summers," "It's A Lie," "My Sister-in-Law," "Why?," "That's Right!," "For Once In My Life," "Thad's Journey," "All The Pretty Little Horses," "I Seen It With My Very Own Eyes."

A Play with music in two acts and twelve scenes. The action takes place in 1870 in the southwestern part of the United States.

General Managers: Norman Kean, Elizabeth McCann
Press: Ben Kornzweig, Karl Bernstein
Stage Managers: Thelma Chandler, Edwin Aldridge

°Closed Sunday, October 13, 1963.
(9 performances)

Henry Grossman Photos

Ave Maria Megna, Danny Lockin, David Aguilar, Patricia Neway
Above: Patricia Neway, Bert Convy in "Morning Sun"

CHERRY LANE THEATRE

Opened Tuesday, October 8, 1963.°
(Moved Sunday, December 22, 1963, to
Village South Theatre)
Theatre 1964 (Richard Barr, Clinton Wilder,
Edward Albee) presents:

CORRUPTION IN THE PALACE OF JUSTICE

By Ugo Betti; Translated by Henry Reed;
Directed by Richard Altman; Designed by William Ritman.

CAST

Malgai	Wyman Pendleton
Erzi	Leonardo Cimino
Bata	John Hetherington
Persius	Sy Travers
Maveri	Russell Gold
Cust	David Hooks
Croz	C. K. Alexander
Porter	Lance Cunard
Vanan	Muni Seroff
Elena	Maria Tucci
A Nurse	Dianne Turley

UNDERSTUDIES: Cust, John Hetherington;
Croz, Sy Travers; Erzi, Russell Gold; Vanan,
Wyman Pendleton; Bata, Maveri, Persius, Malgai, Lance Cunard; Elena, Dianne Turley;
Porter, Nurse, Brent K. Sutton.

A Drama in three acts. The action takes place
at the present time in the Palace of Justice in
a foreign city.

General Director: Michael Kasdan
Press: Howard Atlee, Michael Sean O'Shea,
Paul Solomon
Stage Managers: Robert Currie, Brent K. Sutton
°Closed Sunday, January 5, 1964. (103 performances)

Alix Jeffry Photo

Jimmy Randolph, Ossie Davis, Sylvia Moon
Above: Ray Gilbert, Jim Trotman, Ossie Davis,
Eugene Edwards in "Ballad For Bimshire"

C. K. Alexander, Maria Tucci, Muni Seroff in
"Corruption In The Palace Of Justice"

MAYFAIR THEATRE

Opened Tuesday, October 15, 1963.°
Ossie Davis, Bernard Waltzer and Page
Productions present:

BALLAD FOR BIMSHIRE

Book by Irving Burgie and Loften Mitchell;
Lyrics and Music, Irving (Lord Burgess) Burgie;
Directed by Ed Cambridge; Choreography, Talley
Beatty; Settings, Donald Ryder; Costumes, Mozelle Forte; Musical Director, Sammy Benskin;
Arrangements, Dick Vance; Lighting, Verdon
Enoch.

CAST

Vendor	Alyce Webb
Iris Boyce	Miriam Burton
Daphne Byfield	Christine Spencer
"Captain" Neddie Boyce	Frederick O'Neal
Grafton	Ural Wilson
Spence	Jim Trotman
Dennis Thornton	Bobby Dean Hooks
Howie	Clebert Ford
Millie	Sylvia Moon
Johnny Williams	Jimmy Randolph
Sir Radio	Ossie Davis
Matron	Fran Bennett
Arthur Roundville	Robert Dolphin
Maude	Lauren (Gloria) Jones
Hilda	Hilda Harris
Watchman	Charles Moore
Lead Man	Eugene Edwards

CHORUS: Barbara Alston, Leu Camacho, Ray
Gilbert, Gloria Higdon, Lauren Jones, Hilary
Kelley, Joan Peters, Geri Seignious.
ORCHESTRA: Sammy Benskin (Leader), Fred
King, Rector Bailey, Major Holley.
MUSICAL NUMBERS: "Ballad For Bimshire,"
"Street Cries," "Fore Day Noon In The Mornin',"
"Lately I've Been Feeling So Strange," "Deep
In My Heart," "Have You Got Charm?," "Hail
Britannia," "Welcome Song," "Belle Plain,"
"I'm A Dandy," "Silver Earring," "My Love
Will Come By," "Chicken's A Popular Bird,"
"Vendor's Song," "Pardon Me, Sir," "Yesterday
Was Such A Lovely Day," "The Master Plan,"
"Chant," "We Gon' Jump Up."

A Musical Comedy in two acts with prologue
and sixteen scenes. The action takes place on
the Windward Island of Barbados in the recent
past.

General Manager: Joseph R. Burstin
Company Manager: Sidney Bernstein
Press: Chester Fox, Max Karper
Stage Manager: Carl W. Byrd
°Closed Sunday, December 15, 1963. (74 performances)

Bert Andrews Photos

PLAYERS THEATRE

Opened Thursday, October 24, 1963.°
Sherman Wayne presents:

PENNY CHANGE

By Helen Eisner; Directed by Roger Sullivan;
Settings and Lighting, David Ballou; Costumes,
Ann Keely.

CAST

Henny_____Chevi Colton
Jim_____Roger Barrett
Rosa_____Carmela
Papa_____Ronald Dawson
Hotel Manager_____Gene Pellegrini
Miss Vanderhook_____Lucy Landau
Mr. Cracobbetti_____Gene Pellegrini
Mishko_____Michael Enserro
Walter_____Gene Pellegrini
Yvette_____D. Sigel
Harry_____Joseph Mascolo
Barry_____Borah Silver
Blossom_____Marilyn Raphael
Iris_____Maria Rathay
Waiter_____Bob MacDonald

A Fantasy Comedy in two acts and five scenes.
The action takes place at the present time in
Rome, Florence, and Paris.

General Manager: Daniel R. Cohen
Press: David Lipsky
Stage Manager: William DeSeta

°Closed Thursday, October 24, 1963. (1 performance)

Alix Jeffry Photo

Philip Bruns, Frederic Tozere in "Mr. Simian"

ASTOR PLACE PLAYHOUSE

Opened Monday, October 21, 1963.°
Christina Productions presents:

MR. SIMIAN

Written and Directed by Sheppard Kerman;
Designed by Philip Rosenberg; Lighting, Robert
Brand; Costumes, Marian Lathrop; Movement,
Rhoda Levine; Executive Producer, Robert J.
Moore, Production Assistant, Robin Loggie.

CAST

Alfred Morgan_____Ramon Bieri
Evelyn Davies_____Niels Miller
Hubert Angelo_____Thomas Barbour
Barney Fiddler_____Frederic Tozere
Clara Fiddler_____Ruth Manning
Mr. Simian_____Philip Bruns

A Drama in three acts and six scenes. The
action takes place at the present time on the
deck of the cargo ship Fading Star.

General Manager: Muriel Morse
Press: Seymour Krawitz, Merle Debuskey,
Madi Ross
Stage Manager: George Manasse

°Closed Saturday, November 9, 1963. (22 performances)

Friedman-Abeles Photo

GREENWICH MEWS THEATRE

Opened Monday, October 28, 1963.°
The Greenwich Players, Inc., Stella Holt-
Roscius Productions present:

WALK IN DARKNESS

By William Hairston; Based on the Novel by
Hans Hobe; Staged by Sidney Walters; Scenery
and Lighting, Ming Cho Lee; Incidental Music,
George Fischoff; Costumes, Irish Ayres; Associate Producer, Frances Drucker.

CAST

Soldier_____Don Hudson
Jim_____Wayne Grice
Ira_____Roger Robinson
Sam_____James Murray Arnold
Washington Roach_____Clarence Williams 3rd
Father Durant_____Glenn Kezer
Sgt. Redding_____Richard Ward
Capt. Liscomb_____Stanley Sayer
Mama_____Virginia Donaldson
Eva_____Barbara Schneider
Kurt_____Ronald Willoughby
Sgt. Poznanski_____James Woodall
Cpl. Harris_____Michael DeSimone
Lt. Saunders_____David Roberts
Stefan_____Allen Royce
Robert von Weber_____Robert Fass
Dick_____Harry White
Gus_____Ian Jenkins

A Drama in three acts. The action takes place
in a Bavarian village with the Army of Occupation after World War II.

Press: David Lipsky
Stage Manager: Robert Fass

°Closed Saturday, November 23, 1963. (24 performances)

Bert Andrews Photo

Center Above: Lucy Landau, Chevi Colton,
Roger Barrett in "Penny Change"

Barbara Schneider, Clarence Williams
in "Walk In Darkness"

MIDWAY THEATRE

Opened Tuesday, October 29, 1963.°
The Footnotes Company in association with
Marilyn Thorson presents:

"GOD, MAN AND YOU BABY!"

By Philip S. Gelb; Staged by Mr. Gelb; Light-
ing, Fred Allison; Scenic Design and Effects by
Don MacGlashan and Myron Odegaard; Signs,
Daryle Ann Corr; Production Assistants, Bette
Craig, Carole Russo, Marjorie Wallace, Robert
Wetterstrom, Willie J. Woods.

CAST

Bob Broadway	Peter Harris
Irma Hurley	Linn Mason

Don Pomes

Program

ACT I: "What The Hell Holds It Together?,"
"Non Communication," "The American Revol-
ution," "Southern Justice," "God, Man and You,
Baby!"
ACT II: "Abominable No-Man," "Abraham and
Isaac," "Hard Sell Made Easy," "Academy of
A.P.E.S."

A Comedy Drama-Revue in two acts and
eight scenes.

Press: Max Eisen
Stage Managers: Myron Odegaard, Marjorie
Wallace

°Closed Wednesday, October 30, 1963. (2 performances)

SHERIDAN SQUARE PLAYHOUSE

Opened Thursday, October 31, 1963.°
Judith Rutherford Marechal presents:

IN WHITE AMERICA

By Martin B. Duberman; Directed by Harold
Stone; Designed by Robin Wagner; Costume
Supervision, Patricia Quinn Stuart; Musical Di-
rection, Oscar Brand; Music performed by Billy
Faier.

CAST

Gloria Foster	Claudette Nevins
James Greene	Michael O'Sullivan
Moses Gunn	Fred Pinkard

Presented in two acts, the material in this
production, except for connecting narration,
consists entirely of authentic documents. They
are presented exactly as originally written or
spoken. Occasionally, two or three words have
been added, paraphrased or re-arranged, in order
to provide necessary clarity or transition. None
of the documents are used in their entirety.

Production Manager: Charles Maryan
Press: Samuel J. Friedman

° Still playing May 31, 1964.
(248 performances)

Gloria Foster, Michael O'Sullivan
in
"In White America"

MAIDMAN PLAYHOUSE
Opened Tuesday, October 29, 1963.°
Gene Dingenary and Jane Gilliland present:

THE STREETS OF NEW YORK

Book and Lyrics by Barry Alan Grael; Based on Play by Dion Boucicault; Music, Richard B. Chodosh; Directed by Joseph Hardy; Choreography and Musical Numbers Staged by Neal Kenyon; Musical Arrangements and Direction, Jack Holmes; Setting and Lighting, Howard Becknell; Costumes, W. Thomas Seitz; Wigs by Dorman Allison.

CAST

Gideon Bloodgood	Ralston Hill
Badger	Barry Alan Grael
Captain Fairweather	Ian Brown
A Guide	Ken Roberts
Mr. Puffy	Don Phelps
Alida Bloodgood	Barbara Williams
Edwards	Fred Cline†1
Mark Livingston	David Cryer
Lucy Fairweather	Gail Johnston
Bridget	Joan Kroschell
Kathleen	Ann Clements
Moira	Eleanor Bergquist†2
Mrs. Fairweather	Margot Hand
Mrs. Puffy	Janet Raymond†3
Mexicans	Ian Brown, Ken Roberts, Tom Urich
Maids	Eleanor Bergquist, Ann Clements, Joan Kroschell
Police Officer	Robert Edwards

TOURISTS, GUESTS, ETC.: Eleanor Bergquist, Ann Clements, Joan Kroschell, Ian Brown, Fred Cline, Robert Edwards, Ken Roberts, Tom Urich.
AT THE TWIN PIANOS: Lanny Meyers, Jack Holmes.

MUSICAL NUMBERS: "Prologue," "Tourist Madrigal," "He'll Come To Me Crawling," "If I May," "Aren't You Warm," "Where Can The Rich and Poor Be Friends," "California," "Christmas Carol," "I May Blush From Anger," "Arms For The Love Of Me," "Close Your Eyes," "Love Wins Again," Finale.

A Musical Comedy in two acts and fourteen scenes. The action takes place in New York in the 1880's.

Press: Howard Atlee, Michael Sean O'Shea, Robert Larkin, Paul Solomon
Stage Managers: Dorothy Fowler, Dell Lewis
° Still playing May 31, 1964.
(246 performances)
† Succeeded by: 1. I. W. Klein, 2. Nina Miller, 3. Karen Looze

Bert Andrews Photos

Margot Hand, Gail Johnston, David Cryer

202

Ralston Hill (C) Top Left: Robert Edwards, Don Phelps, Janet Raymond, Ralston Hill

GATE THEATRE

Opened Tuesday, November 5, 1963.°
Yal Company presents:

THE THEATRE OF PERETZ

The Works of Isaac Loeb Peretz Adapted and
Staged by Isaiah Sheffer; Lighting, Don Sussman; Songs Composed by Michael Gelbard.

CAST

Zvee Scooler as Peretz
and
Nancy Franklin
Isaiah Sheffer

PART I: If Not Higher, A Man's Gotta Pray,
Alien Rose, Lullaby, Death Of A Musician,
All For A Pinch Of Snuff, The Judgement Of The
Court, Cabalists.
PART II: A Domestic Idyll, The Melamed of
Chelm, In Marble Palaces, I Don't Believe You,
The Pious Pussycat, Ivan The Sabbath Handyman, Wings.

Press: Chester Fox, Max Karper
Stage Manager: Daniel Goldman

°Closed Sunday, February 16, 1964. (102 performances)

Avery Willard Photo

Zvee Scooler, Nancy Franklin, Isaiah Sheffer
in "The Theatre Of Peretz"

BOUWERIE LANE THEATRE

Opened Thursday, November 7, 1963.°
Bruce Becker presents:

THE IMMORALIST

Adapted from Andre Gide by Ruth and Augustus Goetz; Directed by George Keathley; Designed by Peter Harvey; Lighting, Robert Brand;
Incidental Music Composed by Elliot Kaplan;
Production Assistant, Geri Lardiere.

CAST

Marcelline	Marcie Hubert
Dr. Robert	Tom Klunis
Bocage	Albert M. Ottenheimer
Michel	Frank Langella
Bachir	Richard Manuel
Dr. Garrin	David Metcalf
Sidma	Marian Carr
Moktir	Cal Bellini
Akur	Paul Gennel†1
Dolit	Ric Fields†2

A Drama in three acts and eight scenes. The
action takes place in Normandy, France, and in
Biskra, North Africa, in 1900 and 1901.

Press: Tommy Brent, Betty Lee Hunt,
Earl Butler
Stage Managers: James McKinney, Paul
Gennel, Ric Fields

°Closed Sunday, May 10, 1964. (210 performances)
†Succeeded by: 1. Caesar Melandandri, 2. Russell Stagg.

Herb Breuer Photo

Marcie Hubert, Frank Langella
in "The Immoralist"

THEATRE DE LYS

Opened Monday, November 11, 1963.°
Gene Persson in association with Fred Coe
presents:

JOURNEY TO THE DAY

By Roger O. Hirson; Directed by Fred Coe;
Sets and Lighting, Charles Evans; Associate
Producer, Julian Cohen; Produced by Gene Persson and Nicholas Hyams.

CAST

Dr. Gutera	Michael Baseleon
Dr. Sobik	Harold Herbstman
Dr. Endicott	Robert Pastene
Nurse	Kay Mitchell
Cooper	Jack Hollander
Katherine	Shirley Knight
Helen	Flora Campbell
Billy	Peter deVise
Arthur	Paul Sand
Martha	Rose Gregorio

A Drama in three acts and six scenes. The
action takes place in the recreation room of a
State Hospital at the present time.

General Manager: Robert Kamlot
Press: Gertrude Kirschner, Violet Welles,
Judith Lusk
Stage Managers: Robert Borod, Judith Alperin

°Closed Sunday, December 1, 1963. (29 performances)

Henry Grossman Photo

Shirley Knight, Rose Gregorio, Paul Sand
in "Journey To The Day"

203

ALDANA THEATRE
Opened Thursday, November 14, 1963.°
The Aldana Theatre presents:

THE MAIDS

By Jean Genet; Translated by Bernard Frecht-
man; Directed by Aldo Bruzzichelli; Settings,
Don Manfredi; Sound, Earle Brown and James
Tenney; Sound Technician, Les Barkdull.

CAST
Claire..............................Kathleen Widdoes
Solange..............................Lee Grant
Madame..............................Eunice Anderson
Understudy: Sloane Shelton

A Drama presented without intermission.

Administrator: Paul Libin
Press: Ben Kornzweig, Karl Bernstein
Stage Manager: Robert Moss

°Closed Sunday, January 5, 1964. (62 performances)

Robert Galbraith Photo

**Left: Lee Grant, Eunice Anderson
in "The Maids"**

WRITERS STAGE THEATRE
Opened Friday, November 15, 1963.°
Play-Pix Productions, Inc. (Leonard Davis,
Robert A. Goldston, Nancy W. Green) pre-
sents:

TELEMACHUS CLAY

By Lewis John Carlino; Directed by Cyril
Simon; Lighting, Jules Fisher; Production Coordinator, Betty Goldsmith; "Jimmy-Joe" Composed by J. J. Patterson.

CAST
George Coe   Clayton Corbin
Scottie MacGregor   Carolan Daniels
Jordan Charney   Gerald McGonagill
Bonnie Bartlett   Nancy Barrett
John Tracy   Lew Horn
            Mitchell Jason
UNDERSTUDIES: Marilyn Roberts, James Car-
ruthers.

A College for Voices in two acts.

Production Manager: Robert Woods
Press: Solters, O'Rourke and Sabinson,
        Bud Westman
Stage Manager: Peter A. Maloney

°Closed Sunday, March 1, 1964. (125 performances)

Sam Siegel Photo

**John Tracy, Clayton Corbin, Carolan Daniels
in "Telemachus Clay"**

JAN HUS PLAYHOUSE
Opened Tuesday, November 19, 1963.°
Bari and Bennett Productions present:

BURN ME TO ASHES!

By Nikos Kazantzakis; Translated by Kimon
Friar; Directed by Anthony Michales; Designed
by Leo Kerz; Music, Serge Tcherepnine; Assistant to the Producers, Donald Gastwirth.

CAST
The Voice..............................Ronald Bush
Abraham..............................Don Gunderson
Lot..............................Michael Del Medico
Ruth..............................Brenda Lesley
Rachel..............................Phoebe Dorin
The Angel..............................Neil Vipond
The Slave..............................Morton S. Silverman
The Queen..............................Julie Seastrom
The King..............................Ronald Bush
Understudy: Carol Morell

A Drama in two acts with prologue. The
action takes place in Sodom and Gomorrah on
the night of their destruction on the roof of
Lot's Tower, and in the palace.

General Manager: Jeff Britton
Press: Max Eisen
Stage Manager: David F. Sell

°Closed Sunday, December 8, 1963. (23 performances)

Dolores Gudzin Photo

**Michael Del Medico, Julie Seastrom, Morton S.
Silverman in "Burn Me To Ashes!"**

GRAMERCY ARTS THEATRE

Opened Tuesday, November 19, 1963.*
John T. Weems, Robert Buccolo, Constance Macomber present:

THISTLE IN MY BED

By Gudrun Powers; Directed by Howard Da Silva; Assistant Director, Rhoda Levine; Scenery and Lighting, Richard Casler; Costumes, Budd Hill; Incidental Music, Mark Bucci; Associate Producer, Janie C. Lee; Production Assistant, Emily Ward.

CAST

The Vicar	Larry Swanson
The Sin Eater	John A. Coe
Dawnthea	Joanna Merlin
Timothy	John Cullum
Wessy	Sam Waterston
Sally	Judith Doty
Benjamin	David Margulies
Mrs. Pudd	Barbara Waltuch
Junius	Michael Miller
Ichabod	William Herndon
Virgil	Burris Debenning
Jack	Philip Proctor
The Bear	Larry Swanson
The Gypsy	Brendan Fay

A Farce in two acts. The action takes place in a village in England in 1800, and a birth later.

Press: Max Eisen
Stage Manager: Edward D. Shelton

*Closed Thursday, November 21, 1963. (3 performances)

Alix Jeffry Photo

Top Left: Sam Waterston, Joanna Merlin, John Cullum in "Thistle In My Bed"
Left: Patrick O'Neal, Margaret Phillips in "The Ginger Man"

ORPHEUM THEATRE

Opened Thursday, November 21, 1963.*
Ivor David Balding and Leo Garen (in association with The Establishment Theatre Company, Inc., and Hitchcock-Balding Productions, Ltd.) present:

THE GINGER MAN

By J. P. Donleavy; Directed by Leo Garen; Scenery and Costumes Designed by Ed Wittstein; Lighting, Jules Fisher; Music and Songs, John Duffy; Lyrics, J. P. Donleavy; Sound Created by Gigi Cascio; Chorus Director, Clifford Clark; Assistant to Producers, Claude Leston; Technical Direction, William West, John Morris; Technical Coordinator, Jeff Siggins.

CAST

Sebastian Belfe Dangerfield	Patrick O'Neal
Kenneth O'Keefe	Stefan Gierasch
Marion Dangerfield	Margaret Phillips
Miss Frost	Marian Seldes

A Comedy in two acts and seven scenes. The action takes place at the present time in Dublin, Ireland.

Company Manager: Spofford J. Beadle
Press: Bill Doll, Robert Ganshaw
Stage Manager: Eli Ask

*Closed Sunday, January 5, 1964. (52 performances)

Marian Seldes, Patrick O'Neal
in "The Ginger Man"

THEATRE EAST

Opened Tuesday, November 26, 1963.°
Eaton Associates present:

THE PLOT AGAINST THE CHASE MANHATTAN BANK

Music, Richard R. Wolf; Lyrics, Frank Spiering, Jr.; Sketches, Carl Larsen; Choreography, Karen Kristin, Bick Goss; Musical Direction, Joe Bousard; Designed by Robert T. Williams; Costumes, Sylvia Kalegi; Directed by Tom Gruenewald.

CAST

Renee Gorsey Joan Shepard
Liz Otto Doyle Newberry
Fred Jackson Brian Watson

PROGRAM

ACT I: Let The Play Begin, Goat Play, There's Nothing Left To Give Away, Our Little Family, Freedom Riders, Reach Out and Touch Her, The Director, Only Fool, The Plot Against The Chase Manhattan Bank, The Hour Is Ripe, The Seal.
ACT II: He She We, No Exit, Pamplona, The Clocks, The Three Horsemen of The Metropolis, Only Two Allowed, Josephine, Thoughts By A River, Almost Real, The Closing.

Company Manager: Elliott Goldberg
Press: Samuel J. Friedman, M. Nathanson
Stage Manager: Andrew Mihok

°Closed Sunday, December 8, 1963. (15 performances)

John McLain Photo

PHOENIX THEATRE

Opened Wednesday, November 27, 1963.°
T. Edward Hambleton, Norris Houghton by Arrangement with Kermit Bloomgarden and Philip Barry, Jr., present:

NEXT TIME I'LL SING TO YOU

By James Saunders; Directed by Peter Coe; Setting and Lighting, David Hays; Costumes, Patricia Zipprodt; Suggested by a theme from the book, "A Hermit Disclosed," by Raleigh Trevelyan; Production Assistant, Leslie Kiss; Assistant to the Producers, Richard Kirschner.

CAST

Meff....................................Jered Barclay
Dust....................................Harris Yulin
Lizzie..................................Estelle Parsons
Rudge...................................James Earl Jones
Hermit..................................William Needles

A Drama in two acts.

General Manager: Norman Kean
Press: Ben Kornzweig, Karl Bernstein
Stage Managers: Gordon Davidson, Tom Sawyer, Ken Costigan

°Closed Sunday, December 15, 1963. (23 performances)

Henry Grossman Photo

YORK THEATRE

Opened Tuesday, December 3, 1963.°
Edwin Wilson presents:

THE BURNING

By Wallace Hamilton; Directed by Stephen Aaron; Sets and Lighting, Robin Wagner; Costumes, Patricia Quinn Stuart; Associate Producer, Hyman Silverman; Sound Technician, Earle Edgerton.

CAST

The Bishop of Limoux.................Guy Sorel
Father Henri........................Clint Atkinson
Father Gilbert......................Jonathan Frid
Father Marat........................Bill Daprato
Brother Charles.....................Jerome Guardino
Albert DuBois.......................Richard Nicholls
Jean LaMarch........................Jeno Mate
Torget..............................Clifton James
Bernard.............................Alan Oppenheimer
Felice..............................Kristina Callahan
Guillaume...........................Arland Schubert
Jacques.............................Michael McGuire
Griselle............................Jean LeBouvier
Robert..............................Ed Gasper
Eloise..............................Mary Cass
Guards..............Maurice Whitener, Walter Smith

A Drama in three acts. The action takes place in and around the town of Limoux and at the leper house of San Raoul in southern France in 1321.

Press: Sol Jacobson, Lewis Harmon, Anne Sloper
Stage Managers: Clint Atkinson, Maurice Whitener

°Closed Sunday, December 29, 1963. (31 performances)

Alix Jeffry Photo

Estelle Parsons, James Earl Jones, William Needles, Jered Barclay, Harris Yulin in "Next Time I'll Sing To You"
Top: Liz Otto, Brian Watson in "The Plot Against The Chase Manhattan Bank"

Above Center: Kristina Callahan, Clifton James, Jerome Guardino in "The Burning"

VILLAGE THEATRE

Opened Tuesday, December 10, 1963.°
WBW Productions (Joseph Burstin, Bernard
Waltzer, Milt Warner) present:

BURLESQUE ON PARADE

Directed by Charlie Robinson; Choreographer,
Elna Laun; Costumes, Peter Joseph; Musical
Direction and Music, David Fleischman; Lyrics,
Eric Blau; Orchestrations, Russ Case; Lighting,
Walter S. Russell; Consultant to the Producers,
Eric Blau; Production Supervisor, Peter Xantho.

CAST

Blaze Starr	Charlie Robinson
Dick Dana	Billy Reed
Ken Martin	Charley Schultz
June Knight	Jean Carroll
Paul Brown	Thelma Pelish

and The New Village Corps De Burlesque:
Erin Adair, Patti Boxall, Juanita Boyle, Pamela
Burrell, Judy Cassmore, Altovise Gore, Billie
Mahoney, Nomi Mitty, Linda Shoop, Renee
Slade, John Cashman, Robert St. Clair; and La
Troupe Classique: Lorraine DeLong, Joan Lynn,
Deeda Hymes.

PROGRAM

ACT I: Prologue, Talking Man, Parade, Flirtation
Scene, Lollitapop, Arabella, Bright Footed,
Moanin' Low, Easy Does It, Stage Door, Circus.
ACT II: Calendar Girls, Pantomime Wine, Kiss
Off, Jazz Games, I Love Paris, Dishes, Funny
Bunny, Court Room Scene, Passing Parade,
Passion Street, Finale.

Company Manager: Bill Levine
Press: Max Ernest Hecht
Stage Managers: Walter S. Russell, Jim Boyd
°Closed Sunday, December 29, 1963. (33 per-
formances)

Friedman-Abeles Photo

CARNEGIE RECITAL HALL THEATRE
Opened Wednesday, December 4, 1963.°
Lyn Ely and Norman Kean present:

THE WORLDS OF SHAKESPEARE

Arranged and Selected by Marchette Chute
and Ernestine Perrie; Staged by Miss Perrie;
Scenery and Costumes by Paul Morrison; Production Assistant, Joseph Eppert.

CAST

Vinie Burrows   Earle Hyman

A Program of scenes from Shakespeare's works
presented in two parts with a prologue by the
actors. Part I, The World of Love; Part II, The
World of Music.

Company Manager: George Zorn
Press: Sol Jacobson, Lewis Harmon,
Anne Sloper
Stage Manager: Jerald Funk
°Closed Sunday, December 22, 1963. (24 per-
formances)

Friedman-Abeles Photo

MERMAID THEATRE

Opened Monday, December 16, 1963.°
Keith Rockwell in association with Richard
Gates presents:

OLE! OLE!

Directed by Keith Rockwell; Production Designed by Charles Lisanby; Lighting, Jules
Fisher; Technical Director, Marjorie Wallace.

CAST

Pepa Reyes	Cruz Luna
Ciro†1	Rosa Montoya†2
	Adonis Puertas

Theatre Flamenco presented in two parts.

PROGRAM

PART I: "Rumores de la Caleta," "Fandango
de Hueha," "Farruca," "Soleares," "Rumba,"
"Solo de Guitarra," "Malaga, Spain."
PART II: "Alegrias," "La Cana," "Panaderos,"
"Seguiriya," "Zapateado," "Solo de Guitarra,"
"Buerias."

Press: Bob Perilla Associates, Marc Olden
° Still playing May 31, 1964.
† Succeeded by: 1. Goyo Reyes, 2. Pepita

Goyo Reyes, Pepita in "Ole! Ole!"
Top: Ken Martin, Blaze Starr, Dick Dana
in "Burlesque On Parade"

**Above Center: Earle Hyman, Vinie Burrows
in "The Worlds of Shakespeare"**   **207**

RODALE THEATER

Opened Tuesday, December 17, 1963.*
J. I. Rodale presents:

THE STONES OF JEHOSHAPHAT

By J. I. Rodale; Music and Lyrics, Deed
Meyer; Directed by John Glines; Set and
Lighting, Chuck Eisler; Costumes, Freida Evans;
Choreography, Eleanor Chapin.

CAST

Jeduthun	Ernie Adano
Jedidiah	R. D. Blitz
Jonadab	John Clifton
Menahem	Robert Hewes
Keturah	Rochelle Marek
Jehoshaphat	Robert Morea
Riblah	Prima Stefanini
Slave, Soldier, Groom	David Sigel

MUSICAL NUMBERS: "Opening," "A Man
Who Speaks For Himself," "The Psalm of
Jehoshaphat," "Riblah's Lament," "A Talk
With One's Conscience," "The Stones of Jeho-
shaphat," "I Could Go With The Wind,"
"Song Of The Witch," "The Jester's Tale,"
"The Wedding Celebration," "Beauteous Is The
Bride," "Look Through The Moongate," "Jeho-
shaphat Makes Up His Mind," "Long Live The
Greedy," Finale.

A Musical Comedy in two acts and sixteen
scenes.

General Manager: Daniel Landau
Press: Max Eisen, Carl Samrock
Stage Manager: Chuck Eisler

*Closed Thursday, Dec. 26, 1963.
(6 performances)

Friedman-Abeles Photo

Margaret Webster in "The Brontes"

208

CRICKET THEATRE

Opened Monday, December 16, 1963.*
Cynthia Baer presents:

CRIME AND CRIME

By August Strindberg; Translation by Eliz-
abeth Sprigge; Director, Tom Brennan; Sets,
Peter Wingate; Costumes, Henry Heymann;
Lighting, Ken Kothe; Production Assistant, Shawn
Stuart.

CAST

Mourner	Jacqueline Bartone
Cemetery Keeper	Van Dexter
Jeanne	Monica Lovett
Abbe	Donald Marye
Marion	Laurie Kenney
Emile	John Braden
Maurice	Donald Hotton
Madame Catherine	Ann Hennessey
Henriette	Olympia Dukakis
Adolfe	Louis Zorich
Waiter	Van Dexter
Headwaiter	Ken Kothe
Commissaire	Myron Mitchell
Gendarme	David Tabor
Detectives	Ken Kothe, David Tabor
Luxembourg Gardenkeeper	Van Dexter
Servant Girl	Jacqueline Bartone

A Drama Comedy in four acts and eight
scenes. The action takes place in Paris in the
1890's.

Company Manager: Cynthia Baer
Press: Lawrence Witchel Associates
Stage Managers: Frank Geraci, David Tabor,
Jacqueline Bartone

*Closed Monday, December 16, 1963. (1 per-
formance)

Bert Andrews Photo

PHOENIX THEATRE

Opened Friday, December 20, 1963.*
T. Edward Hambleton, Norris Houghton by
Arrangement with the New York Chapter
of ANTA presents:

THE BRONTES

Arranged and Adapted by Margaret Webster.

CAST

Margaret Webster

A Dramatic Portrait of Charlotte, Emily, and
Anne Bronte, presented in two parts.

General Manager: Norman Kean
Press: Ben Kornzweig, Karl Bernstein
Stage Managers: Gordon Davidson, Robert
Moss, Tom Sawyer

*Closed Sunday, January 5, 1964, after a lim-
ited engagement of 20 performances.

Avery Willard Photo

**Center Above: R. D. Blitz, Rochelle Marek
in "The Stones Of Jehoshaphat"
Top Left: Olympia Dukakis, Ann Hennessey,
Monica Lovett in "Crime and Crime"**

ASTOR PLACE PLAYHOUSE

Opened Saturday, December 21, 1963.*
(Moved to One Sheridan Square January 22, 1964)
Theodore Mann in association with Will B. Sandler presents:

TRUMPETS OF THE LORD

A musical adaptation by Vinnette Carroll of James Weldon Johnson's "God's Trombone"; Directed by Donald McKayle; Musical Director, Howard Roberts; Setting, Ed Wittstein; Lighting, Nicola Cernovich; Costumes, Normand Maxon; Associate Producer, Jay Stanwyck; Production Assistant, Robert Greenwald.

CAST

Rev. Ridgley Washington............Al Freeman, Jr.†
Henrietta Pinkston.....................Theresa Merritt
Rev. Bradford Parham...................Lex Monson
Rev. Marion Alexander..................Cicely Tyson
Female Voices: Elizabeth Brown, Berniece Hall.
Male Voices: Bill Glover, Garwood Perkins, William Stewart.
Accompanist and Singer, Michael Hinton.
Percussionist, Ralph McDonald.

MUSICAL NUMBERS: "So Glad I'm Here," "Call To Prayer," "Listen Lord," "Amen Response," "In His Care," "The Creation," "God Lead Us Along," "Noah Built The Ark," "Run Sinner Run," "Didn't It Rain," "The Judgement Day," "In That Great Gettin' Up Morning," "God Almight Is Gonna Cut You Down," "Soon One Morning," "There's A Man," "Go Down Death," "He'll Understand," "Were You There," "Calvary," "Crucifixion," "Reap What You Sow," "We Shall Not Be Moved," "We Are Soldiers," "Woke Up This Morning," "Let My People Go," "We Shall Overcome," "Jacob's Ladder," "God Be With You."

Press: David Lipsky, Lawrence Witchel
Stage Managers: Ellis Haizlip, Dana White, Robin Loggie

*Closed Sunday, May 17, 1964.
(160 performances)
†Succeeded by Ed Hall

Bert Andrews Photo

MIDWAY THEATRE

Opened Sunday, December 22, 1963.*
Exile Productions presents:

THE BRIG

By Kenneth H. Brown; Directed by Judith Malina; Designed by Julian Beck; Production Assistant, Reginald House; Lighting Technician, Ann Oelschlaeger.

CAST

Guards and Prisoners:

Viktor Allen	Henry Howard
Jim Anderson	Steven Ben Israel
George Bartenieff	Ed Kenmore
Rufus Collins	Tom Lillard
Mark Duffy	Gene Lipton
Carl Einhorn	Richard Nusser
Michael Elias	Paul Prensky
Warren Finnerty	Henry Proach
Jim Gates	Luke Theodore
Gene Gordon	Jim Tiroff

Because of the unusual challenges in the roles, and in order to emphasize the totality of the ensemble playing called for by the play, the company alternated in the roles.

A Drama in two acts and five scenes. The action takes place in the Brig of the U.S. Marine Corps Camp, Fuji, Japan, on a day in March 1957.

Press: Howard Atlee
Stage Manager: LeRoy House

*Closed Sunday, February 16, 1964.
(68 performances)

Karl Bissinger Photo

"The Brig"
Top: Cicely Tyson in
"Trumpets Of The Lord"

209

CIRCLE IN THE SQUARE

Opened Monday, December 23, 1963.°
Theodore Mann presents:

THE TROJAN WOMEN

By Euripides; Translated by Edith Hamilton;
Staged and Choreographed by Michael Cacoy-
annis; Music, Jean Prodromides; Costumes,
Theoni V. Aldredge; Lighting, Jules Fisher;
Chorus Master, Erin Martin.

CAST

Hecuba........................Mildred Dunnock†
Talthybius........................Alan Mixon
Cassandra........................Carrie Nye
Andromache........................Joyce Ebert
Astynax.........Christopher Man or Michael Walker
Helen........................Jane White
Menelaus........................Robert Mandan
Trojan Women.............Kay Chevalier, Carolyn
Coates, Elaine Kerr, Karen Ludwig, Erin
Martin, Linda Martin, Dixie Marquis, Dimitra
Steris, Maria Tucci, Gretchen Kanne, Marilyn
McKenna, Florence Peters.
Greek Soldiers .... James O'Hanlon, Alan Wendl
The Voice of Poseidon recorded by Rod Steiger

A Drama presented without intermission. The
action takes place outside the walls of Troy
following the fall of Troy.

Press: Lawrence Witchel, David Lipsky
Stage Manager: Don Garner

° Still playing May 31, 1964.
(184 performances)
† Succeeded by Carolyn Coates.

Bert Andrews Photos

Top: (L) Alan Mixon, Carrie Nye
(R) Robert Mandan, Joyce Ebert

Mildred Dunnock, Carrie Nye, Alan Mixon

210

CHERRY LANE THEATRE

Opened Saturday, January 4, 1964.°
Theatre 1964 (Richard Barr, Clinton Wilder, Edward Albee) presents:

PLAY

By Samuel Beckett; Director, Alan Schneider; Scenery, William Ritman; Costumes, Fred Voelpel.

CAST

W1	Frances Sternhagen
W2	Marian Reardon
M	Michael Lipton

and

THE LOVER

By Harold Pinter; Director, Alan Schneider; Scenery, William Ritman; Costumes, Fred Voelpel; Assistant Director, Melvin Bernhardt.

CAST

Sarah	Hilda Brawner
Richard	Michael Lipton
John, The Milkman	Charles Kindl

The action takes place in the summer in a detached house near Windsor.

General Director: Michael Kasdan
Press: Howard Atlee, Michael Sean O'Shea, Anne Woll, Paul Solomon
Stage Managers: Robert D. Currie, Charles Kindl
°Closed Sunday, March 22, 1964.
(89 performances)

Alix Jeffry Photos

Right: Marian Reardon, Michael Lipton, Frances Sternhagen in "Play"
Top: Hilda Brawner, Michael Lipton in "The Lover"

GRAMERCY ARTS THEATRE

Opened Monday, January 6, 1964.°
Gerald Krone and Dorothy Olim present:

PIMPERNEL!

Music, Mimi Stone; Book and Lyrics, William Kaye; Based on "The Scarlet Pimpernel"; Director, Malcolm Black; Musical Direction, Robert Rogers; Musical Staging, Sandra Devlin; Scenery and Lighting, Lloyd Burlingame; Costumes, Sonia Lowenstein; Arrangements, Julian Stein; Assistant to Producers, Monica Killoran.

CAST

Jellyband	Richard Marr
Sally	Gelia Heinemann
Sir Anthony Dewhurst	Buff Shurr
Sir Andrew Ffoulkes	John Cunningham
Comtesse de Tournay	Jane Lillig
Suzanne Tournay	Jeanne Devine
Spies	Francis Dux, Dick Latessa
Sir Percy Blakeney	David Daniels
Lady Marguerite Blakeney	Leila Martin
Armand St. Juste	John Canemaker
Chauvelin	William Larsen
Porteous	Budd Mann
Brogarde	Stephen Pearlman
Comte de Tournay	Richard Marr
French Mother	Joan Kenley
French Grandmother	Jane Lillig

GUESTS, CITIZENS: John Canemaker, Gelia Heinemann, Joan Kenley, Jane Lillig, Richard Marr, Budd Mann, Stephen Pearlman.
MUSICAL NUMBERS: "This Is England," "Dangerous Game," "A la Pimpernel," "Le Croissant," "Touch Of Paris," "Everything's Just Devine," "A Woman," "Le Bon Mot," "As If I Weren't There," "Liberty, Equality & Fraternity," "Love Of Long Ago," "What A Day For Me," "I'm Seeing Things," "Sing, Jacques, Sing," "Nose Ahead," Finale.

A Musical Comedy in two acts and eight scenes with prologue. The action takes place in England and France.

Press: Lawrence Witchel, David Lipsky
Stage Manager: Mark Furness
°Closed Wednesday, January 8, 1964.
(3 performances)

Bert Andrews Photo

Leila Martin, Buff Shurr, David Daniels, Jeanne Devine in "Pimpernel!"

THE SANCTUARY

Opened Sunday, January 12, 1964.°
Greenwich Players Inc. in co-ordination
with CORE, NAACP, and SNCC presents:

JERICO-JIM CROW

By Langston Hughes; Directed by Alvin Ailey
and William Hairston; A Stella Holt Production;
Costumes and Lighting, Ves Harper; Music Di-
rector, Hugh Porter; Associate Producer, Frances
Drucker; Assistant To The Producers, David
Goldstein; Organist, Marion Franklin.

CAST

Young Man	Gilbert Price
Young Girl	Micki Grant
Old Man	Joseph Attles
Old Woman	Rosalie King
Jim Crow	William Cain
Woman	Dorothy Drake

GOSPEL SINGERS: Virginia Davis, Eleanor
Howell, Dorothy Brazzle, Sylvia Terry, Vivian
Moore, William Coleman, Marquette Miller, Bob
Broadway, Brock Williams, Johnny Riddley,
Moses Brown, Lamont Washington.

STANDBYS: Ted Butler, Sylvia Terry, Bob
Broadway.

MUSICAL NUMBERS: "A Meeting Here To-
night," "I'm On My Way," "I Been 'Buked
and I Been Scorned," "Such A Little King,"
"Is Massa Gwine To Sell Us Tomorrow?," "How
Much Do You Want Me To Bear?," "Where
Will I Lie Down?," "Follow The Drinking
Gourd," "John Brown's Body," "Battle Hymn
of The Republic," "Slavery Chain Done Broke
At Last," "Oh! Freedom!," "Go Down, Moses,"
"Ezekiel Saw The Wheel," "Stay In The Field,"
"Freedom Land," "God's Gonna Cut You
Down," "Better Leave Segregation Alone," "My
Mind On Freedom," "We Shall Overcome,"
"The Battle of Old Jim Crow," "Come and Go
With Me."

A Musical Play presented without intermission.

General Manager: Stella Holt
Press: Max Eisen
Stage Manager: James Woodall
°Closed April 26, 1964. (32 performances)

Bert Andrews Photos

Gilbert Price, Hilda Harris
Top: Joseph Attles, Hilda Harris, Rosalie
King, Gilbert Price, Dorothy Drake

EAST END THEATRE

Opened Tuesday, January 14, 1964.°
Theatre 1964 (Richard Barr, Clinton Wilder, Edward Albee) presents:

FUNNYHOUSE OF A NEGRO

By Adrienne Kennedy; Directed by Michael Kahn; Settings and Lighting, William Ritman; Costumes, Willa Kim.

CAST

Funnyhouse Lady	Ruth Volner
Funnyhouse Man	Leonard Frey
Mother	Leslie Rivers
Sarah	Billie Allen
Queen Victoria Regina	Cynthia Belgrave
Duchess of Hapsburg	Ellen Holly
Patrice Lumumba	Gus Williams
Jesus	Norman Bush

UNDERSTUDIES: Hugh Hurd, Merlyn Purdy.

A Drama in one act.

General Manager: Michael Kasdan
Press: Howard Atlee, Michael Sean O'Shea, Anne Woll, Paul Solomon
Stage Managers: Mark Wright, Richard Nesbitt
°Closed Sunday, February 9, 1964.
(46 performances)

Alix Jeffry Photo

MAYFAIR THEATRE

Opened Monday, January 20, 1964.°
Jeff Britton presents:

A LOVELY LIGHT

Adapted by Dorothy Stickney; Directed by Howard Lindsay; Setting and Lightings, Anders Meyer; Gowns by Helene Pons.

CAST

Dorothy Stickney

A Dramatization of the Poems and Letters of Edna St. Vincent Millay presented in three acts.

General Manager: Jeff Britton
Press: Harvey Sabinson, Betty Lee Hunt, Phillip Bloom, Earl Butler
Stage Manager: Anders Meyer

° Closed Sunday, February 16, 1964, after a limited engagement of 32 performances.

Alfredo Valente Photo

Above Center: Fred Jackson, Naomi Riseman, Barbara Cole in "Will The Mail Train Run Tonight?"

NEW BOWERY THEATRE

Opened Thursday, January 9, 1964.°
Jon Baisch presents:

WILL THE MAIL TRAIN RUN TONIGHT?

Book and Lyrics, Malcolm L. LaPrade; Music, Alyn Heim; Based on Play by Hugh Nevill; Staged by Jon Baisch; Scenery, Gene Czernicki; Costumes, Joe Crosby; Choreography, Lynne Fippinger; Lighting, Joseph Kreisel; At the Piano, Helen Smith; Production Assistant, Sally Heim.

CAST

Truman Pendennis	Fred Jackson
Harold Stanfast	Jerome Zeffren
Simon Darkway	Peter Lombard
Dirk Sneath	Ross Gifford
Mrs. Hopewell	Naomi Riseman
Prudence	Barbara Cole
Carlotta Cortez	Lela Lawrence

MUSICAL NUMBERS: "So Much To Be Thankful For," "Dearer To Me," "Nature's Serenade," "Honeymoon Choo-Choo," "Hickory, Dickory," "Comes The Dawn," "Paper Matches," "To Dream Or Not Dream," "Prudence, Have Faith," "Villainy," "Three Cowards Craven," "Vengeance," "The Decadent Age," "Heroism," "A Slip Of A Girl," "Remember Him," "I'll Walk Alone," "The Fall of Valor," "Age Of Miracles," "Bitter Tears; No Sacrifice," "Finale."

A Musical Comedy in two acts and twelve scenes with prologue. The action takes place in the 1890's in upper New York State.

Press: Sol Jacobson, Lewis Harmon
Stage Manager: Ross Gifford
°Closed Friday, January 17, 1964.
(8 performances)

Victor Studio Photo

Dorothy Stickney
Top: Gus Williams, Billie Allen, Cynthia Belgrave in "Funnyhouse Of A Negro"

213

**Dick Schaal, Severn Darden, Barbara Harris
in "Open Season At Second City"**

PLAYERS THEATRE

Opened Thursday, January 30, 1964.°
John T. Weems, Robert Buccolo, Constance
Macomber present:

THE CARETAKER

By Harold Pinter; Directed by Fred Herbert;
Lighting, Marvin March; A Weems-Buccolo
Production; Associate Producer, Janie C. Lee.

CAST

Mick..Norman Bowler
Aston...Donald Moffat
Davies......................................Leonardo Cimino

A Drama in three acts and eight scenes. The
action takes place in a house in west London.

Press: Abner D. Klipstein
Stage Manager: Thomas Burrows

° Closed Sunday, April 19, 1964. (94 performances)

Alix Jeffry Photo

SQUARE EAST

Opened Wednesday, January 22, 1964.°
Bernard Sahlins and Paul Sills presents:

OPEN SEASON AT SECOND CITY

Scenes and Dialogue created by the Cast;
Music Composed and Played by Tom O'Horgan;
Directed by Paul Sills and Arnold Weinstein.

CAST

Barbara Harris
Severn Darden
Bob Dishy
Dick Schaal
Avery Schreiber
Ben Keller

The sixth edition of theatrical scenes, games,
and improvisations by the Second City Company.

General Manager: Allen Levine
Press: Seymour Krawitz, Merle Debuskey,
Madi Ross

°Closed Sunday, April 12, 1964.
(156 performances)

Friedman-Abeles Photo

214

**William Martel, John Baylis, Marion
Marlowe, James Harder
in "The Athenian Touch"**

JAN HUS PLAYHOUSE

Opened Tuesday, January 14, 1964.°
David Brown in association with Ronald
Toyser presents:

THE ATHENIAN TOUCH

Book, Arthur Goodman and J. Albert Fracht;
Music, Willard Straight; Lyrics, David Eddy;
Costumes, Don Foote; Scenery and Lighting,
Robert T. Williams; Musical Direction, Glen
Clugston; Orchestrations, Glen Clugston, Willard
Straight; Directed and Choreographed by Alex
Palermo.

CAST

Flictus......................................John Baylis
Lamia....................................Betsy Durkin
Kita....................................Annette Brandler
Thea......................................Marty Clarke
Ora....................................Butterfly McQueen
Rhodia....................................Lois Rooks
Attalea..................................Marion Marlowe
Polycharides............................James Harder
Cleon....................................William Martel
Colonis....................................John Kordel
Aristophanes............................Robert Cosden
Socrates....................................Will Richter
Nicias......................................Bill Caskey
Citizen-Soldiers... Ronn Hansen, Mark Holliday,
Richard Ianni

MUSICAL NUMBERS: "There Goes Time,"
"Today's The Day," "No Garlic Tonight,"
"Have A Little Sooth On Me," "Harmony,
Sweet Harmoni," "The Singer and The Song,"
"When You Write Greek Comedy," "What Is
A Woman," "Elelue," "Look Away," "There
Goes Time," "Love, You Are So Difficult," "A
Lady Of Leisure," "An Awkward Little Boy,"
"An Agent's Blood," "Lysistrata," "All We
Need To Know."

A Musical Comedy in two acts and eight
scenes. The action takes place in Athens in the
third year of the 88th Olympiad.

Press: Martin Shwartz, Bob Ullman,
Ronald Muchnick
Stage Manager: Bill Caskey

°Closed Tuesday, January 14, 1964. (1 performance)

Henry Grossman Photo

**Leonardo Cimino, Norman Bowler
in "The Caretaker"**

PHOENIX THEATRE

Opened Wednesday, January 15, 1964.°
T. Edward Hambleton and Norris Houghton present:

TOO MUCH JOHNSON

By William Gillette; Adapted and Directed by Burt Shevelove; Scenery, William and Jean Eckart; Costumes, Patricia Zipprodt; Lighting, Klaus Holm; Music Arranged and Played by Arthur Kleiner.

CAST

A Steward	Gene Nye
A Purser	Charles Durning
Mrs. Billings	Nancy Berg
Miss Faddish	Nancy Haywood
Mr. Mackintosh	Grover Dale
Mrs. Batterson	Mary Finney
M. Dathis	Pierre Epstein
Mr. Faddish	Dom De Luise
Mr. Billings	John McMartin
Mr. Frederick	Josip Elic
A Cuban	Charles Durning
Another Cuban	Gene Nye
Mr. Johnson	Dolph Sweet
Mr. Looton	Niels Miller

A Comedy in three acts. The action takes place aboard the Tropic Queen, and at the Columbia Plantation in 1896.

General Manager: Norman Kean
Press: Ben Kornzweig, Karl Bernstein
Stage Managers: Gordon Davidson, Robert Moss, Gene Nye

° Closed Sunday, February 2, 1964. (23 performances)

Friedman-Abeles Photos

Top: (L) John McMartin, Nancy Berg
(R) Nancy Berg, John McMartin,
Grover Dale, Nancy Haywood

Grover Dale, Nancy Haywood
Above: John McMartin, Nancy Berg

215

GREENWICH MEWS THEATRE

Opened Tuesday, January 21, 1964.°
Arthur Whitelaw and Leo Friedman present:

CABIN IN THE SKY

Book, Lynn Root; Music, Vernon Duke; Lyrics, John Latouche; Director, Brian Shaw; Musical Numbers Staged and Choreographed by Pepe DeChazza; Settings and Costumes, Alan Kimmel; Musical Direction, Arrangements, and Orchestrations, Eric W. Knight; Vocal Direction and Additional Dance Arrangements, Bobby Banks; Lighting, Daniel Forer.

CAST

Lily	Helen Ferguson
Brother Green	Joseph Attles
Georgia Brown	Ketty Lester
Dr. Jones	Albert Popwell
Petunia Jackson	Rosetta Le Noire
Headman	Bernard Johnson
Henchmen	Harold Pierson, Morton Winston
"Little Joe" Jackson	Tony Middleton
The Lord's General	Sam Laws
Fleetfoot	D'Urville Martin
Angels	Cleo Quitman, Jeannet Rollins De Ramos
Dude	Vernon Washington
Messengers	Harold Pierson, Morton Winston
John Henry	Joseph Attles
Domino Johnson	Albert Popwell

MUSICAL NUMBERS: Overture, "Wade In The Water," "We'll Live All Over Again," "The Man Upstairs," "Taking A Chance On Love," "Cabin In The Sky," "Gospel: Great Day," "Do What You Want To Do," "Fugue," "Not A Care In The World," "Not So Bad To Be Good," "Love Me Tomorrow," "Love Turned The Light Out," "Cross Over—Off To John Henry's," "Living It Up," "Honey In The Honeycomb," "Savanna."

A Musical Fantasy in two acts and nine scenes. The action takes place Then and Now.

Business Manager: Florence DiRe
Press: Max Eisen, Carl Samrock
Stage Managers: Frederick Edell, Mike Herzog, Peter Smith

° Closed Sunday, March 1, 1964. (47 performances)

Tony Middleton, Ketty Lester
in "Cabin In The Sky"

YORK PLAYHOUSE

Opened Tuesday, January 28, 1964.°
Peter Bogdanovich presents:

ONCE IN A LIFETIME

By Moss Hart and George S. Kaufman; Directed by Peter Bogdanovich; Scenery, Ed Wittstein; Costumes, Polly Platt; Lighting, Joe Pacitti; Production Assistant, Leslie Brooks.

CAST

George Lewis	Sandy Baron
May Daniels	Eve Roberts
Jerry Hyland	Ted Tingling
Porter	John McCurry
Helen Hobart	Tomi Romer
Susan Walker	Joanna Miles
First Man	William Finley
First Girl	Jennifer Rains
Second Man	Anthony T. Kent
Second Girl	Tisa Baronne
Coat Check Girl	Deborah Pierce
Cigarette Girl	Mary Cass
Phyllis Fontaine	Cynthia Silliman
Florabel Leigh	Heidi Fithian
Phyllis' Maid	Lee Janell
Florabel's Maid	Susan Strickland
Phyllis' Chauffeur	Gerald Denning
Florabel's Chauffeur	John Heywood
Bellboy	Roy London
Mrs. Walker	Carole Kingsley
Weisskopf	Anthony T. Kent
Girl with Weisskopf	Tisa Baronne
Ernest	Robert Levine
Meterstein	William Finley
Miss Chasen	Jennifer Rains
Policemen	Paul Cole, Clinton Dunn
Herman Glogauer	James S. Tolkan
Schlepkin Brothers	Robert Levine, John Beebout, Anthony T. Kent, William Finley, Jon Burnett, Paul Cole
Miss Leighton	Tisa Baronne
Lawrence Vail	George Morfogen
Pages	Paul Cole, Roy London
Sullivan	Gerald Denning
Moulton	John Beebout
Fulton	Clinton Dunn
Voice Pupil	Lee Janell
Rudolph Kammerling	Lionel Wilson
Electricians	John Heywood, John Beebout
Mr. Flick	Robert Levine
Bridesmaids	Cynthia Silliman, Heidi Fithian, Mary Cass, Deborah Pierce
Cameramen	Gerald Denning, Anthony T. Kent
Truckman	John McCurry
Lightmen	Jon Burnett, William Finley
Leading Man	Clinton Dunn
Bishop	Robert Levine
George's Secretary	Susan Strickland
Script Girl	Lee Janell
Painter	Robert Levine
Biographer	Heidi Fithian
Tie Man	Gerald Denning
Reporters	John Heywood, Clinton Dunn

A Comedy in three acts and seven scenes. The action takes place in 1927 in New York and Los Angeles.

General Manager: Michael Brandman
Press: Martin Shwartz, Bob Ullman
Stage Managers: William DeSeta, Jon Burnett

° Closed Tuesday, January 28, 1964. (1 performance)

Friedman-Abeles Photos

Eve Roberts, Sandy Baron, Ted Tinling
in "Once In A Lifetime"

ORPHEUM THEATRE

Opened Wednesday, February 12, 1964.°
Victoria Crandall presents:

JO

Book and Lyrics by Don Parks and William
Dyer; Based on the Novel "Little Women" by
Louisa May Alcott; Music, William Dyer; Direc-
ted by John Bishop; Choreography, Chele Abel
and Gerald Teijelo; Musical Direction, Jane
Douglass White; Arrangements and Choral Di-
rection, Robert Page; Scenery, Gordon Micunis;
Costumes, Evelyn Norton Anderson; Lighting,
Miller-Moffatt; At the Twin Pianos, Jane Doug-
lass White, Rita Segree; Percussionist, Anthony
Cirone.

CAST

Hannah	Joyce Lynn
Beth	Judith McCauley
Amy	April Shawhan
Meg	Susan Browning
Jo	Karin Wolfe
Marmee	Joy Hodges
Freddie	Paul Blake
Mr. Laurence	Myron Odegaard
John Brooke	Lowell Harris
Sallie Gardiner	Salicia Smith
Harriet King	Joyce MacDonald
Laurie	Don Stewart
Aunt March	Mimi Randolph
Mr. March	Joseph Davies
Editor	Paul Blake
Geordie	Alan Zemel
Kitty	Jania Rozhen
Minna	Renee Tetro
Professor Bhaer	Bernard F. Wurger
Maid	Salicia Smith
Ned Moffat	Joel Pitt
Frank Vaughn	Jack Fletcher

MUSICAL NUMBERS: "Harmony, Mass.,"
"Deep In The Bosom Of The Family," "Hurry
Home," "Let's Be Elegant Or Die!," "Castles
In The Air," "Friendly Polka," "Time Will Be,"
"What A Long Cold Winter!," "Afraid To Fall
In Love," "A Wedding! A Wedding!," "I Like,"
"Genius Burns," "If You Find A True Love,"
"Nice As Any Man Can Be," "More Than
Friends," "Taking The Cure."

A Musical in two acts and seventeen scenes.
The action takes place in Harmony, Mass., during and after the Civil War, and in New York
and Europe.

General Manager: Joseph Beruh
Press: Bob Ullman, Robert Larkin,
Martin Shwartz
Stage Managers: Jerry Arrow, Myron Odegaard
° Closed Sunday, April 5, 1964. (63 perform-
ances)

Henry Grossman Photos

Top: Don Stewart, Karin Wolfe

Susan Browning, Judith McCauley,
April Shawhan, Karin Wolfe (also above)

217

Sylvia Sidney, Donald Woods
in "Riverside Drive"

EAST END THEATRE

Opened Monday, February 24, 1964.°
Robert D. Simons, M. Lloyd Carter, Jay
Stanwyck present:

SQUAT BETTY and THE SPONGE ROOM

By Keith Waterhouse and Willis Hall; Staged
by Robert D. Simons; Designed by Stewart
Chaney; Production Coordinator, Rosalyn Boulter.

"The Sponge Room"

CAST

Leslie Edwards......................... James Coco
Hilary Shepherd........................ Joan Darling
Colin Broughton..................... Leslie Redford

The action takes place at the present time in
the Sponge Room of the Natural History Mu-
seum in London.

"Squat Betty"

CAST

Stanley Mintey........................ James Coco
Elizabeth Mintey....................... Joan Darling
Jonathan Pearce..................... Leslie Redford

The action takes place in late autumn in the
Open Roads Hostel in Hillside, Cumberland,
England.

General Manager: M. Lloyd Carter
Press: Samuel J. Friedman, R. Lycett,
Jane Friedman
Stage Manager: Carl Clark

° Closed Sunday, April 5, 1964.
(49 performances)

Friedman-Abeles Photo

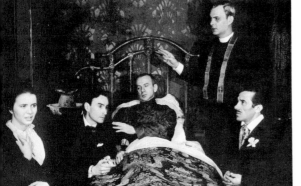

218

Madge Grant, Lance Gore, A. J. Embie,
Fred Hodges, Jason Spartos
in "Finis For Oscar Wilde"

THEATRE DE LYS

Opened Tuesday, February 4, 1964.°
Stan Raiff and Sandy Farber present:

RIVERSIDE DRIVE

Two plays by John Donovan; Directed by
Douglas Seale; Settings and Lighting, Leo Kerz;
Production Assistant, Suzanne Aaron.

"Damn You, Scarlett O'Hara"

CAST

Beatrice Wright....................... Sylvia Sidney
Ashley Brewster....................... Donald Woods

The action takes place late in the afternoon
on a cold October day in a basement apartment
on Riverside Drive.

"All My Pretty Little Ones"

CAST

Leslie Ross............................ Sylvia Sidney
Harrison Ross......................... Donald Woods

The action takes place in a Riverside Drive
penthouse with a commanding view of the
Palisades.

UNDERSTUDIES: Josephine Nichols, Edward
Fuller.

General Manager: David Wyler
Press: Ben Kornzweig, Karl Bernstein
Stage Manager: Tony Manzi

° Closed Sunday, February 16, 1964. (15 performances)

Leslie Redford, Joan Darling, James Coco
in "Squat Betty"

BLACKFRIARS' THEATRE

Opened Friday, February 14, 1964.°
The Blackfriars' Guild presents:

FINIS FOR OSCAR WILDE

By Rev. Edward A. Molloy; Directed by
Walter Cool; Settings and Lighting, Allen Edward Klein; Costumes, Alice Merrigal.

CAST

Oscar Wilde............ A. J. Embie, Alan Lysander
Joy Ellsworth .... Madge Grant, Jill Kenworthy
Jules Dupoirier........... Jack Heller, Gilbert Roper
Jacques Dupoirier.... Jason Spartos, Armand Storace
Lord Alfred Douglas................ Ray Fisher,
Richard Anders
Doctor Tucker................... Harold Anderson,
Barry Dunleavey
Robert Ross......... Lance Gore, Kermit Brown
Edward Carson .... Duane Morris, Robert Milton
Father Cuthbert Dunne............. Fred Hodges,
J. Mark Curran

A Drama in two acts. The action takes place
either in Oscar Wilde's room or in the corridor
just outside his room in the Hotel d'Alsace in
Paris, on November 28 and 29, 1900.

Stage Managers: Robert Charles, Judy Smith

° Closed Sunday, April 12, 1964. (50 performances)

Braun Photo

EAST 78th STREET PLAYHOUSE

Opened Monday, February 17, 1964.°
(Moved March 20, 1964, to the York
Theatre)
Charles Hollerith, Jr., and Jerry Devine
present:

THE AMOROUS FLEA

Book by Jerry Devine; Based on Moliere's
"School For Wives"; Music and Lyrics, Bruce
Montgomery; Staged by Jack Sydow; Sets, Bill
Hargate; Costumes, Donald Brooks; Lighting,
Jane Reisman; Orchestrations, Lou Busch; Mu-
sical Direction, Ted Simons.

CAST

Arnolphe	Lew Parker
Chrysalde	David C. Jones
Alain	Jack Fletcher
Georgette	Ann Mitchell
Agnes	Imelda De Martin
Horace	Philip Proctor
Oronte	Ted Tiller
Enrique	Bryce Holman

MUSICAL NUMBERS: "All About Me," "All
About He," "All About Him," "Learning Love,"
"There Goes A Mad Old Man," "Dialogue On
Dalliance," "March Of The Vigilant Vassals,"
"Lessons On Life," "Man Is A Man's Best
Friend," "The Other Side Of The Wall," "Close-
ness Begets Closeness," "It's A Stretchy Day,"
"When Time Takes Your Hand," "The Amor-
ous Flea," Finale.

A Musical Comedy in three acts. The action
takes place on a street and in a secluded garden
in 17th Century Paris.

General Manager: Mary Jordan
Press: Mary Bryant, Warren Pincus
Stage Managers: John Fenn, Vera Cochran

° Closed Sunday, May 10, 1964.
(93 performances)

Van Williams Photos

Imelda De Martin, Lew Parker

**Top: (L) Ann Mitchell, Jack Fletcher
(R) Philip Proctor, Imelda De Martin**

219

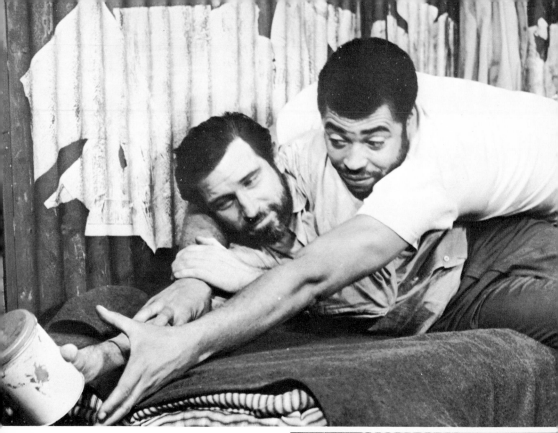

CRICKET THEATRE
Opened Monday, March 2, 1964.°
Sidney Bernstein and Lucille Lortel,
Prod., Inc., present:

THE BLOOD KNOT

By Atholl Fugard; Directed by John Berry;
Setting, John Bury; Costumes, Martha Gould;
Lighting, Harold Baldridge; Production Associate, Michael Perloff.

CAST

Morris Pieterson_____J. D. Cannon†1
Zachariah Pieterson_____James Earl Jones†2

A Drama in three acts. The action takes place
at the present time in a shack in the colored
section of Korsten on the outskirts of Port
Elizabeth, South Africa.

Press: Max Eisen, Jeanne Gibson Merrick
Stage Manager: Ed Cambridge

° Still playing May 31, 1964.
    (102 performances)
† Succeeded by: 1. Nicholas Coster, Atholl
Fugard, 2. Louis Gossett.

Martha Swope Photos

J. D. Cannon, James Earl Jones (also at top)

ASTOR PLACE PLAYHOUSE

Opened Tuesday, March 17, 1964.°
John Ben Tarver, Jose Crespo, Jay Broad,
Jerome Metz, and Laurence Goldstein by
special arrangement with Eric Bentley under
the sponsorship of Teatro Espanol of New
York present:

LA VIDA ES SUENO

(LIFE IS A DREAM)

By Pedro Calderon de la Barca; English Ver-
sion by Roy Campbell and Directed by Jay
Broad; Spanish Version Directed by Jose Crespo;
Designed by Vincent Piacentini, Jr.; Costumes,
Richard Seger; Executive Producer, John Ben
Tarver; Assistant to Spanish Director, Paco Vil-
lar; Production Assistant, Elias Yorshis; Tech-
nical Director, Ray Schmidt.

ENGLISH CAST

Rosaura	Sally Kemp Gossage
Clarion	David Margulies
Segismund	Michael Higgins
Clotaldo	Richard Kuss
Astolpho	Richard Waring
Stella	Cavada Humphrey
Basil	Khigh Dhiegh
First Gentleman	Michael Shoztic
Second Gentleman	David Harris

SPANISH CAST

Segismundo	Raul Davila
Rosaura	Maruja Mas
Basilio	Jose Crespo
Clotaldo	Manuel Aparicio
Clarin	Carlos Rafart
Astolfo	Raul Julia
Estrella	Myrna de Casenave
Criado 1	Elieser Escalante
Criado 2	Rodolfo De La Madrid
Soldado 1	Felix Estremera
Soldado 2	Radames Lopez
Bufon	Kathy Chamorro

DAMAS, CABALLEROS, SOLDADOS, RUE-
BLO: Ana Marta Morales, Leonor Vetulli,
Eduardo Hernandez, Rodolfo De La Madrid,
Azarael Cabrera, Ali Colom.

A Drama in two acts. The action takes place
during the Medieval age in the Court in Poland,
and the surrounding mountains.

General Manager: Howard Scott
Press: Abner D. Klipstein, Maxine Keith
Stage Manager: Milt Commons

° Closed Monday, May 11, 1964.
(83 performances)
Alternate performances by the English and Spanish casts.

Bert Andrews Photos

STAGE 73

Opened Monday, March 16, 1964.°
Fanny Bradshaw with Sherman Wayne
presents:

THE WHITE ROSE AND
THE RED

By William Shakespeare; Arranged by Fanny
Bradshaw; Directed by Edwin Sherin; Set, Robin
Wagner; Costumes, Stanley Simmons; Lighting,
Martin Aronstein; Music, Hubert Dorris; Assist-
ant to Producers, Robert MacDonald.

CAST

Shirley Blanc	Earle Hyman
Staats Cotsworth	Carl Jacobs
David Ford	Nicholas Kepros
Jonathan Frid	Jack Ryland
Joseph Hammer	Rebecca Thompson
John Hillerman	Ted Van Griethuysen
Betty Lou Holland	

A Sweep of History derived from "Henry V,"
"Henry VI," and Richard III presented in two
acts with a prologue.

General Manager: Sherman Wayne
Press: Bob Ullman, Fred Weterick, Robert
Larkin, Irving Suss
Stage Manager: Rusty McGrath

° Closed Sunday, April 12, 1964.
(31 performances)

Henry Grossman Photo

Raul Davila, Carlos Rafart (Spanish Cast)
Above: Richard Waring, Khigh Dhiegh,
Michael Higgins, Richard Kuss (English Cast)
of "Life Is A Dream"

Rebecca Thompson, Ted Van Griethuysen
in "The White Rose and The Red"

PHOENIX THEATRE

Opened Wednesday, March 4, 1964.°
T. Edward Hambleton and Norris Houghton by Arrangement with Association Of Producing Artists presents in repertory:

RIGHT YOU ARE IF YOU THINK YOU ARE

By Luigi Pirandello; English Version by Eric Bentley; Directed by Stephen Porter; Set Designed by James Tilton; Costumes, Nancy Potts; Music Composed and Played by Conrad Susa.

CAST

Lamberto Laudisi	Paul Sparer
Amalia Agazzi	Nancy Marchand
Dina	Jane McArthur
Butler	Gordon Gould or George Bari
Sirelli	Keene Curtis
Signora Sirelli	Jane Farrand
Signora Cini	Eve Roberts
Councillor Agazzi	Richard Woods
Signora Frola	Joanna Roos
Ponza	Sydney Walker
Signora Nenni	Christine Pickles
Police Commissioner Centuri	Joseph Bird
Governor of the Province	Ellis Rabb or Gordon Gould

A Comedy in two acts. The action takes place in the parlor of the home of Councillor Agazzi in 1916.

THE TAVERN

By George M. Cohan; Directed by Ellis Rabb; Setting, Lloyd Burlingame; Costumes, Nancy Potts; Music Arranged and Played by Conrad Susa.

CAST

Zach	Clayton Corzatte
Sally	Jane McArthur
Freeman	Sydney Walker
Willum	William Larsen
The Vagabond	Ellis Rabb
The Woman	Nancy Marchand
Lamson	Richard Woods
Mrs. Lamson	Joanna Roos
Virginia	Christine Pickles
Tom Allen	John Ragin or Paul Sparer
Sheriff	Keene Curtis
Sheriff's Men	Donald Briscoe, Gordon Gould, George Bari, George Pentecost
Stevens	Joseph Bird

A Melodrama in two acts. The action takes place in Freeman's Tavern.

IMPROMPTU AT VERSAILLES

By Moliere; Translated and Directed by Stephen Porter; Costumes, Nancy Potts.

CAST

Moliere	Paul Sparer
Brecourt	Richard Woods
La Grange	George Pentecost
Du Croisy	Keene Curtis
Mlle. Du Parc	Joanna Roos
Mlle. Bejart	Eve Roberts
Mlle. De Brie	Christine Pickles
Mlle. Du Croisy	Jane McArthur
Mlle. Moliere	Jan Farrand
La Thorilliere	Ellis Rabb
A Courtier	Donald Briscoe

with

SCAPIN

By Moliere; Translated by Stephen Porter and Ellis Rabb; Directed by Stephen Porter; Set by James Tilton.

CAST

Octave	George Pentecost
Sylvestre	Joseph Bird
Scapin	Keene Curtis
Hyacinthe	Jane McArthur
Argante	Sydney Walker
Geronte	Ellis Rabb
Leandre	Clayton Corzatte
Carle	Gordon Gould
Zerbinette	Christine Pickles
Nerine	Eve Roberts

THE LOWER DEPTHS

By Maxim Gorki; New Translation by Alex Szogyi; Staged by Ellis Rabb; Set Designed by James Tilton; Costumes, Nancy Potts.

CAST

The Baron	Ellis Rabb
Kvashnya	Eve Roberts
Bubnov	William Larsen
Andrei	Gordon Gould
Nastya	Jan Farrand
Anna	Joanna Roos
Satin	Paul Sparer
An Actor	Clayton Corzatte
Mikhail Ivanovich Kostilyov	Richard Woods
Vassily	John Ragin
Natasha	Jane McArthur
Luka	Sydney Walker
Alyoshka	George Pentecost
Vassilissa Karpovna Kostilyova	Nancy Marchand
Abram Ivanich Medvyedyev	Joseph Bird
The Tartar	Keene Curtis

A Drama in four acts presented in two parts; The action takes place in a flophouse in provincial Russia early in the spring of 1902.

General Manager: Norman Kean
Press: Ben Kornzweig, Karl Bernstein
Stage Managers: Bruce Hoover, Gordon Davidson, Robert Moss

° Still playing May 31, 1964.

Friedman-Abeles Photos

Joanna Roos, Christine Pickles in "The Tavern"
Top Right: Clayton Corzatte, Sydney Walker in "The Lower Depths"

Keene Curtis, Paul Sparer, George Pentecost, Joseph Bird, Ellis Rabb in "The Lower Depths"
Top: (L) Keene Curtis, Ellis Rabb in "Scapin"
(R) Nancy Marchand, Joanna Roos, Jan Farrand in "Right You Are If You Think You Are"

YORK PLAYHOUSE

Opened Sunday, March 15, 1964.°
The Actors Studio, Inc., presents:

DYNAMITE TONIGHT

Libretto by Arnold Weinstein; Music, William
Bolcom; Directed by Paul Sills and Arnold
Weinstein; Designed by Willa Kim; Lighting,
Peter Hunt; Musical Director, Charles Turner;
Special Art Curtain Designed by Tom Keogh,
Marisol, Ernest Trova and Andy Warhol; Chor-
eographic Supervision, Syvilla Fort; Production
Assistant, William Deeb; Production Coordinator,
Mary Jordan.

CAST

Captain	David Hurst
Sergeant	Anthony Holland
Smiley	Gene Wilder
Prisoner	George Gaynes
Soldiers	Lou Gilbert, James Noble, John Harkins
Tlimpattia	Barbara Harris

A Comic Opera for Actors performed without
intermission. The action takes place in a Bunker
under an unspecified battlefield in a more unspecified war in a less specified time.

General Manager: Arthur Waxman
Press: Samuel Lurie, Judith S. Davidson,
Stanley F. Kaminsky
Stage Manager: Don Moreland
° Closed Sunday, March 15, 1964.
(1 performance)

Martha Holmes Photo

Barbara Harris (C), George Gaynes (R)
in "Dynamite Tonight"

ACTORS PLAYHOUSE

Opened Monday, March 16, 1964.°
Northwestern Productions presents:

LITTLE EYOLF

By Henrik Ibsen; Translated by R. V. Fors-
lund; Directed by Marshall W. Mason; Settings,
Robert Thirkield; Costumes, C. M. Nelson; Lighting, Dennis Parichy.

CAST

Alfred Allmers	Mark Lenard
Rita Allmers	Savannah Bentley
Asta Allmers	Claris Erickson
Eyolf	Scott Moore, Jr.
Engineer Borgheim	Ronald Willoughby
The Rat-Wife	Dorothy Peterson

Understudies: Mary Tahmin, Janda Lee, Linda
Eskenas.

A Drama in three acts. The action takes place
in 1894 on a country estate near a small port
in Norway.

Business Manager: Mary Jordan
Press: Seymour Krawitz, Merle Debuskey,
Madi Ross
Stage Manager: James Haire
° Closed Tuesday, April 14, 1964.
(33 performances)

Bert Andrews Photos

Ronald Willoughby, Savannah Bentley,
Claris Erickson
Above: Mark Lenard, Savannah Bentley
in "Little Eyolf"

GATE THEATRE

Opened Thursday, March 19, 1964.°
Stuart Weiner presents:

CINDY

Book by Joe Sauter and Mike Sawyer; Lyrics and Music, Johnny Brandon; Directed and Choreographed by Marvin Gordon; Orchestrations and Musical Direction, Clark McClellan; Musical Conductor, Sammy Benskin; Scenery, Robert T. Williams; Costumes, Patricia Quinn Stuart; Lighting, Martin Aronstein; Associate Producer, Jerry Grace; Production Assistant, Robert Tyson.

CAST

Storytellers:

Thelma Oliver	Herself
Tommy Karaty	Himself
Mark Stone	Himself
Cindy Kreller	Jacqueline Mayro
Lucky	Johnny Harmon†
Della Kreller	Dena Dietrich
Golda Kreller	Amelia Varney
Papa Kreller	Frank Nastasi
David Rosenfeld	Mike Sawyer
Mama Kreller	Sylvia Mann
Ruth Rosenfeld	Lizabeth Pritchett
Chuck Rosenfeld	Joe Masiell

ORCHESTRA: Sammy Benskin, Piano; Haywood Henry, Reeds and Woodwinds; Drums, Herb Lovelle; Trumpet, Dud Bascomb.

MUSICAL NUMBERS: Overture, "Once Upon A Time," "Let's Pretend," "Is There Something To What He Said?," "Papa, Let's Do It Again," "A Genuine Feminine Name," "Cindy," "Think Mink," "Tonight's The Night," "Who Am I?," "Ballroom Sequence," "Entr'Acte," "Opening," "If You've Got It, You've Got It," "The Life That I Planned For Him," "If It's Love," "Got The World In The Palm Of My Hands," "Call Me Lucky," "Laugh It Up," "What A Wedding," Finale.

A Musical Fantasy in two acts and twelve scenes.

Press: Max Eisen, Jeannie Gibson Merrick, Lisa Henri
Stage Manager: Nathan Caldwell, Jr.

° Still playing May 31, 1964.
(86 performances)
† Succeeded by Tommy Karaty

LITTLE FOX THEATRE

Opened Wednesday, March 25, 1964.°
Peter Goldfarb presents:

IN THE SUMMER HOUSE

By Jane Bowles; Directed by Alfred Ryder; Sets, Oliver Smith; Costumes, Ann Roth; Lighting, Tom Skelton; Music Arranged by Nito San Miguel; Production Supervisor, Lyn Austin; Musical Adviser, Margarita Madrigal; Production Associate, Ann McIntosh.

CAST

Gertrude Eastman-Cuevas	Estelle Parsons
Molly	Susan Tyrrell
Esperanza	Coco Ramirez
Frederica	Jan Tanzy
Nito	Nito San Miguel
Mrs. Lopez	Rosemary DeAngelis
Mr. Solares	James Farentino
Lionel	Dennis Cooney
Figure-Bearers	Philip Magdalany, Peter Gerety
Chauffeur	Eric Sydney
Vivian Constable	Kay Frey
Mrs. Constable	Leora Dana
Inez	Mary Grace Canfield

A Drama in two acts and four scenes. The action takes place in Gertrude Eastman-Cuevas' Garden, somewhere on the coast of Southern California.

General Manager: Robert Cherin
Press: Bob Ullman, Fred Weterick, Robert Larkin, Irving Suss
Stage Manager: John Cornell

° Closed Sunday, April 5, 1964.
(15 performances)

Henry Grossman Photos

Tommy Karaty, Thelma Oliver in "Cindy"

Leora Dana, Estelle Parsons, James Farentino
Above: Dennis Cooney, Leora Dana, Susan
Tyrrell in "In The Summer House"   225

CHERRY LANE THEATRE

Opened Tuesday, March 24, 1964.°
Theatre 1964 (Richard Barr, Clinton Wilder,
Edward Albee) presents:

THREE AT THE CHERRY LANE

"Play"

By Samuel Beckett; Directed by Alan
Schneider; Designed by William Ritman.

CAST

W1..Alice Drummond
W2..Marian Reardon
M...Ray Stewart

"The Two Executioners"

By Fernando Arrabal; Directed by Edward
Parone.

CAST

Executioner 1..................................Ron Mack
Executioner 2.............................Peter Michaels
The Mother (Frances)...............Marian Reardon
Ben...David Spielberg
Maurice.................................George Anderson
The Husband (John)..................Charles Kindl

"Dutchman"

By LeRoi Jones; Directed by Edward Parone.

CAST

Clay...Robert Hooks
Lula..Jennifer West
Passengers........George Anderson, Lynn Bernay,
Charles Kindl, Ron Mack, Peter Michaels,
David Spielberg

General Director: Michael Kasdan
Administrative Director: Joseph Call
Press: Howard Atlee, Anne Woll, Paul Solomon
Stage Managers: Robert D. Currie, Charles Kindl
° "The Two Executioners" and "Play" were
withdrawn on Sunday, April 19, 1964, after
32 performances for the former and 121 for
the latter. "The American Dream" was re-
vived.

THE AMERICAN DREAM

By Edward Albee; Directed by Alan Schneider;
Designed by William Ritman.

CAST

Mommy.......................................Jane Hoffman
Daddy......................................John C. Becher
Grandma.......................................Sudie Bond
Mrs. Barker.............................Nancy Cushman
The Young Man.........................Robert Gentry
° Still playing May 31, 1964.

Alix Jeffry Photos

David Spielberg, Marian Reardon, George
Anderson in "The Two Executioners"

Robert Hooks   Jennifer West

Robert Hooks, Jennifer West (also above)
in "Dutchman"

226

MASQUE THEATRE

Opened Tuesday, March 31, 1964.°
Ray Salerno and Danorm Productions
presents:

THE SALAD OF THE MAD CAFE

Written and Directed by Danny Logan; Set
and Lighting, Jim Rule; Costumes, Rita Bottom-
ley; Musical Director, Donald Chan; Hair Stylist,
Robert Lando.

CAST

Danny Logan   Susan Murphy
Marguerite Davis   Mark Malone
          Norman Farber

ACT I: "Opening," "A Cocktail Party," "Dal-
las," "The Auditions," "Apartment For Rent,"
"Marlon Of The Plaza," "The Salad Of The
Mad Cafe," "Makin' Whoopee," "Rolf Hoch-
huth Speaks," "Academy Awards," "The Sui-
cide," "The Zulu Stomp."
ACT II: "Not Tonight," "This Was The Week
That Wasn't," "Judy!," "DeGaulle," "Boy and
Girl At The Movies," "Maggie," "Miss Amer-
ica," "A Poem," "Ann Devine," "Rex and
Julie," "The Les Less Show," "The Finale—A
Medley Of Current Hits."

A Satirical Revue with Music in two parts
with twenty-four scenes.

Press: David Lipsky, Lawrence Witchel,
          Ted Goldsmith
Stage Managers: Norman Farber, John Hedges
° Closed Sunday, April 12, 1964.
(16 performances)

JAN HUS HOUSE

Opened Tuesday, April 14, 1964.°
Fryer, Carr and Harris, Inc., with John
Herman present:

A DREAM OF SWALLOWS

By Paul Zindel; Directed by Michael Simone;
Scenery and Lighting, Boyd Dumrose; Original
Music, Bob Harris; Lyrics, Frank Reardon; Cos-
tume Coordinator, Joanna Beck; Technical Di-
rector, George Blanchard; Production Assistant,
James Davis; Guitarist, Don Rodney; A Majestic
Production.

CAST

Margaret	Sally Schermerhorn
Olla Robinson	Nancy R. Pollock
Uncle Edward	Eugene R. Wood
Randolph Chesterton	Humphrey Davis
Timothy	Robert Berdeen
Mrs. Fields	Kate Harrington
Little Judith	Charlotte Jones

UNDERSTUDIES: Olla, Mrs. Fields, Alberta
Cuozzo; Margaret, Jo Ann Forman; Timothy,
James Davis.

A Drama in two acts and six scenes. The
action takes place at the present time in Olla
Robinson's country house.

General Manager: Jay Rosenblatt
Press: David Lipsky, Lawrence Witchel,
          Ted Goldsmith
Stage Manager: Delmar Hendricks
° Closed Tuesday, April 14, 1964.
(1 performance)

Friedman-Abeles Photo

**Eugene R. Wood, Sally Schermerhorn,
Robert Berdeen in "A Dream Of Swallows"**

SECOND CITY AT SQUARE EAST

Opened Wednesday, April 15, 1964.°
Charles Rubin, Murray Sweig and Al
Weinstein present:

THE WRECKING BALL

Scenes and Dialogue Created by The Com-
pany; Directed by Bob Dishy; Theatre and
Stage Designed by Ralph Alswang; Music
Composed and Played by Tom O'Horgan;
Lighting, Dan Butt; Co-Directors, Alan Arkin,
Peter Kass.

CAST

Roger Bowen   Mina Kolb
Jack Burns   Dick Schaal
Bob Dishy   Avery Schreiber
          Mitzie Welch

An evening of theatrical scenes, games and
improvisations. Everything is subject to change
. . . with or without notice.

General Manager: Felice Rose
Press: Seymour Krawitz, Merle Debuskey,
          Madi Ross
°Still playing May 31, 1964. (84 performances)

Friedman-Abeles Photo

**Roger Bowen, Jack Burns, Mitzie Welch
in "The Wrecking Ball"
Top: Marguerite Davis, Mark Malone
(Back) Danny Logan, Susan Murphy in
"The Salad Of The Mad Cafe"**

GRAMERCY ARTS THEATRE

Opened Thursday, April 16, 1964.°
Nimara Productions in association with
Alex Hassilev present:

DIARY OF A MADMAN

By Nikolai Gogol; Adapted from the French
by Roger Coggio and Sylvie Luneau; English
version by Eric Rudd; Directed by William
Hickey; Settings and Lighting, Richard Hay;
Costumes, Patricia Quinn Stuart; Music, Georges
Delerue; Associate Lighting Designer, Robert
Brand; Russian Consultant, Zoya Voinov.

CAST

Poprichtchin .... Zack Matalon
Alternate Cast
Poprichtchin .... William Hickey

A Drama in three acts. The action of the play
takes place in St. Petersburg, Russia, in the
1830's.

Press: Sol Jacobson, Lewis Harmon,
Earl Butler
Stage Managers: Judd Hirsch, Michael Henry
° Closed Sunday, April 26, 1964.
(8 performances)

Friedman-Abeles Photo

Zack Matalon in "Diary Of A Madman"

WRITER'S STAGE THEATRE

Opened Monday, April 20, 1964.°
Jones Harris presents:

BILLYGOAT EDDIE

By James Grady; Directed by Lawrence Kornfeld; Sets and Lighting, Joel Cook; Costumes,
Sally Gifft; Technician, Joel Wolfe.

CAST

Prof. Parkenkirchen .... Louis J. Camuti, Jr.
Eddie Lauer .... Charles C. Welch
Agatha-Dorothea Higginson .... Nancy Nugent
Howard deVraie Harper .... James Antonio
Optic O. Higginson .... Hal Burdick
Waldo Winter .... Sheldon Baron
Mrs. Hortense Higginson .... Grace Carney
Ethel Chicken Schmidt .... Joyce Aaron
Matilda .... Mary Boylan
Hepzabah .... Lucille Benson
Comfort .... Betty O'Rear

A Comedy in three acts and four scenes. The
action takes place in Cambridge, Mass., in the
Spring of 1840.

General Managers: Dorothy Olim, Gerald
Krone
Press: Max Eisen, Jeanne Gibson Merrick
Stage Manager: William E. Dauphin
° Closed Tuesday, April 21, 1964.
(2 performances)

"Billygoat Eddie"

EAST END THEATRE

Opened Monday, April 27, 1964.°
Northwestern Productions presents:

ARMS AND THE MAN

By G. B. Shaw; Directed by Johan Fillinger;
Settings, Michael Devine; Lighting, Dennis
Parichy; Production Consultant, Maude Fran-
chot; Costumes, Charlotte Lefson.

CAST

Raina Petkoff .... Kathryn Loder
Katherine Petkoff .... Philippa Bevans
Louka .... Joan Bassie
Captain Bluntschli .... Frederic Bradlee
Russian Officer .... Ivan Rider
Nicola .... J. S. Johnson
Major Paul Petkoff .... Carl Don
Sergius .... John Wynne-Evans

UNDERSTUDIES: Howard Bennett, Annette
Krasko, Jeanne Devine, Madeleine Fisher, Norton
Wittstein.

A Comedy in three acts. The action takes
place on the Petkoff Estate in Bulgaria in November 1885.

Business Manager: Mary Jordan
Press: Joe Wolhandler, Mickey Mackay
Stage Manager: Ivan Rider
° Closed Sunday, May 17, 1964.
(23 performances)

Bert Andrews Photo

John Wynne-Evans, Kathryn Loder,
Carl Don, Philippa Bevans in
"Arms And The Man"

THEATRE DE LYS

Opened Monday, May 4, 1964.°
Cheryl Crawford and Roger L. Stevens
present:

DOUBLETALK

By Lewis John Carlino; Directed by Cyril
Simon; Designs and Lighting, Boyd Dumrose;
Costumes, Julia Lusk; Musical Score, Al Cohn;
Production Associate, Richard R. Chandler.

"Sarah and The Sax"

CAST

Sarah..Ruth White
The Sax..............................Clarence Williams III

The action takes place in a small park in
New York on the morning of a late spring day.

"The Dirty Old Man"

CAST

Old Man...Franchot Tone
Mary..Amy Taubin
Chuck...................................Gregory Rozakis

The action takes place on a promontory over-
looking a stretch of deserted Northern California
coast in the fall.

Company Manager: Herbert Cherin
Press: Bob Ullman, Warren Pincus
Stage Managers: Peter Maloney, Norman Bush

° Closed Sunday, May 17, 1964.
(16 performances)

Martha Holmes Photos

Clarence Williams, Ruth White
Top: Amy Taubin, Franchot Tone

229

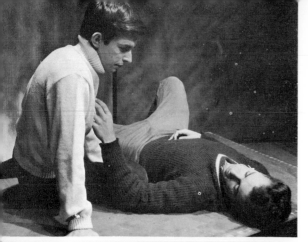

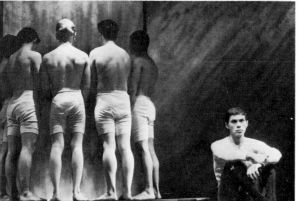

Avery Willard Photos

**Robert Schumacher, Philip Mancuso, Barry
Bonner, Carmine Stipo, Barry Fortus,
Ira Lewis in "The Awakening of Spring"**

ACTORS PLAYHOUSE

Opened Tuesday, May 5, 1964.°
Bonard Productions in association with
Howard Atlee present:

DARK CORNERS
and MR. GROSSMAN

By Stanley Koven; Directed by Joseph Hardy;
Designed by William Wall; Sound Created by
James Reichert; Production Assistant, Gordon
Gray; Assistants to the Producers, James Fra-
sher, Paul Solomon; An American Stage For
Writers and Actors, Inc., production.

"Dark Corners"

CAST

Bert_____Henderson Forsythe
Charlotte_____Haila Stoddard
The action takes place at the present time
in a cheap theatrical hotel in New York City.

"Mr. Grossman"

CAST

Ruana_____Cynthia Belgrave
Cherry_____Audree Rae
Messenger_____Frank Geraci
Dick Piper_____Joel Fabiani
Mr. Grossman_____Joseph Leon
The action takes place in late October, some
time from now.

General Managers: Parland Productions
Press: Ruth Cage
Stage Manager: Frank Geraci
°Closed Sunday, May 10, 1964. (7 performances)

230

POCKET THEATER

Opened Tuesday, May 12, 1964.°
Theatre Vanguard presents:

THE AWAKENING OF SPRING

By Frank Wedekind; Adapted by Arthur A.
Seidelman and Donald Levin; Directed by
Arthur A. Seidelman; Settings, Gary Zeller;
Costumes, Sally Gifft; Music, George Fischoff;
Sound, Alan Heim; Translation, Mascha Beyo;
Co-Producer, John Savoca; Executive Producer,
Arthur A. Seidelman; Production Consultant,
Barry Hyams; Associate Producer, Eleanor Fort-
us; Assistant to the Producer, Donald Levin;
Production Coordinator, Robert Salvio.

CAST

Anne Woodman_____Lynne Lipton
Mrs. Woodman_____Iris Whitney
Michael Gable_____Ira Lewis
Frances Gable_____Helen Baron
Arthur_____Philip Mancuso
George_____Harrison Hart
Robert_____Carmine Stipo
Eugene_____Robert Schumacher
Joseph_____Barry Bonner
John_____Barry Fortus
Matthew Steifel_____Robert Salvio
Thea_____Naomi Robin
Martha_____Silvana Simoni
Henry_____Gary Britton
Miriam_____Elaine Partnow
Professor Meltzer_____Harrison Hart
Professor Hartshorne_____Philip Mancuso
Professor Digby_____Robert Schumacher
Professor Newdigate_____Carmine Stipo
Hablebald_____Barry Bonner
Minister_____Leonard Hicks
Mr. Steifel_____Robert Colson
Mr. Gable_____Leonard Hicks
Boys in Reformatory_____Robert Schumacher,
Philip Mancuso, Barry Bonner, Carmine Stipo,
Barry Fortus
Doctor_____Robert Colson
Singer and Guitarist_____Angus Godwin
Flutist_____Jayne Rosenfeld
UNDERSTUDIES: Michael, Gary Britton; Mat-
thew, Eugene, Philip Mancuso; Henry, Carmine
Stipo; Professors, Barry Bonner; Peter, Joseph,
Hablebald, Barry Fortus; Messrs. Woodman,
Gable, Odette Capetan; General understudies,
Naomi Robin, Anthony Sano.

A Drama in two acts.

Company Manager: John Savoca
Press: Sol Jacobson, Lewis Harmon,
Earl Butler
Stage Managers: Robert Colson, Anthony Sano,
Barry Bonner, Carmine Stipo, Chenault Spence
° Closed Sunday, May 17, 1964.
(8 performances)

Friedman-Abeles Photo
**Robert Salvio, Lynne Lipton, Ira Lewis, and top
Left: Robert Schumacher, Gary Britton
in "The Awakening Of Spring"**

PROVINCETOWN PLAYHOUSE

Opened Monday, May 11, 1964.*
Orson Bean Productions, Inc., in association
with Judson Poets' Theater present:

HOME MOVIES

Book and Lyrics by Rosalyn Drexler; Music,
Al Carmines; Directed by Lawrence Kornfeld;
Sets, Larry Siegel; Lighting, Nicola Cernovich;
"Home Movies" Costumes, Judith Berkowitz;
"Softly, and Consider The Nearness" Costumes,
Carolyn Maxwell; Production Assistant, Ellen
Levene; Violin, Malcolm Goldstein; French Horn,
Carman Moore.

SHORT SUBJECT
"Softly, and Consider The Nearness"
CAST

Nona	Sudie Bond
Floor Model	George Bartenieff
Stranger	Otto Mjaanes

FEATURE
"Home Movies"
CAST

Mrs. Verdun	Gretel Cummings
Vivienne	Sudie Bond
Violet	Barbara Ann Teer
Peter Peterouter	Fred Herko
Sister Thalia	Sheindi Tokayer
Father Shenanigan	Al Carmines†
Charles Anduit	Otto Mjaanes
John the Truck Driver	Jim Anderson
Mr. Verdun	George Bartenieff

Press: Mary Bryant, Violet Welles
Stage Manager: Neville Powers

* Still playing May 31, 1964.
  (24 performances)
† Succeeded by Orson Bean

Van Williams Photos

**Top: Sheindi Tokayer, Barbara Ann Teer,
Gretel Cummings, George Bartenieff, Jim
Anderson, Sudie Bond, Fred Herko,
Otto Mjaanes, Al Carmines**

Jim Anderson, Gretel Cummings, Fred Herko

231

STAGE 73

Opened Thursday, May 14, 1964.°
The Chronicle Company presents:

THE PLACE FOR CHANCE

Arranged by Winthrop Palmer, Maurice Edwards, and Jean Reavey; Directed by Charles Olsen; Settings and Lighting, William Ritman; Costumes, Martha Gould; Musical Director, Barry Kornfeld; Production Assistant, Linda Simon.

CAST

Sam Greene	Margaret De Priest
Jordan Charney	Russell Gold
Leon B. Stevens	John Horn

Dramatized readings of historical events, men, and women, and documents, presented in two acts.

General Manager: Spofford J. Beadle
Press: Sol Jacobson, Lewis Harmon, Earl Butler
Stage Manager: Patrick Horrigan

° Closed Sunday, May 24, 1964.
(13 performances)

Bert Andrews Photo

Right: Margaret DePriest, Leon B. Stevens, Sam Greene

VILLAGE THEATRE

Opened Thursday, May 21, 1964.°
Trans-World Productions presents:

INTERNATIONAL PLAYGIRLS '64

Entire production conceived and directed by Martin B. Cohen; Musical Director, Joe Cabot; Costumes, Kam Deveraux; Special Material, John Roeburt; Comedy Consultant and Assistant Director, Allan Drake; Production Supervisor and Lighting, Peter Xantho; Choreography, Bhaskar; Assistant to the producer, Arlene Gordon.

CAST

Georgia Sothern	John Conte
Allan Drake	Morocco
Saja Lee	The Albrights
Pamela Hayes	Miss Hollywood
and 12 International Beauties	

PROGRAM

ACT I: Opening Production, Morocco, Marriage License Bureau, Japanese Production, The Demonstrators, John Conte, Paris Artist, Allan Drake, Production Finale.

ACT II. Opening Production, Magician, Miss Hollywood, The Mother-in-Law, John Conte, Allan Drake, Georgia Sothern, Finale.
Press: David Lipsky

° Closed Saturday, May 23, 1964.
(4 performances)

Georgia Sothern

232

THE NEW THEATRE

Opened Wednesday, May 27, 1964.°
The Establishment Theatre Company, Inc.,
presents:

THE KNACK

By Ann Jellicoe; Directed by Mike Nichols;
Scenery, Ed Wittstein; Clothes, Theoni V. Ald-
redge; Lighting, Roger Morgan; Produced by
arrangement with David Black; Assistant to the
Producers, Annie Langdon; Production Assistant,
Andy Amic Angelo; Technical Director, Joe
Pacitti.

CAST

Tom	Brian Bedford
Colin	Roddy Maude-Roxby
Tolen	George Segal
Nancy	Alexandra Berlin

UNDERSTUDIES: Sam Waterston, Carol Booth

A Comedy in three acts. The action takes
place in London at the present time.

General Manager: Ivor David Balding
Press: Bill Doll, Maurice Turet,
Robert Ganshaw
Stage Managers: Eli Ask, Sam Waterston

° Still playing May 31, 1964.
(7 performances)

**Top: Brian Bedford, Alexandra Berlin,
Brian Murray, Roddy Maude-Roxby**

**Brian Bedford, Roddy Maude-Roxby,
Brian Murray, Alexandra Berlin**

THE PREMISE THEATRE

Opened Thursday, May 28, 1964.°
Michael Brandman and Murray Roman, in association with the Premise Rest. Corp, present:

THE THIRD EAR

Set pieces and improvisations devised by the company; Directed by Elaine May; Associate Producer, William DeSeta; Technical Director, Joseph Pacitti.

CAST

Peter Boyle	Louise Lasser
Mark Gordon	Reni Santoni
	Renee Taylor

An Improvisational Revue with "Set" pieces.
Press: Seymour Krawitz, Merle Debuskey, Madi Ross
°Still playing May 31, 1964. (6 performances)

Friedman-Abeles Photo

Right: Renee Taylor, Reni Santoni
in "The Third Ear"

MAYFAIR THEATRE

Opened Thursday, May 28, 1964.°
Keith Rockwell presents:

UNDER THE YUM-YUM TREE

By Lawrence Roman; Directed by Michael Ferrall; Lighting, Gary Zeller; Production Assistant, Bernice Stone.

CAST

Irene Wilson	Marrian Walters
Robin Austin	Marian Hailey
Dave Manning	Bill Bixby
Hogan	Ted Brown

A Comedy in two acts and four scenes. The action takes place in an attic apartment of an aged building on San Francisco's Telegraph Hill at the present time.

Company Manager: Moses Baruch
Press: Harvey B. Sabinson, Leo Stern
Stage Manager: Elsa Walden
°Closed Sunday, May 31, 1964. (6 performances)

Ted Brown, Bill Bixby
Above: Marian Hailey, Ted Brown, Bill Bixby
in "Under The Yum-Yum Tree"

WRITERS' STAGE

Opened Sunday, May 24, 1964.°
The Writers' Stage Company and Seymour Hacker present:

TWO BY IONESCO

By Eugene Ionesco; Translated by Donald Watson; Directed by Michael Kahn; Scenery, Ed Wittstein; Costumes, Ruth Morley; Lighting, V. C. Fuqua; Executive Producer, Judith Peabody; Technical Director, Francis White; Production Assistant, Rufus Collins.

CAST

"The New Tenant"

The Caretaker	Charlotte Rae
The Gentleman	Anthony Holland
1st Furniture Mover	Michael Howard
2nd Furniture Mover	Joseph Chaikin

"Victims of Duty"

Madeleine	Charlotte Rae
Choubert	Michael Howard
The Detective	Joseph Chaikin
The Lady	Sharon Gans
Nicolas	Anthony Holland

Press: Blaine Thompson
Stage Manager: Fred Reinglas
°Still playing May 31, 1964. (8 performances)

Left: Charlotte Rae, Michael Howard, Anthony Holland, Joseph Chaikin in "Victims Of Duty"
Top: Michael Howard, Charlotte Rae, Joseph Chaikin, Anthony Holland in "The New Tenant"

OFF-BROADWAY PLAYS FROM OTHER SEASONS THAT CLOSED DURING THIS SEASON

Play	Opened	Closed	Performances
The Premise	Nov. 22, 19.	Nov. 3, 1963	1490
Pinter Plays ("The Dumbwaiter" and "The Collection")	Nov. 26, 1962	Apr. 12, 1964	578
Riverwind	Dec. 12, 1962	Jan. 5, 1964	443
Desire Under The Elms	Jan. 8, 1963	Dec. 15, 1963	380
Days and Nights of Beebee Fenstermaker	Sept. 17, 1962	June 9, 1963	304
The Brig (Suspended from Oct. 9 to Dec. 19, 1963)	May 13, 1963	Feb. 16, 1964	239
Best Foot Forward	Apr. 2, 1963	Oct. 13, 1963	224
"The Typists" and "The Tiger"	Feb. 4, 1963	July 28, 1963	200
The Importance of Being Earnest	Feb. 25, 1963	July 13, 1963	164
Albee Plays ("The American Dream" and "The Zoo Story")	May 28, 1963	Sept. 29, 1963	143
Do You Know The Milky Way?	Mar. 14, 1963	June 2, 1963	94
A Month In The Country	May 28, 1963	July 7, 1963	48
Yerby Plays ("Save Me A Place In Forest Lawn" and "The Last Minstrel")	May 8, 1963	June 9, 1963	38
Put It In Writing	May 13, 1963	June 2, 1963	24
Along Came A Spider	May 27, 1963	June 13, 1963	21
The Summer of Daisy Miller	May 27, 1963	June 9, 1963	17

BIOGRAPHIES

ADLER, LUTHER. Born in New York City, May 4, 1903. Attended Lewis Inst. Made first appearance in 1908 in "Schmendrick." Other performances include "Night Over Taos," "Success Story," "Alien Corn," "Men In White," "Gold Eagle Guy," "Awake and Sing," "Paradise Lost," "Johnny Johnson," "Golden Boy," "Rocket To The Moon," "The Russian People," "Two On An Island," "Common Ground," "Beggars Are Coming To Town," "Dunnigan's Daughter," "A Flag Is Born," "The Merchant of Venice," "A Month In The Country," "A Very Special Baby," "The Passion of Josef D.," "The Three Sisters."

ALBERTSON, JACK. Born in Revere, Mass. Appeared in vaudeville before making Broadway bow in 1941 in "Meet The People." Other appearances include "Strip For Action," "The Lady Says Yes," "Allah Be Praised," revivals of "The Red Mill" and "The Cradle Will Rock," "Make Mine Manhattan," "High Button Shoes," "Tickets, Please," "Top Banana," "The Subject Was Roses."

ALDA, ALAN. Born in New York City, Jan. 28, 1936. Attended Fordham Univ. and Cleveland Playhouse. Broadway credits include "Only In America," "Purlie Victorious," "Fair Game For Lovers" for which he won a THEATRE WORLD Award, and "Cafe Crown." Off-Broadway credits: "Darwin's Theories," "A Whisper In God's Ear," and "Second City" (1963 edition).

ALDA, ROBERT. Born in New York City, Feb. 26, 1914. Attended New York U. Made many motion pictures and appeared in night clubs before making Broadway bow in 1950 in "Guys and Dolls." Has appeared since in "Harbor Lights," "What Makes Sammy Run."

ALEXANDER, JOHN. Born in Newport, Ky., Nov. 29, 1897. Attended Helen Schuster-Martin Dramatic School, Cincinnati. Among his more recent appearances are "Hilda Crane," "Ondine," "A Visit To A Small Planet," "Never Too Late."

AMES, ED. Born in Boston, Mass., July 9, 1929. Attended Boston Latin School, and trained for the stage at the Herbert Berghof Studio. Broadway appearances include "Carnival," and "One Flew Over The Cuckoo's Nest."

ANDERSON, JUDITH. Born in Adelaide, Australia, Feb. 10, 1898. Made NY debut in 1923 in "Peter Weston," followed by "Cobra," "The Dove," "Strange Interlude," "As You Desire Me," "Firebird," "The Mask and The Face," "Come of Age," "The Old Maid," "Family Portrait," "Hamlet," "Macbeth," "The Three Sisters," "Medea," "Tower Beyond Tragedy," "John Brown's Body," "In The Summer House," "The Chalk Garden," "Comes A Day," and during the past season, toured in a one-woman show.

ANDREWS, JULIE. Born in 1935 in Walton-on-Thames, Surrey, Eng. Made Broadway debut in 1954 in "The Boy Friend," for which she received a THEATRE WORLD Award. Has appeared since in "My Fair Lady" in NY and London, and "Camelot."

ANDREWS, NANCY. Born in Minneapolis, Dec. 16, 1924. Studied at Pasadena Playhouse. Has appeared in "Hilarities," "Touch and Go," for which she received a THEATRE WORLD Award, "Gentlemen Prefer Blondes," "Hazel Flagg," "Plain and Fancy," "Pipe Dream," "Juno," "Christine," "The Three-penny Opera," "Tiger Rag," "Flower Drum Song," "Madame Aphrodite," "Little Me."

ANTONIO, LOU. Born in Oklahoma City, Jan. 23, 1934. Attended U. of Okla. Appeared in stock before NY bow (off-Bdwy) in 1959 in "The Buffalo Skinner" for which he received a THEATRE WORLD Award. Has appeared since in "The Power of Darkness," "The Good Soup," "Cry of The Raindrop," "Garden of Sweets," "Andorra," "Lady of The Camellias," "The Ballad of The Sad Cafe."

ARKIN, ALAN. Born in NYC, March 26, 1934. Attended Los Angeles Junior College, and Bennington College. Won 5 acting scholarships, including Brandeis Arts Inst. Appeared off-Bdwy in "Heloise," "Man Out Loud," and on Bdwy in "From The Second City" (1962), and "Enter Laughing" for which he received a THEATRE WORLD Award.

ASHLEY, ELIZABETH. Born in Ocala, Fla., Aug. 30, 1939. Attended Neighborhood Playhouse. Made Off-Broadway debut in "Dirty Hands," and Broadway bow in "The Highest Tree," followed by "Take Her, She's Mine" for which she received a THEATRE WORLD Award, "Barefoot In The Park."

BADEL, ALAN. Born in Manchester, Eng., Sept. 11, 1923. Attended Burnage School, Manchester, and Royal Academy of Dramatic Arts in London. Made Broadway bow Sept. 23, 1963 in "The Rehearsal."

BAILEY, ROBIN. Born in Hucknall, Nottingham, Eng., Oct. 5, 1919. Attended Henry Mellish School, Nottingham. Trained for stage with Birmingham Repertory Co. Made Broadway bow Oct. 17, 1963 in "Jennie."

BALLANTYNE, PAUL. Born in Boorhead, Iowa, July 8, 1909. Trained at Eva Le Gallienne's repertory theatre. Has appeared more recently in "The Strong Are Lonely," "Richard III," "The Enchanted," (Off-Bdwy,) toured in "Mary Stuart" and "Elizabeth The Queen."

BALLARD, KAYE. Born in Cleveland, Ohio, Nov. 20. Appeared in stock, vaudeville, and night clubs before making NY bow in "The Golden Apple," followed by "Carnival," "The Beast In Me."

BANCROFT, ANNE. Born in NYC, Sept. 17, 1931. Attended American Academy of Dramatic Art. Made Bdwy debut in 1958 in "Two For The Seesaw" for which she received a THEATRE WORLD Award, followed by "The Miracle Worker," "Mother Courage and Her Children."

BANKHEAD, TALLULAH. Born in Huntsville, Ala., Jan. 31, 1902. Made Bdwy debut in 1918 in "The Squab Farm," followed by "39 East," "Footloose," "Nice People," "Her Temporary Husband," "The Exciters." Appeared in London from 1923-30. Returned in 1933 in "Forsaking All Others," followed by "Dark Victory," "Something Gay," "Reflected Glory," revivals of "Rain," "The Circle," "Antony and Cleopatra," "Private Lives," and "A Streetcar Named Desire," in "The Little Foxes," "Clash By Night," "The Skin Of Our Teeth," "The Eagle Has Two Heads," "Dear Charles," "Eugenia," "Crazy October" and "Here Today" on tour, "Midgie Purvis," "The Milk Train Doesn't Stop Here Anymore."

BASELEON, MICHAEL. Born in Tarkio, Mo. Attended Northwestern Univ. Studied with Uta Hagen and Lee Strasberg. Broadway credits include "Caligula," "Night Life," "Dear Me, The Sky Is Falling." Off-Broadway: Phoenix productions of "Hamlet," and "Henry IV Part 2," Papp's Park productions of "Richard II," "Romeo and Juliet," and "The Tempest," "Journey To The Day."

BAURSMITH, PAULA. Born in Pittsburgh, July 26, 1909. Attended Carnegie Tech. Has appeared in "Lean Harvest," "East of Broadway," "The Warrior's Husband," "The Anatomist," "Three-Cornered Moon," "All Good Americans," "Mahogany Hall," "Let Freedom Ring," "Bury The Dead," "Two Hundred Were Chosen," "Twentieth Century," "The Lesson," "Sail Away."

BAXLEY, BARBARA. Born in Porterville, Cal., Jan. 1, 1925. Trained at Neighborhood Playhouse. Has appeared in "Private Lives" (1948), "Out West of Eighth," succeeded Jean Arthur in "Peter Pan," Julie Harris in "I Am A Camera," and Kim Stanley in "Bus Stop," "Camino Real," "The Frogs of Spring," "Oh, Men! Oh, Women!," "The Flowering Peach," "Period of Adjustment," "Brecht on Brecht," "She Loves Me."

| Michael Baseleon | Shannon Bolin | Charles Baxter | Tallulah Bankhead |

BAXTER, CHARLES. Born in Paterson, N. J., Apr. 17, 1924. Attended Washington and Lee Univ. and Yale Drama School. Received training in summer theatres. Broadway credits: "Oklahoma," "Texas Li'l Darlin'," "Stalag 17," "Hook 'n' Ladder," "The Advocate."

BEAL, JOHN. Born in Joplin, Mo., Aug. 13, 1909. Attended U. of Pa. Has appeared in "Wild Waves," "Another Language," "She Loves Me Not," "Russet Mantle," "Soliloquy," "Miss Swan Expects," "Liberty Jones," "The Voice of The Turtle," "Lend An Ear," "The Teahouse of The August Moon," "Our Town" (Off-Bdwy), "Calculated Risk."

BEAN, ORSON. Born in Burlington, Vt., July 22, 1928. Appeared in night clubs before making Bdwy bow in 1953 in "Men of Distinction," followed by "John Murray Anderson's Almanac" for which he received a THEATRE WORLD Award, "Will Success Spoil Rock Hunter?," "Nature's Way," City Center revivals of "Mister Roberts" and "Say, Darling," "Subways Are For Sleeping," "Never Too Late."

BEDFORD, BRIAN. Born in Morley, Yorkshire, Eng., Feb. 16, 1935. Attended Royal Academy of Dramatic Arts. Made NY bow Dec. 2, 1960, in "Five Finger Exercise." Has appeared since in "Lord Pengo," "The Private Ear" and "The Public Eye," "The Knack."

BEL GEDDES, BARBARA. Born in NYC, Oct. 31, 1923. Has appeared in "Out Of The Frying Pan," "Little Darling," "Nine Girls," "Mrs. January and Mr. X," "Deep Are The Roots," for which she received a THEATRE WORLD Award, "Burning Bright," "The Moon Is Blue," "The Sleeping Prince," "Silent Night, Lonely Night," "Mary, Mary."

BELL, MARIE. Born in Bordeaux, France, Dec. 23, 1905. One of the great French tragediennes received her training with the Comedie Francaise. Made Broadway debut with her own company Oct. 20, 1963 in "Phedre" and "Berenice."

BELLIN, OLGA. Born Aug. 18, 1935. Attended Downes College and Northwestern U. Appeared off-Broadway in "The Carefree Tree" and "A Month In The Country." Made Broadway debut in 1956 in "Protective Custody," followed by "A Man For All Seasons."

BERRY, ERIC. Born in London, Jan. 9, 1913. Attended Royal Academy of Dramatic Arts. Made NY bow in 1954 in "The Boy Friend," followed by "Family Reunion," "The Power and The Glory," "Beaux Stratagem," "The Broken Jug," "Pictures In The Hallway," "Peer Gynt," "The Great God Brown," "Henry IV, Parts I and II," "The White House."

BLACKMER, SIDNEY. Born in Salisbury, N.C., July 13, 1895. Attended U. of NC. Made NY bow in 1917 in "The Morris Dance," followed by "The Mountain Man," "The 13th Chair," "The Love Child," "The Moon Flower," "The Carolinian," "Scaramouche," "Love In A Mist," "39 East," "The Springboard," "Chicken Every Sunday," "Wonderful Journey," "Portrait In Black," "Come Back, Little Sheba," "The Brass Ring," "Sweet Bird of Youth," "Take Me Along," "A Case of Libel."

BLEEZARDE, GLORIA. Born in Albany, N.Y., Oct. 12, 1940. Attended Southern Seminary Junior College. Appeared in summer stock and National Co. of "Bye Bye Birdie," and off-Bdwy in "Just For Fun" and "New York Coloring Book." Made Broadway debut Mar. 28, 1964 in "Never Live Over A Pretzel Factory" for which she received a THEATRE WORLD Award.

BOLGER, RAY. Born in Dorchester, Mass., Jan. 10, 1906. Has appeared in "The Merry World," "A Night In Paris," "The Passing Show of 1926," "Heads Up," "George White's Scandals of 1931," "Life Begins At 8:40," "On Your Toes," "Keep Off The Grass," "Three To Make Ready," "Where's Charley?," "All American."

BOLIN, SHANNON. Born in South Dakota, Jan. 1, 1917. Attended Univ. of Maryland. Broadway credits include "Helen Goes To Troy," "The Golden Apple," "Regina," "Only In America," "Damn Yankees," "The Student Gypsy."

BOND, GARY. Born in Alton, Hampshire, Eng., Feb. 7, 1940. Attended Churchers College. Received training at Central School of Speech and Drama, and with Worthing Repertory Co. Made Broadway bow Oct. 1, 1963 in "Chips With Everything."

BOVA, JOSEPH. Born in Cleveland, Ohio. Attended Northwestern U. and Cleveland Playhouse. Has appeared on Broadway in "Once Upon A Mattress," "The Rape of The Belt," "Irma La Douce," and "Hotspot," and Off-Bdwy in revivals of "On The Town" and "The Taming of The Shrew."

BOYER, CHARLES. Born in Figeac, France, Aug. 28, 1899. Appeared on stage and in films in France before making Broadway bow in 1948 in "Red Gloves," followed by "Don Juan In Hell," "Kind Sir," "The Marriage-Go-Round," "Lord Pengo," "Man and Boy."

BRANDON, PETER. Born in Berlin, Ger., July 11, 1926. Attended Neighborhood Playhouse. Has appeared in "Cry of The Peacock," City Center revivals of "Come of Age" and "Tovarich," "Ondine," "The Young and Beautiful," "The Hidden River," "The Infernal Machine," "A Man For All Seasons."

BRETT, JEREMY. Born in Berkswell, Warwickshire, Eng., Nov. 3, 1933. Attended Eaton. Appeared with Old Vic's 1956-57 Broadway productions of "Troilus and Cressida," "Macbeth," "Richard II," and "Romeo and Juliet," followed by "The Deputy."

BROOKES, JACQUELINE. Born in Montclair, N.J., July 24, 1930. Attended U. of Iowa and Royal Academy of Dramatic Arts, London. Has appeared in "Tiger At The Gates," and Off-Bdwy in "The Cretan Woman" for which she received a THEATRE WORLD Award, "The Clandestine Marriage," "Measure For Measure," "The Duchess of Malfi," "Ivanov," "Six Characters in Search of An Author."

BROOKS, DAVID. Born Sept. 24, 1917 in Portland, Ore. Attended U. of Wash. and Curtis Inst. of Music. Made Broadway bow in 1944 in "Bloomer Girl," followed by "Brigadoon," "Mr. President," "The Sunday Man."

BROOKS, MARTIN. Born in The Bronx, Nov. 30, 1925. Attended Penn State and American Theatre Wing. Has appeared in "That Lady," "Smile of The World," "Burning Bright" for which he received a THEATRE WORLD Award, "An Enemy of The People," "I Am A Camera," "Night of The Auk," "The Advocate."

BROWNE, CORAL. Born in Melbourne, Australia, July 23, 1913. Appeared on English stage before making Broadway debut in 1956 in "Tamburlaine," followed by "Troilus and Cressida," "The Rehearsal."

BULL, PETER. Born in London, Eng., Mar. 21, 1912. Attended Winchester College, Eng., and Tours Univ., France. Has appeared on Broadway in "Escape Me Never," "The Lady's Not For Burning," "Luther."

BURNETT, CAROL. Born in San Antonio, Tex., April 26, 1935. Attended UCLA. Made NY debut in 1959 in "Once Upon A Mattress" for which she received a THEATRE WORLD Award. Has appeared since in "Fade Out—Fade In."

BURNS, DAVID. Born in NYC, June 22, 1902. Has appeared in "Polly Preferred," "Wonder Boy," "Face The Music," "The Man Who Came To Dinner," "Pal Joey," "My Dear Public," "Billion Dollar Baby," "Make Mine Manhattan," "Out Of This World," "Two's Company," "Men of Distinction," "A Hole In The Head," "The Music Man," "A Funny Thing Happened On The Way To The Forum," "Hello, Dolly!"

BURR, ROBERT. Born in Jersey City, N.J. Attended Colgate U. Has appeared in "The Cradle Will Rock," "Mister Roberts," "Romeo and Juliet" (de Haviland revival), "Picnic," "The Lovers," "Anniversary Waltz," "Top Man," "Remains To Be Seen," "The Wall," "Andersonville Trial," "A Shot In The Dark," "A Man For All Seasons," "Luther," "Hamlet" (Burton revival).

BURTON, RICHARD. Born in Pontrhydyfen, South Wales, Nov. 10, 1925. Attended Exeter College, Oxford. Made Bdwy bow in 1950 in "The Lady's Not For Burning" for which he received a THEATRE WORLD Award, followed by "Legend of Lovers," "Time Remembered," "Camelot," "Hamlet."

CAMPBELL, FLORA. Born in Oklahoma. Made NY debut with Eva LeGallienne's Civic Repertory Co. Has appeared in "Excursion," "Many Mansions," "The Land Is Bright," "Foxhole In The Parlor," "The Curious Savage," "Only In America," and Off-Bdwy in "Angels of Anadarko" and "Journey To The Day."

CARLIN, THOMAS. Born in Chicago, Dec. 10, 1928. Attended Loyola and Catholic U. Appeared Off-Bdwy in "Thieves Carnival," and on Bdwy in "Time Limit!," "Holiday For Lovers," "The Man In The Dog Suit," "A Cook For Mr. General," "Great Day In The Morning," "A Thousand Clowns," "The Deputy."

CARROLL, DIAHANN. Born in NYC, July 17, 1935. Attended NYU. Made Broadway debut in 1954 in "House of Flowers," followed by "No Strings."

CASS, PEGGY. Born in Boston, May 21, 1926. Attended Wyndham. Has appeared in "Touch and Go," "The Live Wire," "Bernardine," "Phoenix '55," "Othello," "Henry V," "Auntie Mame" for which she received a THEATRE WORLD Award, "A Thurber Carnival," "Children From Their Games."

CASSIDY, JACK. Born in Richmond Hills, L.I., Mar. 5, 1927. Has appeared in "Something For The Boys," "Sadie Thompson," "Around The World," "Inside U.S.A.," "Small Wonder," "Music In My Heart," "Alive and Kicking," "Wish You Were Here," "Sandhog," "Shangri-La," "The Beggar's Opera" (City Center), "She Loves Me," "Fade Out—Fade In."

CHANNING, CAROL. Born in Seattle, Wash., Jan. 31, 1921. Attended Bennington College. Has appeared in "No For An Answer," "Let's Face It," "So Proudly We Hail," "Lend An Ear" for which she received a THEATRE WORLD Award, "Gentlemen Prefer Blondes," "Wonderful Town," "The Vamp," "Show Girl," "Hello Dolly!"

CHAPLIN, SIDNEY. Born in Los Angeles, Mar. 31, 1926. Attended Lawrenceville School. Managed, directed, and acted in Circle Theatre, Hollywood. Made several films before Bdwy bow in 1956 in "Bells Are Ringing" for which he received a THEATRE WORLD Award, followed by "Goodbye, Charlie," "Subways Are For Sleeping," "In The Counting House," "Funny Girl."

CHURCH, GEORGE. Born in Springfield, Mass., Oct. 8, 1912. Studied with Anatole Bourman. Has appeared in "Thumbs Up," "Ziegfeld Follies" (1935), "On Your Toes" (1936 and 1954), "The Boys From Syracuse," "Hold Onto Your Hats," "What Big Ears," "Oklahoma," "110 In The Shade."

COLBERT, CLAUDETTE. Born in Paris, Sept. 13, 1907. Attended NYC public schools. Made Broadway debut in 1925 in "The Wild Westcotts," followed by "The Ghost Train," "Kiss In A Taxi," "The Barker," "The Mulberry Bush," "La Gringa," "Tin Pan Alley," "Dynamo," "See Naples and Die," "Janus," "The Marriage-Go-Round," "Jake, Julia and Uncle Joe," "The Irregular Verb To Love."

COLLINS, RUSSELL. Born in Indianapolis, Oct. 6, 1897. Attended Ind. State, Carnegie Tech, and Cleveland Playhouse. Most recent appearances have been in "The Enchanted," "The Grass Harp," "Sabrina Fair," "A View From The Bridge," "The Greatest Man Alive," "Sunrise At Campobello," "Romulus," "Calculated Risk."

COMPTON, FRANCIS. Born in Malvern, Eng., May 4, 1890. Made NY bow in 1912 in "The Whip," followed by "Idiot's Delight," "The Play's The Thing," "Red Gloves," "Montserrat," "Ring Round The Moon," "The Green Bay Tree," "Gigi," "Kismet," "Small War On Murray Hill," "Under Milkwood," "Lady of The Camellias."

CONLOW, PETER. Born in Philadelphia, July 2, 1929. Studied at American Theatre Wing. Has appeared in "As The Girls Go," "Lend An Ear," "Razzle Dazzle," "Courtin' Time" for which he received a THEATRE WORLD Award, "Three Wishes For Jamie," "The Shoestring Revue," "Copper and Brass," "The Boy Friend" (Off-Bdwy), "Take Me Along."

CONVY, BERT. Born in St. Louis, Mo., July 23, 1935. Graduate of UCLA. Made NY bow in 1959 in "Billy Barnes Revue," followed by "Nowhere To Go But Up," "Morning Sun," "Love and Kisses."

COOK, BARBARA. Born in Atlanta, Ga., Oct. 25, 1927. Has appeared in "Flahooley," "Plain and Fancy" for which she received a THEATRE WORLD Award, "Candide," "The Music Man," City Center revivals of "Carousel" and "The King and I," "The Gay Life," "She Loves Me."

COONEY, DENNIS. Born in NYC, Sept. 19, 1938. Attended Fordham U. Appeared Off-Bdwy in "Whisper To Me" and "Every Other Girl" for which he received a THEATRE WORLD Award. Made Bdwy bow in 1961 in "Ross," followed by "Love and Kisses," "In A Summer House" (Off-Bdwy).

COOPER, ANTHONY KEMBLE. Born in London, Feb. 6, 1908. Made NY bow in 1925 in "Lass O' Laughter," followed by "The School For Scandal," "His Majesty's Car," "The Command To Love," "Quiet, Please," "Anne of England," "Hay Fever," "Mary of Scotland," "Age 26," "Sheppey," "Ten Little Indians," "Sweethearts," "Mr. Pickwick," "Foxy."

CORNELL, KATHARINE. Born Feb. 16, 1898 in Berlin, Ger. Has appeared in "Nice People," "A Bill of Divorcement," "Will Shakespeare," "The Enchanted Cottage," "Candida," "The Green Hat," "The Letter," "The Age of Innocence," "The Barretts of Wimpole Street," "Romeo and Juliet," "St. Joan," "Wingless Victory," "No Time For Comedy," "The Doctor's Dilemma," "The Three Sisters," "Lovers and Friends," "Antigone," "Antony and Cleopatra," "That Lady," "The Constant Wife," "The Prescott Proposals," "The Dark Is Light Enough," "The Firstborn," "Dear Liar."

COSTER, NICOLAS. Born in London, Dec. 3, 1934. Studied at Neighborhood Playhouse and with Lee Strasberg. Made Bdwy bow in "Becket." Off-Bdwy credits: "Epitaph For George Dillon," "Shadow and Substance," "The Thracian Horses," "O Say Can You See."

John Davidson   Olive Deering   David Cryer   Imelda DeMartin

CRONYN, HUME. Born in London, Ont. Can., July 18, 1911. Attended Ridley College, McGill U., American Academy of Dramatic Art. Has appeared in "Hipper's Holiday," "High Tor," "Escape This Night," "Three Men On A Horse," "Boy Meets Girl," "Room Service," "The Three Sisters," "Mr. Big," "Retreat To Pleasure," "The Fourposter," "The Honeys," "A Day By The Sea," "The Man In The Dog Suit," "Triple Play," "Big Fish, Little Fish," "Hamlet" (Burton revival).

CRYER, DAVID. Born in Evanston, Ill., March 8, 1936. Attended DePauw Univ. Appeared in summer theatres and Off-Bdwy in "The Fantasticks" and "The Streets of New York."

DAILEY, IRENE. Born in NYC, Sept. 12, 1920. Attended Sacred Heart Convent. Has appeared in "Nine Girls," "Truckline Cafe," "Miss Lonelyhearts," "Andorra," "The Good Woman of Setuzuan" (Phoenix), "The Subject Was Roses."

DALY, JAMES. Born in Wisconsin, Oct. 23, 1918. Attended Cornell. Has appeared in "Born Yesterday," "Man and Superman," "The Devil's Disciple," "Billy Budd," "Mary Rose," "Major Barbara," for which he received a THEATRE WORLD Award, "St. Joan," "Dark Legend," City Center revivals of "The Merchant of Venice" and "The Glass Menagerie," "Miss Julie" (Phoenix), "Handful of Fire," "J. B.," "The Advocate," "The White House."

DAMON, STUART. Born in Brooklyn, Feb. 5, 1937. Graduate of Brandeis U. Made Broadway bow in "First Impressions," followed by "From A To Z," "Entertain A Ghost," and the Off-Bdwy revival of "The Boys From Syracuse" for which he received a THEATRE WORLD Award.

DANA, LEORA. Born in NYC, April 1, 1923. Attended Barnard College and Royal Academy of Dramatic Arts, London. Has appeared in "The Madwoman of Chaillot," "The Happy Time," "Point of No Return," "Sabrina Fair," "The Best Man," "In The Summer House" (Off-Bdwy).

DANIELS, DAVID. Born in Evanston, Ill., Apr. 10, 1929. Attended Yale and Curtis Inst. of Music. Toured in "Call Me Madam" before making Broadway bow in "Plain and Fancy" for which he received a THEATRE WORLD Award, followed by "Oh, Kay" and "The Banker's Daughter" Off-Bdwy, and on tour in "Carnival."

DANIELS, EDGAR. Born in Raleigh, N.C., June 3, 1932. Attended U. of NC. Has appeared in "New Girl In Town," "La Plume De Ma Tante," "Caligula," "The Affair," "A Man For All Seasons."

DANIELS, WILLIAM. Born in Brooklyn, Mar. 31, 1927. Graduate of Northwestern U. Has appeared in "Life With Father," "Richard II," "Seagulls Over Sorrento," "Legend of Lizzie," "Cat On A Hot Tin Roof" (on tour), "A Thousand Clowns," Off-Bdwy in "The Zoo Story," "The Iceman Cometh," and "Look Back In Anger," "Dear Me, The Sky Is Falling," "One Flew Over The Cuckoo's Nest."

DAVID, THAYER. Born in Medford, Mass., Mar. 4, 1927. Graduate of Harvard. Has appeared in "The Relapse," "King Lear" (City Center), "The Carefree Tree" and "The White Devil" at the Phoenix, "Mister Johnson," "Protective Custody," "Oscar Wilde" (Off-Bdwy), "A Man For All Seasons," "Andorra," National Repertory Theatre revivals of "The Seagull" and "The Crucible."

DAVIDSON, JOHN. Born in Pittsburgh, Dec. 13, 1941. Attended Denison Univ., Ohio. Made Bdwy bow Feb. 16, 1964 in "Foxy."

DAWSON, MARK. Born in Philadelphia, Mar. 23, 1920. Attended Phila. Conservatory. Has appeared in "By Jupiter," "Dancing In The Streets," "Sweethearts," "High Button Shoes" for which he received a THEATRE WORLD Award, "Great To Be Alive," "Me and Juliet," "Ankles Aweigh," "New Girl In Town," "Fiorello," "The Riot Act."

DEERING, OLIVE. Made her Broadway debut in 1932 in "Girls In Uniform," followed by "Growing Pains," "Picnic," "Daughters of Atreus," "The Eternal Road," "Winged Victory," "Skydrift," "The Front Page" revival, "Marathon '33."

DELL, GABRIEL. Born in Barbados, B.W.I., Oct. 7, 1930. Has appeared in "Dead End," "Tickets, Please," "Ankles Aweigh," "Fortuna," City Center revivals of "Can-Can," "Wonderful Town," and "Oklahoma," "Marathon '33," "Anyone Can Whistle."

De LUISE, DOM. Born in Brooklyn, Aug. 1, 1933. Attended Brooklyn College, and Cleveland Playhouse. Made Broadway bow in 1963 in "The Student Gypsy," after Off-Bdwy performances in "The Jackass," "Another Evening With Harry Stoones," "Little Mary Sunshine," "Half Past Wednesday," and "All In Love," "Here's Love."

De MARTIN, IMELDA. Born in Merano, Italy, Sept. 16, 1936. Has appeared in "Plain and Fancy," "My Fair Lady," "Goldilocks," "Gypsy," "Girls Against The Boys," "The Sound of Music," "Jenny," "South Pacific" (City Center), and Off-Bdwy in "The Amorous Flea" for which she received a THEATRE WORLD Award.

DEMAS, CAROLE. Born in Brooklyn, May 26, 1940. Attended U. of Vermont and NYU. Appeared in NY Shakespeare Festival, and Phoenix' "Morning Sun."

DEWHURST, COLLEEN. Born in Montreal, Can. Attended Downer College, American Academy of Dramatic Art, and American Theatre Wing. Has appeared in "Desire Under The Elms," "Tambourlaine The Great," "The Country Wife," "Caligula," Off-Bdwy in "The Taming of The Shrew," "The Eagle Has Two Heads," "Camille," "Macbeth," and "Children of Darkness" for which she received a THEATRE WORLD Award, "All The Way Home," "Great Day In The Morning," "The Ballad of The Sad Cafe."

DILLON, MELINDA. Born in Hope, Ark., Oct. 13, 1939. Trained at Goodman Theatre, Chicago, and Washington Arena Stage. Made Broadway debut in 1962 in "Who's Afraid of Virginia Woolf?" for which she received a THEATRE WORLD Award.

DONAT, PETER. Born in Nova Scotia, Can., Jan. 20, 1928. Attended Acadia U. and Yale. Has appeared in "Highlights of The Empire," "The First Gentleman" for which he received a THEATRE WORLD Award, "The Country Wife," "The Entertainer," Off-Bdwy in "A God Slept Here" and "The Three Sisters," Stratford Shakespeare Festival, "The Chinese Prime Minister."

DOUGLASS, STEPHEN. Born in Mt. Vernon, Ohio, Sept. 27, 1921. Appeared in NY and London companies of "Carousel," and in "Make A Wish," "The Golden Apple," "Damn Yankees," "110 In The Shade."

DRAKE, ALFRED. Born in NYC, Oct. 7, 1914. Attended Brooklyn College. Has appeared in "Two Bouquets," "White Horse Inn," "Babes In Arms," "One For The Money," "Straw Hat Revue," "Two For The Show," "Out Of The Frying Pan," "As You Like It," "Oklahoma," "Sing Out Sweet Land," "Beggar's Holiday," "The Cradle Will Rock," "Joy To The World," "Kiss Me, Kate," "The Gambler," "Kismet," "Kean," "Lorenzo," "Hamlet."

DRIVAS, ROBERT. Born in Coral Gables, Fla. Attended U. of Miami, U. of Chicago. Trained with Greek National Theatre, Athens, and Coconut Grove Playhouse, Fla. Made Bdwy bow in 1958 in "The Firstborn," followed by "Mrs. Dally Has A Lover" (Off-Bdwy) for which he received a THEATRE WORLD Award, "Lorenzo," "The Irregular Verb To Love."

DUKE, ROBERT. Born in Washington, D.C., June 22, 1917. Attended American U. and Mozartium, Salzburg, Austria. Has appeared in "The Winter's Tale," "Antony and Cleopatra," "Anne of The Thousand Days," "Romeo and Juliet," "Gertie," "Sabrina Fair," "Anastasia," "Eugenia," "Miss Isobel," "Auntie Mame" on tour, "Becket."

DUNNOCK, MILDRED. Born in Baltimore, Md. Attended Goucher College, Johns Hopkins U., and Columbia. Made Bdwy debut in 1932 in "Life Begins," followed by "The Corn Is Green," "Richard III," "Only The Heart," "Foolish Notion," "Lute Song," "Another Part Of The Forest," "The Hallams," "Death Of A Salesman," "Pride's Crossing," "The Wild Duck" (1951), "In The Summer House," "Cat On A Hot Tin Roof," "Child of Fortune," "The Milk Train Doesn't Stop Here Anymore," "The Trojan Women" (Off-Bdwy).

DUSSAULT, NANCY. Born in Pensacola, Fla., June 30. Attended Northwestern U. Made Broadway debut in 1960 in "Do Re Mi" for which she received a THEATRE WORLD Award, followed by "The Sound of Music."

ELSTON, ROBERT. Born in NYC, May 29, 1934. Graduate of CCNY and Hunter College. Studied with Herbert Berghof. Has appeared in "Maybe Tuesday," "Tall Story," "Golden Fleecing," "Spoon River Anthology."

ENSERRO, MICHAEL. Born in Soldier, Pa., Oct. 5, 1918. Attended Allegheny College, and Pasadena Playhouse. Has appeared in "Molly and Me," "The Passion of Josef D.," and Off-Bdwy in "Penny Change," "The Fantasticks," and "The Miracle."

EPSTEIN, ALVIN. Born in NYC, May 14, 1925. Attended Queens College, Etienne Decroux School of Mime Theatre, and Habimah Theatre, Tel Aviv. Has appeared with Marcel Marceau, and in "King Lear," "Waiting For Godot," "From A To Z," Off-Bdwy in "Purple Dust," "Pictures In A Hallway," "Clerambard" and "Endgame," "No Strings," "The Passion of Josef D."

EVANS, MAURICE. Born in Dorchester, Dorset, Eng., June 8, 1901. Made NY bow in 1935 as Romeo, followed by "St. Helena," "Richard II," "St. Joan," "Henry IV," "Hamlet," "Macbeth," "Man and Superman," "The Browning Version," "Harlequinade," "The Devil's Disciple," "The Wild Duck," "Dial 'M' For Murder," "The Apple Cart," "Heartbreak House," "Tenderloin," "The Aspern Papers," "Program For Two Players" on tour.

EVANS, REYNOLDS. Began career as extra with Sothern and Marlowe. Has appeared in "Cyrano de Bergerac," "Richard III," "Henry IV," "The Doughgirls," "The Late George Apley," "Metropole," "Fancy Meeting You Again," "The Solid Gold Cadillac," "Eugenia," "Compulsion," "First Love," "Lord Pengo," "The Deputy."

EVERETT, TIM. Born in Helena, Mont., Feb. 4, 1939. Attended Neighborhood Playhouse. Has appeared in "On Your Toes," "Damn Yankees," "Living The Life," "The Dark At The Top Of The Stairs" for which he received a THEATRE WORLD Award, "The Cold Wind and The Warm," "Marathon '33."

FABRAY, NANETTE. Born in San Diego, Cal., Oct. 27, 1922. Studied at Max Reinhardt Workshop. Appeared in vaudeville and in "Our Gang" comedies as a child. Made Broadway debut in 1940 in "Meet The People," followed by "Let's Face It," "By Jupiter," "Jackpot," "My Dear Public," "Bloomer Girl," "High Button Shoes," "Love Life," "Arms and The Girl," "Make A Wish," "Mr. President."

FALK, PETER. Born in NYC, Sept. 16, 1927. Attended Hamilton College and Syracuse U. Has appeared in "St. Joan" (1956), "Passion of Josef D.," and Off-Bdwy in "Purple Dust," "The Iceman Cometh," "Comic Strip," "The Lady's Not For Burning," and "Bonds of Interest."

FERRER, JOSE. Born in Santurce, P.R., Jan. 8, 1912. Attended Princeton. Has appeared in "A Slight Case of Murder," "Brother Rat," "In Clover," "Missouri Legend," "Mamba's Daughters," "Key Largo," "Charley's Aunt," "Vickie," "Let's Face It," "Othello," "Cyrano de Bergerac," "The Silver Whistle," "Twentieth Century," "Volpone," "The Shrike," "Angel Street" (City Center), "Richard III," "Edwin Booth," "The Girl Who Came To Supper."

FICKETT, MARY. Born in Bronxville, N.Y. Attended Wheaton College. Has appeared in "I Know My Love," "The Happy Time," "Tea and Sympathy" for which she received a THEATRE WORLD Award, "Sunrise At Campobello," "Love and Kisses."

FIELD, BETTY. Born in Boston, Feb. 8, 1918. Attended American Academy of Dramatic Art. Made stage debut in 1934 in London company of "She Loves Me Not." Has appeared in "Page Miss Glory," "Three Men On A Horse," "Room Service," "What A Life," "The Primrose Path," "Two On An Island," "Flight To The West," "A New Life," "The Voice of The Turtle," "Dream Girl," "The Rat Race," "Not For Children," "The Fourposter," "Ladies of The Corridor," "Festival," "The Waltz Of The Toreadors," "A Touch of The Poet," "A Loss Of Roses," "Strange Interlude" (1963).

FINNEY, ALBERT. Born in Salford, Lancashire, Eng., May 9, 1936. Received stage training at London's Royal Academy of Dramatic Art, and with Birmingham Repertory Co. During the 1959 Stratford-On-Avon season, played Edgar in "King Lear," Lysander in "A Midsummer Night's Dream," and Cassio in "Othello." Made Broadway bow Sept. 25, 1963 in "Luther."

FITZGERALD, NEIL. Born in Tipperary, Ire., Jan. 15, 1898. Attended Trinity College. Broadway appearances include "Leave Her To Heaven," "The Wookey," "Without Love," "Ten Little Indians," "Plan M," "You Touched Me," "The Play's The Thing," "Design For A Stained Glass Window," "The High Ground," "To Dorothy, A Son," "Mr. Pickwick," "Witness For The Prosecution," "Little Moon Of Alban," Off-Bdwy in "A Portrait of The Artist As A Young Man" and "The Barroom Monks," "Roar Like A Dove."

FLEISCHMAN, MARK. Born in Detroit, Nov. 25, 1935. Attended U. of Mich. Has appeared in City Center revivals of "What Every Woman Knows" and "Lute Song," "The Beautiful People" (off-Bdwy), "Tonight In Samarkand," "A Distant Bell."

Neil Fitzgerald

Bill Galarno

Betty Field

Robert Elston

FONDA, HENRY. Born in Grand Island, Neb., May 16, 1905. Attended U. of Minn. Has appeared in "The Game of Love and Death," "I Loved You Wednesday," "Forsaking All Others," "New Faces of 1934," "The Farmer Takes A Wife," "Mister Roberts," "Point of No Return," "The Caine Mutiny Court Martial," "Two For The Seesaw," "Silent Night, Lonely Night," "Critic's Choice," "A Gift of Time."

FONDA, JANE. Born in NYC, Dec. 21, 1937. Attended Vassar. Studied with Lee Strasberg. Made Broadway debut in 1960 in "There Was A Little Girl" for which she received a THEATRE WORLD Award, followed by "Invitation To A March," "The Fun Couple," "Strange Interlude" (1963).

FONDA, PETER. Born in NYC, Feb. 23, 1939. Attended U. of Omaha. Made Broadway bow in 1961 in "Blood, Sweat and Stanley Poole," for which he received a THEATRE WORLD Award.

FONTANNE, LYNN. Born in London, Dec. 6, 1887. Made NY debut in 1910 in "Mr. Preedy and The Countess," followed by "Dulcy," "The Guardsman," "Goat Song," "At Mrs. Beam's," "The Second Man," "Strange Interlude," "Caprice," "Elizabeth The Queen," "Reunion In Vienna," "Design For Living," "Idiot's Delight," "The Sea Gull," "Amphitryon '38," "There Shall Be No Night," "The Pirate," "O Mistress Mine," "I Know My Love," "Quadrille," "The Great Sebastians," "The Visit."

FORD, PAUL. Born in Baltimore, Nov. 2, 1901. Attended Dartmouth. Made NY bow in 1944 in "Decision," followed by "Lower North," "Kiss Them For Me," "Flamingo Road," "On Whitman Avenue," "Another Part of The Forest," "Command Decision," "The Teahouse of The August Moon," "Whoop-Up," "The Music Man," "A Thurber Carnival," "Never Too Late."

FOSTER, BARRY. Born in Beeston, Nottinghamshire, Eng., Aug. 21, 1927. Attended Southall Secondary School. Received stage training with touring repertory companies. Made Broadway bow Oct. 9, 1963 in "The Private Ear" and "The Public Eye."

FOWLES, DEREK. Born in London, Eng., Sept. 2, 1937. Attended Ashlyns Secondary Modern School, and Royal Academy of Dramatic Arts, London. Made Broadway bow Oct. 1, 1963 in "Chips With Everything."

FRANCE, RICHARD. Born in Chicago, Jan. 6, 1930. Attended YMCA Professional School. Made NY bow in 1951 in "Seventeen," followed by "Wish You Were Here," "By The Beautiful Sea," "Pal Joey" in London, "Kiss Me, Kate" (1956 City Center), "What Makes Sammy Run?"

GALARNO, BILL. Born in Saginaw, Mich., March 1, 1938. Received stage training at Pittsburgh Playhouse. Has appeared Off-Broadway in "Nathan The Wise," and "The Flies," and toured in "Sound of Music."

GARRETT, BETTY. Born in St. Joseph, Mo., May 23, 1919. Has appeared in "Of V We Sing," "Let Freedom Ring," "Something For The Boys," "Jackpot," "Laffing Room Only," "Call Me Mister," "Bells Are Ringing," "Beg, Borrow or Steal," "Spoon River Anthology."

GARRISON, SEAN. Born in NYC, Oct. 19, 1937. Appeared in movies and TV before making Bdwy bow in 1960 in "There Was a Little Girl." Appeared Off-Broadway in "Half-Past Wednesday," for which he received a THEATRE WORLD Award, and "Like Other People," "The Beauty Part," and toured in "The Pleasure of His Company" and "Camelot."

GASSEL, SYLVIA. Born in NYC, July 1, 1923. Attended Hunter College and New School. Studied with Herbert Berghof and Uta Hagen. Made Bdwy debut in 1952, using name of Silva Gaselli, in "The Time of The Cuckoo," followed by "Sunday Breakfast," "Fair Game For Lovers," and Off-Bdwy in "U.S.A.," "Romeo and Juliet," "A Darker Flower," "Electra."

GATES, LARRY. Born in St. Paul, Minn., Sept. 24, 1915. Attended U. of Minn. Made Bdwy bow in 1939 in "Speak of The Devil," followed by "Twelfth Night" (1940), "Bell, Book and Candle," "The Taming of The Shrew" (1951), "The Love of Four Colonels," "The Teahouse of The August Moon," "Sing Me No Lullaby," "The Carefree Tree" (Phoenix), "A Case of Libel."

GAYNES, GEORGE. Born in Helsinki, Finland. May 3, 1917. Studied at Milan Conservatory. Sang opera in France, and City Center. Has appeared in "The Consul," "Out Of This World," "Wonderful Town," "The Beggar's Opera," "Can-Can" (City Center), "Lady of The Camellias," "Dynamite Tonight" (Off-Bdwy).

GAZZARA, BEN. Born in NYC, Aug. 28, 1930. Attended CCNY, and Dramatic Workshop. Toured in "Jezebel's Husband" before making NY bow in 1953 in "End As A Man" for which he received a THEATRE WORLD Award, followed by "Cat On A Hot Tin Roof," "A Hatful Of Rain," "Night Circus," "Strange Interlude" (1963).

GENN, LEO. Born in London, Aug. 9, 1905. Attended Cambridge Univ. Trained with Old Vic Company. Has appeared on Broadway in "The Flashing Stream" (1939), "Another Part of The Forest," "Small War On Murray Hill," "Fair Game For Lovers."

GENTRY, BOB. Born in NYC, Sept. 29, 1940. Attended CCNY. Studied with Irene Dailey and Herbert Berghof. Appeared Off-Broadway in "Blood Wedding," "The Summer Pygmies," "Angels of Anadarko" for which he received a THEATRE WORLD Award, "The American Dream."

GIELGUD, JOHN. Born in London, Apr. 14, 1904. Attended Royal Academy of Dramatic Arts. Achieved great success in England before making NY bow in 1928 in "The Patriot," followed by "Hamlet," "The Importance of Being Earnest," "Love For Love," "Crime and Punishment," "The Lady's Not For Burning," "Medea," "Ages of Man," "School For Scandal," "Homage To Shakespeare."

GILLETTE, ANITA. Born in Baltimore, Aug. 16, 1938. Made NY debut Off-Broadway in 1960 in "Russell Patterson's Sketchbook" for which she received a THEATRE WORLD Award, followed by "Carnival," "All American," "Mr. President."

GINGOLD, HERMIONE. Born in London, Dec. 9. Had long career on English stage before making Bdwy debut in 1953 in "John Murray Anderson's Almanac," followed by "The Sleeping Prince," "First Impressions," "From A To Z," "Milk and Honey," "Oh, Dad, Poor Dad, Mama's Hung You In The Closet and I'm Feelin' So Sad."

GISH, DOROTHY. Born in Massilon, Ohio, Mar. 11, 1898. Made stage debut in 1903 in "East Lynn." After eminent career in films, returned to stage in 1928 in "Young Love," followed by "The Inspector General," "Getting Married," "The Streets of New York," "Pillars of Society," "The Bride The Sun Shines On," "Foreign Affair," "Brittle Heaven," "Missouri Legend," "Life With Father," "The Great Big Doorstep," "The Magnificent Yankee," "The Story of Mary Surratt," "The Man."

GISH, LILLIAN. Born in Springfield, Ohio, Oct. 14, 1896. Made stage debut at 6. After long film career, returned to Bdwy in 1930 in "Uncle Vanya," followed by "Camille," "Nine Pine Street," "The Joyous Season," "Hamlet," "The Star Wagon," "Dear Octopus," "Life With Father," "Mr. Sycamore," "Crime and Punishment," "The Curious Savage," "The Trip To Bountiful," "Family Reunion," "All The Way Home," "Too True To Be Good."

GLOVER, BRUCE. Born in Chicago, May 2, 1932. Attended Wright Jr. College, and Northwestern U. Appeared Off-Broadway in "King of The Dark Chamber," "Billy Budd" (ELT), "Night Of The Iguana," "Mother Courage and Her Children."

GORDON, RUTH. Born in Wollaston, Mass., Oct. 30, 1896. Studied at American Academy of Dramatic Art. Made stage debut with Maude Adams in 1915 in "Peter Pan," followed by "Seventeen," "Clarence," "Saturday's Children," "Serena Blandish," "Hotel Universe," "A Church Mouse," "Three Cornered Moon," "Ethan Frome," "The Country Wife," "A Doll's House," "The Three Sisters," "Over 21," "The Leading Lady," "The Smile of The World," "The Matchmaker," "The Good Soup," "My Mother, My Father and Me."

GOSSETT, LOUIS. Born in Brooklyn, May 27, 1936. Made Broadway bow in 1953 in "Take A Giant Step," followed by "The Desk Set," "Lost In The Stars" (City Center), "Raisin In The Sun," "Tambourines To Glory," and Off-Broadway in "The Blacks," "The Bloodknot."

GOULET, ROBERT. Born in Lawrence, Mass., Nov. 26, 1933. Attended Edmunton. Received training in Canadian theatres. Made Broadway bow in 1960 in "Camelot" for which he received a THEATRE WORLD Award.

GRANGER, FARLEY. Born in San Jose, Calif., July 1, 1928. After appearing in films, stock, and "The Carefree Tree" (Phoenix), made Broadway bow in 1959 in "First Impressions," followed by "The Warm Peninsula," "The King and I" (City Center), "Advise and Consent," "Brigadoon" (City Center), National Repertory Theatre revivals of "The Seagull," and "The Crucible."

GREENHOUSE, MARTHA. Born in Omaha, Neb., June 14. Attended Hunter College and American Theatre Wing. Has appeared in "Sons and Soldiers," Off-Broadway in "Clerambard" and "Our Town," "Dear Me, The Sky Is Falling."

GREGG, MITCHELL. Born in NYC, Jan. 15, 1921. Has appeared in "Panama Hattie," "Music In The Air," "Happy Hunting," "Say, Darling," "The Unsinkable Molly Brown," "No Strings."

GRIMES, TAMMY. Born in Lynn, Mass., Jan. 30, 1934. Attended Stephens College and Neighborhood Playhouse. Appeared Off-Broadway in "The Littlest Revue" and "Clerambard," "The Lark," on tour, made Broadway debut in 1959 in "Look After Lulu" for which she received a THEATRE WORLD Award, followed by "The Unsinkable Molly Brown," "Rattle Of A Simple Man," "High Spirits."

GRIZZARD, GEORGE. Born in Roanoke Rapids, N.C., Apr. 1, 1928. Attended U. of NC. Made Broadway bow in 1955 in "The Desperate Hours," followed by "The Happiest Millionaire" for which he received a THEATRE WORLD Award, "The Disenchanted," "Big Fish, Little Fish," APA Repertory 1961-2, "Who's Afraid Of Virginia Woolf?"

GROVER, STANLEY. Born in Woodstock, Ill., Mar. 28, 1926. Attended U. of Mo. Appeared in "Seventeen," "Wish You Were Here," "Time Remembered," "Candide," "13 Daughters," "South Pacific" (City Center and on tour), "Mr. President."

GUARDINO, HARRY. Born in NYC, Dec. 23, 1925. Attended Dramatic Workshop. Has appeared in "End As A Man," "A Hatful Of Rain," "Natural Affection," "Anyone Can Whistle."

GUINNESS, ALEC. Born in London, Apr. 2, 1914. Attended Pembroke Lodge, Southbourne and Roxborough Schools. Studied for stage with Martita Hunt and Fay Compton. Made Broadway bow in 1942 in "Flare Path," followed by "The Cocktail Party," "Dylan."

HACKETT, JOAN. Born in NYC. Attended St. Bartholomew and St. Jean the Baptist Schools. Has appeared in "Much Ado About Nothing" (1959), Off-Broadway in "A Clearing In The Woods" and "Call Me By My Rightful Name" for which she received a THEATRE WORLD Award.

HAGEN, UTA. Born in Goettingen, Ger., June 11, 1919. Made NY debut in 1938 in "The Sea Gull," followed by "The Happiest Years," "Key Largo," "Vickie," "Othello," "A Streetcar Named Desire," "The Country Girl," "St. Joan," "The Whole World Over," "In Any Language," "The Magic and The Loss," City Center revivals of "Angel Street" and "Tovarich," "A Month In The Country" and "The Good Woman Of Setuzan" at the Phoenix, "Who's Afraid Of Virginia Woolf?" (in NY and London).

HAGMAN, LARRY. Born in Texas, attended Bard College. Appeared in London's "South Pacific," in NY in "Once Around The Block," "Comes A Day," "Career," "God and Kate Murphy" for which he received a THEATRE WORLD Award, "The Nervous Set," "The Warm Peninsula," "The Beauty Part."

HALL, ED. Born in Roxbury, Mass., Jan. 11, 1931. Attended Harvard. Received training in stock and Arena Stage, Washington, D.C. Has appeared in "The Climate of Eden," "No Time For Sergeants," "Raisin In The Sun," Off-Broadway in "The Death of Bessie Smith" and "Trumpets of The Lord."

HALL, MARGARET. Born in Richmond, Va., Graduate of William and Mary College. Made Bdwy debut in 1960 in "Becket." Appeared Off-Broadway in "The Boy Friend," "Fallout," "U.S.A.," "A Midsummer Night's Dream," and "Little Mary Sunshine," "High Spirits."

HANLEY, ELLEN. Born in Lorain, Ohio, May 15, 1926. Attended Juilliard. Made Bdwy debut in "Annie Get Your Gun," followed by "Barefoot Boy With Cheek" for which she received a THEATRE WORLD Award, "High Button Shoes," "Two's Company," "First Impressions," "Fiorello!" "The Boys From Syracuse" (1963 Off-Broadway).

HARDIE, RUSSELL. Born in Griffin Mills, NY, May 20, 1906. Attended St. Mary's College. Made Bdwy bow in 1929 in "Criminal Code," followed by "Pagan Lady," "The Constant Sinner," "Remember The Day," "The Ghost Of Yankee Doodle," "The Primrose Path," "Snafu," "Foxhole In The Parlor," "The Doughgirls," "My Sister Eileen," "Home of The Brave," "The Birds and The Bees," "A Streetcar Named Desire," "Bus Stop," "The Andersonville Trial," "Midgie Purvis."

HARDING, JUNE. Born in Emporia, Va., Sept. 7, 1940. Attended William and Mary College. Appeared with children's theatre, and Off-Broadway in "Vincent," "The Ignorants Abroad," "Cry Of The Raindrop" for which she received a THEATRE WORLD Award, and made Bdwy debut in 1961 in "Take Her, She's Mine."

Arthur Hill

Joan Hackett

Ed Hall

Helen Hayes

HARE, WILL. Born in Elkins, W. Va., Mar. 30, 1919. Studied at American Actors' Theatre. Has appeared in "The Eternal Road," "The Moon Is Down," "Suds In Your Eye," "Only The Heart," "The Visitor," "The Trip To Bountiful," "Witness For The Prosecution," "Marathon '33."

HARRIS, JULIE. Born in Grosse Point, Mich., Dec. 2, 1925. Attended Yale. Made Bdwy debut in 1945 in "It's A Gift," followed by "Henry V" and "Oedipus" with Old Vic, "The Playboy of The Western World," "Alice In Wonderland," "Macbeth," "Sundown Beach" for which she received a THEATRE WORLD Award, "The Young and The Fair," "Magnolia Alley," "Montserrat," "The Member of The Wedding," "I Am A Camera," "Mlle. Colombe," "The Lark," "The Country Wife," "The Warm Peninsula," "The Little Moon of Alban," "A Shot In The Dark," "Marathon '33," "Hamlet" (NY Shakespeare Festival).

HARRIS, ROSEMARY. Born in Ashby, Suffolk, Eng., Sept. 19, 1930. Made Bdwy debut in 1952 in "The Climate of Eden" for which she received a THEATRE WORLD Award, followed by Old Vic's "Troilus and Cressida," "Interlock," "The Disenchanted," "The Tumbler," and in repertory with APA.

HARRON, DONALD. Born in Toronto, Can., Sept. 19, 1924. Attended Toronto U. Made NY bow in 1951 in "A Sleep of Prisoners," followed by "Home Is The Hero," "The Dark Is Light Enough," "Separate Tables," "The Tenth Man," "Everybody Loves Opal," "King Lear" (Central Park).

HAYES, BEN. Born in Chicago. Attended DePaul U. and Goodman Memorial Theatre. Made Bdwy bow in 1962 in "Calculated Risk." Off-Broadway credits: "Children Of Darkness," 1961 Shakespeare Festival productions of "Richard II," "Merchant of Venice," and "Much Ado About Nothing."

HAYES, HELEN. Born in Washington, D.C., Oct. 10, 1900. Attended Sacred Heart Academy. Made stage debut in 1908 in "Babes In The Woods," Broadway bow in 1909 in "Old Dutch," followed by "The Summer Widowers," "Penrod," "Dear Brutus," "Clarence," "To The Ladies," "We Moderns," "Dancing Mothers," "Caesar and Cleopatra," "What Every Woman Knows," "Coquette," "Mary of Scotland," "Victoria Regina," "Twelfth Night," "Candle In The Wind," "Happy Birthday," "The Wisteria Trees," "Mrs. McThing," "The Glass Menagerie" (City Center), "The Skin Of Our Teeth," "Time Remembered," "A Touch Of The Poet," "A Program For Two Players," "The White House."

HAYES, MAGGIE. Born in Baltimore. Has appeared in "I Must Love Someone," "Bright Rebel," "Many Happy Returns," "Little Women," "The Family," "One Shoe Off," "Happily Ever After," "Pink Jungle," "Fair Game For Lovers."

HECKART, EILEEN. Born in Columbus, O., March 29. Attended Ohio State U. and American Theatre Wing. Made NY debut in City Center's "Our Town," followed by "They Knew What They Wanted," "The Traitor," "Hilda Crane," "In Any Language," "Picnic" for which she received a THEATRE WORLD Award, "The Bad Seed," "A View From The Bridge," "The Dark At The Top Of The Stairs," "Invitation To A March," "Pal Joey" (City Center), "Everybody Loves Opal." "A Family Affair," "Too True To Be Good."

HEFLIN, VAN. Born in Walters, Okla., Dec. 3, 1910. Attended U. of Okla. and Yale. Received training at Hedgerow Theatre. Has appeared in "Mr. Moneypenny," "End Of Summer," "Casey Jones," "The Philadelphia Story," "A View From The Bridge," "A Case Of Libel."

HEPBURN, KATHARINE. Born in Hartford, Conn., Nov. 9, 1909. Attended Bryn Mawr. Made Bdwy debut in 1928 in "Night Hostess," followed by "A Month In The Country," "Art and Mrs. Bottle," "The Warrior's Husband," "The Lake," "The Philadelphia Story," "Without Love," "As You Like It," "The Millionairess," Stratford productions of "The Merchant of Venice," "Much Ado About Nothing," "Twelfth Night," and "Antony and Cleopatra."

HERLIE, EILEEN. Born in Glasgow, Scot., March 8, 1920. Starred on London stage before making Broadway debut in 1955 in "The Matchmaker," followed by "The Makropoulos Secret" (Phoenix), "Epitaph For George Dillon," "Take Me Along," "All American," "Photo Finish," "Hamlet" (1964).

HICKMAN, DARRYL. Born in Hollywood, Calif., July 28, 1933. Attended Loyola U. Had long career in films before making Broadway bow Oct. 7, 1963 in "How To Succeed In Business Without Really Trying."

HILL, ARTHUR. Born in Melfort, Can., Aug. 1, 1922. Attended U. of British Col. Has appeared in "The Matchmaker," "Look Homeward, Angel," "The Gang's All Here," "All The Way Home," "Who's Afraid Of Virginia Woolf?" (NY and London).

HINGLE, PAT. Born in Denver, Colo., July 19, 1923. Attended Texas U. Has appeared in "End As A Man," "Festival," "Cat On A Hot Tin Roof," "Girls Of Summer," "The Dark At The Top Of The Stairs," "J.B.," "The Deadly Game," "Strange Interlude (1963)," "Blues For Mr. Charlie."

HOFFMAN, JANE. Born July 24 in Seattle, Wash. Attended U. of Calif. Has appeared in "'Tis Of Thee," "Crazy With The Heat," "Something For The Boys," "One Touch Of Venus," "Calico Wedding," "The Mermaids Singing," "The Rose Tattoo," "The Crucible," "Witness For The Prosecution," "Mother Courage and Her Children," "The American Dream," "Fair Game For Lovers," "A Murder Among Us."

HOLBROOK, HAL. Born in Cleveland, O., Feb. 17, 1925. Attended Denison U. Toured world in his one-man show "Mark Twain Tonight!," and played it Off-Broadway in 1959. Made Bdwy bow in 1961 in "Do You Know The Milky Way?," followed by "Abe Lincoln In Illinois" (Phoenix), "Marco Millions" (Lincoln Center Rep).

HOLLIDAY, JUDY. Born in The Bronx, NY, June 21, 1921. Made Broadway debut in 1945 in "Kiss Them For Me" for which she received a THEATRE WORLD Award, followed by "Born Yesterday," "Dream Girl" (City Center), "Bells Are Ringing," "Hot Spot."

HOLM, CELESTE. Born in NYC, Apr. 29, 1919. Made Bdwy debut in 1938 in "Glorianna," followed by "The Time Of Your Life," "Another Sun," "The Return of The Vagabond," "Papa Is All," "The Damask Cheek," "Oklahoma," "She Stoops To Conquer," "Bloomer Girl," "Affairs of State," "Anna Christie" (1951), "His and Hers," "Interlock," "Third Best Sport," "Invitation To A March," "A Month In The Country" (Off-Broadway).

HOLM, JOHN CECIL. Born in Philadelphia, Nov. 4, 1904. Attended U. of Pa. Has appeared in "Wonder Boy," "Dangerous Corner," "Mary of Scotland," "Midgie Purvis," "Mr. President," "The Advocate." Author of "3 Men On A Horse," "Best Foot Forward" (book), "Brighten The Corner," "Gramercy Ghost" and "Southwest Corner."

HOWES, SALLY ANN. Born in London. Has appeared in New York in "My Fair Lady," "Kwamina," "Brigadoon" (City Center), "What Makes Sammy Run?"

HUSMANN, RON. Born in Rockford, Ill., June 30, 1937. Attended Northwestern U. Has appeared in "Fiorello!," "Greenwillow," "Tenderloin" for which he received a THEATRE WORLD Award, "All American."

HYMAN, EARLE. Born in Rocky Mount, NC., Oct. 11, 1926. Attended New School. Appeared with American Negro Theatre in "Anna Lucasta" and "Three's A Family," and in "Run, Little Chillun," "The Climate Of Eden," "The Merchant of Venice," "Othello," "No Time For Sergeants," "Mister Johnson" for which he received a THEATRE WORLD Award, "Waiting For Godot" (1957), Off-Bdwy in "The Duchess of Malfi," "The White Rose and The Red" and "The Worlds of Shakespeare."

IRVING, GEORGE S. Born in Springfield, Mass., Nov. 1, 1922. Has appeared in "Oklahoma," "Call Me Mister," "Along Fifth Avenue," "Two's Company," "Me and Juliet," "Can-Can," "Shinbone Alley," "Bells Are Ringing," "The Good Soup," "Tovarich," "A Murderer Among Us."

JACKSON, ANNE. Born in Alleghany, Pa., Sept. 3, 1926. Attended Neighborhood Playhouse. Made Bdwy debut in 1945 in "Signature," followed by "Yellow Jack," "John Gabriel Borkman," "The Last Dance," "Summer and Smoke," "Magnolia Alley," "Love Me Long," "The Lady From The Sea," "Never Say Never," "Oh, Men! Oh, Women!," "Rhinoceros," Off-Broadway in "Brecht On Brecht" and "The Tiger" and "The Typists."

JAMESON, HOUSE. Born in Austin, Tex., Dec. 17, 1902. Attended U. of Tex. and Columbia. Has appeared in "St. Joan," "Goat Song," "Grand Street Follies of 1924," "Garrick Gaieties," "An American Tragedy," "The Dark Hours," "We, The People," "Judgement Day," "In Time To Come," "The Patriots," "Requiem For A Nun," "Never Too Late."

JANIS, CONRAD. Born in NYC, Feb. 11, 1928. Made Bdwy bow in 1942 in "Junior Miss," followed by "Dark Of The Moon," "The Next Half Hour," "The Brass Ring" for which he received a THEATRE WORLD Award, "Time Out For Ginger," "The Terrible Swift Sword," "A Visit To A Small Planet," "Make A Million," "Sunday In New York," "Marathon '33."

JANNEY, LEON. Born in Ogden, Utah, Apr. 1, 1917. Child film star. Made Bdwy bow in 1934 in "Every Thursday," followed by "The Simpleton Of The Unexpected Isle," "Parade," "Mulatto," "Foreigners," "Ghost For Sale," "The Flowering Peach," "Madam, Will You Walk," "Measure For Measure," "The Country Wife," "Damn Yankees," "The Gazebo," "Summer Of The 17th Doll," "Nobody Loves An Albatross."

JENS, SALOME. Born in Milwaukee, May 8, 1936. Attended Northwestern U. Has appeared in "The Disenchanted," "A Far Country," "Night Life," and Off-Broadway in "The Bald Soprano," "Deirdre of The Sorrows," "U.S.A.," "The Balcony," "Shadow of Heroes," "Desire Under The Elms," "After The Fall" and "But For Whom Charlie."

JOHNSON, VAN. Born in Newport, R.I., Aug. 25, 1916. Made Bdwy bow in 1936 in "New Faces." Other credits: "Too Many Girls," "Pal Joey" (1940), "Come On Strong," "The Music Man" in London.

JONES, JAMES EARL. Born in Tate County, Miss., Jan. 17, 1931. Graduate of U. of Mich. Has appeared in "The Egghead," "Sunrise At Campobello," "The Cool World," and Off-Broadway in "The Pretender," "The Blacks," "Clandestine On The Morning Line," "The Apple," "A Midsummer Night's Dream," "Moon On A Rainbow Shawl" for which he received a THEATRE WORLD Award, "P.S. 193," "The Last Minstrel," "The Love Nest," "The Bloodknot," "Othello."

JONES, NEIL. Born in Boston, May 6, 1942. Attended Boston Conservatory of Music. Has appeared in summer stock, and in "The Music Man," "Hello, Dolly!"

JORDAN, RICHARD. Born in NYC, July 19, 1938. Attended Sherbourne School, Eng., and Harvard. Made Bdwy bow in 1961 in "Take Her, She's Mine," followed by NY Shakespeare Festival productions of "A Midsummer Night's Dream," "Romeo and Juliet" and Richard II," "Bicycle Ride To Nevada."

JUSTICE, BARRY. Born in Lucknow, India, Aug. 18, 1940. Attended Oundle School, Eng. Received training with Leatherhead Rep. Co., and Old Vic. Made Bdwy bow in 1963 in "Man and Boy."

KASZNAR, KURT. Born in Vienna, Aug. 12, 1913. Studied with Max Reinhardt. Made NY bow in "The Eternal Road," followed by "The Army Play By Play," "Joy To The World," "Make Way For Lucia," "The Happy Time," "Waiting For Godot," "Look After Lulu," "Sound Of Music," "Barefoot In The Park."

KELLY, NANCY. Born in Lowell, Mass., Mar. 25, 1921. Has appeared in "Susan and God," "Flare Path," "The Big Knife," "Season In The Sun," "Twilight Walk," "The Bad Seed," "The Genius and The Goddess," "The Rivalry," "Who's Afraid Of Virginia Woolf?"

KENMORE, EDDIE. Born in New Orleans, La., Nov. 18, 1940. Attended Mota DeLarosa Military Academy, and Metairie High, New Orleans. Appeared in Hollywood stage productions of "All The King's Men," "Dark Of The Moon" and "No Time for Sergeants." Studied with Lee Strasberg and Frank Corsaro. Appeared Off-Broadway in "Like Other People," "The Brig."

KERT, LARRY. Born in Los Angeles, Dec. 5, 1934. Attended Los Angeles City College, and Players Ring Theatre. Made NY bow in "John Murray Anderson's Almanac," followed by "Ziegfeld Follies," "Mr. Wonderful," "Walk Tall," "Look, Ma, I'm Dancin'," "Tickets, Please," "West Side Story," "A Family Affair."

KILEY, RICHARD. Born in Chicago, Mar. 31, 1922. Attended Loyola U. and Barnum Dramatic School. Toured in "A Streetcar Named Desire" before making Bdwy bow in 1953 in "Misalliance" for which he received a THEATRE WORLD Award, followed by "Kismet," "Sing Me No Lullaby," "Time Limit!," "Redhead," "Advise and Consent," "No Strings," "Here's Love."

| Angela Lansbury | Eddie Kenmore | Ketty Lester | Neil Jones |

KIMBROUGH, CLINTON. Born in Sandusky, O., Feb. 14, 1935. Appeared Off-Broadway in "Our Town" and "Camino Real" before making Bdwy bow in 1961 in "Look, We've Come Through," followed by "After The Fall," "But For Whom Charlie."

KING, DENNIS. Born in Coventry, Eng., Nov. 2, 1897. Made NY bow in 1921 in "Claire De Lune," followed by "Romeo and Juliet," "Antony and Cleopatra," "The Vagabond King," "The Three Musketeers," "I Married An Angel," "A Doll's House," "The Three Sisters," "Dunnigan's Daughter," "He Who Gets Slapped," "Medea," "Edward, My Son," "The Devil's Disciple," "Billy Budd," "Music In The Air," "The Strong Are Lonely," "Lunatics and Lovers," "A Day By The Sea," "Affair Of Honor," "Shangri-La," "The Hidden River," "The Greatest Man Alive," "Love and Libel," "Photo Finish."

KING, EDITH. Made Broadway debut in 1915 in "The Boomerang," followed by many productions, including most recently, "Amphitryon '38," "The Taming Of The Shrew," "A Kiss For Cinderella," "Othello," "Legend of Lovers," "Ondine," "Affair of Honor," "Miss Isobel," "Cheri," "Saratoga," "Wildcat," "A Murderer Among Us."

KIRK, LISA. Born in Roscoe, Pa. Has appeared on Broadway in "Goodnight, Ladies," "Allegro," "Kiss Me, Kate," "Here's Love."

LAHR, BERT. Born in NYC Aug. 13, 1895. Appeared in vaudeville and burlesque before making Bdwy bow in 1927 in "Delmar's Revels," followed by "Hold Everything," "Flying High," "Hot-Cha," "George White's Varieties," "The Show Is On," "DuBarry Was A Lady," "Seven Lively Arts," "Burlesque," "Make Mine Manhattan," "Two On The Aisle," "Waiting For Godot," "Hotel Paradiso," "Romanoff and Juliet," "A Midsummer Night's Dream," "The Boys Against The Girls," "The Beauty Part," "Foxy."

LAMPERT, ZOHRA. Born in NYC. Attended U. of Chicago. Has appeared in "Major Barbara" (1956), "Maybe Tuesday," "Look: We've Come Through," "First Love," "Mother Courage and Her Children," "After The Fall, "Marco Millions" (1963).

LANSBURY, ANGELA. Born in London, Oct. 16, 1925. Attended South Hampstead School for Girls, London, and Weber-Douglas School of Dramatic Arts, London. Has appeared on Broadway in "Hotel Paradiso," "A Taste of Honey," "Anyone Can Whistle."

LAURENCE, PAULA. Born in Brooklyn. Has appeared in "Horse Eats Hat," "Dr. Faustus," "Junior Miss," "Something For The Boys," "One Touch of Venus," "Cyrano de Bergerac," "The Liar," "Season In The Sun," "Tovarich," "The Time of Your Life," "The Beggar's Opera," "Hotel Paradiso," "Night of The Iguana," "Have I Got A Girl For You."

LEE, SONDRA. Born in New Jersey. Has appeared in "High Button Shoes," "Peter Pan," "Hotel Paradiso," "Sunday In New York," "Hello, Dolly!"

LeGALLIENNE, EVA. Born in London, Jan. 11, 1899. Attended Royal Academy of Dramatic Arts. Made Bdwy debut in 1915 in "Mrs. Boltay's Daughters." Organized Civic Repertory Co. in 1926 and presented many notable productions before disbanding in 1933. Has appeared in "Lilliom," "The Swan," "The Master Builder," "L'Aiglon," "Madame Capet," "Uncle Harry," "The Cherry Orchard," "Therese," "What Every Woman Knows," "Alice In Wonderland," "Ghosts," "Hedda Gabler," "The Corn Is Green" (City Center), "The Southwest Corner," Phoenix productions of "Mary Stuart" and "Elizabeth The Queen," National Repertory Theatre revivals of "Ring Round The Moon," and "The Sea Gull."

LEIGH, VIVIEN. Born in Darjeeling, India, Nov. 1913. Attended Comedie Francaise, and Royal Academy of Dramatic Arts. Made Bdwy debut in 1940 in "Romeo and Juliet," followed by "Antony and Cleopatra," "Caesar and Cleopatra," "Duel of Angels," "Tovarich."

LEIGHTON, MARGARET. Born in Barnt Gree, Warwickshire, Eng., Feb. 26, 1922. Attended Church of England College. Made Bdwy debut in 1946 with Old Vic Co. Has appeared since in "Separate Tables," "Much Ado About Nothing," "The Night Of The Iguana," "Tchin-Tchin," "The Chinese Prime Minister," "Homage To Shakespeare."

LeMASSENA, WILLIAM. Born in Glen Ridge, NJ, May 23, 1916. Attended NYU. Has appeared in "The Taming of The Shrew," "There Shall Be No Night," "The Pirate," "Hamlet," "Call Me Mister," "Inside U.S.A.," "I Know My Love," "Dream Girl," "Nina," "Ondine," "Fallen Angels," "Redhead," "The Conquering Hero," "The Beauty Part."

LeNOIRE, ROSETTA. Born in NYC. Has appeared in "Bassa Moona," "The Hot Mikado," "Marching With Johnny," "Janie," "Decision," "Three's A Family," "Destry Rides Again," City Center revivals of "Finian's Rainbow" and "South Pacific," Off-Bdwy in "The Bible Salesman," "Double Entry," "Clandestine On The Morning Line" and "Cabin In The Sky," "Sophie," "Tambourines To Glory," "Blues For Mister Charlie."

LESTER, KETTY. Born in Arkansas, Aug. 16, 1938. Appeared in night clubs and summer stock before making NY debut Jan. 21, 1964 in the Off-Bdwy revival of "Cabin In The Sky" for which she received a THEATRE WORLD Award.

LEVENE, SAM. Born in NYC in 1907. Attended American Academy of Dramatic Art. Has appeared in "Three Men On A Horse," "Dinner At Eight," "Room Service," "Margin For Error," "A Sound of Hunting," "Light Up The Sky," "Guys and Dolls," "The Hot Corner," "Fair Game," "Make A Million," "Heartbreak House," "The Good Soup," "The Devil's Advocate," "Let It Ride," "Seidman and Son," "Cafe Crown."

LILLIE, BEATRICE. Born in Toronto, Can. Attended St. Agnes College. Made NY debut in 1924 in "Charlot's Revue," followed by "Oh, Please," "This Year of Grace," "She's My Baby," "The Third Little Show," "Too True To Be Good," "At Home Abroad," "The Show Is On," "Set To Music," "Seven Lively Arts," "Inside U.S.A.," "An Evening With Beatrice Lillie," "Ziegfeld Follies," "Auntie Mame," "High Spirits."

LODEN, BARBARA. Born in Marion, N.C., July 8. Appeared in summer stock before making Bdwy debut in "Compulsion," followed by "Look After Lulu," "The Long Dream," "After The Fall" for which she received a THEATRE WORLD Award.

LUCE, CLAIRE. Born on train passing through Syracuse, N.Y. Made Bdwy debut in 1923 in "Little Jessie James," followed by "Music Box Revue," "Ziegfeld Follies," "Society Girl," "The Gay Divorcee," "Of Mice and Men." Appeared for several years in London. Returned in 1947 in "Portrait In Black," "With A Silk Thread," "The Taming of The Shrew," "Much Ado About Nothing," and Off-Bdwy in "These Are My Loves" and "Feast of Panthers."

LUNT, ALFRED. Born in Milwaukee, Aug. 19, 1893. Attended Carroll College and Harvard. Has appeared in "Clarence," "Outward Bound," "The Guardsman," "Arms And The Man," "Goat Song," "At Mrs. Beam's," "Juarez and Maximillian," "Ned McCobb's Daughter," "The Brothers Karamazov," "The Second Man," "The Doctor's Dilemma," "Marco Millions," "Volpone," "Caprice," "Elizabeth The Queen," "Reunion In Vienna," "Design For Living," "The Taming of The Shrew," "Idiot's Delight," "Amphitryon '38," "The Sea Gull," "There Shall Be No Night," "The Pirate," "O Mistress Mine," "I Know My Love," "Quadrille," "The Great Sebastians," "The Visit."

MACKENZIE, WILL. Born in Providence, R.I., July 24, 1938. Graduate of Brown U. Trained with Stratford, Conn., Shakespeare Festival Theatre Co. Has appeared Off-Bdwy in "Wonderful Town" (1963 City Center), "Put It In Writing" and "Morning Sun."

MADDEN, DONALD. Born in NYC, Nov. 5, 1933. Attended CCNY, Theatre Workshop, and University Playhouse. Made Bdwy bow in 1958 in "Look Back In Anger," followed by "First Impressions," "Julius Caesar" in Central Park for which he received a THEATRE WORLD Award, Off-Bdwy in "Lysistrata," "Pictures In A Hallway," "Henry IV, Part I," "She Stoops To Conquer," "Octaroon" and "Hamlet," "Step On A Crack."

MAGGART, BRANDON. Born in Carthage, Tenn., Dec. 12, 1933. Graduate of U. of Tenn. Has appeared with Radio City Music Hall Glee Club, and Off-Bdwy in "Sing, Muse!," "Like Other People," "Put It In Writing" for which he received a THEATRE WORLD Award.

MAHARIS, GEORGE. Born in Astoria, L.I., Sept. 1, 1928. Studied with Sanford Meisner and Lee Strasberg. Appeared Off-Bdwy in "I, Too, Have Lived in Arcadia," "Deathwatch," "The Saintliness of Margery Kemp," "The Zoo Story" for which he received a THEATRE WORLD Award.

MARCH, FREDRIC. Born in Racine, Wisc., Aug. 31, 1897. Attended U. of Wisc. Made NY bow in 1920 in "Deburau." After several years in Hollywood, returned to Bdwy in 1938 in "Yr. Obedient Husband," followed by "The American Way," "Hope For A Harvest," "The Skin Of Our Teeth," "A Bell For Adano," "Years Ago," "Now I Lay Me Down To Sleep," "An Enemy of The People," "The Autumn Garden," "Long Day's Journey Into Night," "Gideon."

MARIE, JULIENNE. Born in Toledo, Ohio in 1943. Attended Juilliard School of Music. Has appeared in "The King and I," "Whoop-Up!," "Gypsy," "Foxy," and Off-Bdwy revival of "The Boys From Syracuse" for which she received a THEATRE WORLD Award.

MARKEY, ENID. Born in Dillon, Colo. Silent film star before making Bdwy debut in 1919 in "Up In Mabel's Room," followed by many productions among which are "Barnum Was Right," "The Women," "Morning's At Seven," "Ah, Wilderness," "Mr. Sycamore," "Beverly Hills," "Snafu," "Happy Birthday," "The Silver Whistle," "Buy Me Blue Ribbons," "Mrs. McThing," "Mrs. Patterson," "The Southwest Corner," "Only In America," "Ballad of The Sad Cafe."

MARSH, LINDA. Born in NYC, Feb. 8. Attended Bennington College. Made Broadway debut April 9, 1964 as Ophelia in Burton's "Hamlet." Off-Bdwy credits: "The Breaking Wall," "Poppa Is Home" and "The Laundry."

MARTIN, MARY. Born in Weatherford, Tex., Dec. 1, 1914. Attended Ward-Belmont College. Made Bdwy debut in 1938 in "Leave It To Me," followed by "One Touch of Venus," "Lute Song," "Annie Get Your Gun," "South Pacific," "Kind Sir," "Peter Pan," "The Skin of Our Teeth" (1955), "A Sound Of Music," "Jennie."

MASSI, BERNICE. Born in Camden, NJ, Aug. 23. Graduate of Camden Catholic High School. Made professional debut in National Co. of "South Pacific," followed by Bdwy productions of "Wish You Were Here," "Can-Can," "By The Beautiful Sea," "No Strings," "What Makes Sammy Run?"

MATHEWS, CARMEN. Born in Philadelphia. Attended Royal Academy of Dramatic Arts, London. Made Bdwy debut in 1938 in "Henry IV," followed by "Hamlet," "Richard II," "Harriet," "The Cherry Orchard," "The Assassin," "Man and Superman," "The Ivy Green," "Courtin' Time," "My Three Angels," "Holiday For Lovers," "Night Life," "Lorenzo."

McCARTY, MARY. Born in 1923 in Kansas. Was child actress in films. Made Broadway debut in 1948 in "Sleepy Hollow" for which she received a THEATRE WORLD Award, followed by "Small Wonder," "Miss Liberty," "Bless You All," "A Rainy Day In Newark."

McDOWALL, RODDY. Born in London, Sept. 17, 1928. Attended St. Joseph's College, London. Appeared in many films before making Bdwy bow in 1953 in "Misalliance," followed by "Escapade," "The Doctor's Dilemma," "Diary of A Scoundrel," "No Time For Sergeants," "Good As Gold," "Compulsion," "Handful of Fire," "Look After Lulu," "The Fighting Cock," "Camelot."

McEWAN, GERALDINE. Born in Old Windsor, Eng. Received training at Theatre Royal, Windsor. Has appeared on Broadway in "The School For Scandal" (1963), and "The Private Ear" and "The Public Eye."

McGONAGILL, GERALD. Born in Chicago, Mar. 24, 1925. Attended DePaul U. and Goodman Theatre, Chicago. Has appeared in NY Shakespeare Festival productions of "Julius Caesar," "Much Ado About Nothing," "King Lear," "The Merchant of Venice" and "Antony and Cleopatra." Off-Bdwy credits: "Death of Satan," "The Bald Soprano," "The Good Woman of Setzuan," "Electra" and "Telemachus Clay."

McLERIE, ALLYN ANN. Born in Grand Mere, Can., Dec. 1, 1926. Made Bdwy debut in 1943 in "One Touch of Venus," followed by "Where's Charley?" for which she received a THEATRE WORLD Award, "Miss Liberty," "Time Limit!" "Bells Are Ringing" in London, "West Side Story," "South Pacific" (1961 City Center), "The Beast In Me."

McNEIL, CLAUDIA. Born in Baltimore, Aug. 13, 1917. Studied with Maria Ouspenskaya. Appeared in night clubs before making Bdwy debut in 1952 in "The Crucible," followed by "Simply Heavenly," "A Raisin In The Sun," "Tiger Tiger Burning Bright."

Robert Milli

Linda Marsh

Will Mackenzie

Rosemary Murphy

MEACHAM, ANNE. Born in Chicago, July 21, 1925. Attended U. of Rochester, Yale Drama School, and Neighborhood Playhouse. Toured in "The Fatal Weakness" and "The First Mrs. Frazer" before making Bdwy debut in 1952 in "The Long Watch," followed by "Ondine," "The Immortal Husband," "Eugenia," "Legend of Lizzie," "A Passage To India," National Repertory Theatre revivals of "The Seagull," "The Crucible" and "Ring Round The Moon," Off-Bdwy in "Suddenly Last Summer" and "Hedda Gabler."

MEDFORD, KAY. Born in NYC, Sept. 14. Has appeared in "Paint Your Wagon," "Two's Company," "John Murray Anderson's Almanac," "Lullaby" for which she received a THEATRE WORLD Award, "Black-Eyed Susan," "Almost Crazy," "Wake Up, Darling," "Mr. Wonderful," "A Hole In The Head," "Carousel" (City Center), "Handful of Fire," "Bye, Bye, Birdie," "In The Counting House," "The Heroine," "Pal Joey" (City Center), "Funny Girl."

MEEHAN, DANNY. Born in White Plains, NY, Feb. 17, 1933. Attended American Academy of Dramatic Art. Made Bdwy bow in 1958 in "Whoop-Up!," followed by "Do Re Mi," "Funny Girl." Off-Bdwy credits: "Smiling The Boy Fell Dead," "The Thracian Horses," "O Oysters."

MEEKER, RALPH. Born in Minneapolis, Nov. 21, 1920. Attended Northwestern U. Made Bdwy bow in 1945 in "Strange Fruit," followed by "Cyrano de Bergerac," "Mister Roberts" for which he received a THEATRE WORLD Award, "A Streetcar Named Desire," "Picnic," "Cloud 7," "Rhinoceros," "Something About A Soldier," "After The Fall," "But For Whom Charlie."

MERMAN, ETHEL. Born in Astoria, L.I., Jan. 16, 1907. Appeared in vaudeville before making Bdwy debut in 1930 in "Girl Crazy," followed by "George White's Scandals," "Take A Chance," "Anything Goes," "Red, Hot and Blue," "Stars In Your Eyes," "Panama Hattie," "Something For The Boys," "Annie Get Your Gun," "Call Me Madam," "Happy Hunting," "Gypsy."

MERRILL, SCOTT. Born in Baltimore, July 14, 1922. Attended Baltimore College. Made NY bow in "Oklahoma," followed by "Love Life," "Guys and Dolls," "Small Wonder," "Lady In The Dark," "Paint Your Wagon," "Pal Joey," Off-Bdwy's "Threepenny Opera" for which he received a THEATRE WORLD Award, "Seventh Heaven," "Eugenia," "Street Scene" (City Center), "The World of Kurt Weill In Song" (Off-Bdwy).

MICHELL, KEITH. Born in Adelaide, Australia, Dec. 1, 1926. Attended Adelaide Teachers College, and Australian School of Arts and Crafts. Made Bdwy bow in 1960 in "Irma La Douce," followed by "The Rehearsal."

MILLER, BUZZ. Born in Snowflake, Ariz., Dec. 23, 1928. Attended Ariz. State College. Has appeared in "Magdalena," "Pal Joey," "Two's Company," "Me and Juliet," "Pajama Game," "Bells Are Ringing," "Redhead," "Bravo Giovanni," "Hot Spot," "Funny Girl."

MILLI, ROBERT. Born in Brooklyn, March 15, 1933. Graduate of U. of Maryland. M.A. from Catholic Univ. Has appeared in "Write Me A Murder," "Ross," "The Rehearsal," "Hamlet" with Richard Burton.

MITCHELL, ANN. Born in Providence, R.I., Oct. 23. Made Bdwy debut in 1958 in "Make A Million." Off-Bdwy credits: "The Threepenny Opera," "Once Upon A Matress" and "The Amorous Flea."

MITCHELL, JAMES. Born in Sacramento, Cal., Feb. 29, 1920. Attended Los Angeles City College. Made Bdwy bow in 1944 in "Bloomer Girl," followed by "Billion Dollar Baby," "Brigadoon" for which he received a THEATRE WORLD Award, "Paint Your Wagon," Off-Bdwy in "The Threepenny Opera," "Livin' The Life," and "Winkelberg," "Carousel" (City Center), "First Impressions," "Carnival," "The Deputy."

MONTGOMERY, EARL. Born in Memphis, Tenn., Apr. 17, 1921. Attended Harvard. Made NY bow in 1947 in "Galileo," followed by "Summer and Smoke," "The Relapse," "Mr. Pickwick," "Love's Labour's Lost," "The Merchant of Venice," "The Strong Are Lonely," "The Heavenly Twins," "A Visit To A Small Planet," "Look After Lulu," "Lady of The Camellias," "Tovarich," "The Rehearsal."

MORROW, KAREN. Born in Chicago, Dec. 15, 1936. Attended Clarke College, Iowa, and Workshop "M" in Milwaukee. Made NY debut Off-Bdwy in 1961 in "Sing, Muse!" for which she received a THEATRE WORLD Award, followed by 1963 Off-Bdwy revival of "The Boys From Syracuse."

MORSE, RICHARD. Born in Brookline, Mass., May 31, 1927. Attended Principia College and Neighborhood Playhouse. Made NY bow Off-Bdwy in 1955 in "Teach Me How To Cry," followed by "Thor With Angels," "The Makropoulos Secret," "All Kinds Of Giants," "Mother Courage and Her Children."

MORSE, ROBERT. Born in Newton, Mass., May 18, 1931. Made Bdwy bow in 1955 in "The Matchmaker," followed by "Say, Darling" for which he received a THEATRE WORLD Award, "Take Me Along," "How To Succeed In Business Without Really Trying."

MOULDER, WALTER. Born in San Francisco, Nov. 3, 1935. Attended U. of Calif. and Neighborhood Playhouse. Appeared in NY Shakespeare Festival production of "Romeo and Juliet," ELT's "What Every Woman Knows." Made Bdwy bow in 1961 in "Take Her, She's Mine."

MURPHY, ROSEMARY. Born in Munich, Ger., Jan. 13, 1927. Received stage training with Stratford Shakespeare Festival Theatre. Has appeared in "Look Homeward, Angel," "Period of Adjustment," "Any Wednesday."

NAGEL, CONRAD. Born in Keokuk, Iowa, Mar. 16, 1897. Made Bdwy bow in 1918 in "Forever After." After many years in films, returned to stage in "The First Apple," "The Skin of Our Teeth," "Tomorrow The World," "Susan and God," "A Goose For The Gander," "State of The Union," "Goodbye, My Fancy," "Music In The Air," "Be Your Age," "Four Winds," "The Pleasure of His Company," "The Captains and The Kings."

NAISMITH, LAURENCE. Born in Surrey, Eng., Dec. 14. Played 15 years in repertory throughout England before London debut in 1947. Broadway credits: "School For Scandal" (1963) and "Here's Love."

NATWICK, MILDRED. Born in Baltimore, June 19, 1908. Made Bdwy debut in 1932 in "Carrie Nation," followed by "The Wind and The Rain," "The Distaff Side," "End of Summer," "Love From A Stranger," "Candida," "The Star Wagon," "Missouri Legend," "Blithe Spirit," "The Playboy of The Western World," "The Grass Harp," "Coriolanus," "The Waltz of The Toreadors," "The Day The Money Stopped," "The Firstborn," "Critic's Choice," "Barefoot In The Park."

NEWMAN, PAUL. Born in Cleveland, Ohio, Jan. 26, 1925. Attended Kenyon College and Yale. Made Bdwy bow in 1953 in "Picnic" for which he received a THEATRE WORLD Award, followed by "The Desperate Hours," "Sweet Bird of Youth," "Baby Want A Kiss."

NOLTE, CHARLES. Born in Duluth, Minn., Nov. 3, 1926. Attended U. of Minn. and Yale. Made Bdwy bow in 1947 in "Antony and Cleopatra," followed by "Uniform of Flesh," "Caesar and Cleopatra," "Design For A Stained Glass Window" for which he received a THEATRE WORLD Award, "Mister Roberts," "Billy Budd," "The Caine Mutiny Court Martial," "Medea" (1955). Has devoted time to playwrighting, and had his play "The Summer People" produced in 1962 in England.

OLAF, PIERRE. Born in Cauderan, France, July 14, 1928. Attended Lycee. Made Bdwy bow in 1958 in "La Plume de Ma Tante," followed by "Carnival," "A Murderer Among Us."

OLIVIER, LAURENCE. Born in Dorking, Eng., May 22, 1907. Attended St. Edward's School, Oxford, and studied with Elsie Fogarty. Made Bdwy bow in 1929 in "Murder On The Second Floor," followed by "Private Lives," "The Green Bay Tree," "No Time For Comedy," "Romeo and Juliet," "Oedipus," "The Critic," "Uncle Vanya," "Henry IV, Parts I and II," "Antony and Cleopatra," "Caesar and Cleopatra," "The Entertainer," "Becket."

O'LOUGHLIN, GERALD. Born in NYC, Dec. 23, 1921. Attended Lafayette College and Neighborhood Playhouse. Made Bdwy bow in 1952 revival of "Golden Boy," followed by "The Flowering Peach," "A Streetcar Named Desire" (1956 City Center), "The Dark At The Top Of The Stairs," "Shadow Of A Gunman," "A Touch of The Poet," "Machinal" (Off-Bdwy), "A Cook For Mr. General," "Calculated Risk," "One Flew Over The Cuckoo's Nest."

OLSON, JAMES. Born in Evanston, Ill., Oct. 8, 1930. Attended Northwestern U. and Actors Studio. Made Bdwy bow in 1955 in "The Young and Beautiful," followed by "The Sin of Pat Muldoon," "J.B.," "The Chinese Prime Minister," "The Three Sisters" (1964).

O'NEAL, FREDERICK. Born in Brooksville, Miss., Aug. 27, 1905. In 1940 co-founded American Negro Theatre. Appeared in 7 of their productions before making Bdwy bow in 1944 in "Anna Lucasta," followed by "Take A Giant Step," "The Winner," "House of Flowers," and Off-Bdwy in "The Man With The Golden Arm" and "Ballad of Bimshire." Is president of Actors Equity.

O'SHEA, TESSIE. Born in Caerdydd, Great Britain, March 13, 1918. Attended private schools, and made theatrical debut in 1923. Made Bdwy bow Dec. 4, 1963 in "The Girl Who Came To Supper."

O'SULLIVAN, MAUREEN. Born in Roscommon, Ire. Attended Sacred Heart Convent, Dublin. After a long career in films, made Bdwy debut in 1962 in "Never Too Late."

OYSTER, JIM. Born in Washington, D.C., May 3, 1930. Attended Hill School. Has appeared Off-Bdwy in "Coriolanus," "The Cretan Woman" and "Man and Superman," on Bdwy in "The Cool World."

PAGE, GERALDINE. Born in Kirksville, Mo., Nov. 22, 1924. Studied at Goodman Theatre, Chicago. Appeared in many Off-Bdwy plays before making Bdwy debut in 1953 in "Mid-Summer" for which she received a THEATRE WORLD Award, followed by "The Immoralist," "The Rainmaker," "The Innkeepers," "Separate Tables," "Sweet Bird of Youth," "Strange Interlude" (1963), "The Three Sisters" (1964).

PARKER, LEW. Born in Brooklyn, Oct. 29, 1910. Has appeared in "The Ramblers," "Girl Crazy," "Red, Hot and Blue," "Heads Up," "Are You With It?," "The Front Page," "Ankles Aweigh," "The Amorous Flea" (Off-Bdwy).

PARSONS, ESTELLE. Born in Lynn, Mass., Nov. 20, 1927. Attended Conn. College, and Boston U. Law School. Has appeared in "Whoop-Up!," "Beg, Borrow or Steal," and Off-Bdwy in "The Threepenny Opera," "Automobile Graveyard," "Mrs. Dally Has A Lover" for which she received a THEATRE WORLD Award, and "In The Summer House."

PASTENE, ROBERT. Born in Brockton, Mass., Jan. 29, 1918. Attended M.I.T. and Wash. U. Has appeared in "The First Crucus," "Hamlet," "Crime and Punishment," "The Taming of The Shrew" (1951), "St. Joan" (1951), "The Children's Hour" (1952), "In The Counting House," "Journey To The Day" (Off-Bdwy).

PEARCE, JOHN. Born in Gainesville, Ga., Nov. 7, 1931. Attended Northwestern U. Has appeared in "The Ponder Heart," and Off-Bdwy in "Career" and "The Days and Nights of Bebe Fenstermaker."

PENN, BILL. Born in Reading, Pa., June 15, 1931. Attended Franklin and Marshall College, and UCLA. Made NY bow in 1953 in "The Fifth Season," toured in "Stalag 17." Founded Bdwy Chapel Players in 1954 and appeared in "The Boy With A Cart," "Noah," "In April Once," "The Hour Glass," and directed their other productions, as well as "Oscar Wilde," Tempo productions, "Tobacco Road," "Double Entry," "Put It In Writing."

PERKINS, ANTHONY. Born in NYC, Apr. 4, 1932. Attended Rollins College and Columbia. Made Bdwy bow in 1954 in "Tea and Sympathy" for which he received a THEATRE WORLD Award, followed by "Look Homeward, Angel," "Greenwillow," "Harold."

PHILLIPS, MARGARET. Born in Wales, July 6, 1923. Has appeared in "Cry Havoc," "The Late George Apley" for which she received a THEATRE WORLD Award, "Another Part of The Forest," "Summer and Smoke," "The Cocktail Party," "The Heiress," "The Merchant of Venice," "Second Threshold," "Dial 'M' For Murder," "Fallen Angels," Stratford Shakespeare productions, and Off-Bdwy in "The Lady's Not For Burning," "Under The Sycamore Tree" and "The Ginger Man."

PIAZZA, BEN. Born in Little Rock, Ark., July 30, 1934. Attended Princeton and Actors Studio. Made Bdwy bow in 1958 in "Winesburg, Ohio," followed by "Kataki" for which he received a THEATRE WORLD Award, "A Second String," Off-Bdwy in "The American Dream," "Zoo Story" and "Deathwatch," "The Fun Couple," "Who's Afraid of Virginia Woolf?."

PLUMMER, CHRISTOPHER. Born in Toronto, Can. in 1927. Toured with "The Constant Wife" before making Bdwy bow in 1954 in "The Starcross Story," followed by "Home Is The Hero," "The Dark Is Light Enough" for which he received a THEATRE WORLD Award, "Medea," "The Lark," "The Night of The Auk," "J. B.," "Arturo Ui."

POLLOCK, NANCY R. Born in Brooklyn, Feb. 10, 1905. Attended U. of Cuba, Columbia, U. of Mexico, and NYU. Made Bdwy debut in 1950 revival of "Diamond Lil," followed by "One Bright Day," "In The Summer House," "Middle Of The Night," "Period of Adjustment," "Come Blow Your Horn," "In The Counting House," "Have I Got A Girl For You."

| Jim Oyster | Carol Rossen | John Pearce | Maureen O'Sullivan |

PORTER, DON. Born in Miami, Okla., Sept. 24. Attended Oregon Inst. of Technology, and Portland Civic Theatre School. Has appeared on Bdwy in "Calculated Risk," "Any Wednesday."

PRESSMAN, LAWRENCE. Born in Cynthiana, Ky., July 10, 1939. Attended Northwestern U. Studied with Robert Lewis and Elia Kazan. Made Bdwy bow Mar. 28, 1964 in "Never Live Over A Pretzel Factory" for which he received a THEATRE WORLD Award. Off-Bdwy credit: "Go Show Me A Dragon."

PRESTON, ROBERT. Born in Newton Highland, Mass., June 8, 1918. Studied at Pasadena Playhouse. Made many films before Bdwy bow in 1951 in "Twentieth Century," followed by "The Male Animal," "Men of Distinction," "His and Hers," "The Magic and The Loss," "The Tender Trap," "Janus," "The Hidden River," "The Music Man," "Too True To Be Good," "Nobody Loves An Albatross."

PRICE, GILBERT. Born in NYC, Sept. 10, 1942. Graduate of Erasmus High School, Brooklyn. Received training at American Theatre Wing School. Has appeared in "Kicks and Company," "Fly Blackbird," "Jerico-Jim Crow" (Off-Bdwy) for which he received a THEATRE WORLD Award.

PRINCE, WILLIAM. Born in Nicholas, NY, Jan. 26, 1913. Attended Cornell. Has appeared in "Richard II," "Hamlet," "Ah, Wilderness," "Guest In The House," "Across The Board On Tomorrow Morning," "The Eve of St. Mark," "John Loves Mary," "Forward The Heart," "As You Like It," "I Am A Camera," "Affair of Honor," "Third Best Sport," "The Highest Tree," "Venus At Large," "Strange Interlude" (1963), "Ballad of The Sad Cafe."

PROCTOR, PHILIP. Born in Goshen, Ind., July 28, 1940. Graduate of Yale. Received training in Yale Drama School productions and Herbert Berghof Studio. Made Bdwy bow in "A Sound of Music." Off-Bdwy credits: "The Cherry Orchard" (1963), "Portrait of An Artist," "Barroom Monks," "Thistle In My Bed," "The Amorous Flea" for which he received a THEATRE WORLD Award.

RAHT, KATHARINE. Born in Chattanooga, Tenn., May 8, 1904. Attended Bryn Mawr. Has appeared in "Our Town," "The Heiress," "Sabrina Fair," "The Happiest Millionaire," "Love and Kisses."

RAINE, GILLIAN. Born in Gillian, Ceylon. Attended Convent College in England, and Royal Academy of Dramatic Arts. Made Bdwy debut Oct. 7, 1963 in "Semi-Detached."

REDFORD, ROBERT. Born in Santa Monica, Cal., Aug. 18, 1937. Attended U. of Colo., Pratt Inst., and American Academy of Dramatic Arts. Has appeared in "The Highest Tree," "Little Moon of Alban," "Sunday In New York," "Barefoot In The Park."

REDGRAVE, CORIN. Born in London, July 16, 1939. Trained for stage at Royal Court Theatre, London. Made Bdwy bow Oct. 1, 1963, in "Chips With Everything."

REDGRAVE, MICHAEL. Born in Bristol, Eng., Mar. 20, 1908. Attended Clinton and Magdalene Colleges. Appeared in many English films and plays before making Bdwy bow in 1948 in "Macbeth," followed by "Tiger At The Gates," "The Sleeping Prince," "The Complaisant Lover."

RITCHARD, CYRIL. Born in Sydney, Australia, Dec. 1, 1898. Attended St. Aloysius College and Sydney U. Appeared on Australian and London stages before making Bdwy bow in 1947 in "Love For Love," followed by "Make Way For Lucia," "The Relapse," "Peter Pan," "A Visit To A Small Planet," "The Pleasure of His Company," "The Happiest Girl In The World," "Romulus," "Too True To Be Good," "The Irregular Verb To Love."

ROBARDS, JASON, JR. Born in Chicago, July 26, 1922. Attended American Academy of Dramatic Arts. Made Bdwy bow in 1947 with D'Oyly Carte Opera Co., followed by "Stalag 17," "The Chase," Off-Bdwy in "American Gothic," and "The Iceman Cometh," "Long Day's Journey Into Night" for which he received a THEATRE WORLD Award, "The Disenchanted," "Toys In The Attic," "Big Fish, Little Fish," "A Thousand Clowns," "After The Fall," "But For Whom Charlie."

ROBERTS, RALPH. Born in Salisbury, NC, Aug. 17, 1918. Attended U. of NC. Made NY bow in 1948 in City Center's "Angel Street," followed by "Four Chekhov Comedies," "S.S. Glencairn," "The Madwoman of Chaillot," "Witness For The Prosecution," "The Lark," "Bells Are Ringing," "The Milk Train Doesn't Stop Here Anymore."

ROE, PATRICIA. Born in NYC, Sept. 18, 1932. Attended USC, Columbia, American Theatre Wing, and Actors Studio. Made Bdwy debut in 1951 in "Romeo and Juliet," followed by "Cat On A Hot Tin Roof," "Compulsion," "The Beautiful Sea," "Night Circus," "A Distant Bell," "Look After Lulu," "The Night of The Iguana," Off-Bdwy in "The Collection," "After The Fall," and "But For Whom Charlie."

ROEBLING, PAUL. Born in Philadelphia, Mar. 1, 1934. Studied with Stella Adler. Has appeared in "A Girl Can Tell," "The Dark Is Light Enough," "The Lark," "A Desert Incident" for which he received a THEATRE WORLD Award, "This Side of Paradise" (Off-Bdwy), "The Milk Train Doesn't Stop Here Anymore."

ROSSEN, CAROL. Born in Los Angeles, Aug. 12. Attended Sarah Lawrence College. Studied with Lee Strasberg. Made NY debut Off-Bdwy in 1962 in "Entertain A Ghost," followed by "The Egg," "Nobody Loves An Albatross."

ROSSITER, LEONARD. Born in Liverpool, Eng., Oct. 21, 1926. Trained for stage with Bristol, Old Vic and Coventry Players. Made Bdwy bow Oct. 7, 1963 in "Semi-Detached."

ROWLES, POLLY. Born in Philadelphia. Attended Carnegie Tech. Has appeared in "Richard III," "Anne of The Thousand Days," "The Golden State," "The Small Hours," "Gertie," "Time Out For Ginger," "The Wooden Dish," "Goodbye Again," "Auntie Mame," "Look After Lulu," "A Mighty Man Is He," "No Strings."

249

SAND, PAUL. Born in Santa Monica, Calif., Mar. 5, 1935. Attended CCLA. Trained with Marcel Marceau. Made Bdwy bow in 1961 in "From The Second City," followed by "Journey To The Day" (Off-Bdwy).

SANDS, DIANA. Born in NYC, Aug. 22, 1934. Attended High School of Performing Arts. Has appeared in "A Raisin In The Sun," "Tiger Tiger Burning Bright" for which she received a THEATRE WORLD Award, Off-Bdwy in "The World of Sholom Aleichem," "Major Barbara," "The Man With The Golden Arm," "Land Beyond The River" and "Brecht On Brecht," "Blues For Mister Charlie."

SANDS, DOROTHY. Born in Cambridge, Mass., Mar. 5, 1900. Attended Radcliffe College. Has appeared in "Grand Street Follies," "The Seagull," "The Stairs," "All The Comforts of Home," "Papa Is All," "Tomorrow The World," "A Joy Forever," "Bell, Book and Candle," "Misalliance," "Quadrille," "The First Gentleman," "Moonbirds," Off-Bdwy in "Mary Stuart" and "Whisper To Me," "Once For The Asking."

SCOFIELD, PAUL. Born in Hurstpierpoint, Sussex, Eng., Jan. 21, 1922. Attended Vardean School, Brighton. Trained at London Mask Theatre Studio. Made Bdwy bow in 1961 in "A Man For All Seasons," followed by "King Lear" (1964).

SCOTT, GEORGE C. Born in Wise, Va., Oct. 18, 1927. Attended U. of Mo. Appeared Off-Bdwy in "Richard III" for which he received a THEATRE WORLD Award, "As You Like It," "Children of Darkness," and "Desire Under The Elms." Made Bdwy bow in 1958 in "Comes A Day," followed by "The Andersonville Trial," "The Wall," "General Seeger."

SCOTT, MARTHA. Born in Jamesport, Mo., Sept. 22, 1914. Attended U. of Mich. Made NY debut in 1938 in "Our Town," followed by "Foreigners," "The Willow and I," "Soldier's Wife," "The Voice of The Turtle," "It Takes Two," "Design For A Stained Glass Window," "The Remarkable Mr. Pennypacker," "Cloud 7," "A Distant Bell," "The Tumbler," "The 49th Cousin," "Never Too Late."

SEYMOUR, ANNE. Born in NYC, Sept. 11, 1909. Attended Cathedral School and American Laboratory Theatre School. Has appeared in "Mr. Moneypenny," "At The Bottom," "The Seagull," "Puppet Show," "School For Scandal," "Sunrise At Campobello."

SEYMOUR, JOHN D. Born in Boston, Oct. 24, 1897. Attended Colgate U. Made NY bow in 1918 in "Out There," followed by "Richard III," "Dearest Enemy," "Blood Money," "The Barretts of Wimpole Street," "Sweet Adeline," "Cyrano de Bergerac," "Pride and Prejudice," "Susan and God," "The Moon Is Down," "Eastward In Eden," "The Vigil," "Light Up The Sky," "The Sacred Flame," '1963 City Center revivals of "Pal Joey" and "The King and I."

SHATNER, WILLIAM. Born in Montreal, Can., Mar. 22, 1931. Attended McGill U. Appeared with Canadian Repertory Co. and Stratford Shakespeare Festival of Can. before making NY bow in 1956 in "Tamburlaine The Great," followed by "The World of Suzie Wong" for which he received a THEATRE WORLD Award, "A Shot In The Dark."

SHEEN, MARTIN. Born in Dayton, Ohio, Aug. 3, 1940. Received training with The Living Theatre. Made Bdwy bow in 1964 in "Never Live Over A Pretzel Factory," followed by "The Subject Was Roses." Off-Bdwy credits: "The Connection," "Many Loves," and "In The Jungle of Cities."

SHUTTA, ETHEL. Born in NYC, Dec. 1, 1896. Attended public schools. Has appeared in "The Ziegfeld Follies," "The Passing Show of 1923," "Marjorie," "Louis XIV," "Whoopee," "My Dear Public," "Jennie."

SILVERS, PHIL. Born in Brooklyn, May 11, 1911. Appeared in vaudeville and burlesque before making Bdwy bow in 1939 in "Yokel Boy," followed by "High Button Shoes," "Top Banana," "Do Re Mi."

SKULNIK, MENASHA. Born in Poland, May 15, 1898. Began career at 10. Was favorite on Yiddish stage for many years before making Bdwy bow in 1953 in "The Fifth Season," followed by "The Flowering Peach," "Uncle Willie," "The 49th Cousin."

SMITH, LORING. Born in Stratford, Conn., Nov. 18, 1895. Made Bdwy bow in 1917 in "Leave It To Jane," followed by "Kiss The Boys Goodbye," "Glamour Preferred," "George Washington Slept Here," "A Joy Forever," "Junior Miss," "Over 21," "John Loves Mary," "The Happiest Years," "Texas Li'l Darlin'," "Of Thee I Sing," "The Solid Gold Cadillac," "The Matchmaker," "The Gay Life," "A Murderer Among Us."

SMITHERS, WILLIAM. Born in Richmond, Va., July 10, 1927. Attended Hampden-Sydney College, and Catholic U. Made Bdwy bow in 1951 in "Romeo and Juliet" for which he received a THEATRE WORLD Award, followed by "Legend of Lovers," "End As A Man," "The Troublemakers," "The Seagull," "The Square Root of Wonderful," "The Shadow of A Gunman," "Man and Boy."

STANDING, MICHAEL. Born in London, Eng., June 19, 1939. Attended Secondary Modern Medical College, and Royal Court Theatre, London. Made Bdwy bow Oct. 1, 1963 in "Chips With Everything."

STANLEY, KIM. Born in Tularosa, N. Mex., Feb. 11, 1925. Attended U. of N. Mex. and U. of Tex. Made Bdwy debut in 1949 in "Montserrat," followed by "The House of Bernarda Alba," "The Chase" for which she received a THEATRE WORLD Award, "Picnic," "The Traveling Lady," "Bus Stop," "A Clearing In The Woods," "Cat On A Hot Tin Roof" in London, "A Touch of The Poet," "Cheri," "A Far Country," "Natural Affection," "The Three Sisters" (1964).

STANYON, BRYAN. Born in Staffordshire, Eng., July 3, 1941. Received training with Bristol, Worthing, and Dundee repertory theatres. Made Bdwy bow Oct. 7, 1963 in "Semi-Detached."

STAPLETON, JEAN. Born in NYC, Jan. 19, 1923. Attended Hunter College and American Theatre Wing School. Made Bdwy debut in 1953 in "In The Summer House," followed by "Damn Yankees," "Bells Are Ringing," "Juno," "Rhinoceros," "Funny Girl."

STAPLETON, MAUREEN. Born in Troy, NY, June 21, 1925. Toured in "The Barretts of Wimpole Street" before making Bdwy debut in 1946 in "The Playboy of The Western World," followed by "Antony and Cleopatra," "Detective Story," "The Bird Cage," "The Rose Tattoo" for which she received a THEATRE WORLD Award, "The Emperor's Clothes," "The Crucible," "Richard III," "The Seagull," "27 Wagons Full of Cotton," "Orpheus Descending," "The Cold Wind and The Warm," "Toys In The Attic."

STEVENS, CRAIG. Born in Kansas City, Mo. Attended U. of Kansas and Pasadena Playhouse. Appeared in many films before making Broadway bow Oct. 3, 1963 in "Here's Love."

STEVENS, PAUL. Born in Los Angeles, June 17, 1924. Attended UCLA, Max Reinhardt Workshop, and Pasadena Playhouse. Has appeared Off-Bdwy in "The Crucible," "Romeo and Juliet," "Two Gentlemen From Verona," "As You Like It," "Much Ado About Nothing," "Ivanov," and on Bdwy in "Compulsion," "Girls of Summer," "General Seeger," "Andorra," "The Advocate."

STEWART, DAVID J. Born in Omaha, Neb. Attended Neighborhood Playhouse and Actors Studio. Has appeared in "Antigone," "Antony and Cleopatra," "That Lady," "The Rose Tattoo," "Barefoot In Athens," "Camino Real," "The Immoralist," "The Making of Moo" (Off-Bdwy), "A Man For All Seasons," "Marco Millions," "After The Fall."

STEWART, DON. Born in Staten Island, NY, Nov. 14, 1935. Attended Wichita U. Made Bdwy bow in "Camelot," followed by "The Student Gypsy." Off-Bdwy credits: "The Fantasticks," "Jo."

| Diana Sands | Bryan Stanyon | Ann Wedgeworth | D. J. Sullivan |

STICKNEY, DOROTHY. Born in Dickinson, S.D., June 21, 1900. Attended Northwestern Dramatic School. Made NY debut in 1926 in "The Squall," followed by "Chicago," "March Hares," "The Beaux Stratagem," "The Front Page," "Philip Goes Forth," "Another Language," "On Borrowed Time," "Life With Father," "Life With Mother," "The Small Hours," "To Be Continued," "Kind Sir," "The Honeys," "The Riot Act," "A Lovely Light" (solo show).

STRASBERG, SUSAN. Born in NYC, May 22, 1938. Made debut Off-Bdwy in 1953 in "Maya," followed by "The Diary of Anne Frank" for which she received a THEATRE WORLD Award, "Time Remembered," "The Shadow of A Gunman," "The Lady of The Camellias."

STREISAND, BARBRA. Born in Brooklyn, Apr. 24, 1942. Made Bdwy debut in 1962 in "I Can Get It For You Wholesale," followed by "Funny Girl."

STRIDE, JOHN. Born in London, July 11, 1936. Attended Royal Academy of Dramatic Arts. Made NY bow in 1962 Old Vic productions of "Macbeth" and "Romeo and Juliet" for which he received a THEATRE WORLD Award, followed by "The Lady of The Camellias."

STRIMPELL, STEPHEN. Born in NYC, Jan. 17, 1937. Graduate of Columbia Law School. Appeared with American Shakespeare Festival Co., in Phoenix revivals of "A School For Scandal" and "Henry IV, Part I," "Dumbell People In A Barbell World," and made Bdwy bow in 1964 in "The Sunday Man."

SULLIVAN, D. J. Born in NYC, Sept. 22, 1937. Graduate of Harvard. Studied with Lee Strasberg. Made Bdwy bow in 1957 in "Compulsion." Off-Bdwy credit: "Ardele."

SWANN, ELAINE. Born in Baltimore, Md., May 9. Attended U. of NC. Received training with Maryland Hilltop Theatre. Made Bdwy debut in 1957 in "The Music Man," followed by "Greenwillow," "A Thurber Carnival," "My Mother, My Father and Me," "Jennie."

SWENSON, INGA. Born in Omaha, Neb., Dec. 29, 1932. Attended Northwestern. Made Bdwy debut in "New Faces of 1956," followed by "Twelfth Night," "The First Gentleman" for which she received a THEATRE WORLD Award, American Shakespeare Festival productions, "110 In The Shade."

SWENSON, SWEN. Born in Inwood, Iowa, Jan. 23, 1932. Has appeared in "Great To Be Alive," "Bless You All," "As I Lay Dying," "Ulysses In Nightown" (Off-Bdwy), "Destry Rides Again," "Wildcat," "The Golden Apple" (1962 Off-Bdwy), "Little Me" for which he received a THEATRE WORLD Award.

TANDY, JESSICA. Born in London, June 7, 1909. Made NY debut in 1930 in "The Matriarch," followed by "The Last Enemy," "Time and The Conways," "Geneva," "Jupiter Laughs," "Anne of England," "Yesterday's Magic," "A Streetcar Named Desire," "Hilda Crane," "The Fourposter," "The White Steed," "The Honeys," "A Day By The Sea," "The Man In The Dog Suit," "Triple Play," "Five Finger Exercise," Stratford American Shakespeare Festival, and Minneapolis Festival productions.

TEITEL, CAROL. Born in NYC, Aug. 1, 1929. Attended American Theatre Wing School. Has appeared Off-Bdwy in "The Way of The World," "The Plough and The Stars," "The Anatomist," "A Country Scandal" and "Under Milkwood," and in "The Country Wife," "The Entertainer," Burton's "Hamlet" (1964).

TONE, FRANCHOT. Born in Niagara Falls, NY, Feb. 27, 1906. Attended Cornell. Made Bdwy bow in 1928 in "The Age of Innocence," followed by "Cross Roads," "Red Dust," "Hotel Universe," "Green Grow The Lilacs," "Pagan Lady," "The House of Connelly," "Night Over Taos," "The Gentle People," "Success Story," "The Fifth Column," "Hope For The Best," "Oh, Men! Oh, Women!," "Moon For The Misbegotten," "Mandingo," "Strange Interlude" (1963), "Bicycle Ride To Nevada," Off-Bdwy in "Uncle Vanya" and "The Dirty Old Man."

TORN, RIP. Born in Temple, Tex., Feb. 6. Attended U. of Tex. Studied with Lee Strasberg. Appeared Off-Bdwy in "Chaparral" for which he received a THEATRE WORLD Award, followed by "Cat On A Hot Tin Roof," "Sweet Bird of Youth," "Daughter of Silence," "Strange Interlude" (1963), "Blues For Mister Charlie."

TRACY, JOHN. Born in Des Moines, Iowa, Jan. 11, 1938. Attended U. of Iowa, and studied with Lee Strasberg. Made NY bow Off-Bdwy Nov. 15, 1963 in "Telemachus Clay" for which he received a THEATRE WORLD Award.

TRAVERS, BILL. Born in Northumberland, Eng., Jan. 3, 1922. Received training with repertory theatres in Eng. Starred in films and on English stage before making Bdwy bow in 1961 in "A Cook For Mr. General," followed by "Abraham Cochrane."

TRUEMAN, PAULA. Studied at Neighborhood Playhouse. Has appeared in "Grand Street Follies," "Sweet and Low," "Grand Hotel," "You Can't Take It With You," "George Washington Slept Here," "Kiss and Tell," "Violet," "For Love Or Money," "Gentlemen Prefer Blondes," "The Solid Gold Cadillac," "Mrs. McThing," "Wake Up, Darling," "A Family Affair," "Wonderful Town" (1963 City Center), "The Sunday Man."

TUCKER, FORREST. Born in Plainfield, Ind., Feb. 12, 1919. Appeared in burlesque before making many films in Hollywood. Toured with National Co. of "The Music Man." Made Bdwy bow Feb. 10, 1964 in "Fair Game For Lovers."

VACCARO, BRENDA. Born in Brooklyn, Nov. 18, 1939. Attended Neighborhood Playhouse. Made Bdwy debut in 1961 in "Everybody Loves Opal" for which she received a THEATRE WORLD Award, followed by "The Affair," "Children From Their Games."

VAN PATTEN, JOYCE. Born in Kew Gardens, L.I. Made Bdwy in 1941 in "Popsy," followed by "This Rock," "Tomorrow The World," "The Perfect Marriage," "The Wind Is Ninety," "The Desk Set," "A Hole In The Head," "Between Two Thieves," "Spoon River Anthology."

VERDON, GWEN. Born in Culver City, Calif. Has appeared in "Alive and Kicking," "Magdalena," "Can-Can" for which she received a THEATRE WORLD Award, "Damn Yankees," "New Girl In Town," "Redhead."

VOSKOVEC, GEORGE. Born in Sazava, Czech., June 19, 1905. Attended Dijon College, France, and Charles U. in Prague. Made NY in 1945 in "The Tempest," followed by "The Love of Four Colonels," "His and Hers," "The Sea Gull," "Festival," "Uncle Vanya" (Off-Bdwy), "Do You Know The Milky Way?," Burton's "Hamlet" (1964).

WALLACH, ELI. Born in Brooklyn. Attended CCNY, U. of Tex., and Neighborhood Playhouse. Has appeared in "Henry VIII," "Androcles and The Lion," "Alice In Wonderland," "Yellow Jack," "What Every Woman Knows," "Skydrift," "Antony and Cleopatra," "Mister Roberts," "The Lady From The Sea," "The Rose Tattoo" for which he received a THEATRE WORLD Award, "Mlle. Colombe," "The Teahouse of The August Moon," "Major Barbara," "The Chairs," "The Cold Wind and The Warm," "Rhinoceros," Off-Bdwy in "The Typists" and "The Tiger."

WARREN, KENNETH J. Born in Parramatta, New South Wales, Australia, Sept. 25, 1929. Attended Julian Ashton Art School. Has appeared on Bdwy in "The Summer of The 17th Doll" and "Luther."

WARREN, LESLEY. Born in NYC, Aug. 16, 1946. Studied with Stella Adler. Made Broadway debut Oct. 24, 1963 in "110 In The Shade."

WATERS, ETHEL. Born in Chester, Pa., Oct. 31, 1900. Sang in night clubs before making Bdwy debut in 1927 in "Africana," followed by "Lew Leslie's Blackbirds," "Rhapsody In Black," "As Thousands Cheer," "At Home Abroad," "Mamba's Daughters," "Cabin In The Sky," "Blue Holiday," "The Member of The Wedding," "At Home With Ethel Waters."

WATSON, DOUGLAS. Born in Jackson, Ga., Feb. 24, 1921. Attended U. of NC. Made Bdwy bow in 1947 in "Antony and Cleopatra" for which he received a THEATRE WORLD Award, followed by "The Leading Lady," "Richard III," "The Happiest Years," "That Lady," "The Wisteria Trees," "Romeo and Juliet," "Desire Under The Elms," "Sunday Breakfast," "Cyrano de Bergerac," "The Confidential Clerk," "Portrait of A Lady," "The Miser," "The Young and The Beautiful," "Little Glass Clock," "The Country Wife," "A Man For All Seasons," "The Chinese Prime Minister," Stratford American Shakespeare Festival Productions.

WATSON, MORAY. Born in Kent, Eng., May 25, 1930. Attended Eton College. Received training with Liverpool Repertory Co. Made Broadway bow Oct. 9, 1963 in "The Public Eye."

WAYNE, DAVID. Born in Traverse City, Mich., Jan. 31, 1916. Attended Western State U. Made Bdwy bow in 1938 in "Escape This Night," followed by "Dance Night," "The American Way," "Scene of The Crime," "The Merry Widow," "Peepshow," "Park Avenue," "Finian's Rainbow" for which he received a THEATRE WORLD Award, "Mister Roberts," "The Teahouse of The August Moon," "The Ponder Heart," "The Loud Red Patrick," "Say, Darling," "Send Me No Flowers," "Venus At Large," "Too True To Be Good," "Marco Millions" (1964), "But For Whom Charlie."

WEAVER, FRITZ. Born in Pittsburgh, Jan. 19, 1926. Attended U. of Chicago. Appeared Off-Bdwy in "The Way of The World," "The White Devil" and "The Doctor's Dilemma" before making Bdwy bow in 1955 in "The Chalk Garden" for which he received a THEATRE WORLD Award, followed by "Protective Custody," "Miss Lonelyhearts," Phoenix productions of "The Family Reunion," "The Power and The Glory," "The Great God Brown," "Peer Gynt," and "Henry IV, Parts I & II," "All American," "Lorenzo," "The White House."

WEBB, ALAN. Born in York, Eng., July 2, 1906. Attended Royal Naval College, and Dartmouth. Made NY in 1936 in "Tonight At 8:30," followed by "George and Margaret," "The Winslow Boy," "Nina," "The Deep Blue Sea," "The Genius and The Goddess," "The Night of The Iguana," "The Chinese Prime Minister."

WEDGEWORTH, ANN. Born in Abilene, Tex., Jan. 21. Attended U. of Tex. Has appeared on Bdwy in "Make A Million," "Blues For Mister Charlie." Off-Bdwy credits: "Chaparral," "The Crucible," "The Days and Nights of Bebe Fenstermaker."

WEST, JENNIFER. Born in Ft. Smith, Ark., Sept. 22, 1939. Attended CCLA. Made NY debut March 24, 1964 Off-Bdwy in "Dutchman," followed by "After The Fall."

WHITE, JANE. Born in NYC, Oct. 30, 1922. Attended Smith College, and New School. Made Bdwy debut in 1945 in "Strange Fruit," followed by "Razzle Dazzle," "The Insect Comedy," "The Climate of Eden," "Take A Giant Step," "Jane Eyre," "The Power and The Glory," "Once Upon A Mattress," Off-Bdwy in "Hop, Signor!" and "The Trojan Women."

WICKWIRE, NANCY. Born in Harrisburg, Pa., Nov. 29, 1925. Attended Carnegie Tech, and Old Vic School, London. Has appeared in "Jane," "Dial 'M' For Murder," "St. Joan," "The Grand Prize," Off-Bdwy in "The Way of The World," "The Cherry Orchard," "Measure For Measure," "The Girl Of The Golden West," "As You Like It," "A Clearing In The Woods," and "Rosmersholm," "Seidman and Son," "The Golden Age," "Abraham Cochrane."

WILLIAMS, BARBARA. Born in Milwaukee, Wisc., May 24. Attended Northwestern U. Has appeared in "Damn Yankees," "The Music Man," "The Streets of New York" (Off-Bdwy).

WILLIAMS, EMLYN. Born in Mostyn, Flintshire, Wales, Nov. 26, 1905. Attended Christ Church School, Oxford. Made NY bow in 1927 in "And So To Bed," followed by "Criminal At Large," "Night Must Fall," "Montserrat," "Readings From Charles Dickens," "Bleak House," "A Boy Growing Up," "Daughter of Silence," "A Man For All Seasons," "The Deputy."

WILLIAMS, JOHN. Born in Chalfont, St. Giles, Eng., Apr. 15, 1903. Attended Lancing College. Made NY bow in 1924 in "The Fake," followed by "The Ghost Train," "Mixed Doubles," "The High Road," "Ten Minute Alibi," "Dodsworth," "Call It A Day," "No Time For Comedy," "Claudia," "Anne of The Thousand Days," "The Velvet Glove," "Venus Observed," "Dial 'M' For Murder," "The Dark Is Light Enough," "Ross," "The Chinese Prime Minister."

WILLIAMS, MICHAEL. Born in Stratford, Manchester, Eng., July 9, 1935. Attended St. Edward's College, Liverpool. Trained at Royal Academy of Dramatic Arts, London, and with Nottingham Rep. Co. Made NY bow in 1964 with Royal Shakespeare Co. in "King Lear" and "Comedy of Errors."

WINTERS, MARIAN. Born in NYC, Apr. 19, 1924. Has appeared in "Dream Girl," "I Am A Camera," "Auntie Mame," "Tall Story," "49th Cousin," "The Cherry Orchard" (Off-Bdwy), "Nobody Loves An Albatross."

WOOD, PEGGY. Born in Brooklyn, Feb. 9, 1894. Made Bdwy debut in 1910 in "Naughty Marietta," followed by "The Lady of The Slipper," "Love O' Mike," "Maytime," "Candida," "Trelawney Of The Wells," "The Merchant of Venice," "Bitter Sweet," "Old Acquaintance," "Blithe Spirit," "The Happiest Years," "Getting Married," "Charley's Aunt" (1954 City Center), "The Transposed Heads" (Phoenix), "Girls In 509," "Opening Night" (Off-Bdwy).

YURKA, BLANCHE. Born in St. Paul, Minn., June 19, 1893. Began long and successful career in 1907. Most recent appearances include "The Wind Is Ninety," Phoenix productions of "The Carefree Tree" and "Diary of A Scoundrel," "Jane Eyre," ELT revival of "The Corn Is Green."

PORTRAIT DOLLS by Mary Green, New York artist from the Daniel Blum Collection: Richard Burton as Hamlet; Gertrude Hoffman in "Sumurun," Maude Adams in "The Little Minister," Guy Robertson in "The Circus Princess."

Photo by Dan Entin Studio

253

OBITUARIES

Frank Albertson

Phil Baker

Brendan Behan

ALBERTSON, FRANK, 55, stage and film actor, died in his sleep in his Santa Monica, Calif., home, Feb. 29, 1964. His career spanned 35 years. Besides his many films, his Broadway credits include "Late Love," "Seventeen," "Mr. Adam," "The More The Merrier," "Brother Rat," and "The Walrus and The Carpenter." He is survived by his widow and two sons and two daughters. Burial was in Holy Cross Cemetery, Hollywood.

AMAYA, CARMEN, 50, a top flamenco Spanish dancer, died of a kidney ailment at her home in Bagur, Spain, on Nov. 19, 1963. She made her first appearance in New York in 1941 in a night club and created a sensation. Besides night club engagements, she appeared in concerts in Carnegie Hall. Her one Broadway appearance was in 1942 with Ed Wynn in "Laugh, Town, Laugh." She was buried in a small cemetery of Bagur, a Mediterranean village. She is survived by her husband, Juan Antonio Aguero, who usually accompanied her on the guitar.

APPEL, ANNA, 75, veteran Yiddish character actress, died of a heart attack in Bellevue Hospital, NYC, Nov. 19, 1963. She devoted 50 years to the Yiddish theatre. Her Broadway credits include: "Did I Say No," "Good Neighbors," "All You Need Is One Good Break," "Highway Robbery," "Abie's Irish Rose" (1954 revival), "Comic Strip," and "The Golem."

BAKER, PHIL, 67, stage and radio comedian, died in his home in Copenhagen, Denmark, Dec. 1, 1963. He played in vaudeville and night clubs before Broadway claimed him. He appeared in Ziegfeld's "Midnight Follies," "Music Box Revue" (1922), "Greenwich Village Follies," "Artists and Models," a series of the "Passing Shows," "A Night In Spain," "Calling All Stars," "Priorities of 1942," "Crazy Quilt," and "All In Fun." He had great success as a quizmaster on "Take It Or Leave It," a radio program. Surviving are a widow, Irmgard, three sons and three daughters.

BARTHELMESS, RICHARD, 68, famous silent screen star, died of throat cancer, Aug. 17, 1963, in his summer home in Southampton, L.I., N.Y. His film career was illustrious, and spanned 25 years. His only stage appearance was in 1936 when he starred on Broadway in "The Postman Always Rings Twice." Burial was in Ferncliff Cemetery, Hartsdale, N. Y.

BEHAN, BRENDAN, 41, Irish playwright, died of many complaints aggravated by his renowned bouts with drink, on March 20, 1964, in Meath Hospital, Dublin. Two of his plays, "The Quare Fellow" and "The Hostage," have been produced in New York. His third play, "Richard's Cork Leg," under option to the Theatre Guild, is yet to be produced. He is survived by his wife Beatrice and an infant daughter.

BLITZSTEIN, MARC, 58, composer, died Jan. 22, 1964, after being beaten and robbed by three seamen in the public square of Fort-de-France, Martinique, West Indies. His Broadway credits include "The Cradle Will Rock," "No For An Answer," "Regina," and "Juno." He is survived by his mother and sister.

BLUM, GUSTAV, 76, producer in the 'twenties and 'thirties, died of a heart attack in Monticello, N.Y., July 29, 1963. Among his Broadway productions were "The Shame Woman," "Caught," "Gertie," "Her First Affair," "Spring Song," "Truly Valiant," "Don't Look Now," "That Ferguson Family," and "Walk Hard."

BRENDEL, EL, 73, film comedian, died of a heart attack at Hollywood Presbyterian Hospital on Apr. 9, 1964. Although born in Philadelphia, he became famous with a comical Swedish accent. Besides his many films, he appeared on Broadway in "Cinderella On Broadway," "Spice of 1922," "Passing Show of 1923," and "New York Whirl." He is survived by his wife Sophie Flo Burt.

CAMPBELL, ALAN, 58, actor and writer, died in his West Hollywood, Calif., home from an apparent overdose of sleeping pills on June 14, 1963. He played small parts in Eva LeGallienne's Repertory Co., and Laurette Taylor's son in "The Furies." He is survived by his widow, Dorothy Parker.

COCTEAU, JEAN, 74, noted Frenchman, died of a heart attack, at his home in Milly-la-Foret, near Paris, Oct. 11, 1963. The "enfant terrible" of French literature was a jack-of-all-arts. He was adept in creating films, plays, paintings, music, poetry, as well as writing novels and essays. He was librettist for Stravinsky's "Oedipus Rex," did ballets for Diaghilev's "Ballet Russe," and adapted Tennessee Williams' "A Streetcar Named Desire" for the Paris stage. He was buried beside the little Sainte Blaize Chapel of Milly-la-Foret.

CONROY, FRANK, 73, stage and film actor, died of a heart ailment in the Bergen Pines Hospital, Paramus, N.J., Feb. 24, 1964. He made his Broadway bow in 1915 in "Helen's Husband." Among his many other appearances include "The Little Foxes," "Strange Interlude," "The Constant Wife," "On Borrowed Time," "Kind Sir," "Point of No Return," "The Potting Shed," "Compulsion," and in 1962 his last play "Calculated Risk." He is survived by his wife Ruth Weeker, and a son Richard.

COTTON, FRED AYRES, 57, a stage actor, and later an executive of Actors Equity, died of a heart attack at University Hospital, NYC, Jan. 29, 1964. His Broadway appearances include "Swing Your Lady," "Brown Danube," "State of The Union," "Joy To The World," "Anne of The Thousand Days," "Affairs of State," and "Winged Victory."

DANIELL, HENRY, 69, stage and film actor, died of a heart attack in his Santa Monica, Calif., home on Oct. 31, 1963. Came to U.S. in 1921 to appear with Ethel Barrymore in "Déclassé." Among his subsequent successes were "Claire de Lune," "The Second Mrs. Tanqueray," "Serena Blandish," "Kind Lady," "Watch On The Rhine," "Murder Without Crime," "Lady Windemere's Fan," "Lovers and Friends," "The Winter's Tale," "That Lady," "The Cocktail Party," "My Three Angels," and his last role in "Lord Pengo" in 1962. Appeared in many films. He is survived by his widow, Ann Knox, a novelist, and a daughter Athalie.

DELF, HARRY, 71, stage and vaudeville comedian, playwright, songwriter, and director, died of a heart attack in his NYC home on Feb. 7, 1964. Appeared in vaudeville and Earl Carroll's "Vanities." Was author and director of 3 early talking films. Plays he wrote include "The Family Upstairs," "Sun Showers," "The Unsophisticates," "The Nebblepredders," and "Atlas and Eve." Wrote songs and sketches for many revues and entertainers, including The Dolly Sisters, and Nora Bayes. Surviving are his son, Harry, Jr., and a daughter, Mrs. Robert Asherman.

DUMKE, RALPH, 64, stage, radio, film, vaudeville, and TV comedian, died of a heart ailment at his home in Sherman Oaks, Calif., on Jan. 4, 1964. He and his partner, Ed East, appeared in vaudeville for 10 years before winning national fame on radio as "The Sisters of The Skillet" in the '30's. His legitimate stage appearances include "By Jupiter," "Helen Goes To Troy," "Mr. Strauss Goes To Boston," "Sadie Thompson," "The Merry Widow," "La Vie Parisienne," and Capt. Andy in the 1946 revival of "Show Boat." Surviving are his wife Greta, and two sons, James and William.

GARRISON, MABEL, 77, American opera singer, died at her Sutton Place, N. Y., home on Aug. 20, 1963. She was one of the leading coloraturas of the Metropolitan Opera between 1914 and 1922. Among the roles she sang were Queen of The Night in "The Magic Flute," Gilda, Martha, Lucia, and Rosina. While at the Met, she sang with Caruso. There are no survivors.

Marc Blitzstein

Jean Cocteau

Frank Conroy

Carol Haney
1924-1964

GALLI-CURCI, AMELITA, 81, famous coloratura soprano opera star, died of emphysemia at her home in La Jolla, Calif., Nov. 26, 1963. Italian-born, she made her American debut in 1916 with the Chicago Opera Co. Later she sang for the Metropolitan Opera Co. For 20 years, she reigned as one of the world's greatest coloraturas, singing such roles as Gilda, Rosina, Lucia, Violetta, Mimi, Lakme, Dinorah, and others. No immediate survivors. Burial was in the Cypress View Mausoleum in San Diego, Calif.

HANEY, CAROL, 39, musical comedy star and choreographer, died of bronchial pneumonia at the NY Hospital, NY, May 10, 1964. She made her first big hit on Broadway with the "Steam Heat" number in "The Pajama Game." She played a straight role on Bdwy in "A Loss Of Roses." Recently she has choreographed "Flower Drum Song," "She Loves Me," "Bravo Giovanni," and "Funny Girl." Her divorced husband, Larry Blyden, was with her when she died. She is survived by two children. Burial was in Old Landing Cemetery, Marion, Mass.

HANDZLIC, JEAN, 41, singer, died of cancer in St. Barnabas Hospital, Bronx, NY, July 9, 1963. She sang with the NYC Center Opera, and the San Francisco Opera Company. On Broadway her credits include "The Mikado" and "How To Succeed In Business Without Really Trying." She is survived by a son Jan.

HECHT, BEN, 70, author of plays, movie scripts, and novels, died Apr. 18, 1964 of a heart attack in his NY apt. Born in NY of Russian immigrant parents, he began his career at 16 on the Chicago Journal. He ultimately wrote about 70 movie scripts, 26 books, 20 plays, and hundreds of short stories, and magazine articles. His best-known plays were "The Front Page" and "Twentieth Century" written in collaboration with Charles MacArthur. Interment was in Oak Hills Cemetery, Nyack, NY. He is survived by his wife Rose and two daughters, Edwina and Jenny, an actress.

JANNEY, RUSSELL, 79, theatrical producer and author, died of natural causes in his NYC apt. on July 14, 1963. Born in Wilmington, Ohio, and graduated from Yale. Best remembered as producer and co-author of the musical "The Vagabond King," and for his novel "The Miracle of The Bells." He wrote material for "Ziegfeld Follies" and worked as a "play doctor," revising plays for others without program credit. Served as a theatrical press agent and manager before producing his first play in 1918, Booth Tarkington's "Seventeen." Other productions include "Marjolaine," "Pomander Walk," "White Eagle," "June Love," "Ballyhoo," and "The O'Flynn."

JOY, NICHOLAS, 80, stage, film, and TV character actor, died of a heart attack after a long illness at the Edwin Forest Home in Philadelphia, Mar. 16, 1964. He had appeared in over 100 plays. Born in Paris of English parents, he came to the U.S. in 1912 after appearing on the London stage. His best-known roles were in "End of Summer," "The Philadelphia Story," "The Iceman Cometh," "Ode To Liberty," "Music In The Air," "The Cat and The Fiddle," "Topaze," "Rain," "Wings Over Europe," "The Doughgirls," "Ten Little Indians," "Yes, My Darling Daughter," "Caesar and Cleopatra" (1949). His widow, Hildreth, survives.

KAZAN, MOLLY, 56, playwright, died at Bellevue Hospital, NY, of a cerebral hemorrhage, Dec. 14, 1963. Plays she wrote include "The Egghead," "Rosemary," and "The Alligator." She is survived by her husband, Elia Kazan, the director, and four children.

KIRKWOOD, JAMES, 80, silent screen star, died in the Motion Picture Country Hospital, Woodland Hills, Calif. He appeared in many films and on Bdwy in "The Fool," "The Country Chairman" revival, "The Devil's Disciple," and on the road in "Tobacco Road." Burial was in the Holy Cross Cemetery, Hollywood.

MALO, GINA, 57, musical comedy actress, died at her home in NYC on Nov. 30, 1963. Her Broadway credits include "George White's Scandals of 1921, "Sons O' Guns," and on tour in "The Merry Wives of Windsor." She is survived by her husband, Romney Brent, and a daughter Victoria.

Amelita Galli-Curci

Nicholas Joy

Clifford Odets

Maynard Morris

Douglass Parkhirst

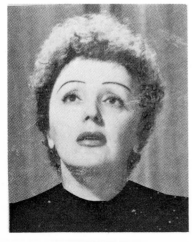

Edith Piaf

MORRIS, MAYNARD, 65, famous theatrical agent, died of a heart attack in his NYC apt., Jan 25, 1964. He was a top agent for Music Corporation of America for 25 years. Among the stars he discovered include Paul Newman, Gregory Peck, Charlton Heston, Joanne Woodward, Robert Goulet, and John Payne. He is survived by his sister, Mrs. James Main.

ODETS, CLIFFORD, 57, playwright, actor, motion picture writer and director, died of cancer in The Cedars of Lebanon Hospital, Hollywood, on Aug. 14, 1963. Was an actor until his late 20's and a member of The Group Theatre. Achieved success with his first play "Awake and Sing," followed by "Waiting For Lefty," "Golden Boy," "Rocket To The Moon," "Night Music," "Clash By Night," "The Big Knife," and "The Country Girl." His last play "The Flowering Peach," was produced in 1954. Went to Hollywood in 1936 and wrote and directed several successful films. His first marriage to Luise Rainer ended in divorce, as did his next to Betty Grayson. A daughter Nora, and son Walt Whitman survive. Interment was in Forest Lawn Memorial Park, Glendale, Calif.

PARKHIRST, DOUGLASS, 50, actor-author, died in Lennox Hill Hospital, NY, May 20, 1964, after a brief illness from a brain tumor. He appeared on Bdwy in "Let Freedom Ring," "200 Were Chosen," "Bury The Dead," "Washington In April," "Love On The Dole," "Brother Rat," "Hymn To The Rising Sun," and "Thunder Rock." For many years was on radio and TV in "Road of Life" and other serials and dramatic shows. Was author of several plays, TV productions, and books. Served as president of the Veterans Hospital Radio and Television Guild for several terms. Interment was in Lebanon, Pa. His mother survives.

PIAF, EDITH, 47, petite French singer, affectionately called "Sparrow of The Streets," died from an internal hemorrhage in her Paris home Oct. 11, 1963 after a long illness. Sang her way from Paris street corners at 15 to international fame. "La Vie En Rose," a song she wrote, became her trademark. Her first and only Broadway appearance was in 1947 with Les Compagnons de la Chanson. Later appeared in many clubs in the U.S. Her last appearance here was in 1959. She is survived by her second husband, and protege, Theo Sarapo. Burial was in the Pere Lachaise Cemetery in East Paris.

PITTS, ZASU, 63, pioneer screen actress, died of cancer in the Good Samaritan Hospital, Hollywood, June 7, 1963. Her film career was long and illustrious. She appeared on Broadway in "Ramshackle Inn" in 1944, and a revival of "The Bat" in 1953. She is survived by her husband, John E. Woodell, a daughter Ann, and an adopted son Donald.

PRICE, GEORGIE, 64, former vaudeville star, died from a heart attack in NYC, May 10, 1964. He was a singer and comic, and was with Gus Edwards' "Song Review," toured with Keith vaudeville circuit, and was on Bdwy in a drama "The Song Writer," and musicals "Spice of 1928," "Artists and Models," and "A Night In Paris." In recent years he was a stock broker. Two sons and two daughters survive.

RAISA, ROSA, 70, famous opera star, died Sept. 28, 1963 in her Pacific Palisades, Calif. home after a long illness. She was the top soprano with the Chicago Opera Co. for 25 years. Her famous roles included Aida, Tosca, Norma, Marschallin, and Valentine. She is survived by her daughter, Mrs. Joseph Segala.

ROCKWELL, FLORENCE, 76, retired actress, died at the Stamford, Conn., Hospital, Mar. 24, 1964. Her Broadway credits included "The Round Up," "The Barrier," "Mills of The Gods," "Jessimy Bride," "D'Arcy of The Guards," and "Fallen Idol." She also appeared in Shakespearean productions. No survivors.

Joseph Schildkraut
1895-1964

Georgie Price

Rosa Raisa

J. J. Shubert

Diana Wynyard

SCHILDKRAUT, JOSEPH, 68, stage and screen star, died in his NY home from a heart attack on Jan. 21, 1964. Had appeared in many films. Broadway credits include "Pagans," "Liliom," "Peer Gynt" (1923), "The Highwayman," "The Firebrand," with the Civic Repertory Theatre, "Camille," "Dear Jane," and "Alice In Wonderland," "Between Two Worlds," "Tomorrow's A Holiday," "Clash By Night," "Uncle Harry," "The Cherry Orchard" (1944), "The Green Bay Tree" (1951), "Love's Labour's Lost," and "The Diary of Anne Frank." At the time of his death he was preparing for a role in the musical version of "Cafe Crown," Surviving is his third wife, Leonora Rogers. Burial was in Beth Olam Cemetery, Los Angeles.

SHUBERT, J. J., 86, producer and director, died Dec. 26, 1963 of a cerebral hemorrhage in his NY penthouse atop Sardi's Restaurant across from Shubert Alley. He was the last and youngest of the three brothers from Syracuse who founded Bdwy's most powerful theatrical dynasty. "Mr. J. J." produced or co-produced 520 plays and musicals, some of which he directed. The most successful were "The Student Prince," "Blossom Time," "Countess Maritza," "The Last Waltz," and "Hellzapoppin." He introduced to Bdwy such stars as Eddie Cantor, Al Jolson, Marilyn Miller, Ed Wynn, Fanny Brice, The Dolly Sisters, Carmen Miranda, Ray Bolger, and Bert Lahr. At one time "The Messrs. Shubert" controlled more than half the theatres in the U.S. He is survived by his second wife Muriel.

SOBEL, BERNARD, 76, press agent, died Mar. 12, 1964 at his home in NYC. He was an aide of Florenz Ziegfeld and Earl Carroll, and publicized many of their stars. He also wrote several one-act plays, books on the history of the theatre, and articles for the NY Herald Tribune. His sister, Mrs. Lorraine Lee, survives.

VAN GORDON, CYRENA, 67, former opera singer, died in NY's Bellevue Hospital, Apr. 4, 1964. A contralto, she made her debut in 1913 with the Chicago Opera Co. as Amneris in "Aida," and her debut at the Metropolitan Opera on Jan. 18, 1934. Among her famous roles were Ortud, Erda, Fricka, Brunnhilde, Azucena, Venus, and Delilah. A brother, Joseph McGriff, survives.

WYNYARD, DIANA, 58, British star, died from a kidney ailment in St. Paul's Hospital, London, May 13, 1964. She appeared in many Hollywood films. Her Broadway appearances include "The Devil Passes," "Cue For Passion," and "Heartbreak House" revival. At the time of her death she was rehearsing for a revival of "The Master Builder" in London. No survivors.

INDEX